Sociology and Pragmatism

BOOKS BY C. WRIGHT MILLS

Sociology and Pragmatism (1964)

Power, Politics and People (1963)

The Marxists (1962)

Listen, Yankee: The Revolution in Cuba (1960)

Images of Man (edited) (1960)

The Sociological Imagination (1959)

The Causes of World War Three (1958)

The Power Elite (1956)

Character and Social Structure (1953)
(with H. H. Gerth)

White Collar (1951)

The Puerto Rican Journey (1950)
(with Clarence Senior and Rose Goldsen)

The New Men of Power (1948)

From Max Weber: Essays in Sociology (1946)
(edited and translated with H. H. Gerth)

SOCIOLOGY AND PRAGMATISM

THE HIGHER LEARNING IN AMERICA

C. WRIGHT MILLS

Edited with an introduction
by Irving Louis Horowitz

New York
OXFORD UNIVERSITY PRESS
1969

The best claim we can make for the higher education, the best single phrase in which we can tell what it ought to do for us, is that it should enable us to know a good man when we see him.

WILLIAM JAMES

Contents

Preface

Introduction   The Intellectual Genesis of C. Wright Mills   11

SOCIOLOGY AND PRAGMATISM:
The Higher Learning in America

PART I

1. Division of Labor, Religion and Educational Institutions   35
2. Types of Men and the New Schools   57
3. Graduate Schools and Professionalization   67
4. The Personnel of American Philosophy   75
5. Biographical Composition of the Metaphysical Club   84

PART II

6. Charles Peirce   123
7. The Laboratory Style of Inquiry   150
8. The Practical in Peirce   168
9. The Realist Definition of Society   191
10. Social Components of Peirce's Perspective   206

PART III

11. William James   215
12. Three Vocabularies of Social Practice   232
13. The Polarization of Science and Religion   248
14. Psychological Liberalism   260

PART IV

15. John Dewey   279
16. Hull House and Consequent Writings   307
17. John Dewey's Reading Public   325
18. Professionalization of Teaching   338
19. The Philosophic Public and Professional Ascent   347
20. Meanings and Moorings in Dewey   356
21. Modulations of Action   391
22. Freedom and Culture   426
23. Social Psychology: Model for Liberals   447

Postscript: Some Last Reflections on Pragmatism   464
Name and Subject Index   468

Preface

The justification for the belated publication of the dissertation of C. Wright Mills on *Sociology and Pragmatism* is manifold. The first and foremost reason is that this is a very sound piece of scholarship. The wide readership it has enjoyed in its dissertation form can be attested to by its considerable use at the University of Wisconsin dissertation archives. The second reason is that sociological research on the theme Mills chose, remains at relatively the same point as it was a quarter century ago. Indeed, the study of the ideological and institutional fabric of philosophy has receded as a theme in the sociological literature. Were it not for the work of European trained scholars like Hans H. Gerth, Kurt H. Wolff, Max Horkheimer, and Georges Gurvitch, among others, it would be well nigh impossible to "legitimate" such a study at all. The third reason that the publication of this book at this time must be considered fortuitous is the growth of interest in the process of professionalization — the transformation of a discipline into an occupation, and the corresponding transformation of the intellectual into an academic. It is my personal judgment that the book will find a more ready and responsive audience than it would have twenty five years ago. The fourth reason, and the one which closes the need for further rationalization is that Wright Mills wanted *Sociology and Pragmatism* to be published. In spare moments, he would go over the manuscript for purposes of style and formulation. As a matter of fact, he had submitted his dissertation to various commercial publishers, but no arrangements were arrived at which could prove mutually satisfactory.

There is an additional reason for the publication of this volume, which must be considered as a point apart. With the publication of *Sociology and Pragmatism* the corpus of Mills' finished writings are now available for public inspection. We can now see him in an original "pristine" form, and compare and contrast this with his later efforts. In my Introduction I have attempted to state the case for regarding Mills' writings as a continuum. Given the natural adaptation to styles of doing sociology which penetrated Mills' consciousness at a later stage, and as a consequence of a wide network of professional and intellectual associates, it is remarkable that the themes introduced in *Sociology and Pragmatism* remained a constant source of inspiration and utilization in his subsequent writings. Clearly, even the natural enthusiasm of an editor for his project cannot lead to a judgment of this as a "great and classic book" — but then again, this designation, so often assigned to the trivial and the transitory, has really lost its meaning. It is sufficient to say, and without fear of contradiction, that this book is an exceedingly perceptive account; and if the author of this dissertation had never produced any other work, it richly deserves publication and critical attention.

Those who know the original dissertation will be aware of certain changes. First, the title of the dissertation, *A Sociological Account of Pragmatism*, has been changed to *Sociology and Pragmatism: The Higher Learning in America*. This is not only a commercially more viable title, but better reflects Mills' main concern in the dissertation, the professionalization of philosophic education in the United States, and also his enormous indebtedness to the work of Thorstein Veblen.

The technical changes, from a more orderly presentation of chapters and sections to changes in content, have been held to a minimum, and have yielded to the guide lines established by Mills in his own notations. They are in no way central, and anyone doubting this, is quite at liberty to compare this published edition with the dissertation itself. It must frankly be said that there were a number of points where the editor was tempted to make changes or add explanatory notes, but this procedure was resisted for the obvious reason that such alterations would have violated the essential purposes of publication. And I have little assurance that such changes would necessarily have been for the better.

Thus, aside from the rather standard editorial services any good book deserves, the reader can rest assured that this is an authentic and accurately transcribed book of Mills.

The Postscript, "Some Last Reflections on Pragmatism" is the title I have given to a commentary Mills made on his own dissertation. This set of remarks is in the nature of a self criticism written by Mills so as to obviate the need for a complete rewriting of the dissertation without having digested new materials and methods of improving the original effort. Yet it is not merely a self-criticism but also an implied critique of the sociological profession or that portion of it that had not yet come to terms with the American intellectual tradition which had so much to do with shaping modern sociology. It is submitted in this volume as a Postscript rather than as an Appendix because it represents Mills' last thoughts on his dissertation as well as his first thoughts on the enterprise which remains open for future sociologists of knowledge. This Postscript is, I might add, noteworthy as an example of *intellectual* modesty; a characteristic frequently overlooked in Mills because of his *personal* extravagances.

C. Wright Mills was a "controversial" figure in American intellectual and academic life. To the degree that such controversy has been based upon an incomplete knowledge of what it was that Mills actually said, this volume will serve to ground controversy in increasing solidity, and with the passage of time, decreasing heat. It is neither desirable nor beneficial that the conflict of ideas be in any way blunted. But it is desirable and beneficial that such a clash of opinions be based on a maximum amount of information. Thus, it is to Mills' critics — friendly and otherwise — that this book is dedicated. Let the curtain open!

I. L. H.

Washington University
St. Louis, Missouri
November 10, 1963

Sociology and Pragmatism

The Intellectual Genesis of C. Wright Mills

IRVING LOUIS HOROWITZ

"Anything that obscures the fundamentally moral nature of the social problem is harmful, no matter whether it proceeds from the side of physical or of psychological theory. Any doctrine that eliminates or even obscures the function of choice of values and enlistment of desires and emotions in behalf of those chosen weakens personal responsibility for judgment and for action. It thus helps create the attitudes that welcome and support the totalitarian state."

John Dewey—*Freedom and Culture*

"There is no way in which any social scientists can avoid assuming choices of value and implying them in his work as a whole. Problems, like issues and troubles, concern threats to expected values, and cannot be clearly formulated without acknowledgement of those values. Increasingly, research is used, and social scientists are used, for bureaucratic and ideological purposes. This being so, as individuals and as professionals, students of man and society face such questions as whether they are aware of the uses and values of their work, whether these may be subject to their own control, whether they want to seek to control them ... All social scientists, by the fact of their existence, are involved in the struggle between enlightenment and obscurantism."

C. Wright Mills—*The Sociological Imagination*

It has been wisely said that a man never really overcomes his first love. I take this to be the case in intellectual matters no less than in romantic affairs. Mills' first intellectual attraction was for pragmatism. As a young scholar, it was for him a way of life and

11

a set of propositions about the nature of the world. From his first effort, to his last unpublished writings, C. Wright Mills retained a lively interest in the social and intellectual values of pragmatism. He was the embodiment of Jamesian Man; complete with a heroic definition of self. Like William James, he invested his political beliefs with a highly personal content. He inveighed against American intervention in Latin America quite in the same way, and with the same motives, as James' activities in the Anti-Imperialist League. His faith in intellectual activity as a basic way out of the morass of power was articulated in a manner made famous by James' words: "Les intellectueles unite!" At the same time, Mills' mistrust of narrow professionalism rings a familiar note to those acquainted with James' indictment of higher academicism. The similarities between Mills and James are so patently clear, it is disconcerting to see how thoroughly the connection has been missed.

During his lifetime and after, Mills was accused by some of being a Manichean, by others as a Machiavellian, and by yet others as a Marxian. He was racked for being a thinker saturated with a love of power, and at the same time criticized for his super-intellectualism, his idealistic disregard of real factors of power such as the economic system. The picture offered by critics is one which doesn't "tally". One reason may be that the early career of Mills remains shrouded in some mystery. Perhaps, with the publication of *Sociology and Pragmatism,* a number of ghosts can be laid to rest; and a full picture of his sociological ideas can be realized.

It seems to be the fate of significant figures that the size and extent of the caricature to which they are subjected is itself an inadvertent accolade. Mills, for his part, has been likened to Ernest Hemingway and Andre Malraux in literature; to Charlie Parker and Jack Kerouac in the world of marginal men, and to everyone who is anyone in the past history of socialism. In some circles it was fashionable to speak of Mills as the "Trotsky of Texas". The simple truth is that Mills was trained in philosophy and then in sociology; and that his mentors in philosophy were the pragmatists. That his appreciation for the "classicists" in sociology, of Durkheim, Weber, Veblen, Pareto, and Michels among others, should be so pronounced, is in good measure a consequence of his philosophic criteria of what good sociology should contain. His interest in Marx was a relatively late development. Indeed, it came well after his working acquaintance with the orothodox movements within sociology, and it was stimulated by the brilliant group of sociologists (particularly Hans Gerth) who had gathered at the University of Wisconsin after the Nazi rise to power, and reinforced by men like Theodore Adorno, Max Horkheimer and especially his colleague at Columbia, Franz Neumann. They made up the core of the exiled group which created the *Institute of Social Research* after having settled in the United States during World War Two. It is important to place these influences in time and space in order to highlight the central fact: Mills' initial intellectual contact was with the pragmatists. It was through their writings that his concern with problems of social action, political freedom in an industrial universe, and no less, his life-long contempt for all forms of metaphysics, was brought to fructification in a unique sociological approach.

Before offering an account of how this pragmatic inheritance shaped the content and contours of all of Mills' later writings, it might be useful to state the aims and purposes of his dissertation (SP).°

The major work of Charles Sanders Peirce, William James, and John Dewey are examined in an effort to explain their central conceptions in terms of their respective careers, publics, and general social-historical context. An historical account of the transformation of the higher learning and the professionalization of philosophy since 1860 provides a social structural background for more detailed problems. Relevant features of the personnel of academic philosophy and the intellectual and biographical composition of the Metaphysical Club are presented.

The position of Charles Sanders Peirce as a scientific technician and a philosophical outsider is found useful in reconstructing his perspective. Inquiry, doubt, belief, action, and sociality, the pragmatic maxim and logical realism are the central aspects of Peirce's style of thinking that are examined. The publics and associates of William James are developed and one of his key problems, the "pragmatistic" mediation of science and religion, is imputed to this construction. The translation of the pragmatic maxim into the sphere of personal life-styles is considered in detail. And from this consideration it becomes clearer both how and why Mills "internalized" pragmatism as a way of life, even after "abandoning" it as a theoretically adequate system of thought.

The most extensive analysis is given to John Dewey's work. Four of his publics, and several of his circles are presented; the foci of his attention from 1882 to 1939 and a full account of his career are given. Class, occupational, and demographic features of the American social structure are found to be relevant to an understanding of his generic perspective. All phases of his work are included in the analysis. The major concern is with Dewey's theory of logic and its component conceptions. It is significant to note that the two works which Dewey wrote just prior to Mills' work, *Logic: The Theory of Inquiry* (1938) and *Freedom and Culture* (1939), had the greatest impact on the early efforts of Mills to link language, logic and culture.

Naturally enough, Mills' earliest published writings reveal a persistent reflection on pragmatic themes. Now that these essays have been gathered and republished in *Power, Politics and People,* the extent of Mills' obligations to the pragmatic tradition can be more adequately gauged. In his study of "The Language and Ideas of Ancient China" Mills tries his hand at explaining why a scientific tradition is stunted in the Asian East, while flowering in the European West.

> In America, this type of generalization from laboratory and craft facts has gone further than anywhere else. American pragmatism from Peirce through Dewey, and the core of Veblen has been built squarely around the technological laboratory and industrial domain of culture. The Chinese did not. Thus, although the means-ends, the physically technical logic, was no doubt implicit in the craft work of the Chinese, this logic was not raised to form part of the circle of official canons of truth and reality. The thinking elite were concerned with other domains of culture: the moral, liturgical, and political. The conceptions and structure of Chinese thought cannot be explained in terms of technological domain and experiences. (PPP:499)

Undoubtedly, Mills' judgments on the nature of Chinese scientific work, based as it was on the pioneering efforts of Marcel Granet, is subject to drastic revision in the light of the later researches of Joseph Needham and others. But the point to note is how convinced Mills was that what the European West calls scientific is no less and no more than what the scientific tradition in America called pragmatic. It was the fusion of hand and head, of craft and intellect, which from the outset defined Mills' vision of the true scientist. This concentration on "intellectual craftsmanship" is an experienced participation in events, and not the sort of nostalgic commitment to organic labor common to the English Edwardians and Victorians.

An early paper by Mills on "Language, Logic and Culture" reveals with perfect clarity how deeply he was enmeshed with pragmatism — not simply as a mode of philosophic discourse, but more importantly, as a philosophy which sets forth the right sociological problems. The work of Peirce, Mead, and Dewey forms the warp and woof of his discussion. Language is seen "as a system of social control". Following closely Mead's *Mind and Society*, a symbol is defined as "an event with meaning, because it produces a similar response from both the utterer and the hearer." Communication is likewise defined operationally as the setting up of "common modes of response" in which the meaning of language "is the common social behavior evoked by it." The definition of mind as "the interplay of the organism with social situation mediated by symbols" likewise derives from Peirce and Mead. The capstone of this sociotics is the Deweyan definition of language and vocabulary as "sets of collective action" which are a consequence of social norms and values. (PPP:423-38).

Indeed, this particular paper of Mills reads like a digest of everything sociologically relevant which the pragmatists said about language and culture. By designating his work as "sociotics", Mills sought to encompass all sociological phenomena involved in the function of language; the ways in which language channelizes, limits, and elicits thought. But as Mills readily acknowledges, sociotics derives from the work of Charles W. Morris on the *Foundations of the Theory of Signs*. It is nothing more than the relations of signs to their users — what Morris called pragmatics — seen from a sociological perspective. From this vantage point, rather than from Marx or Mannheim, Mills came to a study of the sociology of knowledge. This is why we find Mills emphasizing the social basis for the *discovery of truth*, rather than the economic basis for the *uncovery of error*.

In his paper, "The Methodological Consequences of the Sociology of Knowledge," Mills argued from pragmatist assumptions that the relativism of the sociology of knowledge is not necessarily an argument against this branch of sociology since "the imputation of the sociologist of knowledge may be tested with reference to the verificatory model generalized, *e.g.*, by Peirce and Dewey", that is by probability and warranted assertions about the world. It was Dewey's *Logic* rather than Marx's *German Ideology* that led Mills to a full acceptance of the sociology of knowledge.

> The assertions of the sociologist of knowledge escape the 'absolutists's dilemma' because they can refer to a degree of truth and because they may include the *conditions* under which they are true. Only conditional assertions are translatable from one perspective to another. Assertions can properly be stated as probabilities, as more or less true. And only in this way can we account for the fact that scientific inquiry is self-correcting. (PPP:463)

Mills fully accepts Peirce's definition of a technical-intellectual elite, that is, those persons engaged in doubting, criticizing, and fixing beliefs. He had little difficulty in moving toward a sociological investigation of how beliefs are fixed, under what conditions doubt is institutionalized, and when criticism is tolerable. Indeed, Mills criticizes Mannheim for being inconsistent and ambiguous because, unlike Dewey, he confused factual examinations with the general relativistic aspects of knowledge.

> We need here to realize Dewey's identification of epistemology with methodology. This realization carries the belief that the deriving of norms from some one type of inquiry . . . is not the end of epistemology. In its 'epistemologic function' the sociology of knowledge is specifically propaedeutic to the construction of sound methodology for the social sciences. (PPP: 464)

On the other hand, Mills also employs Mannheim to criticize Dewey's notion of experiment as a form of scientific verification. In particular, he finds Dewey's physicalism as "informed by failure to see fully and clearly the difficulties and the ambiguities associated with the physical paradigm of inquiry and particularly 'experiment,' when applied to social data. Experiment in a societal situation does have characteristics and problems which experiment in a laboratory does not." (PPP:466). Therefore, as early as 1940 we find Mills using European *Wissenssoziologie* to overcome empiricism; and the American pragmatic tradition to overcome oracular rationalism. This was crystallized in Mills' *Sociological Imagination,* and in his collection of papers on *Images of Man.* The "classic tradition" was one which embodied a spectrum extending from Dewey to Veblen, as well as from Marx to Mannheim.

Throughout Mills' earlier efforts there is a dialogue with Dewey — sometimes direct and conscious, at other times elliptical and unconscious. Interestingly, getting beyond Dewey generally meant moving from an epistemological to a sociological pespective, and not, as might be imagined, moving away from pragmatism as such. Motives are imputed or avowed to be answers to questions interrupting acts or programs. But the model offered by Dewey is rejected by Mills for being "nakedly utilitarian". In fact, Mills writes, the determination of action is not only based on anticipation of differential consequences, but more concretely, is determined by different *social* consequences. The trouble with Dewey's theory of valuation from Mills' standpoint is that "there is no need to invoke 'psychological' terms like 'desire' or 'wish' as explanatory, since they themselves must be explained socially." (PPP:442). Dewey, to be sure, has the *terminology* of motive well in tow, but since "motives vary in content and character with historic epochs and societal structures," sociology is needed to locate the *vocabularies* of motives.

Since these essays form the solid core of Mills' early contributions to sociology, it is scarcely possible to dismiss the claim that pragmatism served him as a tool for understanding the critical importance of society. Further, it provided a way into the study of social-psychological problems on the basis of pragmatism, a vein which was already being mined by George Herbert Mead. Pragmatism always remained for Mills "the nerve of progressive American thinking for the first several decades of this century"; even though it took "a rather severe beating" from "fashionable leftism" and from "religious and tragic views of political and personal life." Pragmatism is defined as the "emphasis upon the power of

man's intelligence to control his destiny". (PPP:292). No matter
how critical Mills was of Dewey's world, in which there is no final
end to sustain life, he is far more critical of those, like Charles W.
Morris, who abandon pragmatism in a vain and empty effort to
locate some providentially directed *telos*.

> Dewey has not 'solved the problem of value', but sociologic-
> ally, one must ask: for whom does such a problem really ex-
> ist? If men in the large were as snarled as the ethicists and
> religionists make themselves out to be, there would not be any
> human action and we should probably all starve . . . Just what
> the goals, the course, the means of the Promethean today
> should be I cannot say in full. But *this* is our general condi-
> tion. It ought not to compel us to make the surrender and
> dish up, in our own minds, messianic world religions. Rather
> it should lead us to remain frustrated and attendant until we
> are in a position to see how to have the knowledge and the
> power to remake the social orders which trap us. He who can
> bear frustration may be able to use it at least intellectually; he
> who cannot stand it and yet has not the grace of silence,
> will only clutter up the work at hand. (PPP:168-69)

In the long pull, Mills stood with a pragmatism which could not
be "legitimated" over and against a pragmatism which sought legitimation in religion. The naturalism of a blurred pragmatism was
more appealing than the supernaturalism of an abandoned pragmatism. (PPP:168-69). Particularly in Dewey's hands, pragmatism
had a Durkheimian emphasis on social contexts of behavior which
in some way facilitated Mills' transition from philosopher to sociologist. The thought of abandoning pragmatism of such a sort in
favor of a religious vision was not possible without a corresponding abandonment of the sociological. And this direction Mills was
certainly never prepared to take. Thus, while Mills left philoso-
ophy, in part this was a consequence of the pragmatic prompting
to confront the world in its hard social forms. It never became a
"revolt" against pragmatism such as occurred with Charles Morris
and later Eliseo Vivas.

The kind of progressivism and populism Mills came to be identified with was to some degree foreshadowed in *The New Men
of Power*. The final chapter of the book is entitled "The Power and
the Intellect"; and it is essentially a plea for their fusion. The key

phrase, and one which appears at least once in every subsequent work of Mills, is that "as the labor leader moves from ideas to politics, so the intellectual moves from ideas to career" (NMP:281). Precisely this bifurcation, this great dualism between theory and practice, is what the mainstream of American pragmatism addressed itself to. While pragmatism has often been accused of undue emphasis on action at the expense of theory, it is more nearly the case that as pragmatism matures, the specific frame of reference moves toward the other direction. For as Mills points out in *Sociology and Pragmatism*, men like James and Dewey were from the outset tied to educational reform and to intellective functions.

Mills' high regard for "labor intellectuals" stems in some measure at least from a pragmatic base.

> Unlike many non-union intellectuals of more academic or journalistic types, the union-made intellectuals compete with each other in terms of the activity to which their ideas lead. They are not intellectuals for the sake of being intellectuals or because they have nothing else to do. They are union thinkers, with a big job on their hands. Such men are in themselves a link between ideas and action; this affects the healthily extrovert shape of their mentality. With them the gap between ideas and action is not so broad as to frustrate and turn their minds inward; they compete by having their ideas acted out, for better or for worse; they are not just waiting and talking. (NMP:286)

What is so very interesting in this summary formulation is Mills' clear regard for action which is experientially derived, and his relative disregard for a general theory of action as such. He speaks of the "healthily extrovert shape" of labor intellectuals, not of theoretical moorings as such. Labor is a creative process. Labor intellectuals are in the midst of this process, hence they have a "big job on their hands" in contrast to intellectuals who are not at the same time social actors. And even though Mills had a longstanding interest in the sociology of knowledge, his separation from the European tradition is made clear by his total unconcern with raising the problem of "interest bound" and "ideological aspects" of an action orientation. For Mills, labor has a historic decisiveness which the middle classes can no longer claim. Hence, his regard for their ideas is considerably more estimable. He speaks of "the main drift" rather than of ideas as such. The good labor leader is one who has a sense of the main drift. What this main drift is at any given point remains vague and unconvincing.

Having already imbibed the lessons of Weber and Michels on bureaucracy and elite, Mills sought a fusion between that sociological tradition and the pragmatic contours of American thought. He views the essential task of labor leaders "to allow and initiate a union of power and the intellect." Furthermore, "they are the only ones who can do it." Perhaps the least euphoric aspect of this analysis is Mills' final statement: "Never has so much depended upon men who are so ill-prepared and so little inclined to assume the responsibility." In short, the fusion of actor and intellectual, of behavior and thought, is hardly inherent in the labor movement as such. It is a desirable moral consequence of the good labor leader. Even in Mills' most extreme expression of "sociological empiricism" there is a strong moralistic turn — but it was a moralism which followed closely the Deweyan model for industrial reform through working class participation first expressed in *Human Nature and Conduct.* Blue collar socialization had a therapeutic value in itself; independent of imagined long-range revolutionary potential.

The context in which pragmatism arises in Mills' *White Collar* is of special significance. This work, which both completed the stage of Mills' enchantment with empiricism and introduced a more global view of social problems, shows that he continued to view pragmatism as essentially a protest philosophy of the minority intellectual. After severely castigating the conduct of scholars during the World War Two period as that moment during which intellectuals "broke with the old radicalism" to become "liberals and patriots, or give up politics altogether" Mills goes on to note how this act of betrayal (and he left no question that he viewed the unconditional support of the war effort an unbecoming posture for men of ideas) was connected to a revolt against reason as such. He saw this in philosophic terms as a movement in ideas from John Dewey to Soren Kierkegaard.

> No longer can they (the intellectuals) read, without smirking or without bitterness, Dewey's brave words, 'every thinker

puts some portion of an apparently stable world in peril' . . .
Now they hear Charles Péguy: 'No need to conceal this from
ourselves: we are defeated. For ten years, for fifteen years,
we have done nothing but lose ground. Today in the decline,
in the decay of political and private morals, literally we are
beleaguered . . . ' What has happened is that the terms of acceptance of American life have been made bleak and superficial at the same time that the terms of revolt have been made
vulgar and irrelevant. The malaise of the American intellectual is thus the malaise of a spiritual void.

In *White Collar* the pragmatic acquiescence of MacLeish,
Mumford, and Brooks is seen as *trahison* to the optimistic, rationalist, and progressive picture of the world provided by early pragmatism. It is interesting that during a period when Marxist philosophers were berating pragmatism as the "philosophy of imperialism" and other such nonsensical formulations, and when Conservatives were in full search of essentialist modes of thought,
Mills should have seen the plight of intellectuals, ideologically at
least, as a loss of nerve and of the cutting edge, that were typified
in the thought of Dewey and Mead, as well as Marx and Freud.

However tinged with nostalgia Mills might have been, he was
sociologist enough to know that "the liberal ethos, as developed
in the first two decades of this century by such men as Beard,
Dewey, Holmes, is now often irrelevant, and that the Marxian
view, popular in the American 'thirties, is now often inadequate."
They remain "important and suggestive as beginning points", but
nonetheless obsolete. Then what is to replace such views? Even
if we grant that Mills adopts Max Weber's analysis of bureaucracy
and Karl Mannheim's description of social consciousness, the character of his social philsophy at the stage *White Collar* was written,
remains under a shroud. Already present were Mills' critique of
the power elite, his condemnation of the political party system
which only argued over symbols and issues concerned with who
gets what within the social order, his appreciation of the function of *anomie* as a middle class, as well as a working class phenomenon, etc. But there was no real replacement of the pragmatic canons which initially shaped Mills. The very intimate and
personal feelings expressed in the book reflects the work of a sociologist *experiencing* truth, rather than one structuring problems
for future (and further) analysis. Mills was still linked to a prag-

matism in which "rationality was formally located in the individual", and not to the "rationality of class" as in the Marxist system. Indeed, he sees "fashionable Marxism" as giving "new life" to the major themes of liberal pragmatism. This was a view to which Mills held firm during the next, and by far the more hectic, decade of his life (WC:142-60).

The Power Elite, perhaps Mills' most controversial and yet enduring book, makes no mention of pragmatism. It does not have to. Implicit in the free-swinging critique of "mindlessness" ... "machiavellianism for the little man" ... "crackpot realism" is the sort of open-ended and tough-minded approach that made Mills distinct. No less, pragmatism became part of his definition of "the democratic man". It has been said, and often, that Mills' view of democracy was nostalgic, something which looked backward; based not on criteria of social class but on criteria of personal experience. This is to some degree accurate. What is important is not so much the presence of nostalgia, since a backward glance or two is characteristic of even the most wild-eyed futurist, but the quality of this nostalgia. It was not the mimicry by the poor of the rich, nor the vicarious enjoyment of the powerless in the exploits of the powerful, which enticed and engaged Mills' attention. He was too critical of the stupefying ignorance of the poor to be much of a populist (he certainly fashioned no "myths of the happy worker"), and he was too concerned with the machinery and agencies of domination and control to have much faith in the power of reason to change society (Mills' "mass" was in contrast to "publics" — the mass had so little that a cultural apparatus had even to provide them with their "identity"!).

His vision of democratic man therefore was still basically pragmatic; John Fiske's educated publics which made policy in the town halls of America remained at the seat of Mills' definition of responsibly exercised power. We must remember that Mills had much more than a common sense view of pragmatism. For him, it did not mean mindless trial and error, or conscious anti-intellectualism. The concept of a pragmatic life meant tough-minded pursuit of democratic life-styles. This would give the "articulate and knowledgeable public" the help needed to keep leaders of society responsive and responsible.

That Mills' nostalgia is selective rather than a general motivating principle is indicated in an interesting note on the fashioning of American ideology by the American historians.

> The 'good' historians, in fulfilling the public role of the higher journalists, the historians with the public attention and Sunday acclaim, are the historians who are quickest to reinterpret the American past with relevance to the current mood, and in turn, the cleverest at picking out of the past, just now, those characters and events that most easily make for optimism and lyric upsurge . . . In truth, and without nostalgia, we ought to realize that the American past is a wonderful source for myths about the American present. (PE:358ff)

Mills, so fond of criticizing the "liberal rhetoric," nevertheless ends *Power Elite* with it. He wants a civil service linked with the world of knowledge and responsibility, men shaped by nationally responsible parties that carry forth open debates, men subject to a plurality of voluntary associations. In short, he wants the social forces which the power elite have stamped out.

The Causes of World War Three is really an embellishment on themes raised in *The Power Elite;* and from the point of view of political sociology does not represent any new theoretical principles. What can be said of this "middle period" in Mills' writings is that he retained a basic regard for liberal values, if not for the liberals who sought to carry forth such values; and a basic regard for pragmatic philosophies, if not for the pragmatists who acquiesced in the "conservative mood" of the "political directorate".

Altogether new influences penetrated Mills' consciousness throughout the fifties. Beginning with Theodore Adorno, Max Horkheimer and especially Franz Neumann, Marxism, heavily textured with Freudianism became a central pivot for him. Of course, even prior to this acquaintance, Mills benefited from his contact with European trained scholars at the University of Wisconsin — especially Hans H. Gerth. Nor can it be ignored that the profession of sociology made its own claims on the shape of Mills' thought — so that his early reading in James, Peirce, and Dewey was not much reinforced by trends within the profession. However, contact with philosophy was not altogether absent, as is witnessed in his friendship with Charles Frankel of the department of philosophy at Columbia. The "classic" tradition in soci-

ology nonetheless revealed increasing divergencies from the pragmatic tradition. This severence was particularly feasible, since few
Europeans knew much or cared about American pragmatism;
while men like Mills revered sociological ancestors like Durkheim,
Simmel, Weber and Mannheim.

Under these circumstances, one of two reactions might have
been anticipated: either a full critique of pragmatism from a
Marxian point of view, castigating the encouragement pragmatism
rendered to European fascism, and to American foreign policy, or
a fading from consciousness of pragmatism. Neither was forthcoming. Mills was quite appraised of Marxian criticisms of pragmatism, and basically thought them erroneous. While the continued attention to pragmatism shown in *The Sociological Imagination* tends to seriously call into question the second possibility.

The final statement made by Mills on sociological theory is still
permeated with the attitudes he held as a young man. When he
notes in *The Sociological Imagination* "the motivations of men,
and even the varying extents to which various types of men are
typically aware of them, are to be understood in terms of the vocabularies of motive that prevail in a society and of social changes
and confusions among such vocabularies", he speaks very much
as the pragmatist. (SI:162). The widespread use of this sort of
Peircian semiotics in a chapter on the "uses of history" is indicative of the voluntaristic position Mills took in relation to events
in history. Even the phrase "events in history" fails to correspond
to this view, since the more likely formulation would be "history
as experienced occurrences." If Weber and Marx framed the essential contours of Mills' political sociology, Peirce, Mead and
Dewey framed his social psychology. "It may well be," Mills
writes, "that the most radical discovery within recent psychology
and social science is the discovery of how so many of the most
intimate features of the person are socially patterned and even
implanted". In Mills' view, human emotions take place with continual reference to "social biography" which in turn is part of an
"experienced social context". This is neither a neo-Freudian language of genetic types nor a neo-Marxian language of alienation.

Indeed, he was discontent with the "small-scale setting" of most
varieties of psychoanalysis, the tendency to make values reside
in the supposed needs of individuals in isolation and apart from

a meaningful social context. Once more we find Mills making an appeal to the pragmatic tradition for a sanction of his sociologism; this time to the work of George Herbert Mead. "The social element in the lens of psychoanalysis was greatly broadened, especially by what must be called sociological work on the super-ego. In America, to the psychoanalytic tradition was joined one having quite different sources, which came to early flower in the social behaviorism of George H. Mead." (SI:160). The basis of a sound social psychology involved plugging the humanism of the pragmatic tradition into the stricter confines of the psychoanalytic tradition.

One of the confusions extant with respect to *The Sociological Imagination* is the assumption by a number of critics — left and right — that this work represented a theoretical work "on the road" to a "Marxist world outlook". This is simply not the case. Marxism always remained part of the social science tradition for Mills — and not the other way around. If anything, the final chapter "On Politics" in this volume displayed a powerful sentiment in favor of "politics of exposure" rather than towards a "science of politics". Social scientists are said to be involved in "the struggle between enlightenment and obscurantism" the way Dewey held that all philosophers are involved in a struggle between living in an open tentative world of experience and a closed world of dogmatism and certitude. Even if it is proper to note that Mills was touched by "nostalgia for the past" the "past" remains to be defined. Here it becomes perfectly clear that his faith in the will of enlightenment to conquer power makes it implausible to define him in terms of the neo-machiavellian school of Franco-Italian sociology. The thought of power did not intoxicate or saturate Mills. If anything, Mills was infatuated with the potential of reason to redirect the irrational rush of raw power. This is not Manicheanism, but old-fashioned rationalism. And if *The Sociological Imagination* reveals a declining reference to pragmatists as such, it is because in their modern form they became celebrators rather than critics of the American experience, and not because of a declining interest in them. In the vacuum created by the modern pragmatists — their increasing ideological stridency in political matters and their decreasing intellectual involvement in social questions — Mills naturally enough began to place a new emphasis on the

radical aspects of the "classic tradition" in sociology from Marx to Mannheim. Thus, in his macroscopic work Mills moved away from a pragmatic framework, and into a more universal concern with contributions of radical European thought. The parochialism of pragmatic discourses on politics and society could not but have dismayed Mills as the years moved on. It became an unsuitable vehicle for his theories of power.

But if he moved away from pragmatism as a theory, he moved nearer to it as a way of life. He "internalized" the behavior of pragmatic man — at least of Jamesian man. This is plainly evident in Mills' one man crusade to present the truth about the Cuban Revolution to the American public in much the same fashion that William James lectured up and down the Atlantic Coast in 1898 in an effort to alert Americans to the dangers of the take over of Cuba by American imperialism. James' efforts on behalf of the Anti-Imperialist League were perhaps as much inspired by his personal dislike of Theodore Roosevelt as it was for any real knowledge of Cuba. And I venture to say that Mills' crusading zeal on behalf of the Cuban Revolution, particularly after the Bay of Pigs invasion attempt, was motivated by an equally *personal* (rather than political) dislike of the President. The force of personalities is important to the pragmatic mind. This is diametrically opposed to the impersonal force of history that is important for the dialectical mind. It is the difference between a philosophy which begins with personal *experience* and another which has its starting point in objective *existence*. In this sense, Mills certainly remained a firm adherent to the pragmatic canons of truth as involvement.

The portrait of Castro which emerges from the pages of *Listen Yankee* lends weight to his interpretation. For Castro is seen not as a model of theoretical acumen, but in terms of tough-minded practicality. "Revolution is construction". Indeed, the revolution is not so much an historic act as it is a creative act. "The revolution is a way of defining reality" an informant says. "The revolution is a way of changing reality — and so of changing the definition of it. The revolution is a great moment of truth". And while Mills describes this kind of thinking as "revolutionary euphoria" he leaves little doubt that this is a euphoria which he personally takes great pleasure in, a shared euphoria. (LY:114-15). The revolution is a "connection". It becomes a therapeutic device for linking dreams and reality; an enterprise which has direct personal benefits. The Cuban economy is described as an almost spontaneous agrarian reform, a "do it yourself" type of economic development. Castro is said to have given a check to the Commandante of agriculture and told to produce. The Commandante in turn asks the peasants what they want to do. Produce beans is the answer. And so it came to pass that the agricultural sector of Cuba was socialized without the sacrifice of human lives, and without recourse to rigorous planning characteristic of the East European Soviet bloc States. Spontaneity was said to be everything. Produce and it was done. Consume less and it was done. Defend the revolution against the insurgents and it was done. All on a voluntary basis, and all with the sort of spontaneity which characterizes the pragmatic criteria of truth as *praxis*.

The position of the Cuban revolutionist as drawn by Mills is not much different from the picture of the good man as drawn by Dewey in *Freedom and Culture* twenty years earlier.

> Our idea of freedom is different from that of the reactionaries who talk of elections but not of social justice. Without social justice, democracy is not possible, for without it men would be slaves of poverty. That is why we have said that we are one step ahead of the right and of the left, and that this is a humanistic revolution, because it does not deprive man of his essence, but holds him as its basic aim. Capitalism sacrifices man; the Communist state, by its totalitarian concept, sacrifices the rights of man. That is why we do not agree with any of them. Each people must develop its own political organization, out of its own needs, not forced upon them or copied. (LY:99)

The final words of Mills on this score, concerning his "worries for Cuba" would suggest that it is just these liberal values that he thought might be subverted by the charismatic leader. "I do not like such dependence upon one man as exists in Cuba today". His view was that the United States had an obligation to assist Cuba in passing through its euphoric and essentially monolithic stage.

What is at stake here is not the factual correctness of Mills' position, or even the soundness of his policy recommendations. This is, after all, an introduction to his dissertation, not to his final political views. What is relevant is the constancy of the pragmatic thread in Mills' thought — considering pragmatism as an ethos no less than as a technical system of philosophy. It is the judgment that the critics rather than the celebrators who will, in the long pull of time, be seen to have remained loyal to the basic philosophic and social commitments of the founders of American pragmatism. The fact that "fundamentalists" in American education have spent a decade attempting to displace pragmatism as a style of teaching and learning would indicate that the political potency and main drift of pragmatism is still toward mass democracy.

Who, after all, did the pragmatists influence? It most certainly was not, as Mills shows, the great unwashed. The impact of American pragmatism was popular only in the sense that the select publics who imbibed its lessons were concerned with social affairs and with demonstrating that public action can have public consequences. The muck-raking tradition of Upton Sinclair, Lincoln Steffens, and Ida Tarbell was not directed toward the "overthrow of capitalism" but toward the exposure of the meat-packing industry; and it was not directed toward the "liberation of women" but toward universal suffrage and sexual equality. In this sense, early pragmatism was sociological and not philosophical. It paid scant attention to "fundamentals". Its theoretical energies were focused on the practical, the immediate, and the reformable.

That it should be educators and journalists who responded to the pragmatic challenge was thus something in the nature o. an inevitability. And it is precisely this strain that had the greatest impact on Mills. If, at the outset, Mills seemed anxious to use pragmatism systematically, by the close of his career, he had begun to use pragmatism journalistically. The long trek from sociotics to muck-raking involved many sociological improvizations. But there can be little question that the major motif and theme undergirding these improvizations was remarkably constant. Mills was not a "half-baked" follower of Weber, Michels, or Marx. He was a fully developed pragmatic man. Seen from such a vantage-point, much of the criticism pointed at Mills has to be judged as largely irrelevant and off the mark. The reviewers of Mills' writings in the professional journals were unsympathetic and unresponsive, in the same way and with the same lack of comprehension, as the reviewers were fifty years earlier, of the writings of Steffens, Sinclair, and Tarbell. The irony of the situation is that the "true reformer" (which Mills certainly was) suffered at the hands of the true believer turned true scientist, while at the same time he found himself celebrated by the journalists and columnists.

It would be an error to conclude from these remarks that Mills was uniquely determined by the pragmatic factor. The chief personal influences on Mills — Clarence Ayres at Texas who taught him the values of Veblen, Hans Gerth at Wisconsin who was responsible for Mills' initial appreciation of the German sociological tradition, the years Mills spent at Maryland which instilled an appreciation of the economic factor in social history, his contacts at the Bureau of Applied Social Research at Columbia which deepened his technical understanding — would make it clear that Mills was something less (or something more) than a pragmatist fallen among sociologists. His later appreciation of the critical role of Marx in political sociology and Freud in social psychology further served to remove Mills from the pragmatic position.

Reinforcing this separation from pragmatism is the failure of nerve of the practitioners of the doctrine. Increasingly, pragmatism came to stand for acquiescence in the social order. In the assumption that the evolutionary process supplants rather than is a part of the revolutionary process. The pragmatists also came to lose the need for communication. The increasing professionalization of philosophy meant its relative isolation from its earlier search for a public forum. The new pragmatism linked arms with logical positivism in the essential details. It turned its gaze inward, and attempted to serve as a philosophical justification of scientism rather than social reform. In addition to which, the increasing concern with technical problems of epistemology and ontology led pragmatism to move a considerable distance away from the social and reform impulses of its pioneers. As Mills himself realized, this process already begins in the work of Peirce. It was completed during the decades Mills did his chief researches.

Furthermore, it needs to be said that Mills in *Sociology and Pragmatism* is not writing a philosophic study of interconnections, but a resoundingly *sociological* examination of how philosophy in America becomes professionalized, and the role of pragmatism, from the viewpoint of the sociology of knowledge taken in its most exact sense of how new social forces give rise to different intellectual styles. The variables in this study are sociological: the social origins of the thinker, the structure of the academic community, the requirements of the social context, etc. The philosophical criticisms of pragmatism are largely eschewed. This is not a study in the *truth* of pragmatism, but rather a study in its *utility*. The only comparable work in the sociological literature is Georges Sorel's *De l'utilité du pragmatisme*. But this latter volume is not genuinely of the same order since its chief focus is ideological and sweeping, whereas Mills' is institutional and intimate.

These qualifications registered and accounted for, it remains an ineluctable fact that Mills' early work on pragmatism was not simply a dissertation written for the purpose of acquiring a degree, or for the purpose of taking a simple or obscure topic so that a board of academic advisors would certify it out of blithe ignorance. Quite the contrary: Mills had his troubles with the dissertation — first in convincing his advisors that the topic had merit; second in the absence of the sort of hard data usually regarded as necessary in dissertation topics, and finally, in the resistance of the dissertation review board to pass on it until after innumerable delays. It is reliably reported that with the exception of one advisor, the examination board did not even know the work of Charles Sanders Peirce, and only had a fleeting knowledge of the work of Dewey.

That Mills would incur such professional risks in order to do this dissertation must therefore signify a profound belief in its value, in the importance of settling with one basic sphere of the American intellectual inheritance.

If this introduction has sought to make explicit the nature of Mills' connection with American pragmatism, it is not simply because this is a useful prelude to reading *Sociology and Pragmatism*, but because it might provide a basic starting point in the general understanding of this major figure in modern social science.

This volume is submitted as part of a continuing effort to place before the interested reader the major writings of C. Wright Mills. However, it should not be thought that this is either the primary or exclusive motive for the belated presentation of a dissertation written nearly a quarter of a century ago. For if this was the case,

Sociology and Pragmatism could interest only a few archaeologists of ideas. The chief reason for its publication at this time is the intrinsic merits of the dissertation; its always lively and sometimes brilliant linkage of two currents in philosophy and sociology which are distinctly American. There are precious few volumes which deal so thoroughly, and so deeply, with the origins of present-day American social thought. The fine work done by Henry Steele Commager, Ralph Barton Perry, Philip Paul Weiner, Morton D. White, and Richard Hofstadter in the social history and social implications of pragmatism are well known. To this list must now be added the work of C. Wright Mills. Known up to now as a sociologist and as a social critic, we can, belatedly to be sure, see him in his first form — as an historian of ideas and as a sociologist of philosophy.

°The code used for the specific books referred to is as follows: (NMP) *The New Men of Power;* (PRJ) *The Puerto Rican Journey;* (WC) *White Collar;* (CSS) *Character and Social Structure;* (PE) *The Power Elite;* (WWT) *The Causes of World War Three;* (SI) *The Sociological Imagination;* (IM) *Images of Man;* (LY) *Listen Yankee;* (TM) *The Marxists;* (SP) *Sociology and Pragmatism;* (PPP) *Power, Politics and People.*

PART I

1

Division of Labor, Religion and Educational Institutions

Since the Civil War the total social structure of the United States has expanded and become industrialized. It has shifted its occupational composition and professional groups have arisen within it. During the same period American philosophy had changed its foci of attention and several different styles of thought have become dominant.

Our most generic problem consists in explaining the relations between one type of philosophy, pragmatism, and the American social structure, "between" philosophy and society; operating as a crude but most tangible link are the educational institutions of higher learning. The professionalization of philosophy within American institutions of learning is the most obvious social anchorage of the field. There have been movements, groups, individuals interested in philosophy living outside the halls of learning, notably Transcendentalism and the St. Louis Movement, but they have been caught up in the drift of academic affairs and their philosophic bearings were perpetuated in the schools. From the standpoint of higher education we can at once study the changing social structure and the shiftings of philosophical doctrines.

Given such general impressions of the social structure of the United States since the Civil War as *background* this essay is therefore set forth in terms of the growth and qualitative transformations of educational institutions. Later, in appropriate contexts, more detailed structural features of the larger scene will be noted. What is needed first is some knowledge of the more immediate settings in which American philosophy developed in the last quarter of the nineteenth century. The history of pragmatism is, in part, a history of the academic profession in America.

The development if not the origins of pragmatism is a segment of the development of graduate school education in America. With the exception of Chauncy Wright, Oliver Wendell Holmes, Jr., and Charles S. Peirce, and very important exceptions, the major protagonists of pragmatism have been academicians: graduate students and later professors in American Universities. And it is precisely because they are outside the *universities* that Wright, Holmes and Peirce gain importance for our present concern. The more mature proliferation of pragmatism has gone on in universities at the hands of university men, but it was initiated by men outside of universities. We shall see that its transit wrought differences in its orientation and problems. One major social difference between Peirce on the one hand and James, Dewey and Mead on the other, which leads to intellectual variations around the pragmatic theme lies precisely in philosophy's affiliation with the schools, with its definite public, its direction of attention via courses and the circles and their social location into which it brought James, Dewey and Mead.

These are two immediate links binding pragmatists, and possibly pragmatism in its Deweyan phase, to the educational scene. First, as noted, the chief pragmatists, with the exception of Peirce, were part of the personnel of universities. With all of his mobility the center of William James' active life and work was at Harvard. Upon maturity, when he travelled, it was to universities to give lectures, and it was back to a university that he always came. He was a professor of philosophy. John Dewey was also a professor. He has done much more than teach, but it has been from universities that he came into larger communities to tell what he thought. The hours of George H. Mead's life were spent largely upon the campus and in the classrooms of The University of Chicago. The stronghold and locus of the development of pragmatism in the United States are linked to the situations of the American university since the Civil War; these make up the immediate social structure in which all but one of the major pragmatists directly lived and wrote. It furnished their incomes. In terms of what was happening there they saw their career chances and took them along these channels. Therefore, in understanding

American pragmatism sociologically, the transformations of the universities must be considered the most immediate situation of the pragmatic movement.

There is another link of the movement to the changing educational situation. Pragmatism, particularly in its later, and most influential phase, focused intellectually upon what was happening in the theory, policy, and organizational practice of educational institutions. Education became for Dewey, on his own avowal, his major interest, the center of his thought. In the proper place, this link will be examined in detail.

In a general orienting statement of the higher learning after the Civil War, we shall first link its new content and elective range of courses to the division of labor in society; second, note several mechanisms which secularized it; and third, outline the development of scientific and professional schools. Then taking three schools as typical, we shall trace the careers of two types of men, the new educational managers and the gilded philanthropists who were financial midwives of many of the specialized and scientific educational centers. A skeleton history of the graduate school and the Ph.D. degree in America will be presented. Finally, something of the social extraction and professionalization of the typical personnel in philosophy itself will be noted.

It is not a sociological principle that colonial societies fighting a wilderness necessarily fail to develop institutions for intellectual life. It depends upon the elements of the culture they bring with them. In Mexico and Peru the first universities in the new world were grandly established as early as 1553. This occurred within a generation after the conquest by Spain. Back of these universities lay the richest states in the world at that time. They were learned appendages to "a mighty monarch and a powerful church." The Puritans in Massachusetts founded an institution for higher learning in 1636. "No other commonwealth of the English-speaking world, even our western states, attempted to provide for higher learning so soon after its foundation."[1] Cotton Mather thought it was "the best thing that ever New England thought upon." Although the Anglican (through William and Mary in 1693) and the Roman Catholic Churches provided two other lines of academic descent in America, they will not concern us here.

It is widely agreed that the College at Cambridge was estab-

lished in order to train a "learned ministry to take the place of
Oxford and Cambridge graduates in New England, as they died
off." However, Morison contends that the root motive was broader than that. Some of the Baconian advancement of "learning"
figured in the venture. "Less than half the alumni of Seventeenth
Century Harvard entered the sacred calling." Theology was studied *professionally* only after the bachelor degree was taken, which
involved the seven arts and the three philosophies. Many became
schoolmasters, but in the schools there were religious duties. In
proper seventeenth century fashion, the object of education was
to attain greater knowledge of God through knowledge of his
works, and, secondly, the incorporation of "good conduct" or "right
action." It is Morison's contention that social distinctions among
those who entered have been greatly exaggerated. Yet, the total
graduates of the seventeenth century amounted to 475; and there
were 17,800 people in New England colonies in 1650; 106,000 in
1700.

The intellectual elite of seventeenth century New England
was predominantly clerical in occupation.[2] Lawyers were, of
course, a "despised class without professional status." The center
of intellectual attention was religious. Intellectual production was
largely expended in the oratory of the pulpit before a highly articulate and critical public. Given such audiences, the puritan ministry required logic. Particularly was this so since the branch of
Puritanism that founded New England was Congregational, with
its latent democracy, which was "an exceptionally heavy cross for
the autocratically inclined parsons to carry." In the face of such
audiences, logic was supplied at an early date in William Brattle's
manual, which was strictly Cartesian.[3] It is precisely against Descartes that Peirce is to revolt two centuries later.

The availability of listening publics probably decreased the size
of a readership, despite other elements in Protestantism. There
were no publishers, in the modern sense, in English speaking
countries until the eighteenth century. An author dealt directly
with a printer, publishing upon the professed persuasion of his
friends. Yet from 1655-1672 about 190 books and pamphlets (15
in Indian languages) were issued from Cambridge presses. No
matter how it is examined, the intellectual life of New England,

its personnel, its interests, and its organization, went on within the "embrace of Puritanism."

It is a very long way from Cambridge or Boston in 1700 to Baltimore, Maryland, where Johns Hopkins was begun in 1876. "Farming, fishing, shipping, trading" sustained the intellectual life in the seventeenth century. In the late nineteenth century modern finance, reared in the interstices of a machine industry, was providing the gilded, material base. Much had happened within the movement from an agrarian to an industrial, social structure. I am not here concerned with this total transmutation nor with many of its significant imports. Only as it ramifies institutions of higher learning and the intellectual scene does it come into my focus.

In general, the enlightenment of the eighteenth century was not reflected in any central way in the curriculum of the American colleges. There were some shifts in the direction of specialization and in the additions of scientific and commercial topics, but they could not be called inroads, although the seeds of such things as the system of election lay in Franklin's theory in Pennsylvania.[4] Those features of the higher learning that are distinctive for our purposes are nineteenth century outcomes, and in the main they come to fruition only after the Civil War.

But the growth of many of the implements of learning was continual. The 100 books and pamphlets issued from Cambridge presses in the third quarter of the seventeenth century were dwarfed by the flood of books in the second quarter of the nineteenth. The profession of writing could exist now without direct subsidy. Prescott made around $100,000 from royalties. Cooper and Hawthorne made more with their pens than most preachers. With increased education, there was a market for writers. The line of mercantile and professional families had two generations of fortune-accumulation back of them since the Declaration of Independence and hence could and did supply men and women with leisure to write. Not only were there more books, presses, writers, and markets for them, but all these factors existed within the confines of America; they were no longer dependent upon England. "In 1820 not quite one-third of the publications issued in the United States came from American writers; before the middle period had reached its close more than four-fifths were of domestic origin."[5]

The United States was developing the social organs indispensable to an intellectual life; the factors contributing to this development grew stronger after 1800. After the Civil War, in the last steps of the chronological road from Cambridge to Baltimore, the movement came to life not only steadily but with a glitter and a hugeness. Still practically buried in a mass of print were the first philosophical journals to be printed in America: *The Journal of Speculative Philosophy* was first circulated in 1867. It was followed by the second American philosophical periodical in 1892, which bore the title *The Philosophical Review*. Such publications and what they meant to professional personnel and in public, had to wait upon changes in the institutional bases of intellectual life.

The increase in student population and in wealth, both public and private, expended on organized higher learning after the Civil War, did not occur within the inherited forms of educational practice. Back of that wealth and its acquisition lay *qualitative* changes in the occupational structure of society in the United States. After the Civil War this structure was reflected in the older schools. It formed the scaffolding for many newly founded institutions.

The increase and complexity of the divisions of labor, and consequent specialization, ultimately meant, for the higher schools, the *elective system*. Introduced in Harvard in 1869 by the young chemist, Charles Eliot, by the end of the century it was a duly installed feature of all universities and colleges worthy of the name.[6] The essential arguments for the elective system had been made prior to the Civil War,[7] but only during the last half of the nineteenth century did occupational proliferations make the elective system imperative to the survival and growth of the schools and universities. R. Freeman Butts, in examining 15 representative colleges, indicates that during the last half of the nineteenth century they transited from the prescribed to the elective principle, to new subjects; from "traditional, classical studies" to "the sciences, history, and modern languages."[8]

The content of these elective systems was related to the emergent industrial and business divisions of occupation. It was increasingly *scientific, utilitarian,* and *professional.*

If the quantitative motif of what happened in the universities was swift growth, in content they moved from a predominantly religious orientation to a secular one. As an integral feature of this general movement there occurred the specialization and professionalization of higher learning. A pivotal issue of such movements, for our concern, is the rise of graduate schools and consequent professionalization of domestic philosophy.

In America a relatively unique historical feature of the education system has been the opportunity to go unilaterally from the lower grades through college.[9] Underlying colleges, no matter how they are sustained, is the elementary school system. Since the days of old Cambridge, the public schools had boomed into large proportions. Everything in the social-historical structure, especially after the turn of the nineteenth century, seemed to facilitate the growth of public schools.[10]

> "America" wrote Max Weber in 1906, "has no old aristocracy; hence there do not exist the tensions caused by the contrast between authoritative tradition and the purely commercial character of modern economic conditions. Rightly it celebrates the purchase of the immense territory in whose centre we are here, as the real historical seal imprinted upon its democratic institutions . . ."[11]

Among these institutions were the public schools. The absence of a fixed landed aristocracy, of clerical or military vested interests permitted them to take a "practical turn." The lower classes, including poorer farmers, were enfranchised; they had a certain economic surplus and these characteristics, even in the first half of the nineteenth century, facilitated the establishment of public schools. Both in the industrial east and in the western states public schools grew. For a number of reasons the push was not for sectarian schools on the elementary levels.

Apart from the general proliferation of secular occupations in an expanding *and* industrializing society, there was the high cost of maintaining individual religious schools. Protestantism, however, adopted early the habit of educating its children as an insulation against other doctrines, inculcating loyalty to one creed.[12] Secularization of the schools was forwarded by the heavy competition among the many Protestant sects, each of which wished to proselytize all pupils with particular versions of God, creed, and salvation. Agreement was possible only upon schools supported publicly, freed completely from direct clerical control. In his *First Report* to the Massachusetts Board of Education in 1838 Horace Mann wrote:

> ". . . to debar successive teachers in the same school, from successively inculcating hostile religious creeds, until the children in their simple-mindedness should be alienated, not only from creeds, but from religion itself; the statute of 1826 specially provided, that no school books should be used in any of the public schools 'calculated to favor any particular religious sect or tenet.' "[13]

Where there is too much religion and especially too many kinds, you may end up with none. In a dissertation at the Catholic University of America, B. Confrey speaks of ". . . the secularization of the public schools through the jealousy of religious factions . . ."[14] State constitutions forbade religious tests for entrance to state schools and appropriated no money to sectarian and denominational schools. With uniform adoption of texts, state- or county-wide, plus the lack of denominational homogeneity, no sectarian text could work out. In order to effect state and county certification of teachers, no religious texts for school officials, teachers, or pupils could be used.[15]

The immigration of Catholic families to the United States became socially visible in the 1830's. This created a new problem for Protestant communities. "Protestants feared that Catholics might . . . get the parochial schools into the public . . . system and secure state support for them. . . ."[16] Control was passing from the clergy.

Although by the forties the movement for public schools was a widely institutionalized achievement, the *higher* learning was still largely supported by "fees and endowments." Yet where students come from may affect the higher institutions into which they go.

Modern universities may be establishments of the state, of churches, or they may be maintained by private groups. Somewhat in contrast to other nations, universities in the United States have been predominantly of the latter two types. Until 1785 only denominational colleges existed. The University of Georgia was founded in that year. Michigan's legislature drafted plans for an educational system from the first grades through a university in

1817. Upon admission to statehood in 1837 it realized its university, and in 1870 it opened its doors to women.[17] This was the school where Dewey and Mead were to teach in the eighties and early nineties. Harvard was first Congregationalist, later it became Unitarian. Yale, founded in 1701, was Congregational; whereas Columbia (1754) and William and Mary (1693) were Episcopal. Brown (1767, called the College of Rhode Island) was Baptist; whereas Princeton was established in 1746 as a Presbyterian school. State institutions often developed from denominational schools, the initiative being taken in 1825 by the University of Virginia, which had been founded by Jefferson in 1816. New colleges were founded as the people moved west during the nineteenth century. And by the time John Brown made his raid there were in the United States 182 colleges and universities. Only twenty-one of them were state institutions.[18]

In the decades immediately prior to the Civil War, there was continual movement of the population westward. Among them and with them spread religious evangelism: Presbyterians, Congregationalists, Baptists — and these denominations founded colleges.[19] The evangelism brought many converts, and the colleges trained loyal young ministers to hold them, care for them, attract more. The Awakening may be polarized against the French importation of rational Deism, against the infidel in general, and against the Catholic immigrant. One set of institutional organs for the Awakening were these denominational colleges.

No matter in what kind of Unitarian guise worn by Harvard to conceal eighteenth century deistic leanings, these denominational colleges in the thirties and forties reincarnated the older religious aim. The stronghold and "mother" of the orthodox Congregational colleges was Yale; of the orthodox Presbyterian colleges, Princeton.[20]

> "Yale College," said Porter, its president, "was founded avowedly as a Christian college. All its . . . . arrangements have been inspired and controlled by the definite purpose that the education imparted here should be emphatically Christian."[21]

These two, Yale and Princeton, probably "furnished the largest number of presidents and professors to the colleges of the west and south."[22] It is revealing that even at Yale, later, in 1884, Sumner, an ordained minister, was blasting at the old curriculum, which by training people in the classics encouraged them to "think that they prove something when they quote somebody who has once said it."[23]

But in the West new state universities also arose. Says Beard, "The monopoly of the higher learning, once enjoyed mainly by the prosperous, was punctured at the expense of the tax-payers," which is only half the story considering that the larger proportion of students were in privately endowed schools. But it is true that the state universities as vehicles of social ascent facilitated the chances of the sons of farmers and mechanics who rose into the broadening middle classes of the new cities and into the ranks of the lesser professions. Public money expended on public schools rose from seventy million in 1871 to 200 million at the century's close, at which time it about equalled the funds privately endowed upon the higher learning. By 1894 all states south and west of Pennsylvania had state universities.[24] There are political and legal reasons why the educational upsurge from the West and from the lower ranks of the Northeast could not break the near monopoly of the higher learning by private institutions.

> ". . . . an attempt to conquer the older colleges by political control was defeated by Chief Justice Marshall in the celebrated Dartmouth College case, decided in 1819 — a spectacular event more important in American educational history than the founding of any single institution of higher learning. By securing the boards of trustees of endowed educational institutions against political interference, the Dartmouth decision in effect decreed that a large part of the terrain of the higher learning should be forever occupied and controlled by private corporations composed of citizens empowered to select their own successors, collect and disburse money, choose presidents and professors, and more or less directly determine the letter and spirit of the curriculum."[25]

Hence the way out for the lower and middle classes lay in the founding of the state universities. Yet, even "at the end of the century the private colleges and universities of the U.S. had endowments yielding revenues approximately equal to those derived from public funds by the state institutions of higher learning."[26]

In 1889-90, 315 universities and colleges had productive funds amounting to seventy-four million, in 1899-1900, 488 institutions had endowments amounting to 166 million. In 1928 the endowments had risen to one billion, 150 millions distributed to 1,076 institutions. From the late nineties to the mid-twenties Johns Hopkins had an endowment increase of from three to twenty-four millions; Yale, from four to fifty-eight millions; Columbia, from nine to sixty-three millions; Harvard, from ten to eighty-six millions. Such increases are typical of the privately supported institutions which still sustain two-thirds of the students in universities and colleges throughout the United States. There has also been a flow of private endowment to state controlled universities, as at Michigan, with a gift of twelve millions.[27]

Between old Cambridge and the new Johns Hopkins lay major developments in science. They had been particularly heavy in the first half of the nineteenth century. Watt had done his work. In 1844 Morse had successfully completed a telegraph line. Harvard subsidized Louis Agassiz, zoologist; Yale, Benjamin Silliman, mineralogist and chemist;[28] the Federal naval observatory gave research leisure to Matthew F. Maury.[29] Asa Gray led a flock of botanists to the study of North American flora; by 1850 they had the situation well in hand. In 1847 "The American Association for the Advancement of Science" crowned the specialist societies that had arisen on a national scale since 1815 among geologists, geographers, and statisticians. In 1846 James Smithson of England had made a bequest upon which the federal government built the Smithsonian Institution in Washington, a project with which Peirce's father was affiliated. Out of such work and organizations came textbooks in science: Cleveland's (mineralogy and geology in 1816) and Gray's and Silliman's texts in 1842 and 1830 respectively.[30]

Even though the graduate schools were to incorporate science in earnest only after the Civil War, there were separate scientific schools previous to this time. Founded in 1824 by Stephen van Rensselaer, The Rensselaer Polytechnic Institute had by 1850 become a regular four-year center of engineering work. Technologic training was "securely laid in the fabulous 40's and fermenting 50's."[31]

Prior to the middle of the nineteenth century such specialists or professionals, if you will, as "actuaries, surveyers, realtors, secretaries, patent attorneys, and accountants" as well as large groups of engineers who united chemistry and physics with materials and products of practical use were virtually unknown in Anglo-Saxon countries.[32] The occupational and social structure lying back of the rapid rise of such professions in America, as elsewhere, had been transformed by the mechanical revolution resting on technological science. In America there was no law nor class strong enough to stop the march of industry across the continent after the Civil War nor to complicate the contact of industrial growth and exploitation with naked resources. It grew. It built machines and technically trained personnel was needed to man them. It spread across the continent. Charles S. Peirce surveyed "in the wilds of Louisiana"; later G. H. Mead surveyed and engineered. Institutions arose to supply such personnel to serve machine industry. "Parallel courses" grew within the framework of those traditional colleges which could not bear to finance separate schools. "Independent technical schools" arose, such as the above mentioned Rensselaer Polytechnic Institute. The Worcester Polytechnic appeared in 1865 as well as the Massachusetts Institute of Technology, where John Dewey's brother was later to teach. There were also scientific schools established alongside some of the traditional colleges, such as the Sheffield Scientific School at Yale, financed by a charter member of the New York and New Haven Railroad, the Lawrence Scientific School at Harvard and the Chandler School at Dartmouth.[33] These were the three such schools existing prior to 1860.

In 1864 the Columbia School of Mines was opened. Significantly enough, it was in this technical school that Columbia gave its first Ph.D. Other scientific schools that arose in the great cluster after the Civil War were Lehigh University (1866), Stevens Institute of Technology (1870), the Case School of Applied Science (1881), Rose Polytechnic Institute (1874), Brooklyn Polytechnic Institute (1874). Of the sixteen privately controlled technical schools examined by E. V. Wills, thirteen arose after the Civil War.[34] One reason, given by Butts, for the interests of the colleges in scientific and practical courses was the beginning of the technological education on a high level as represented in the founding of Rensselaer Polytechnic Institute, which had the avowed purpose of ". . . affording an opportunity to the farmer, the mechanic, the clergyman, the lawyer, the physician, the merchant, and in short, to the man of business or of leisure, of any calling whatever, to become practically scientific."[35]

By the nineties science was part and parcel of large portions of the previous educational structure and had achieved its own institutions to carry its lore, technique, and mood. Not only was it privately endowed in new institutions, incorporated by endowments in older schools, but it was publicly supported in state universities. The growth of science and its firm institutionalization were immeasurably facilitated by the Morrill Act of 1862 which bestowed thousands of acres of land in aid to those states which would set up industrial and mechanical colleges. Science was a steadily growing portion of the universe of education in which philosophers as well as businessmen moved. Science also became an established department of government. From this development, the mind of Charles Peirce was to receive a heavy residue.

Specialization means the development of a distinction between the expert and amateur. For medicine and law, and in America even for such occupations as journalism,[36] it means an increase in the tuition period and it means schools and colleges to make possible and to implement professionalization. To make professions out of occupations you must have specialist schools. Some of them came later to America. The first "school of journalism" was not founded in America until 1908 (at the University of Missouri), but by the years preceding the turn of the third decade the average annual output of men and women graduating into this profession was approaching 1,000.[37]

In 1833 there were only about 150 law school students in the United States. In 1915 there were over 20,000 distributed in 140 professional schools. At present the number is, of course, a multiple of this figure. It is only within the last generation that a majority of the members of the Supreme Court have been men trained in law schools.[38] Oliver Wendell Holmes, Jr., a member of Charles Peirce's Metaphysical Club, was among the first members of the United States Supreme Court with a degree from a "law school." The earlier Puritan contempt for the role of the lawyer was made short shrift of by nineteenth century requirements of business and government.

The incorporation of secular and utilitarian interests was not limited to physical sciences, nor to what are more generally known as the professions. As the United States became less agricultural and more urban, as the occupational structure became loaded with business vocations, as it became a society steered by profitable transactions, and as these operations became not only more numerous but also more complicated, "schools of business" began to spring up. Upon all levels and in all types of schooling commercial courses were introduced, the innovation being most pronounced in the last half of the nineteenth century. In high schools, registration for commercial courses increased from 15,000 in 1893 to more than 75,000 in 1900. This increase was "almost three times as great as the increase in high school enrollment during the same period."[39] By 1900 private commercial schools and, more or less in imitation of them, commercial courses in high schools were firmly established. At a conference of the preparatory schools A. C. Miller pled for "schools of commerce." "It is no mere figure of speech that has long likened business to warfare and called business heads *captains of industry*." He admitted that in his discussion he had "tacitly accepted the ordinary mercantile view that business is followed for gain, that it is solely a money-getting pursuit," and attempted "to show what the higher education could do toward developing business aptitudes."[40] By 1920 the private commercial schools alone enrolled 336,000 students. In 1929 the United States Bureau of Education announced the enrollment of high school commercial courses to be one-third of one million.

The Wharton School of Finance and Economy, established at the University of Pennsylvania in 1881, was not imitated by others of its kind until 1898 when California and Chicago announced such schools.[41] The business schools of colleges and universities enrolled 9,000 in 1915, thirty years later the figure was 60,000.

Among many others, the ex-journalist, J. F. French (1853-1925) was most effective as a pioneer in "commercial education." He trained teachers to teach such subjects and organized and was Dean of the "School of Commerce, Accounts, and Finance of New York University." In 1909 he organized the "Alexander Hamilton Institute" in order to get into more effective contact with persons actually engaged in business. At an early point Harvard, Yale, Columbia, Dartmouth, Princeton, and Williams had added the study of mercantile and business affairs to the old rituals of clerical learning. By the nineties the tie of these schools to business enterprise and to the individualistic desire to augment individual chances with more equipment was clear. "By the end of the Nineteenth Century the universities in ... America ... were closely bound up with the public."[42] At least with the middle classes on the climb. And every step in this direction meant a decrease in direct clerical control, and, increasingly, an orientation within the capitalist system. The commercial value of the college degree is a product of the late nineteenth century. "A Harvard degree," answered a pupil interrogated by Adams, "is worth money to me in Chicago."

Two other developments associated educational agencies with the public and with social trends: adult education and household arts. By the late eighties the adult education movement came out from under the sign of "entertainment" and became linked with the American Library Association of New York. Extension work was introduced at Wisconsin Agriculture College in 1889. During the same year, Teachers College of Columbia University formally inaugurated extension courses. "In the next 15 years such courses became part of the curriculum of universities in all parts of the country." This democratization apparently did not enter deeply enough into the content of the work offered, for effective interest in the movement barely enabled university extension work to survive from 1894 to 1906. A new and successful push then arose. During the World War these courses were adapted to war explanation and were greatly accelerated thereby. In 1919 there were 2,000,000 persons being reached by university extension lectures in the United States; by 1930, the number had risen to 3,000,000. During the same period the number taking formal courses rose from 35,000 to 250,000.[43]

Nineteenth century industrialization, with its stealing of functions from the household economy, made possible courses in "household arts." Inclusions of home economics courses in the curricula of colleges and universities were in the main an eventuation of movements in the west and middlewest sections of the country. They were widespread in the agricultural colleges; being the coeducational refraction of the Morrill Act under which many of the colleges had been founded. When household arts depart-

ments were introduced into the public schools during the 1880's,
teachers were needed and these were recruited and trained
by schools of education, such as those at Columbia and later at
Chicago. Manual training was also introduced into public schools
during the eighties. The "vocational" aspect of such courses did not
come into the picture until around 1910.[44]

The secularization of learning in America was not some vague
mood and principle that was suffused through educational institutions. There was a set of rather specific social mechanics underlying and promoting the secularization, and they can be enumerated:

(1) Directly back of the educational changes on all levels lay a
shifting division of labor, which was cradled in the movement of a
total social structure from agrarian to urban industrialization. The
elective system of the colleges was a response to this shift in occupational structure and in turn enhanced its trend toward complication, specialization, and utilitarian rationality.

(2) Not only did this change existing institutions but it led to an
increase in the proportionate innovation of schools which had as
their purpose and practice the training of scientists and engineers, as well as institutions for the professions, for business and
other "practical" training.

(3) The schools became increasingly dependent financially,
upon the industrialists and the businessmen, not upon religious
sects nor upon public funds. At first the bulk of the new schools
were privately endowed; all the leading ones were, and a good
deal of the money for the qualitative expansion of the older ones
came from private fortunes. The huge industrial fortunes of the
Gilded Age and after, were overwhelmingly philanthropized into
"education," when they were philanthropized at all.[45] We glimpse
the newness of the rise of these endowments and educational plants
when we recall that less than sixty-five years ago D. C. Gilman, later President of Johns Hopkins, resigned the librarianship of Yale,
because he "could not obtain an assistant and had . . . to light the
fire in the stove every morning — a stove fire in a combustible
building."[46]

(4) Moreover, the rise of *state* universities definitely made for
the introduction of more secular and utilitarian subjects. It must
be asked "for what these institutions were educating?" The answer

is: for laymen of all sorts, for middle class occupational chances; certainly not for clerical careers. It follows that they should be manned by laymen and not by preachers, and we find this to have been the case. "They advance and enable industries," wrote E. E. Brown, of state universities, they "build up the professions."[47] Dr. H. P. Tappen, President of the University of Michigan, asserted that he wished "to adapt the University to the present wants of the community." Therefore, "scientific" courses, a "school of civil engineering," an "agricultural school", etc. were to be established.[48]

(5) As the proportion of endowed money was taken up by the originally denominational schools, their management, curricula, and content moved away from clerical hands and perspective. This occurred regardless of pronouncements. The University of Chicago, after all, was and is a "Baptist school." The trustees of universities and colleges more and more became businessmen, less and less clerical. The management of the schools was decreasingly dependent financially upon their conformity to church doctrine and perspective.

(6) Since the source of these endowments was not local, the management of the colleges and universities became less dependent upon local religious opinions. This is one reason why the larger universities in and near cities put much less emphasis upon religious conceptions than did the smaller ones. "See to it," said the *Catalogue of Central College* at Fayette, Missouri, in 1891, "that the mother's religion, the father's faith, the sweet influences of the pious home, are not discredited by the 'philosophy, falsely so called,' of the arrogant professor. Put your son into the care and keeping of Christian teachers, if you value his soul."[49]

(7) As long as there were only a handful of students, a school could the more easily concentrate upon training them religiously, for ministerial careers. But with increasing numbers of students, diversified and secular vocational chances had to be included in curricula considerations under penalty of institutional extinction.

The fact of having money with which to handle these students, particularly when taken in conjunction with the other mechanisms and the source of the money, smeared the restricted plan of the neat classical curricula with sheer growth. In the last quarter of the nineteenth century the number of students in colleges more than doubled.[50] Attendance in colleges and universities between

1890 and 1924 increased 352 per cent, whereas the total population increase was seventy-nine per cent.[51] The number of pupils studying college preparatory courses more than tripled between 1878 to 1898.[52] The number of students in colleges, not including normal schools and teachers colleges was in 1900, 104,098; in 1910, 174,213; in 1920, 341,082; and in 1930, 753,827. Should we include normal and teachers colleges the total for 1930 would be 1,033,022.[53] Increased enrollments in conjunction with the newer and widening occupational chances, plain for persons of all ranks to see, made for new subjects which would be ladders into these newer occupations. There was a student "demand" for such secular training and the educator produced wares to "supply" the demand.

(8) It should be remembered that the students who went to college were increasingly trained in grade and high schools that were public, that were in no direct way controlled by the competing religious sects. The growth of public educational systems for grade and high schools did not conduce to a clerical content of higher education. The mechanics back of the *public* character of the lower educational ranks have been set forth above. To them may be added further political and legal facts: *e.g.*, universal manhood suffrage, was a factor in the trend toward public education. With such a basis of control the state could not "entrust its civic and national welfare . . . to any agents except its own."[54] President Grant, the "official" spokesman for the Gilded Age, resolved in 1875 "that not one dollar" should be "appropriated to the support of any sectarian school."[55] No longer interested in preparing an educated ministry, the middle class citizenry after 1850 shifted the goal of public education towards the training for civil and industrial occupations.

(9) The increased number of foreign trained men was a factor making for secularization in the higher branches of learning. These men will be discussed below in connection with the growth of graduate schools. But here it should be noted that the possibility of receiving the Ph.D. degree on American soil, a possibility resting upon the existence of graduate schools, cut into the numbers of those who might otherwise have taken the Doctor of Divinity.

(10) It has been concluded by a most detailed study of the sec-

ularization of United States education: "After considering the civil administration in its entirety in so far as it is related to our schools, we see not the intention to oppose religion but the prevention of discrimination between denominations."[56] This seems true, but to it should be added the fact of the growth of indifference to religion which directed attention elsewhere.

The mechanics and structures which *set* the institutional base on an intellectual milieu "go on behind the backs" of the individuals participating in them. Nor are such shifts necessarily due to anybody's intention. The secularization of the schools in the United States was not primarily due to any sudden or gradual turn *against* religion. It was due, negatively, to inter-sect conflict and, positively, to those middle class chances for ascent that were manifested by qualitative changes in the occupational structure, and which directed interests to the side of the complex of religious conflicts and careers.

1. Morison, S. E., *The Puritan Pronaos*. (New York 1936) p. 24f. These published lectures along with Morison's *Harvard College in the Seventeenth Century*, (Cambridge 1936) and *Three Centuries at Harvard*, (Cambridge 1936), constitute the best factual account of intellectual organizations in colonial times. *See* also, I. W. Riley, *American Philosophy, The Early Schools*, 1907.

2. Morison, S.E., *The Puritan Pronaos*, p. 152, also 162.

3. William Brattle (1662-1717). This was the first text on logic by an American. It was used at Harvard until around 1765. *See* A. L. Jones, *Early American Philosophers*, Columbia University contributions. Volume II, No. 4 (June, 1898) pp. 11-12.

4. Cf. R. F. Butts, *The College Charts Its Course*, (New York 1939) p. 72.

5. This paragraph epitomized from Charles A. and Mary R. Beard, *The Rise of American Civilization* (one volume edition). (New York 1936).

6. Judging by the courses announced in the catalogues for the liberal arts colleges of universities, their number has continued steadily to increase. By 1900 Harvard was announcing 543, in 1930, 1,114; during the same period the University of Chicago rose from 960 to 1,897; Stanford from 373 to 1,095; and the University of Alabama from 46 to 437. Taken from a table by Charles Judd, *Recent Social Trends in the United States* (one volume edition). (New York 1933) p. 338.

7. R. Freeman Butts, *The Development of the Principle of Election of Studies in American Colleges and Universities*, Thesis (Ph.D.), University of Wisconsin, 1935. This is the most capable display of factual materials concerning the elective system.

8. *The College Charts its Course*, pp. 131-42.

9. Relatively. *See*, however, G. S. Counts' careful study, *The Selective Character of American Secondary Education*, "Supplementary Educational Monographs," No. 19, University of Chicago Press, 1922, and his Inglis Lectures of 1929, *Secondary Education and Industrialism*, Harvard University Press.

10. *See* Charles A. and Mary R. Beard, *op. cit.* p. 810f.

11. Max Weber, "The Relations of the Rural Community to Other Branches of Social Science", *Congress of Arts and Science*, Vol. VII. (Boston 1906) p. 745.

12. *See* Charles A. Beard, "Individualism and Capitalism", *Encyclopedia of the Social Sciences*, Vol. I, p. 150.

13. Quoted from R. B. Culver, *Horace Mann and Religion in the Massachusetts Public Schools*. (New Haven, 1929), p. 41.

14. Burton Confrey, *Secularism in American Education*, (Ph.D. Thesis), 1931, p. 126.

15. *Ibid.*, pp. 145-46. *See* Chapter III and pp. 124-25 for chart showing precise dates of such shifts to non-religious texts by States.

16. *Ibid.*, pp. 145 and 147.

17. For interesting light upon appointments of college presidents, *see From Vermont to Michigan: Correspondence of James B. Angell, 1869-1871* (University of Michigan Press, 1936).

18. For dates and numbers, *see* S. D'Irsay, "Universities and Colleges," *Encyclopedia of the Social Sciences*, Vol. 15, and Mary R. and Charles A. Beard, *op. cit.*, pp. 184-85.

19. D. G. Tweksbury, *The Founding of American Colleges and Universities Before the Civil War*, (New York, 1932).

20. R. Freeman Butts, *op. cit.*, pp. 98 and 117.

21. "The Christian College", *Fifteen Years in the Chapel of Yale College* (New York 1888) p. 382. Quoted in Joseph Dorfman's *Thorstein Veblen and his America* (1934) p. 42.

22. George P. Schmidt, *The Old Time College President*, (New York 1930) p. 96. Cited by R. Freeman Butts, *op. cit.*, p. 118.

23. *The Princeton Review*, March 1884, cited by Josef Dorfman, *op. cit.*

24. Mary R. and Charles A. Beard, *op. cit.*, Vol. II, pp. 467-68.

25. *Ibid.*, Vol. I, p. 819

26. *Ibid*, Vol. II, p 469.

27. *See* W. A. Orton, "Endowments and Foundations", *Encyclopedia of the Social Sciences*, Vol. V, pp. 532-33.

28. *See* George P. Fischer, *Life of Benjamin Silliman*, Scribner's (New York 1866).

29. *See* D. F. M. Corbin, *A Life of Matthew Fontaine Maury* (London 1888).

30. *See* Asa Gray, *The Botanical Textbook*, (New York, Wiley & Putnam); later in 1858, he did *Botany For Young People and Common Schools* (New

York, Ivison, Blakeman, Taylor and Co.) B. Silliman, *Elements of Chemistry, in the order of the Lectures given in Yale College.* H. Howe (New Haven 1830-31) 2 vols.

31. *See* the Beards' sweeping portrayal. Mary R. and Charles A. Beard, *op. cit.,* Vol. I, p. 814f.

32. A. M. Carr-Saunders and P. A. Wilson, "Professions", *Encyclopedia of the Social Sciences,* Vol. 12, pp. 476, 480.

33. The three routes and some of the schools mentioned are given by R. F. Butts, *op. cit.,* pp. 129-30.

34. E. V. Wills, *Growth of American Higher Education* (New York 1936). *See* chart, p. 108.

35. From a circular purporting to be the first prospectus of a school of science in the English language, quoted in U.S. *Bureau of Education, Circular of Information* (Washington 1900) No. 3, p. 484. Cited by R. F. Butts, *op. cit.* p. 130.

36. Allen Nevins, "Journalism", *Encyclopedia of the Social Sciences,* Vol. I, p. 420f.

37. *Ibid.,* p. 422.

38. *See* Max Radin, "Legal Profession and Legal Education", *Encyclopedia of the Social Sciences,* Vol. III, p. 108.

39. *See* article by L. S. Lyon, *Encyclopedia of the Social Sciences,* Vol. III, p. 108.

40. *Chicago University Records,* (December 8, 1899) p. 220. Quoted by J. Dorfman, *op. cit.,* p. 153.

41. L. S. Lyon, *op. cit.,* p. 109.

42. S. D'Irsay, *op. cit.,* p. 184.

43. *See* Donald Slesinger's and Elizabeth Mead's article, *Encyclopedia of the Social Sciences,* Vol. XV, p. 187f.

44. *See* Hazel Kyrk's article, *Encyclopedia of the Social Sciences,* Vol. VII, p. 427f.

45. Concrete figures are more readily available for more recent years. The Twentieth Century Fund reported in 1930 that the annual disbursement of American Foundations for educational purposes was $30,500,000; "individual aid" second with only nine million, and "pure scientific" research third with seven million. *Annual Report, 1930,* (New York 1932) p. 35ff.

46. A. Flexner, *Universities: American, English, German,* (New York 1930) p. 76. *See* below.

47. "The Origin of American State Universities", *University of California Publications, Education* (April 1903) Vol. 3, p. 39.

48. H. P. Tappen, *Review of his Connection with the University of Michigan,* p. 5. Quoted by R. F. Butts, *op. cit.,* pp. 154-55.

49. Quoted in R. F. Butts, *op. cit.,* p. 224.

50. *National Education Association, Journal of Proceedings and Addresses,* 1900.

51. H. F. Clark, *Encyclopedia of the Social Sciences*, Vol. V, p. 429.
52. *National Education Association, op. cit.*
53. Charles Judd, *op. cit.*, p. 342.
54. Burton Confrey, *op. cit.*, p. 145.
55. *Ibid.*, p. 148.
56. *Ibid.*, p. 150.

2

Types of Men and the New Schools

Emerging from a panorama of figures, dates and trends into a closer view, we can do no better than reconstruct typical events as they occurred in the lives of two types of men. The careers of these two types are especially important to our understanding of the situation of higher learning in America after the Civil War.

The most conspicuous type is the "educator" who arose to plan, institute, and administer the new universities that emerged or to take over previously existing colleges. They were presidents of the schools. Five of these presidents are representative: J. B. Angell of the University of Michigan, C. E. Eliot of Harvard, D. C. Gilman of Johns Hopkins, White of Cornell, and W. R. Harper of the University of Chicago. These men played key roles in building the educational structure. It is significant that to mention four of their (*their* is used advisedly) institutions is to point to settings where pragmatists went to school and taught and thought out their view of life. Such types of educators were not limited to those named above. Of the same stamp and perhaps as important were such presidents as: Jordan of Stanford, Wheeler of California, Hall of Clark, Van Hise of Wisconsin, MacLean of Iowa, Alderman of Virginia, Wilson of Princeton, Thomas of Ohio State, Hadley of Yale, Butler of Columbia.[1] Some of these men made their careers in state universities, some in private institutions. Wherever they were, a difference between them and the generation of administrators preceding them in the academies was the fact that these men had money to spend. As active "administrators" most of these new men were too busy raising and managing money and taken up with public relations to teach "philosophy" as had previous college presidents.

Several of them were active outside of their academies. For example, James B. Angell, President of the University of Michigan, was "minister plenipotentiary to revise treaties" with China in 1880-82, and in 1897 was minister to Turkey.

A second type of man who figured in the transformation of educational agencies after the Civil War was the capitalist philanthropist. This type directly links the school to economic changes and to the new industry. He was the economically necessary and immediate precipitant of those schools most important to the pivotal shiftings in education. Chicago's Rockefeller was an oil man; Hopkins, a rich Baltimore merchant. Such men, extracting great wealth from the vicissitudes and expanding exploitations of the Gilded Age, handed fractions of it to the managerial educators who guided their philanthropic investments. Carnegie was persuaded by Gilman not to found another college but instead a Foundation. Cornell (1865) was endowed by Ezra Cornell, Boston University (1869) by Isaac Ridi, Jacob Sleeper, and others; Vanderbilt was remade in 1872 by a gift from "Commodore" Cornelius Vanderbilt.

Perhaps if we grasp how the careers of Rockefeller and Harper, and of Johns Hopkins and D. C. Gilman crossed, we shall see more clearly the mechanics of the new organizations for learning. And if we round it out with a brief statement of President Eliot's career at Harvard, we shall have a grasp of the representative institutions of the new schools.[2] It is not irrelevant nor coincidental that we shall also have the major settings of the pragmatists. James, Peirce and Mead were students at Harvard. James taught there from 1880 until his death in 1910. Peirce lectured at Johns Hopkins and Dewey got his degree there. And it was at Rockefeller's Chicago plant that Mead and Dewey worked out the major elements of their brands of pragmatism.

In the background of William Rainey Harper ". . . we look in vain for a great line of forbears. There was no wealth in the family . . . he had to make his own way in the world."[3] He was born in Ohio and, quite properly, in a house of logs. His father was "the merchant" of New Concord, which harbored a population of from 600-800 and which was inhabited by "a peculiar people," *i.e.*, they were United Presbyterians. William Harper went to Yale, and in January, 1879, "Dr. Harper, Ph.D.," began to teach Hebrew at Morgan Park, in the Baptist Union Theological Seminary. A little later he taught a summer session, then he began to teach Hebrew by correspondence. He sent out the first "lesson" in 1881. John D. Rockefeller had been giving money to the seminary; he was vice-president of its Board of Trustees. When, in 1886, Yale made a bid for Harper, Rockefeller wrote to the seminary advising them of this "movement." During this year Harper was teaching Hebrew to "1,000 men" by mail. He was organizing things. Yale College wrote him three letters in one week.[4] They telegraphed, and though Harper was interviewed in New York by John D. Rockefeller in the interests of the seminary, he went to Yale in 1886. But Rockefeller was settling upon the idea of founding "a big college or a university". As the idea focused for realization, he again sought out Harper. By 1889 plans were begun in earnest for "not a college, but a university".[5] There was a lot of milling around with the idea. Harper wanted "an additional million" to insure that the place would be a "university to begin with". Then on September 6, 1890, Rockefeller wrote: "Gentlemen: I will contribute one million dollars to the University of Chicago..."[6] That was the beginning. Down to 1919 Rockefeller had given a little over thirty four and a half million to the institution that President Harper built.[7]

Examination of the degrees held by professors, associate and assistant professors whom Harper selected for his first faculty, reveals that out of a total of about seventy five, only twelve of them had D.D.'s or B.D.'s. The rest had earned the Ph.D. degree, LL.D., or merely B.A. and M.A.[8] President Harper himself had the D.D. only honorarily, after his career had been well set in its direction.

18,936 Bachelor Degrees were awarded during the years 1893 through 1930-31. The comparison of the occupations of the fathers of these students with the occupations eventually pursued by the graduates is most illuminating:

TABLE 1. OCCUPATIONS OF UNIVERSITY OF CHICAGO
GRADUATES AND OF THEIR FATHERS, 1893 - 1931

Occupations	Per cent		Per cent	
	Fathers	Sons	Fathers	Daughters
Professional Services ....24......62..			..28........73....	
Business, Commercial ......40......32.			..44........15....	
and Proprietary				
Services				
Others ....36...... 6..			.28........11....	

Taken in time "the percentage from the commercial [element]
increased consistently from 1901 to 1930 and the percentage from
the proprietary and agricultural groups decreased consistently
during this period."[9] During this period no changes in other groups
were noted. Of the sixty-two per cent of the graduates who became
professional, twenty-seven per cent were teachers, about thirteen
per cent of them in colleges and universities; whereas nine per cent
of the thirty-two per cent of those who had gone into business were
"managerial."[10] In the period from 1893 to 1930 nearly two-thirds
of the graduates "financed part or all of their college training by
working their way..."[11]

Not only within the University of Chicago, but off its campus
this ascent pattern and aim were furthered. Sociologically, correspondence schools are anchored in a faith that individuals can advance their life chances and personal fortunes through increased
vocational and "social" competence. The president of Chicago had
begun correspondence work in the early eighties, and when Chicago University was opened, he quickly established a correspondence department.[12]

Such, in brief, was the educational situation in which John Dewey developed his pragmatism and in which which G. H. Mead
and James Tufts worked at its implications. The student audience
with which they all worked, among whom were many of those
younger men who were first to bear the pragmatic *oriflamme*, was
moving from the older middle class stratum of commercial and
business careers into the newer professions and skilled groups. The
Chicago school of pragmatism was developed in the center of a
major vehicle of (1) class ascent and (2) professionalization. Its
first public was drawn from those on the make within these two
patterns.

Daniel Coit Gilman was the son of a prosperous New England

manufacturer and business enterpriser.[13] He was of the Yale class of 1852, then for a time he was a Harvard graduate student. In 1853, he sailed with A. D. White for Europe as "attachés" of a United States Legation at St. Petersburg.[14] He attended the Universal Exposition at Paris in 1855. Then he came back home, to become Assistant Librarian at Yale. He remained at New Haven for seventeen years. During the early part of his life he was undecided as to whether or not he would preach. Although he applied for a license under external circumstance, he did not attend any theological school.[15] At Yale he was employed in raising funds for the scientific school. He had a family connection with Professor Silliman, one of whose daughters was married to Gilman's brother. He became "Professor of Physical Geography" in the scientific school in 1863, teaching there for nine years, but he was even then organizing and executing clubs and art displays and functioning on building committees. He resigned the Librarianship in 1865, writing: "I am quite discouraged."[16] President Woolsey advised him that perhaps Yale was not the place for his talents. These talents were used in a truncated manner at The University of California as President of that institution. But, in the meanwhile, something was happening on the East Coast.

In Baltimore a "large minded man" was acquiring "his fortune by slow and sagacious methods." Born in 1794, of a family which had been for several generations members of the "Society of Friends," John Hopkins "came to Baltimore without any capital but good health, the thrifty habits . . . capacity for a life of industrious enterprise."[17] "By his economy, fidelity, sagacity, and perseverance he rose. . ." Gilman later wrote that he was ". . . a merchant who had accumulated . . . by . . . industry and frugality, and by great financial ability."[18] He was a wholesale grocer who became a financial capitalist. He did not marry. He became president of a bank, a Director of the Baltimore and Ohio Railroad. In 1873 he died, leaving several millions for a "university and a hospital." The trustees who managed the fund included: two "merchants of the highest credit" who "sailed their ships on distant seas;" two judges of the Supreme Bench in Baltimore, one who "observed the heavens" and "practiced photography" and "attended scientific lectures",[19] another who had been a mayor of the City. There was also among them the President of the Baltimore and Ohio Railroad. In addi-

tion there were seven businessmen." Seven of the twelve trustees
were Friends. There did not seem to have been any clergyman on
the Board of Trustees. These men proceeded very cautiously: in
1874 the trustees read books on colleges, visited them. In December they elected D. C. Gilman president. He was selected upon the
unanimous advice of Eliot of Harvard, A. W. Andrews, and Angell
of Michigan.[20] Gilman left his presidency of the University of
California and went to Europe, conferring there with university officials. Then almost wholly unrestricted, he sought out a faculty:
"in the selection of the faculty...we endeavored to consider especially the devotion of the candidate to some particular line of
study, and the certainty of his eminence in that specialty..."[21]
Gilman contacted a young man, an "assistant instructor" in the
Rensselaer Polytechnic. He looked promising. Gilman wrote to the
Trustees, and they replied: "Engage that young man and take him
with you to Europe, where he may follow the leaders of his science and be ready for a professorship." Thus Henry A. Rowland
was employed.[22] Benjamin Peirce wrote Gilman to get J. J. Sylvester, English geometrist.[23] And Sylvester was employed. In the list
of twenty-nine "professors in the philosophical faculty" appointed
at Johns Hopkins from 1874 to 1893, there is not one listed as a
D.D.; they are Ph.D.'s, L.L.D.'s or Sc.D.'s The same holds for all
the associate professors throughout this period.[24] At the inauguration, no less a Darwinian than T. H. Huxley made the address,
blessing the institution as no clergyman ever could.

As the first of guiding principles, it was written that "All sciences are worthy of promotion."[25] At his inauguration, Gilman
said that "men of science and of affairs" concede that geographical,
meteorological, geodetical, etc., surveys are needed in the United
States. "If our University can provide instructions in these departments . . . it will do a good service."[26] At Chicago's convocation in
1903, Gilman again hailed science: "Science is accepted as synonymous with exact knowledge. Truth takes the place of tradition."[27]
The Johns Hopkins University at Baltimore was not founded by
any "commonwealth" nor by any church. The whole thing was of
the new order. In spite of Harvard, a university in the typically modern sense did not exist in America before 1876, during which year
Johns Hopkins began.[28] For twenty years Hopkins was the most distinctive center of learning in America, and the most stimulating in

its effects upon other institutions. It had a medical school, a *faculty of philosophy;* it founded journals and "series" for the dissemination of monographic endeavors. It was a research center for mature professional scholars. Its undergraduate school, established later, has only been an appendage. It inaugurated graduate and professional schools.

The figures on its growth of faculty and students fail to show its tremendous influence on the structure and animus of the higher learning in America.

TABLE 2. JOHNS HOPKINS: TEACHERS, STUDENTS, AND
DEGREES, 1876-1893*

Year	Teachers	Total Number of Students	Ph.D.'s Conferred
1876-77	29	89	0
1877-78	34	104	4
1880-81	39	176	9
1881-82	43	175	9
1883-84	49	249	15
1892-93	72	551	28

*Adapted from *Ninth Annual Report of the President,* Johns Hopkins University, Baltimore, 1884.

Since the tables and figures throughout are not intended to serve any comparative or causal purposes, it does not seem necessary to control increases by references to growths of any other populations. That the field of Hopkins' magnet worked across the nation is shown by the fact that only 21.8 per cent of the graduate students at Johns Hopkins received their first degree in Maryland, whereas 64.4 per cent of those at Harvard received theirs in Massachusetts, and 56.6 per cent of those at the University of Michigan received theirs in Michigan.[29]

Among these figures for "Ph.D.'s conferred" at Hopkins was a young man from Vermont named John Dewey. Among the student body was the immigrant's son, Thorstein Veblen. The longest academic connection held by Charles Peirce was at Hopkins. Yet even here Charles Peirce could not become established on the inside. He was listed as a "lecturer."

When Reverend Thomas Hill resigned the presidency at Harvard in 1868, a great discussion arose over whether the new president should be a "clergyman" or a "professional educator." In *The Atlantic Monthly* of 1869, there appeared two articles under the title of "The New Education," which set forth "the need of a high grade technical education for the youth of America." It was written by Charles William Eliot, then a Professor of Chemistry and Mineralogy at Massachusetts Institute of Technology, who was a recently elected member of the Board of Overseers of Harvard College, and the content of whose article "coincided, in the main, with recommendations made by a report of a Committee of the Overseers..."[30] Attention went to Eliot for the presidency of Harvard. In March, 1869, he was chosen by the corporation, and his choice was sanctioned by the Board of Overseers in May. The same year Ulysses S. Grant became president of the United States.

Charles William Eliot was born in Boston, 1834, two years after Charles Peirce. He graduated from Harvard in 1853 and the following year was a tutor in mathematics. By 1858 he was assistant professor of mathematics and chemistry, and in 1861 had charge of the chemistry laboratory of Lawrence Scientific School.[31] He went to Europe, coming back in time to turn down in 1865 a $5,000 per year offer to become superintendent of a cotton mill at Lowell.[32] He went to the Massachusetts Institute of Technology and from there to Harvard. Harvard in 1879 felt the competition of rival, newer schools which were not hampered by traditions. "Age was no safeguard... in pulsating young America." The clerical tradition at Harvard had been broken by Quincy's election,[33] but the new president was not only not a clergyman, he was a physical technician who in his inaugural address expressed the view: "Philosophical subjects should never be taught with authority. They are not established sciences... [they are] full of... bottomless speculation."[34] Eliot was an enthusiast for civil service reform; he steadily opposed protectionism.

Illustrative of Eliot's efforts to secure financial support for Harvard's growth is the story told by Charles Kendall Adams in *The Chronicle* (February, 1885): "I remember a few years ago it was said that whenever a rich man of Boston saw President Eliot coming, he reached for his check-book and anxiously asked: 'and how much must it be?' "[35]

The roots and the import of the elective system, with which Eliot's name is correctly linked, have already been discussed. He was of the new educational scene, indeed, a landmark in its conquest. It should, however, be mentioned that it was not until "the decade of the 1890's that the Harvard Graduate School began to exert an influence comparable to that of the Johns Hopkins University..."[36] Nevertheless, from 1873-1928, 1,596 young men earned the Ph.D. degree from Harvard.[37]

1. Drawn from a list given by Walton C. John in *Graduate Studies in Universities and Colleges, Educational Bulletin* (Department of Interior 1934), No. 20.

2. These three men are most usually given as the "chief makers of the American University".

3. T. W. Goodspeed, *William R. Harper* (Chicago 1928) p. 3.

4. *Ibid.*, pp. 57 and 59.

5. *Ibid.*, p. 86.

6. T. W. Goodspeed, *A History of the University of Chicago, 1891-1916* (Chicago 1917) p. 163.

7. *Ibid.*, p. 498.

8. *Ibid.*, counted from listing of faculty for 1892-93.

9. *Ibid.*, p. 9.

10. *Ibid.*, pp. 65-66.

11. *Ibid.*, p. 104.

12. Many of the one hundred fifty academic institutions and the three hundred privately owned correspondence schools (with their combined enrollment of 1,400,000 in 1929) were directly steered or partially financed by business corporations... See Herbert Salow, *Encyclopedia of the Social Sciences*, Vol. III, p. 444f. For a brief glimpse at the *status* aspect of private correspondence schools, see Ella Woodyard, *Culture at a Price: A Study of Private Correspondence School Offerings* (New York 1940).

13. Fabian Franklin, *Life of D. C. Gilman*, (New York 1910) p. 3.

14. *Ibid.*, p. 15.

15. *See* his letter to his elder brother who was a Congregational minister, *Ibid.*, pp. 36-37.

16. Letter to President Woolsey, *Ibid.*, p. 77.

17. D. C. Gilman, *The Johns Hopkins University* (Baltimore 1893), no title page, p. 1.

18. D. C. Gilman, *The Launching of a University*, Dodd Mead & Co. (New York 1906) p. 27.

19. *Ibid.*, p. 31.

20. D. C. Gilman, *The Johns Hopkins University*, p. 1.

21. *Ibid.*, p. 4.

22. Fabian Franklin, *op. cit.*, pp. 197-98.

23. *Ibid.*, pp. 214-15.

24. Tallied from data in, D. C. Gilman, *op. cit.*

25. *Ninth Annual Report of the President*, Johns Hopkins University, (Baltimore 1884) p. 59.

26. *Addresses at the Inauguration of D. C. Gilman* (Baltimore 1876) p. 45.

27. D. C. Gilman, *The Launching of a University*, p. 251.

28. A. Flexner, *op. cit.*, p. 42.

29. *See* table in *U.S. Bureau of Educational Report, 1889-90* (Washington, D.C. 1893) Vol. 2, p. 826.

30. *See* S. E. Morison, *Three Centuries of Harvard* (Cambridge 1936) pp. 325-26. Also *see* John Spencer Clark's *John Fiske: Life and Letters* (Boston and New York 1917) Vol. I, pp. 343-44.

31. Henry James, *Charles William Eliot* (Boston and New York 1930) Vol. I, p. xv.

32. S. E. Morison, *op. cit.*

33. *Ibid.*, Begin pp. 323-24, 327.

34. S. E. Morison, *Development of Harvard*, p. lxiii.

35. *The Chronicle* (February 1885) quoted by R. F. Butts, *op. cit.*, p. 177.

36. C. H. Haskins, "The Graduate School of the Arts and Sciences" in Morison, *op. cit.*, p. 456.

37. *Ibid.*

3

Graduate Schools and Professionalization

"In the modern sense, American universities and colleges carried on relatively little graduate study and research until after the Civil War."[1] There were, of course, from an early date, M.A.'s given: degrees above the B.A. were honorary. For example, at Harvard in 1825 anyone who had taken a B.A. degree there and "kept good moral character for three years" could pay a fee and therewith entitled to the Master's degree. Such seems to have been the case at Harvard until 1872. Indeed, in 1880 there were 119 honorary M.A. Degrees conferred in the United States: in 1885, 140.[2] In 1874 there was awarded at Harvard an earned M.A. degree. Harvard's graduate school was only a name in 1872. It began, in fact, in 1877-78.[3] Wills asserts that it was "relatively undeveloped" until the early nineties.[4] And it is true that in 1887-88 there were only seven doctorates awarded, and there were 217 graduate students enrolled, including both the M.A. and the Ph.D. level.[5] During the early years of Yale, also, the M.A. was automatic upon payment of a fee. Not until 1876 did Yale confer an earned Master of Arts degree. Yale's graduate school was really organized in 1872.[6] For Princeton, the first M.S. was conferred in 1879; at the University of Pennsylvania, 1891. However, the University of Michigan granted its first M.A. on the basis of course work and thesis in 1859; its first Ph.D. was conferred in 1876. The University of North Carolina was also a forerunner, granting an earned M.A. degree in 1856. In 1858 Henry Barnard, then associated with the University of Mississippi, wrote a proposal to the Trustees to add to the regular prescribed B.A. course a post-graduate course leading to the M.A. and including "scientific and literary" subjects.[7] Thus the growth of graduate schools at least in one place was a phase of the shift from prescribed to elective courses, permitting a modified retention of the former. It is significant of the character of the trend toward the Ph.D. that Columbia's first Ph.D. (1875) was granted under the School of Mines.[8]

Among the state universities, the University of Nebraska was first in organizing graduate work, having set up a graduate school in 1886.[9] However, the Ph.D. was not offered until 1896. The newness of the organization of graduate schools is shown in the following dates:[10]

Columbia University	1880
Harvard University	1890
University of Wisconsin	1892
Princeton University	1901
University of Illinois	1906
University of California	1909
University of Michigan	1915

The graduate emphasis at the newer institutions is evidenced in that at the opening of the University of Chicago in 1892 forty per cent of the staff (exclusive of the Divinity School) were members of the graduate faculty, although only twenty-eight per cent of the students were doing graduate work. There were, however, some forty graduate fellowships available at Chicago.[11]

"Made possible" by gifts from Jonas Gilman Clark,[12] Clark University opened in 1889 as a "purely graduate institution." There was no undergraduate school until 1900 when one was endowed by the will of Clark. There was no philosophy department installed at Clark. The only degree offered was the Ph.D., 192 of which were granted from 1891-1914, ranging from one a year to a top of sixteen.[13] Of these 192, 117 were given in the Department of "Psychology and Education." In the original departments the nearest thing to philosophy was "Psychology (including Education and Anthropology)." Examination of the titles of theses accepted in this Department shows them to have been heavily experimental, but they are in general a trendless mixture.

Figures on the number of graduate students in the United States reveal a steady growth. In 1870-71, forty-four graduate students were rej orted. The rise in numbers is steady:

1871-72	198
1872-73	219
1879-80	411
1884-85	869
1888-89	1,343

The number more than doubled from 1871 to 1879, tripled in the period 1880-89.

1890	2,382
1900	5,832
1910	9,370
1920	15,612
1930	47,255

From 1890 to 1920 there occurred a doubling each decade; from 1920-30 there was a tripling.[14]

Taking the country at large, the Ph.D.'s granted rise steadily:

TABLE 3

Number of Institutions Offering the Ph.D. Degree and Number of Ph.D. Degrees Conferred from 1876 to 1940[15]

Year	Number of Institutions	Number of Ph.D. Degrees Conferred
1876	25	44
1890		164
1900		342
1910	38	409
1920	44	532
1930	74	2,024
1935		2,649
1940		3,088

Lord Bryce wrote in 1886 that in any rigorous sense there were "not more than twelve, and possibly only eight or nine" American

universities among the "enormous total of degree granting
bodies."[16] The growth of graduate instruction in the United States
may be divided into three typical periods:[17] (1) between
1642 and 1860 the M.A. degree was supreme and in the main it
was an honorary affair. (2) The period from 1860 to 1900 is made
up of "the growth and development of the Ph.D. degree." (3) The
period from 1900 to the present, which continues the second while
adding a further diversification of degrees. I have documented its
growth above. The *character* of the Ph.D. degree and the social
mechanisms which impelled its growth were set by the needs of
industry for scientifically trained personnel: "the influence of modern science . . . was greatly accelerated by the urgent need for industrial and agricultural research and received its greatest single
impetus from the large number of newly organized land grant colleges and state universities."[18] And:

> "the extraordinary expansion of agriculture, industry, com-
> merce, and education, especially between 1870 and 1900,
> greatly encouraged the establishment of graduate schools
> throughout the country . . . as the nature of the social-economic
> problems of the time demanded not mere theory, but prac-
> tical results, the interests of research and graduate study were
> naturally turned in the direction of the applications of truth
> and knowledge. . . ."[19]

In the development of the significance of the Ph.D. degree in
America, it should be noted that from 1872-1900 the Ph.D. was
granted *"honoris causa"* to some extent. But after 1891 this ritual
declined in frequency. In 1898 it amounted to only three per cent
of the total Ph.D.'s awarded; whereas in 1894 it was 12.4 per cent.[20]

The conferring of the Ph.D. by *"honoris causa"* was opposed by
several agencies and groups who had a stake in seeing it professionalized. This period witnessed the rise of scholarly societies
which were composed of men interested in the advancement of
their profession, many of them in the younger age brackets. In 1869
the American Philological Association was formed, and it was quite
active in the movement to professionalize the degree. Other societies sprang up; the dates of their establishment run as follows:

American Historical Association	1884
American Economic Association	1885
American Mathematical Society	1890
American Psychological Association	1892
American Philosophical Association	1901
American Sociological Society	1905
American Political Science Association	1906

In addition to these professional organizations the more general "American Association for the Advancement of Science" was established in 1880. It embraced the physical, biological, and earth sciences. Several of the societies listed above came into being as more specialized outgrowths of previously formed associations. For instance, Associate Professor H. B. Adams promoted the American Historical Association from the membership of the American Social Science Association; Ely promoted the American Economic Association from among the members of the American Historical Association.

In the early nineties, The Affiliated Clubs of Graduate Students were formed. They met in New York and formally inveighed against the conferring of honorary degrees.[21] The Association of the American Universities, formed by the presidents of leading universities, in the absence of any governmental agency, joined the movement for the professionalization of the Ph.D. in 1900.

The process of professionalization was carried by (a) professional learned societies, (b) graduate students, (c) the university heads themselves. All groups having anything to do with the matter agreed that uniform standards should be set up, and by the early decades of the twentieth century the Ph.D. was a research degree.

There is one other feature of American intellectual life which furthered the growth of graduate schools and the consequent professionalization of disciplines. These processes occurred in America under the heavy influence of German models of research. The full influence of the German university system with its animus of specialization and research was mediated by American scholars who studied in German universities and by German professors who came to teach in American universities.

Benjamin Franklin visited Göttingen in 1766. A German university, Göttingen, granted a degree in medicine to B. S. Barton of Pennsylvania in 1789.[22] These, however, were driblets. The stream began shortly after 1815 when four Americans went to Göttingen. There were then eminent teachers in the Hanoverian University: the Grimms, Heeren, Gauss. To this university, went four American scholars: Edward Everett, George Tichnor, George Bancroft and J. G. Cogswell. Tichnor in America had had a difficult time gathering together a textbook, a grammar, a dictionary in order to learn the German language.[23] Tichnor is given credit by many for Harvard's later fully installed elective system. Each of these men returned to America to assume leading roles in the American universities and libraries. Between 1800 and 1850 less than 200 American students were matriculated in all German universities. "In the fifth decade, the number came to exceed one hundred, and in the sixth, it increased at least three fold." In the seventies there were more than 1,000 students.[24]

We must remember that it was not until the nineties that American graduate schools could supply deans and professors with Ph.D.'s. It was only with graduate schools that the domestic Ph.D. degree could supplant the prestige of the degree of divinity. In the period from 1890 to 1900, the number of German Ph.D.'s conferred on Americans declined. From then until World War I it steadily diminishes. Graduate schools were arising in the United States. But this migration had performed its task. It was quite largely in the hands of these men that the direction of higher learning in the United States after the sixties was entrusted.[25] All but a few of Johns Hopkins' fifty-three professors and lecturers had at least studied in Germany. "One went to Germany," wrote Josiah Royce, "still a doubter as to the possibility of the theoretic life: one returned ... determined to contribute his *scherflein* to the massive store of human knowledge, burning for a chance to help to build the American University."[26] Another one said: "My German studies gave me the capacity and the habit of considering social facts from two points of view rather than a single one, and I gained thereby ... in objectiveness."[27] As for what studying in Germany accomplished for young American philosophers, the following statement, which Santayana wrote to James from Berlin in 1887, is typical and revealing: "Since I have been in Germany I have become optimistic about the prospects in philosophy...."[28]

In addition to the Americans with German degrees there have been "hundreds" of Germans who have taught in American schools. Thwing selects several as especially influential on American academic life and intellectual endeavor:[29] Francis Lieber, who was in the United States in 1827 and who served at the University of South Carolina and then, from 1857 to his death in 1872, at Columbia; Charles Follen, who was in America between 1824 and 1840 teaching at Harvard. H. von Holst, with a Heidelberg doctorate came to the United States in 1867, went back to Germany, finally became professor at Chicago in 1892. Philip Schiff came in 1844; Albert Michelson, who was at the Case School of Applied Science, at Clark University, ended finally at the University of Chicago.

1. Walton C. John, *op. cit.*

2. From National Education Association Proceedings for 1889, quoted by Walton C. John, *ibid.*, p. 9.

3. S. E. Morison, *op. cit.*, p. 454.

4. E. V. Wills, *op. cit.*, p. 455.

5. Charles H. Haskins, *op. cit.*, in Morison, *op. cit.*, p. 455.

6. E. V. Wills, *op. cit.*, p. 190.

7. Given in R. Freeman Butts, *op. cit.*, p. 128.

8. Walton C. John, *op. cit.*, p. 11.

9. B. J. Horton, *The Graduate School* (New York 1940) p. 74.

10. *Ibid.*, p. 77.

11. F. W. Reeves, *et al.*, *The University Faculty*, (Chicago 1933) Vol. III, pp. 7-8.

12. E. V. Wills, *op. cit.*, p. 150.

13. "Degrees Granted at Clark" compiled by L. N. Wilson, *Clark University Library Publication* (Worcester, Mass. 1914-15).

14. These figures were compiled by Walton C. John, *op. cit.*, pp. 12-13, from the United States Commission of Education Annual Reports. *See* also the *United States Bureau of Education Report, 1889-90* (Washington, D.C., 1893) Vol. 2, p. 818.

15. The first six rows adapted from table built by Walton C. John, *op. cit.*, p. 19, from *United States Commissioner and Office of Education Reports and Biennial Surveys*. The last two rows are from *List of American Doctoral Dissertations Accepted*. Washington, Annual volumes. The number of women included here has increased gradually, amounting to seventeen per cent of the total in 1930.

16. James Bryce, *The American Commonwealth*, revised ed. (New York 1910) Vol. II, p. 715.

17. Walton C. John, *op. cit.*, p. 59.

18. Walton C. John, *op. cit.*, p. 59.

19. *Ibid.*, p. 215.

20. *Ibid.*, pp. 19-21.

21. Walton C. John, *Ibid.*, p. 24f.

22. A detailed account of the traveling scholars and of the German influence on American universities and scholarships is to be found in C. F. Thwing, *The American and the German University* (New York 1928). *See* also B. A. Hinsdale, "Notes on the History of Foreign Influence upon Education in the United States, "*U.S. Commissioner of Education Report, 1897-1898* (Washington 1898) Part I, pp. 591-629.

23. G. S. Hillard, *Life, Letters and Journals of George Tichnor* (New York and London 1896) Vol. I, p. 26.

24. C. F. Thwing, *op. cit.*, p. 42.

25. *See* Mary R. and Charles A. Beard, *op. cit.*, Vol. II, p. 476f.

26. *Atlantic Monthly* (1891) quoted by L. F. Snow in a thesis at Columbia, *The College Curriculum in the United States* (1907) p. 161.

27. C. W. Thwing, *op. cit.*, p. 49.

28. Quoted by Ralph Barton Perry, *The Thought and Character of William James* (Boston 1935) Vol. I, p. 404.

29. C. F. Thwing, *op. cit.*, p. 78f.

4

The Personnel of American Philosophy

There does not exist any Dictionary of American Philosophers which contains data on sociological extraction. The only Dictionary is *Who's Who in Philosophy* (1942) which contains very little indeed of sociological relevance. The general *Dictionary of American Biography* lists a total of fifty seven individuals as "philosophers"; of those only thirty five were born after 1830, a year chosen to mark the lower limit of the first generation of pragmatists. Of these thirty five, there is much sociologically relevant information that is excluded. Quite a few of these biographies, *e.g.*, contain no information or very fragmentary information concerning the occupation and economic level of the fathers of the subjects. The exact method of their selection is not available. Five of those given may be considered pragmatists in general viewpoint. On this fragmentary material, about all that can be said is this: in these data there appear to be few significant differences between the social *derivation* of the pragmatists and non-pragmatists. However, this statement should not be taken as statistically definitive. The data are not all in, and this compilation is not possible for me at the present time. Going beyond the *Dictionary of American Biography* as a source, the occupations of some of the fathers of the major pragmatists are:

C. S. Peirce: eminent college professor
William James: free lance religionist and rentier
John Dewey: small grocery owner
G. H. Mead: seminary teacher
James Tufts: preacher and private teacher[1]

The original economic levels of all save Dewey are rather high. Peirce alone experiences descent in his life span. Mead and James remained at about the same level. Dewey rose from small, old middle class to professional upper-middle. The general pattern of the younger pragmatists around Dewey at Chicago, A. H. Lloyd and A. W. Moore, e.g., was probably in accord with the pattern for the general student body at Chicago:[2] from farmers and businessmen to professionals.

As for the non-pragmatic "philosophers" listed in the *Dictionary of American Biography,* born after 1830, there appears to be five general occupational groups from which they typically derive: Teachers, Clergymen, Farmers, Business Proprietors, Local officials, such as Justice of the Peace. The proportions derived from these social sources are about equal except for the clergymen, which appears to have not quite doubled the number from any one of the other groups. There may be proportionately, though slightly, fewer pragmatists deriving from clergymen's families, although given *these* data, I am not in a position to push the point. These data are entirely too fragmentary to warrant the construction of trends or the attempt at comparison. Even to tally them would be a mislocated precision.

As seems to be the case for college teachers in general in America, the philosophers appear to derive from rather wide sources. I am dubious of the common flat assertion that college professors in general and philosophers in particular have derived from clergymen. It may well be so. It has by no means been proved by anybody and should be a moot point until it is. In a population, however, growing as rapidly as that of the United States and with a tremendous increase in the teaching profession, it would be mathematically difficult to derive all of this growth from persons trained during the early nineteenth century in seminaries. The wholesale training of ministers occurred in the middle and latter decades of the century.[3] To my knowledge there exists only one study encompassing data on the occupational extraction of college professors of philosophy. It was done in 1936 by B. W. Kunkel.

This study was based upon 4,667 replies (41.5 per cent of those circularized) from members of the A.A.U.P.[4] Among this group 122 were in "philosophy and ethics". The total average age was 47.9 plus .11. One third of the total group was born before 1885, one third between 1885-1894 inclusive, and one third since 1894. Forty three per cent of those born prior to 1885 were born in New England; seventy eight per cent of the total number had the Ph.D. degree; 94.2 per cent of those teaching in "philosophy and ethics" had the doctorate degree; Harvard, Columbia, and Chicago contributing the most of these degrees in the order listed.

TABLE 4. Occupations of Fathers of 4,667 Academicians by Three Age Groups.[5]

Occupation of Fathers:	Born prior 1885	Born after		Total
		1885-1894	1894	
Businessmen	25.1%	27.0%	33.8%	26.6%
Farmers	31.2	25.0	15.2	24.7
Manual workers	11.6	11.7	12.0	12.1
Clergymen	10.8	10.6	10.4	10.6
Teachers	4.9	5.6	4.2	5.1
Physicians	4.6	5.0	5.1	5.1
Lawyers	4.0	4.2	3.9	4.1
Professors	2.4	3.7	5.8	3.9
Chemists and Engineers	2.0	2.5	4.4	3.0
Public officials	1.4	2.1	3.2	1.9
Editors and writers	1.2	1.4	1.0	1.2
Artists and musicians	1.1	1.1	1.0	1.0

In these tallies only 122 are in "philosophy and ethics", which makes the data much less valuable for our purposes. Also, only fifty-three of the 4,667 were born between 1855-65, roughly Dewey's generation or the second generation of pragmatists; forty two per cent of those born prior to 1884 were born in New England, whereas only 28.5 per cent of those born after 1884 originated in this region. For the younger academicians, the Middle Atlantic, Gulf and Pacific Coast contributed more as age decreases. Indeed, "An examination of the origins of parents of the teachers in American Colleges shows that the distribution of birth places is in accordance with the population of the various sections of the country in their generation."[6]

Table 4 shows, as we would expect from demographic and occupational data, that "farmers" drop off, being replaced largely by businessmen and professionals. Notice that the extraction from clergymen is constant. This, however, does not mean anything definite for the 122 philosophers included, for we *might* expect them to make up a disproportionate number of those so derived. Besides a rather wide base of extraction, this table suggests that college professors in general have very probably experienced ascent. However, for at least 25.2 per cent of those born prior to 1884 (those from the professions) this cannot be asserted, for among the professions, except primary and secondary teaching, teaching is quite low in pay and, very likely proportionately, in prestige.

Cattell's study of the "Families of American Men of Science"[7] is of interest in gaining *general* knowledge of the social sources of intellectuals in America. Also some, we do not know what proportion, of the scientists were in universities. His results are not radically different from Kunkel's. Forty three of the fathers of 885 scientists born around 1850 were professional men; of these ten per cent were clergymen, twenty one per cent of the fathers were in agriculture; whereas 35.7 per cent were in the rather loose category of "manufacturing and trade."[8]

"It is clear that a majority of scientific men come from the so-called middle and upper classes, forming about one-thirtieth of the population, and undoubtedly they tend to be sons of the more successful professional men."[9]

Comparing these materials, insofar as they may be taken as representative, the "academicians" probably experienced more occupational ascent than "scientists;" this inference should, however, be very carefully and tentatively held, for "academicians" received less income and prestige than scientists, both in and out of the academies.

One way in which data on the social extraction and careers of philosophers, full enough to be sociologically useful, could be obtained is by primary circularization of the members of the American Philosophical Association, which was organized in 1901. Many, indeed most, of its former members of Dewey's generation are dead. Their relatives are unknown to me and are not readily available. Therefore, another method of gathering these data was evolved; so far it has been unavailing. Test letters were sent to several university registrars, who it was thought would have personal data on file on their former faculties (although it is known in several cases that extraction data are not available at all, not even in obituary notices in *The Philosophical Review*). These registrars undoubtedly have much material. But it cannot be obtained by mail. Perhaps it would be forthcoming if a study was supported by some reputable foundation or by the United States Department of Education. In the meantime, we must rest with the fragmentary information displayed above and with that to be presented below.

Several indices of the professionalization of philosophy in the United States are available. One is, of course, the degree composition of those who have taught this subject. By examining the catalogues of various colleges we see that the regular B.A. degree or theological degrees diminish and are, in the last half of the nineteenth century, displaced by the Ph.D. We also see that the presidents of the colleges discontinue teaching philosophy during these fifty years and, that "the average curriculum in philosophy in the old American college" was quite meager.[10]

At Amherst College "Professors of Mental and Moral Philosophy"[11] were either A.B.'s, L.L.D.'s, or D.D.'s until 1890 when President M. E. Gates with a Ph.D. is listed; however, it was not until 1903 that a non-president Ph.D. is listed. Since that date, Amherst's philosophers have had Ph.D.'s. The last President to teach philosophy at Amherst ceased to do so in 1899.

At Brown University[12] the situation was mixed Ph.D., L.L.D. and D.D. until late in the second decade of the twentieth century; however, a Ph.D. was instructor of philosophy in 1895-96. Since then their proportion of Ph.D.'s has increased.

At Cornell[13] there were A.B.'s and M.A.'s. A Ph.D. was first appointed to teach philosophy in 1890-91, in which year "The Sage School of Philosophy" was founded; until 1886 a D.D., who was also a "registrar", is listed as a "Professor of Moral and Intellectual Philosophy."

At the University of Wisconsin[14] F. C. Sharp, Ph.D., was appointed in 1893, B. H. Bode in 1900 and E. B. McGilvary, also with a Ph.D., in 1905. Wisconsin began conferring the Ph.D. in philosophy in 1892. President Bascom was listed as a teacher of philosophy at Wisconsin until 1887.

Columbia University[15] established its formal "Faculty of Philosophy" in 1890. Up until 1881 one man, who was also a professor of English, handled all the philosophy courses. N. M. Butler came to the president's chair via the philosophy department, in which he taught from 1887 to 1889. In 1892 James H. Hyslop, Ph.D., was appointed. In 1896 there were eight instructors offering a total of twenty four courses. Since then all major appointments have had non-theological degrees except G. S. Fullerton in 1904 with a B.D., but he also possessed a Ph.D.

At Harvard more details are available,[16] but the situation at Harvard was not typical of the history of philosophy in American universities, although it did, of course, share many features with the general pattern. The men who made up the "first well rounded staff for teaching philosophy . . . in this country" — James, Royce, Santayana, Perry, *et al* — were not born before James' generation, and most of them in Dewey's, that is in the late fifties and early sixties. Prior to this influx of men with domestic Ph.D.'s or degrees from abroad (and from abroad in personal origin) the situation of philosophy at Harvard was not too dissimilar from other schools: D.D.'s manned a course of study that was predominantly historical. All work in philosophy was prescribed until 1868-69. Philosophy began with Eliot's regime. We shall discuss this later.[17]

The typical pattern emerging from these data taken from catalogues is twofold: First, in the last quarter of the nineteenth century teachers of philosophy began to be professionally qualified by the Ph.D. degree and not the D.D. Second, those who taught philosophy became full-time philosophers, and not Presidents of the schools who also taught philosophy. There are other rough indices of the professionalization of philosophy which occurred in the generations of James and Peirce, but which came to fruition in Dewey's time.[18] Perhaps the most important of these is the founding of a professional association which will be discussed.

One point concerning the religious affiliations of academic personnel and especially philosophers in America must be noticed. I have stated above that it has not been proved that their *extraction* was so overwhelmingly from clerical occupations. However, this does not exhaust the matter, for there is evidence that they themselves were rather heavily trained in seminaries. On this point there are two sources which I have used. First, the degree compositions and trends as displayed by the catalogues of the colleges all show a genetic connection. Second, we have impressions set forth by philosophers in memoirs. This would seem equally as important, if not more so, as the exact statistical facts, for *no matter*

*what the occupational facts, the operating atmopshere lived in by
philosophers, as set forth by them, seemed to have been built up
from a personnel of clergymen.*

Thus, Dewey (in 1886) wrote that the philosophy taught in
"the ordinary American college" is a "survival" of a time when its
aim was "to furnish to the community well-fortified ministers of the
gospel." Writing from Michigan, he adds that only at Harvard and
Michigan are "the philosophical interpretations and criterion of
the principles of modern science known and taught."[19] And in
1929, writing of the later nineteenth century, he says:

> "Teachers of philosophy were at that time, almost to a man,
> clergymen; the supposed requirements of religion, or theology,
> dominated the teaching of philosophy in most colleges."[20]

The American Philosophical Association was organized at a conference in New York, November 2, 1901.[21] Creighton's *Philosophical Review* was elected to print the proceedings of the Association
and abstracts of papers read. This initial report lists the complete
membership. They total ninety-eight persons; all but four are
listed as members of university staffs. The Association was an off-
shoot from the American Psychological Association, which had
been founded in 1891. Since at least 1896 there had been difficulties over scheduling of papers at the annual meetings and various
other tensions between the psychologists and philosophers. Professor Creighton of Cornell seems to have taken the initiative, however Professor Thilly of Missouri, who the year before had founded
the Western Philosophical Association, was also an agent of the
split.[22] By 1926 there were around 250 papers read before the Association.

For a number of years the A.P.A. represented only the eastern
states, as there were similar associations for other sections: the already mentioned Western Philosophical Association (founded
1900); the Southern Society for Philosophy and Psychology
(founded 1904); Philosophical Society of the Pacific Coast (founded 1925). In 1919 a nominal reorganization of the Eastern, Western, and Southern divisions into an inclusive Association was effected, but was non-operative. In 1927 a federation was agreed

upon by the Eastern, Western and Pacific societies to bear the name American Philosophical Association. The Southern Society was not a party to the federation. In the year 1927 the members of all three divisions totalled approximately 450. From 1927 until 1930 it seems to have grown very slightly.[23]

1. *See* Table 5 below for members of Peirce's "Metaphysical Club."

2. *See* above data, Table 1

3. In 1850 there were 26,842 clergymen in the United States; in 1870, they numbered 43,874; in 1910 they numbered 118,018; in 1920, 127,270; in 1930, 148,848. *United States Census*, Seventh, Ninth and later. *See* later figures on academic personnel.

4. *Association of American Colleges Bulletin 23* (1937) pp. 465-514, condensed in "A Survey of College Teachers", *Bulletin of American Association of University Professors 24* (1938) pp. 249-62.

5. "Upwards of eighty seven different occupations were cited, which ranged alphabetically from accountants and advertising agents to undertakers, watchmen, and writers." p. 510.

6. *Association of American Colleges Bulletin 23* (1937) p. 509.

7. *Popular Science Monthly* (January-June 1915) 86, pp. 504-15.

8. The census of 1852 gives these occupational compositions for white males: professional, 3.1; agriculture, 44.1; trade, manufacturing, etc., 34.1. Thus, professions contributed out of all proportion to their number, whereas farm boys did not stand nearly so high a chance to become scientists.

9. *Popular Science Monthly, op. cit.,* p. 509.

10. *See* A. C. Armstrong Jr., "Philosophy in American Colleges," *Educational Review* (January 1897) Vol. XIII. pp. 10-22.

11. *Amherst College General Catalogues, 1821-1910* (Amherst 1910). Also from *1910 Amherst College Biographical Record,* edited by R. Fletcher and M. O. Young (Amherst 1939).

12. *The Historical Catalog of Brown University, 1764-1934.* Published by the University (Providence 1936).

13. *Annual Catalogs, Cornell,* from 1868-91.

14. *Wisconsin University, General Catalog,* 1849-1907.

15. *Columbia University, General Catalog,* 1754-1906. (New York) Published for the University, 1916.

16. S. E. Morison, *Development of Harvard,* and Benjamin Rand, "Philosophical Instruction in Harvard University from 1636 to 1900", in the *Harvard Graduates' Magazine,* Vol. 37, No. 145.

17. *See* also above section on Eliot.

18. Incidentally, the number of Ph.D'.s conferred in philosophy in the United States was not centrally available until 1926-38. The number per year during this span was never below forty three nor above sixty six. Harvard and Columbia seems to have contributed a disproportionate number

of these. *See* the annual *List of American Doctoral Dissertations,* Library of Congress. (These began in 1912 but consist only of those whose thesis was printed) and *Doctoral Dissertations Accepted by American Universities* (New York). For further figures on number of philosophers, *see* below on American Philosophical Association.

19. John Dewey, *"Inventory of Philosophy Taught in American Colleges"*, *Science Supplement* (Friday, April 16, 1886) pp. 353-55.

20. John Dewey, "From Absolutism to Experimentalism", *Contemporary American Philosophers* (New York 1929).

21. *Philosophical Review*, (April 1902) Vol. XI, p. 264.

22. H. N. Gardiner, "The First Twenty-Five Years of the American Philosophical Association", *Philosophical Review*, Vol. 35, (1926) pp. 145-58.

23. *American Philosophical Proceedings and Addresses*, Vols. 1-4, (1927-1930).

5

Biographical Composition of the Metaphysical Club

"It was in the earliest seventies,"[1] wrote C. S. Peirce in the most complete description of the Metaphysical Club extant, "that a knot of us young men in Old Cambridge, calling ourselves, half-ironically, half-defiantly, 'The Metaphysical Club,' — for agnosticism was then riding its high horse, and was frowning superbly upon all metaphysics — used to meet, sometimes in my study, sometimes in that of William James. It may be that some of our old-time confederates would today not care to have such wild-oats-sowings made public, though there was nothing but boiled oats, mild, and sugar in the mess. Mr. Justice Holmes, however, will not, I believe, take it ill that we are proud to remember his membership; nor will Joseph Warner, Esq. Nicholas St. John Green was one of the most interested fellows, a skillful lawyer and a learned one, a disciple of Jeremy Bentham. His extraordinary power of disrobing warm and breathing truth of the draperies of long worn formulas, was what attracted attention to him everywhere. In particular, he often urged the importance of applying Bain's definition of belief, as 'that upon which a man is prepared to act.' From this definition, pragmatism is scarce more than a corollary; so that I am disposed to think of him as the grandfather of pragmatism. Chauncey Wright, something of a philosophical celebrity in those days, was never absent from our meetings. I was about to call him our corypheus; but he will better be described as our boxing-master whom we — I particularly — used to face to be severely pummelled. He had abandoned a former attachment to Hamiltonianism to take up with the doctrines of Mill, to which and to its cognate agnosticism he was trying to weld the really incongruous ideas of Darwin. John Fiske and, more rarely, Francis Ellingwood Abbot, were sometimes present, lending their countenances to the spirit of our endeavours, while holding aloof from any assent to their success. Wright, James, and I were men of science, rather scrutinizing the doctrines of the metaphysicians on their scientific side than regarding them as very momentous spiritually. The type of our thought was decidedly British. I, alone of our number, had come upon the threshing-floor of philosophy through the doorway of Kant, and even my ideas were acquiring the English accent. Our metaphysical proceedings had all been in winged words (and swift ones, at that, for the most part), until at length, lest the club should be dissolved, without leaving any material *souvenir* behind, I drew up a little paper expressing some of the opinions that I had been urging all along under the name of pragmatism. This paper was received . . . unlooked-for kindness. . . ."[2]

The men whose career-lines crossed to make up the membership of the Metaphysical Club were from diverse social strata and were to participate in quite diverse publics and institutions. It was at a university that they met, all of them were "university men," but only one was a professional philosopher of the academies. Grossly, the only experience which they possessed in common was four years at Harvard, and, as we shall see, each of them took this experience in an individualized manner. In terms of diversity of social extraction and career heterogeneity these men are to be enrolled in the membership of a relatively free intelligentsia. The immediate audence in intellectual discourse with whom C. S. Peirce prepared his first statement of the pragmatic doctrine was composed of three lawyers and jurists, two scientists, the American popularizer of the Spencerian model of science, a leader in a radically deviant humanist religion, who fell out with congregations and religiously free-lanced most of his life, was the nearest to a clergyman among them.[3] Peirce and James, and to a lesser extent Wright and Holmes were to make a pragmatic style of thought part of their intellectual lives, although each of them used it in different contexts and for diverse purposes and gave it a varied form. We want briefly to catch the pragmatic mood and style of thought, in so far as it exists, in each of the members of the Metaphysical Club. In this effort we shall be especially interested in the variations of the pragmatic style as a function of varying political positions and in its several mixtures with other intellectual affiliations, pieties, and usages.

We do have C. S. Peirce's statement that his paper was prepared directly for this group. He did not, at this time, intend to publicize it beyond the confines of their discussion. Indeed, it was not until "1875 or 1876" that Peirce met "old William Appleton, on a steamer" who offered him "a good round price for some articles for *The Popular Science Monthly*." Peirce then "patched up the piece" and "it appeared November, 1877."[4] These seven men constitute the first explicit public of what later became pragmatism. From all indications, it was against them and with them that C. S. Peirce was thinking during the writing of his statement. Hence they are important to an understanding of Peirce's pragmatism.

Several of them are also important for a more direct reason: their reflection was informed by this style of thinking and they were to use it in varied manners. The membership of the Club claims our attention for another, a more general reason.

By grasping the lives of these men, their opinions and interests, their positions in the social structure of nineteenth century New England, we are enabled to catch the larger secular and professionalizing movement of intellectual affairs. These men, born in the thirties and forties, carried the seeds of multi-sided futures within them. Their careers and their intellectual modes are, therefore, worthy of examination as indices as well as intrinsically.

> "I see not how the great God prepares to satisfy the heart in the new order of things." — Emerson, quoted by Abbot in *Scientific Theism*, p. 216.

Francis Ellington Abbot: In 1875 C. S. Peirce wrote James a letter in which he had occasion to draw a circle and place F. E. Abbot within it: "I don't speak of the philosophical *canaille*, but I mean you, Frank Abbot and myself."[5] The admiration of Peirce for Abbot was a persistent feature of their relation; in 1904 Peirce wrote that Abbot was "one of the strongest thinkers I ever encountered. . . . ."[6] Fortunately, we are able to determine precisely what it was in Abbot's thinking that C. S. Peirce esteemed so highly. It was his enthusiastic espousal of "logical realism."

Abbot was born in 1836, the son of a Boston teacher.[7] His family was replete with "intellectual energy and strenuous Puritanism." He properly attended the Boston Latin School. He graduated from Harvard College in 1859 and joined the Harvard Divinity

School, but only for several months. During the years 1860-63 he taught at and attended the Meadville Theological School, attaining a degree in '63. Leaving Meadville, he was pastor for a while at Beverly, Massachusetts; from 1864 he was pastor of the "Unitarian Church" at Dover, New Hampshire.

It was not long, however, before he discovered "creedal limitations in the constitution of the National Unitarian Conference." By '67 he was at the head of those, among them Frothingham, who were creating the Free Religious Association. This society aimed at replacing "God in Christ" by "God in Humanity."[8] In '68 Abbot resigned his pastorate of the Unitarian Church at Dover, N. H. A majority of the parish wished to retain him even to the point of changing the name of the church to the "First Independent Religious Society," but a majority legally defeated the move.

Abbot supported himself by tutoring. He gave free public speeches in the City Hall. A Unitarian church in Toledo, Ohio, changed its affiliation to secure Abbot as pastor. It was at Toledo that he began editing the *Index*, the paper of the Free Religious Association. Promptly it went into debt. He went to Cambridge in '73, continuing the editorship there until 1880. He tried to teach in New York. He tried to establish a classical boys school in Cambridge. He came into a legacy in 1892, and then he could free-lance, writing out two volumes of very abstruse pages: an example of the contents; "Personal Ethicality is the Law of the Utterance or Realization of Personal Concepts in Personal Words...."[9] From 1872-76 he was organizing "local resistance groups" into a National Liberal League to fight a proposed amendment of the national constitution which would have attempted to make the Bible into law. In '94 he was estranged from the Free Religious Association because of "its refusal to avow independence of all historical religions."[10] He poisoned himself and was found upon his wife's grave in 1903. His two volumes received unfavorable notices and were almost immediately buried. The pages of the copies in the Library of Congress were uncut in 1941.

In each of the four areas of endeavor which make up Abbot's life he encountered constant opposition, abuse, or simply indifference: (1) within the established churches; (2) with reformist religious and quasi-political groups; (3) as a philosophical writer; (4) within the academic world. As to this later context, two in-

cidents are worth recounting. There exists a set of letters dated
"Boston: 1879," entitled "Testimonials", and then, "Privately
printed — not published." It is "copyrighted by F. E. Abbott." It
contains a set of eulogies of Abbot, most of them in connection
with his desired appointment as Professor of Moral Philosophy at
Cornell. No less a man than Emerson is among the authors. The
last two letters in the book are from President White turning his
appointment down: "An older man would better become the Professorship."

In 1888 Abbot taught at Harvard as a substitute for Josiah
Royce. He published his lectures in a little book, *The Way out of
Agnosticism* (1890). In the *International Journal of Ethics* for October, 1890, Royce sharply attacked the book. Among many other
things he issued a "professional warning" to the philosophical community against Abbot, the "pretender." Royce was an editor of the
Journal. Abbot's response was not given entirely free access to the
Journal's pages. He caused to be circulated a protest to the overseers of Harvard, registering redress from libel. The venture was
without success. In *The Nation,* C. S. Peirce wrote a signed letter.
It was a very rough epistle, a fierce, hot blast at Royce, whose
"cruel purpose never left his heart."[11] But, said Peirce, one should
expect a student of ethics, like Royce, to acquire "conceptions of
right and wrong that the rest of the world cannot understand."

William James answered C. S. Peirce's letter in the next issue,
November 19, of *The Nation.* First, of course, he thinks it "unfortunate" that Peirce's letter has brought the subject "before the
larger public." He definitely defends "Professor Royce," imputing
a "pathological" motive to Abbot's conduct.[12]

Then, in the next issue, comes a letter from J. B. Warner, the
Boston lawyer, who had been retained as "Professor Royce's coun-
sel." In *The Nation* he causes to be reprinted his lawyer-like letter
to Abbot which is kindly and professional but suggests straight out
that if Abbot publishes and circulates a certain manuscript
against Royce "it may . . .entail a serious legal responsibility."[13]
This defense of Royce makes Abbot appear like a temperamental
bad boy.

Finally, in the next week's issue of *The Nation,* December 3,
1891, Abbot enters. Of Warner's letter, he writes that it is "evidence
of nothing but the lawyer's attempt to put forward his own baseless

assumptions in his client's behalf as if they were assured facts."[14] At the end of his two column letter there runs in brackets: "We cannot print any more letters respecting this controversy. — Editor, *The Nation*."[15]

As regards the Free Religious Association, it represented a definite loosening up the older Protestantism in the face of new urban congregations. It dignified "The Dignity of Human Nature," seeking the law within, revolting against any "external law." It had faith in "man as a progressive being." It aimed to "convert the human race into a vast cooperative union devoted to universal ends." It was a humanist movement, religiously radical.[16]

Regardless of Abbot's difficulties in the school and his affiliation with deviant religious sects, it is not true that he was in any general sense of the word irreligious. On the contrary, his *Scientific Theism* is one of the most skillful attempts of religionists to meet the threat of "science." It is accomplished by accepting fully "the presuppositions of scientific method" and then by showing that they strictly involve "scientific theism."[17] The book grew from lectures given before the Concord Summer School of Philosophy in 1885. Such men as Fiske and W. T. Harris were there.

It is this book that C. S. Peirce cites. In 1871 Peirce had "acknowledged that the tendency of science has been toward nominalism; but the late Dr. Francis Ellington Abbot in the very remarkable introduction to *Scientific Theism* showed on the contrary, quite conclusively, that science has always been at heart realistic, and always must be so; and upon comparing his writings with mine, it is easily seen that these features of nominalism which I pointed out in science are merely superficial and transient."[18]

This book is an important document in the understanding of one of C. S. Peirce's central views. It is worthy of examination for this reason. It is also convenient to examine it in detail because the pattern of its argument lends itself to an interpretation of concepts and views for which realism and nominalism are surrogates.

". . . the Philosophized Scientific Method creates the only idea of God which can at once satisfy both Head and Heart; and Scientific Theism creates the Real Reconciliation of Science and Religion."[19] Kant's key doctrine that "things conform to cognition, not cognition to things," his "critical philosophy was only the logical evolution and outcome of Medieval Nominalism . . . Wrapped up in . . . Nominalism . . . was the doctrine that things-in-themselves are utterly unknown . . .in short, that the only knowledge possible to man is the knowledge of the *a priori* constitution of his own mind, and the relations which it imposes upon things (if they exist) . . ."[20]

"The historical development of the Critical Philosophy . . . only shows how impossible it is for that philosophy to overstep the magic circle of Egoism with which Nominalism logically environed itself." Likewise the other modern alias of nominalism: associationalism. Both drift inevitably toward "idealistic conclusions which cannot stop short of absolute Solipsism."[21]

The religious and social humanism of Abbot's thinking coincides in his thought with logical realism and these are polarized against "individualism" and logical nominalism. Working on a philosophical plane he equates "solipsism" with "absolute egoism"[22] and his objection to Kantianism is basically that he sees it as logically contracting "human knowledge to the petty dimensions of individual self-consciousness . . ."[23] The nerve of the matter is seen in the following two quotations:

> "Under [the sway of the Nominalistic revolution], philosophy is blind to the race, and beholds the individual alone. What wonder that, in the hands of those who insist on their rights to reduce theory to practice, philosophy is so often found pandering to the moral lawlessness of an Individualism that sets mere personal opinion above the supreme ethical sanctions of the universe? In human society, individual autonomy is universal antinomy . . ."[24]

> "With Nominalism for its root, Idealism for its flower, and Solipsism for its fruit, how can modern philosophy, teaching in both its great schools that the individual mind knows nothing except the states of its own consciousness, discover any law that shall have recognized authority over all consciousness? . . . So far . . . as the social and moral interests . . . are concerned, the present philosophical situation has become simply intolerable."[25]

On the other hand, it is also nominalism that "paralyzed the Scotch School."[26] And then: Enter "Science." Now notice the way he establishes his point by defining "science" so as to *include* his point:

"physical science has immovably planted itself on a new definition of knowledge." Its "temple of truth" is "destined to be coeval with the human race."

Modern science defines knowledge (a) as *"individual knowledge,* or the mind's cognition of its own conscious states *plus* its cognition of the Cosmos of which it is a part," and (b) as *"universal knowledge,* or the sum of all human cognitions of the Cosmos which have been substantiated by verification and certified by the unanimous consensus of the competent. This latter definition may never have been formulated before, but it is tacitly assumed in all [scientific] investigations . . ."[27] Science's "principle of cognition" is "utterly antagonistic to the Nominalism which denies all objectivity to genera and species . . . Scientific Realism [or "Relationism"] teaches that cognition conforms to things . . . This is the philosophical translation of the principle of verifications . . . (It) begins with a Cosmos of which the individual ego is merely a part . . . (It) is objective, in a sense so broad as to include the subjective within itself . . ."[28] In all matters "science" is polarized against "modern philosophy." "Philosophy" should sit "modestly at the feet of science" so it can become "modernized."[29] This polarization of "science" and "philosophy" contains, or rather is a surrogate for "realism" and "nominalism" which in turn involves "humanism" and "individualism."

Abbot wants to make "the foundations, method, and system of philosophy scientific," and vice versa. He wants to "bring [philosophy] into harmony with the now thoroughly established scientific method . . ." And he speaks of "the greatly needed identification of Science and Philosophy."[30]

Notice that "modern sciences" could not have been "produced by an individual"[31] and that one of the chief forms of "philosophy," "the Scotch School taught . . . Nominalism."[32]

"The universal scientific method" constitutes "the only foundation on which the philosophy of the future can be reared; and if, as I profoundly believe, human thought is the architect of all things human, then what the philosophy of the future shall prove to be, that also will be its religion."[33]

Abbot wants to get hold of the "religious outcome" of the scientific method.[34] After fifty pages of abstracted inferences he comes to his point. He not only wants to believe humanistically; he wants to plant it deeply as part of the universe, and his strategy is to lean it against the verity of "scientific method."

> "We seem to have been led by a very straight path, assuming only the validity of the scientific method and of the philosophical presuppositions logically involved in it, to the momentous result that the universe *per se* is an Infinite Self-conscious Intellect, which, though infinitely removed in degrees, is yet essentially identical in kind with the human intellect. This result ... is the constitutive principle of scientific theism; and I see no way to escape it, except by repudiating the scientific method itself."[35]

Science mediates the finite and the infinite. The philosophy of science will be "The Supreme wisdom of Man and the self-evident Word of God."[36] For the universe is "a living and growing organism."[37] What does this *mean?* It means that "the absolute end of Being-in-itself ... is ... the Infinite Creative Life of God."[38] There seems to be occurring an "Eternal Creative Act" and "the infinite organism manifests itself essentially as Moral Being — as a universe whose absolute foundation is Moral Law ... the moral nature of man, derived from this moral nature of the universe itself, is the august revelation of the infinite purity, rectitude, and holiness of God."[39] "Such appears to me to be the conception of the universe which flows naturally, logically, inevitably, from the philosophized scientific method; and such, therefore, appears to me to be the *Idea* of *God* which is the legitimate outcome of modern science."[40]

John Fiske: In the seventies John Fiske was in his early thirties. Fifteen years before, upon the death of his father and the remarriage of his mother, he had legally changed his name. He was born Edmond Fiske Green at Hartford, Connecticut in 1842. His father, E. B. Green, was a lawyer, a journalist, owner and editor of a paper, *The Panama Herald,* in the canal zone; he had been a private secretary to Henry Clay in Washington.[41] Fiske's mother had taught school in New York and in Newark. Her remarriage was to a well-to-do lawyer, and she assisted John Fiske financially. Throughout his childhood Fiske lived in Middletown, Connecticut, with his grandparents, who were prosperous people, the father holding five city offices at once to the "satisfaction of all."[42] After attending private schools there, Fiske entered Betts Acade-

ation, and because he was a successful popularizer his thought
took certain assumptions from his audiences. Around 1870 he
shifted "publics" and his thought moved from tracing out "evolution" in the narrow ranges of philology to setting it forth as a Dynamic Principle of all Cosmic phenomena.[46] Call him what they
may, those contemporaries who really listened to him could not
find any great blow to "religion" in his words. He reconciled science and religion, seeing a divine will that shaped evolution to
ends well liked by all. With him, progress became a cosmic law.
"Teleology is beneficient."[47] "God is the one all-pervading fact of
life . . . ."[48] E. L. Youmans, as a publisher-proselyte of Spencerian
science had sought out Fiske in his early career. These two men as
writer and publisher were chief vehicles of English evolutionism
and Victorian science to the enlarging American public. "In Youmans . . . ear . . . found its John the Baptist. He did more than anyone to prepare . . . America . . . for the great scientific awakening. . . ."[49]

Darwin, Spencer, and Huxley claimed Fiske as an important ally
in the fight for science and the recognition of science, and this
battle was, of course, for many the major polemic of the time. In
his earlier days, considered a radical, an outsider never quite in
the stabler Harvard assumptions, he lived to see the drift of dominant intellectual opinion come to some sort of agreement with
what he fought for. Harvard gave him the LL.D. The University
of Pennsylvania gave him the Litt.D. He lectured in Washington
University from 1881, becoming a professor there in '84. But he
continued his residence in Cambridge to his death in 1901. The life
of John Fiske parallels and is a major component of the way science and evolution came to the intellectual public of America. But
C. S. Peirce and Chauncey Wright did not assimilate "science" in
this, the more popular manner. C. S. Peirce called Spencer's system an "amateurism." And Chauncey Wright went out of his way,
as we shall see, to polemicize against it. William James, in a letter to T. S. Perry in 1905, who was then writing on Fiske, recalled
an event concerning a meeting of The Club: "If you want an ex-
tra anecdote, you might tell how, when Chauncey Wright, Charles
Peirce, St. John Green, Warner and I appointed an evening to discuss the 'Cosmic Philosophy,' just out, John Fiske went to sleep
under our noses."[50] As far as any direct influence of Fiske upon

my in Stamford, Connecticut, at the age of thir
there until the age of fifteen. He was tutored two
gyman, and then he entered Harvard as a sophon
the age of eighteen.

From the standpoint of the Harvard administrat
not do well. He not only read Spencer, but became a
disciple of the English evolutionist. He wrote arti
threatened to expel him. But he took the degree in
the formal course, he read law independently and in
the bar examination. For two years none came under l
have him practice law in their behalf. When Eliot ca
presidency of Harvard in 1869, John Fiske became a
"position" which he held until 1872. He lectured on "
philosophy," dealing mainly with philosophy and w
Outside of Harvard he became known as "the Cambrid
In 1872 he became "assistant librarian" at Harvard, whi
best Eliot could do for him.[43] Dwelling among the boo
gan to turn from philosophy to history. Judging from his
work, the intellectual motive for, or at least result of, th
attention was the desire to study American society from t
point of a Spencerian evolutionist. In fine New England
he evolved American democracy from the New Engla
meeting. His life of writing, lecturing and handling books
brary was broken in 1873, at which time he went to Eng
study. Apparently he was not in any kind of money, for the
or scientific pilgrimage, was made possible by a friendly
$1,000 from some maecenas. There is some evidence that tl
from "philosophy" to "history" may have been motivated
creased financial chances in the latter sphere. In England
moved in definitely scientific circles. The lad from Connectic
Darwin, Huxley, Clifford, Lewes, Tyndall, and above all,
cer.[44]

There is nothing outstandingly original in the intellectual
duction of John Fiske. His role in the intellectual publics of A
ica in the last quarter of the nineteenth century lies unambigu
ly in his championing the scientific world view of Spencer. I
rington describes Fiske as "a philosophical hippopotamus, wa
ing the chill waters of Spencerian science with his prodigi
bulk."[45] He popularized the Spencerian model of science and ev

the pragmatists of the Metaphysical Club is concerned, perhaps this anecdote, along with Peirce's statement of Fiske's aloofness, is sufficiently telling. The style of thought which Fiske represented does not enter as a component of the pragmatic. His presence in the Metaphysical Club may be taken as symbolic of the scientific movement which backgrounds the emergence of pragmatism, but the meaning and the use of "science" by Fiske and by pragmatists are definitely two matters.

Chauncey Wright: Ansel Boleyn Wright was the deputy sheriff and a successful dealer in "West Indian goods and groceries" of Northampton, Massachusetts. The Wrights had settled in Northampton in the early fifties of the seventeenth century. Chauncey Wright, born 1830, was one of nine children. He later wrote that his father was "doubtless . . . descended from a series of English Wrights, who . . . were well known to their friends. . . ."[51] At the age of fifteen, he wrote a letter to his brother which included the following quaint germ of skepticism: "In the beginning God . . . created the earth ages before man with all the heavenly bodies now in existence except maybe a few."[52] He entered Harvard in 1848, studying mathematics, natural science and philosophy. He graduated in 1852 at the age of 18, and on this later edge of golden transcendentalism went to work as a computer and devisor of new and more precise calculations for *The Nautical Almanac*. He held positions with *The Almanac* until his death in 1875; throughout his life it was his chief source of income. He had not only studied but had been directly engaged in scientific work prior to the discussions of the Metaphysical Club.

Judging from Peirce's statement, Chauncey Wright was at the center of the first immediate audience of Peirce's pragmatism. He fought for Darwin's view, and in 1873 set forth a detailed botanical study which advanced an evolutionary explanation of the arrangement of leaves on plants, which received the personal commendation of the number one English evolutionist. With such a focus as he had, rooted not only in formal training but in occupational activity, it is not surprising that philosophically he was drawn to and was deeply influenced by Hamilton and Mill. Of American thinkers he was among the first seriously to study and introduce the methods of British empiricism. It is significant to the understanding of Peirce that he should call Chauncey Wright "our boxing master."[53] For Wright was probably closer to Peirce in style and temper of intellect than any other member of the Metaphysical Club, which is not to say that they were by any means congruent on all important points. "It must have been," writes Peirce, "about 1857 when I first made the acquaintance of Chauncey Wright, a mind about on the level of J. S. Mill ... Wright ... was at that time a thorough Hamiltonian ... Soon after he turned ... a great admirer of Mill ... He and I used to have long and very lively and *close* disputations lasting two or three hours daily for many years."[54]

As a boy Chauncey Wright filled sheets of paper with quasi-mathematical circles, squares and triangles.[55] Later he experimented in legerdemain.[56] He was a skillful juggler, despite his ponderous bulk. Being interested in "the processes by which impressions on the senses are converted into knowledge" led him to an interest in "the psychology of illusion." He observed, analyzed, and then reproduced "the most difficult of Hermann's tricks."[57] Those traits which "distinguished his observation as a physicist were exhibited in his feats of parlor magic." He invented and performed "marvelous games and puzzles of cards."[58] It is interesting to note that C. S. Peirce had precisely the same interest and skill in such matters.

Chauncey Wright never married. He lived quietly in Cambridge. He spent his entire life in the pursuit of science and fulfilling positions in social organizations for the advancement of sciences. He was, for example, recording secretary and editor of the *Annual Proceedings of The American Academy of Arts and Sciences* from 1863-70. From 1870 he lectured at Harvard on psychology and in 1874 became a regular member of the Harvard faculty, teaching mathematics and physics. As a member of the faculty he was definitely of the newer order. He wrote of his acceptance of the appointment as a lecturer that it was a "... romantic incident — rash act of heroic adventure ... something like the German University lecture system is aimed at...."[59] He was a scientist in a university who had won his reputation among scientists, probably in the main from a non-academic group.

Certain of Wright's friends saw "an aspect of tragic futility in his life." Visualizing him, Henry James heard the question, "But what then are you going to do for me?"[60] William James saw in

Wright a "master in the field of scientific thought and tended to accept him as an authoritative exponent of scientific aims and methods."[61] Wright thought that "boyish" was "a well chosen word for James." He was "Jamesonian" in being "crude and extravagant" in the way of his "opinion and more especially his language." Chauncey Wright went on: "I imagine that by laboring with him I shall get him in better shape by and by." And then, characteristically, "One remains a boy longer in philosophy than in any other direction."[62]

"An able critic" wrote in *The Nation* that to Wright "such ideas as optimism or pessimism were alike irrelevant. Whereas most men's interest in a thought is proportional to its possible relation to human destiny, with him it was almost the reverse."[63] "The dramatic interest of the doctrine" of evolution [Spencerian model!], says Fiske, "was to Mr. Wright *prima facie* evidence of its unscientific character."[64] "He was a born positivist" continues Fiske, "he went as far as it was possible for a human thinker to go toward a philosophy which should take no note of anything beyond the content of observed facts."[65] "He always kept the razor of Occam uncased." He had no "emotional excitability," no "aesthetic impulse or needs," he was "utterly insensible to music." He recalled "historic streets in London and Paris only as spots where some happy generalization had occurred to him."[66]

Fiske found that Wright intensely disliked anything teleological. To him there was no tendency in the career of the universe. He called this "purposeless play of events," the "cosmical weather." It was like the capricious wind.[67]

Chauncey Wright believed in the "possibility of an irreligious morality."[68] His interest in the "questions between" himself and Frank Abbot were "almost entirely speculative." He was just reflecting upon Abbot's "apostasy from the orthodox philosophy,"[69] He "believed that the really *essential* positions of morals and religion could be sustained on the 'lower' ground of common sense . . ." Furthermore, he writes:

> "I have always felt that philosophy was concerned with matters of theoretical interpretation rather than with practical matters of fact. Indeed, the history of philosophy hardly ever exhibits any divergence in opinion as to simple questions of practice, as to what should be done next in any given state

of social circumstances, — though it is one of the weapons of the orthodox to deduce the direct practical consquences from their opponents' theories."[70]

The philosophy which Wright held "denies nothing of orthodoxy except its confidence; but it discriminates between the desirability of a belief and the evidence thereof. Faith is in this philosophy what it was with St. Paul, a sentiment, not a faculty of knowledge."[71]

In a letter to Mr. Norton in 1867, Chauncey Wright sets forth with great clarity a distinction between (1) "legal duties" which "have . . . real sanctions in the punitive powers of the state. . . ." (2) "moral duties" which are "without legal sanctions, and are not enforced except by depriving the delinquent of voluntarily . . . rendered benefits . . ." and (3) "the strictly religious duties" which "are above the sanctions of fear or favor, and have their rewards and sanctions either in another life or in themselves — or in the evils of the absence of the requisite motive to them."[72]Specifically, religious sanctions are "either wholly self-subsisting, or sustained by a superstitious faith in another life."[73] This trichotomy is polarized against "The Calvinist" who regards:

> "this life and the next as all one and part of a grand moral scheme, in which obligations, duties, rights, and sanctions are completely balanced and mutually fitted to each other, conceives three different classes of virtues as essentially one, — as all on the type of legal duties, that is, of duties of 'perfect obligation,' with corresponding rights either in human beings or in the Divine Being. This identification of religious and all other obligations with legality is the characteristic of the extreme Protestant or Calvinistic creed."[74]

In this letter he goes on to characterize "strictly religious . . . conduct" in a manner which we shall later see to be similar in one respect to C. S. Peirce's. "Conduct," says Wright, is "strictly religious only when determined by the immediate, peculiar, and supreme happiness, *which the acting for universal ends*, without fear or favor, causes in the mature religious character."[75] He finds those ends to be the test that "conduces to the highest good of the greatest number" and would substitute the unity of this utilitarian morality for the "legal type" of unity of Calvinism. In so doing he would get around locating the test on "the shifting, historic ground of the so-called 'moral sense'."[76]

To Abbot, in 1867, he wrote of his beliefs concerning "a God and the immortality of the soul ... The verdict of 'not proven' is the kind of judgment I have formed on these matters." Then, after noting that this was not "atheism," he continues: "In fact, practical considerations determine that a state of suspended judgment on these themes is the state of stable equilibrium." Again, later, "practical grounds are really the basis of belief in the doctrines of theology." But personally Chauncey Wright had "no desire to wake into a strange, unknown future life," and he could "discover no valid reasons for any confidence in such a waking."[77]

In a very rough and rather personal discussion of "Dr. McCosh's treatment of those thinkers ... who differ from him in fundamental views," Wright wrote that:

> "To use the language of kindliness and magnanimity when every page manifests an intense, though smothered, *odium theologicum,* conceals nothing, and repels more effectively than the most open hostility. Expressions of petty spite, deprecatory epithets, intimations of ill-opinion, readiness to credit evil reports of those who hold unorthodox opinions in philosophy, and misinterpretations of every sign of weakness in them — these characterize Dr. McCosh's treatment...."[78]

To Abbot he wrote a paragraph that is revealing for the new order of things *philosophical* and *theological:*

> "But I hope that I have misunderstood you, and that you will be able to continue, as a religious instructor, to exemplify how irrelevant metaphysics really are to the clergyman's true influence, — quite as much so, I think, as to that of the scientific teacher. The pursuit of philosophy ought to be a side study. Nothing so much justifies that shameful assumption by ecclesiastical bodies of control over speculative opinions as the inconsiderate preaching of such opinions, in place of the warnings, encouragements, sympathies, and persuasions of the true religious instructor. The lessons which he has to deliver are really very easy to understand, but hard to live up to."[79]

Both Wright and Peirce relegate "religion" to the *practical;* they may think it important, but it is *not* accorded the intellectual status of "philosophy" which is viewed *professionally* and which is informed by, or is to be oriented to, the method of *science.*

Chauncey Wright was one of the "minds bred in physical studies" of the age of "experimental philosophy."[80] What is the difference between "ancient and modern science?" asks Wright in seeking orientation. The former verifies by "appeals to the tests of internal evidence, tests of reason, and the data of self consciousness." But the true characterization of modern science lies in its "method" of "verification by sensuous tests, tests of sensible experience — a deduction from a theory of consequences, of which we may have sensible experiences if they be true."[81]

I have not found anywhere among writers who are not usually lumped with "the pragmatists" a statement of a positivistic style of approach that contains in briefer or clearer form the general import of the "pragmatic maxim,"[82] nor one which exhibits the feel for the general push of this manner of thinking. This is no isolated comment of Chauncey Wright's. He goes on to stress *verification* as the hallmark of "science." "Science asks no questions about the ontological pedigree or *a priori* character of a theory, but is content to judge it by performance; and it is thus that a knowledge of nature, having all the certainty which the senses are competent to inspire, has been attained,——" Thus "while ideal or transcendental elements are admitted into scientific researches, though in themselves insusceptible of simple verification, they must still show credentials from the senses, either by affording from themselves consequences capable of sensuous verification, or by yielding such consequences in conjunction with ideas which by themselves are verifiable." And this knowledge of science ". . . maintains a strict neutrality toward all philosophical systems, and concerns itself not at all with the genesis or *a priori* grounds of ideas."[83]

The questions of "philosophy proper are human desires and fears and aspirations — human emotions — taking an intellectual form."[84] Nor was Chauncey Wright vague concerning the *source* of science:

> "Ancient schools of philosophy despised narrow material utilities, the servile arts, and sought no instruction in what moderns dignify by the name of useful arts; but *modern science finds in the requirements of the material arts the safest guide*

to exact knowledge. A theory which is utilized receives the highest possible certificate of truth. Navigation by the aid of astronomical tables, the magnetic telegraph, the innumerable utilities of mechanical and chemical science, are constant and perfect tests of scientific theories, and afford the standard of certitude, which science has been able to apply so extensively in its interpretations of natural phenomena."[85]

This paragraph could have been written in the 1920's by John Dewey. Chauncey Wright goes on to locate such views historically:

"This recognition of the dignity of the useful and of the authority of induction, but still more the subtler perceptions of method in induction by later English thinkers, and especially in the Positivism of Locke, Newton, Herschel, J. S. Mill, have more than anything else given the English their eminence in modern science. The restraints of the speculative spirit in scientific pursuits, determined mainly for a desire for peace with Theology and Philosophy, and accomplished by a division of provinces, have been the chief cause of the easy triumphs of inductive evidences in the modern sciences of physics, astronomy, chemistry, and even geology and biology, over an opposition which, when roused, has carried with it the strength of a desperate self-defense and all the gigantic forces of tradition."[86]

The relations of philosophy and science are put as follows:

"Philosophy proper should be classed with the Religions and with the Fine Arts, and estimated rather by the dignity of its motives, and the value it directs us to, than by the value of its own attainments. To condemn this pursuit because it fails to accomplish what science does, would be to condemn that which has formed in human nature habits, ideas, and associations on which all that is best in us depends, — would warrant the condemnation of science itself, since science scarcely existed at all for two thousand years of civilization, and represented as a distinct department during this period only the interest of the servile arts."[87]

Wright argued off and on with Fiske about Spencer from 1862 to 1875.[88] Notice the *way* Wright confronts Spencer. He says that the man's writings "evince an extensive knowledge of facts...." but "extensive rather than profound, and mainly at second hand."

"It is not, of course, to be expected that a philosopher will be an original investigator in all the departments of knowledge with which he is obliged to have dealings. He must take much at second hand. But original investigations in some department of empirical science are a discipline which best tests and develops even a philosopher's powers . . . . He learns how to make knowledge profitable to the ascertainment of new truths, — an art in which the modern natural philosopher excels. By new truths must be understood such as are not implied in what we already know, or deducible from what is patent to common observation. However skillfully the philosopher may apply his analytical processes to the abstraction of the truths involved in patent facts, the utility of his results will depend not so much on their value and extent as mere abstractions, as on their capacity to enlarge our experience by bringing to notice residual phenomena, and making us observe what we have entirely overlooked, or search out what has eluded our observation. Such is the character of the principles of modern natural philosophy, both mathematical and physical. They are rather the eyes with which nature is seen, than the elements and constituents of the objects discovered. It was in a clear apprehension of this value in the principles of mathematical and experimental science, that the excellence of Newton's genius consisted . . . "[89]

Mr. Spencer's method proceeds on "the supposition that the materials of truth have all been collected." But in *science* "nothing justified . . . abstract principles . . . but their utility in enlarging our concrete knowledge. . . ." Scientific "ideas" are . . . "working ideas." They are "finders, not merely summaries of truth."[90] ". . . selection is the prime function of the intellect."[91] But Spencer "uses abstractions and abstract modes of thought for moral ends."[92] In a letter to Abbot in 1867, Wright asserted, concerning the foundation of experientialism, that he agreed:

"that experience includes more than a heterogeneous mass of particular sensuous impressions, and cannot be explained by a mere 'law of association' among such impressions. Our cognitions are indeed more than the mere chronicles of a sensuous history. There are orders and forms in them which do not come directly from the transient details of sense-perceptions. Indeed, without the constant reaction of the mind through memory upon the presentations of the senses, there could arise nothing worth the name of knowledge. If our memories were only retentive and not only cooperative with the senses, only associations of the very lowest order could be formed. We should not each know the same world, but only each his own world."[93]

Spencer does not have "that precision in apprehension . . . which comes chiefly from a successful cultivation of experimental and mathematical research. . . ."[94] He possesses an "incompetency for the further development of his encyclopedic abstractions."[95]

It is also this stress upon *method* with which Wright confronts McCosh:

> " . . . 'inductions,' the name he gives (without adequately explaining the process) to what most other modern thinkers call, and try to explain by the name, 'intuitions *a priori.*' In this Dr. McCosh has doubtless confounded the effect of re- peated assertions and professions of belief with the force in producing universal beliefs of invariably repeated particular experiences — an effect enforced by that modern factitious moral obligation, 'the duty of belief'; a duty which though urged upon us by modern religious teachers . . . was far from being felt or admitted by . . . great teachers. Their service to us was in teaching *how* rather than *what* to think and be- lieve."[96]

There seems to be a linking of logical nominalism with political individualism and of logical realism with *not* political socialism but with "sentimentalism" or "sociality" as with C. S. Peirce[97] or the similar humanism as with Abbot. Chauncey Wright follows with some reservations what he took to be J. S. Mill's position:

> " . . . ascribing myths to a disease of language, by which words with forgotten meanings become personal or proper names . . . a thousand . . . important superstitions spring from that most pernicious disease, — afflicting the maturity as well as the infancy of language, — 'realism,' by which a general name becomes the name of a reality, different from the ob- jects or the qualities which it denotes in common. It is in this way that 'society' has appeared to have claims which the in- dividuals that compose it do not have; *and thus a reform in logic became necessary for the overthrow of many social and religious superstitions.* In fact, the two warfares, the philo- sophical and the social, or the theoretical and the practical, have been carried on side by side from the days of the school- men; and it is not an accident, but an historical consequence,

that Mr. Mill is the modern champion at once of *nominalism
in logic* and of *individualism in sociology.*"[98]

Here are some characteristic phrases and expressions of Wright's
social views taken from his letters: "In the long run, the privileges
of wealth" and he adds a phrase reminding us of his first letter
about God creating the heavenly bodies, "—that is, most of them—
conduce to the benefit of society."[99]

> "Of course, our rulers may make fatal mistakes, as the Ro-
> mans did. One fatal mistake would be in not sustaining the
> class of prosperous and independent yeomanry, the true back-
> bone of civilized communities as now constituted. Yet the
> privileges of wealth ought to be — will have to be — circum-
> scribed. The rapacity of wealth is, of course, the taproot of
> all these evils, the source of the hostility which threatens so-
> cial revolutions. We have got to amend the great Roman in-
> vention, the laws of property, as well as the constitutions of
> large cities and the management of their populations. But a
> scientific study of the subject from the point of view of utili-
> tarian political economy will, I am convinced, meet the de-
> mands of the revolutionists at a point far short of their pro-
> gramme. It would be easier for it to do so, but for the com-
> plication introduced by the city problem . . . But so far as
> the laws of property are inherently, or through changed cir-
> cumstances have come to be productive, not of increased gains,
> but of a large and permanent class of unproductive consu-
> mers, so far they are devices of legalized robbery, and must
> be abrogated or amended, if justice is ever to be effected by
> legislation, through whatever political powers."[100]

Yet to Wright it was "perhaps unfortunate that the problem will
have to be solved through democratic agencies. . . ." For this involves the "ascendency of the will of the masses in political matters."[101]

Nevertheless, "our great men are the wise and painstaking pro-
moters and guardians of extensive interests,"[102] and "Individualism is vindicated as a means to an end — the end of social improvement."[103] He links individualism with a view of evolution:
"The possibility of monstrosities in nature is also the possibility of
amelioration."[104] Thus, Wright's "liberalism" is hesitant. He was
inclined to attribute "social problems" to "mismanagement."[105]
Correspondingly, he was interested in "electoral reforms." He

gave his private sanction, in a letter, to a scheme for such reform on the grounds that it would prevent "logrolling" by minorities and would encourage "the assumption of responsibility by majorities." He believed that the scheme would effect a "cure" of "some of the worst of our political evils." In addition, it would afford a solution "of the woman's suffrage question."[106] Wright was in favor of woman's suffrage, not as a question in itself but as an element in the greater question of rights.[107] It was not "for the benefit of woman, but simply for liberty's sake, that I would demand for her this right."[108] The social-political point that is significant in connection with Chauncey Wright's style of thinking is not, it seems to me, his characteristic caution, nor even his slight stress on a "managerial" or "administrational" interest in the workings of society. Rather it is the linkage of *logical nominalism* with *political individualism.* In Peirce and Abbot "scientific method" involves *logical realism* and neither Abbot nor Peirce is "individualistic" politically.

What I want to point out about this blue-eyed Puritan of Cambridge is (1) that he was bred and lived in active scientific work. (2) As an intellectual, he did not feel the force of science in terms of its results, but as a *method.* (3) That in stating this method, in using it polemically, especially against the Spencerian mode of thought, he generalized it and stated *abstractions, ideas,* in terms of verificatory modes which can truly be called pragmatic. (4) That he was closely associated with C. S. Peirce. Later I shall detail the import of his central role in C. S. Peirce's public for the first articulation of "pragmatism."

Lawyers: Nicholas St. John Green was a lawyer and a jurist. He was born in Cambridge in 1830 and died in 1876. He graduated from Harvard in 1851 and took the LL.B. in '53. His practicing of law was interrupted by the Civil War, during which he was a "major and paymaster." He instructed "philosophy and political economy" at Harvard in 1870 and 1871, lectured at the Harvard Law School from 1870 to 1873, was Dean and lecturer at the Boston University Law School from 1872 to his death. Engaging in official tasks, he edited the first two volumes of "Massachusetts Reports" published in 1874.[109] That his was more than a strictly legal mind is indicated by his intellectual behavior in *Essays and Notes.*[110] He quotes Dun Scotus on causation,[111] writes on "the distinction between mistake of fact and mistake of law,"[112] and quotes from the Port Royal Logic: "Maxims are to be distrusted ... " I find in his writing no *direct* influence or citation from Bain. In the *American Law Review* of 1869-70, Green published an essay "Proximate and Remote Cause"[113] in which he praises the school-man for "separating and defining ideas." Fisch suggests that the following passage from Green's essay points at the facts with which law deals, which may have suggested a pragmatic or prediction theory of law: "We cannot add clearness to our reasoning by talking about proximate and remote causes and effects when we mean only the degree of certainty or uncertainty with which the connection between cause and effect might have been anticipated." Since Peirce mentions that Green was interested in Alexander Bain's work, and in the same passage calls Green the "grandfather of pragmatism," it is well to examine briefly the relevant opinions of Bain.

Alexander Bain was the son of an Aberdeen "hand-loom weaver."[114] The book containing the references to belief and action is his *The Emotions and the Will*.[115] In this work he writes that ". . . belief has no meaning, except in reference to our actions . . . no mere conception that does not directly or indirectly implicate our voluntary exertions, can ever amount to the state in question . . . The primordial form of belief is expection of some contingent future about to follow on our action."[116] "While action is the basis, and ultimate criterion, of belief, there enters into it as a necessary element some cognizance of the order of nature, of the course of the world."[117] Yet action . . . [is] the only test, and essential import of the state of conviction . . . there is no other criterion . . . When I believe . . . if I am not repeating an empty sound, or indulging in idle conception, I give it out that if any occasion should arise for putting this fact in practice, I am ready to do so."[118]

Joseph B. Warner graduated from Harvard in 1869. He was a lawyer in Boston, and a life-long friend of the James family. He died in 1923.[119] He seems to have worked with Holmes on Kent's *Commentaries*.[120] None of the available biographical dictionaries contain his name.

The disproportionate number of lawyers in the Metaphysical Club has been noted. It has been suggested by M. H. Fisch that the methods of the practicing lawyer had at least as much to do with the development of "pragmatism" as did Kant.[121] The evidence offered by Fisch for such an imputation is Peirce's reference to Green in the quotation above, and certain characteristics of Holmes' thought. In addition there are the activities engaged in by four members of the Club during its meetings. Holmes, Green, and Gray[122] were all practicing lawyers and all three were lecturing and/or writing on law; Warner was a law student. As Fisch indicates, this period also witnessed the introduction by Langdell of the "case method" of instructing law, which, of course, intrinsically conceived of law as "growing."[123]

Let us focus a little more sharply upon these legal activities and lawyer memberships of the Metaphysical Club. We can do so the more sharply by examining the career of Oliver Wendell Holmes, Jr.

Of the three lawyers of the Metaphysical Club, undoubtedly the most important is Holmes. His career was not academic. By examining his life and thought we can observe in a professional context certain formulated usages of his variant of a pragmatic style of thinking. He was born in 1841, one year before James, and came to articulation in Boston, Massachusetts. His father was a professional writer, physician, a wit and a poet who moved within the central circle of Boston's literary elite without losing his touch with school "marms" and plebians. Holmes' mother was a daughter of a member of the Supreme Court of Massachusetts. Holmes, Jr., attended a Latin school in Cambridge and took the A.B. from Harvard in 1861. He fought in the Fourth Battalion infantry during the Civil War and was wounded three times. By the middle sixties he was back in Cambridge "wrangling" with William James.[124]

By 1868 James was calling Holmes one of his "best friends so far."[125] And the next year Holmes was coming "out" to James and "we jaw once a week."[126] But James thought Holmes' "cold-blooded, conscious egoism and conceit" poisoned his "noble qualities."[127] Holmes "debauched o' nights in philosophy" and then it was "law-law-law."[128] He read Kant; he read Tyndall on *Heat,* but all the time he was working very hard at law. In 1869 he was engaged in the two-year task of editing Kent's *Commentaries.* He had, said Mrs. James, perhaps a little appalled, "a fearful grip upon his work."[129]

"Law" seemed to be somewhat apart from the traffic in general ideas which went on between James and Holmes. The academic circle was only one of Holmes' circles, the Metaphysical Club only one of his clubs. As his career went on, he was more and more drawn into official spheres of action, and more than ever philosophy became a "hobby" and thinking had to include for Holmes certain tough facts of which James never dreamed. In 1883 Holmes had taken an associate seat in the Supreme Judicial Court of Massachusetts, in 1899 he was its Chief Justice. In 1902, Theodore Roosevelt appointed him to the Supreme Court of the United States. He held this position until 1932, resigning at the age of 91. James had written to "Wendell" in 1868 that he was glad to see him embracing "the very bowels of the law and grapple them to your soul with hooks of steel...." But he was even gladder that Holmes could still see "the blue Jove above...."[130] The "blue Jove," as James saw it, was to dwindle in Holmes. James and Holmes had enjoyed certain commonalities, as Perry says, in a philosophical adolescence which they shared. But their thought was to drift apart as did their careers. In 1866-67 William James had written a memorandum to be read *at* Holmes: "it contained a defense of optimism against the negations of agnosticism."[131] In 1872 James wrote that Holmes' "mind resembles a stiff spring, which has to be abducted violently from . . . his law . . . and which every instant it is left to itself flies tight back."[132]

As far as the legal context of the emergence of pragmatism is concerned, which I have mentioned above, it should be noted that about the time of the Metaphysical Club, Holmes was "University Lecturer on Jurisprudence." Hence, as Fisch has indicated, Holmes had probably not only to define legal concepts, but "law" itself. Fisch suggests that this "was the need under pressure of which both the prediction theory of law and pragmatism took form." I am not ready to so telescope "pragmatism's" origin, but as for the prediction theory of law the point undoubtedly holds. Fisch has shown that this theory was in probability invented between 1870 and 1872."[133] It is during these years that the pragmatic maxim of Peirce was advanced. We find a sentence written by Peirce, probably in 1902, in a discussion of English rationality, which asserts the prediction theory of law: "The actual law consists in that which the court's officers will sustain."[134] Whether this pragmatic maxim is "a generalization of the prediction theory of law," we must refrain from saying until our more detailed examination of Peirce. I think it may well have been the other way around. It is also relevant that in a letter to Pollock, Holmes acknowledged Chauncey Wright as the *general* source of "probabilism":

> "Chauncey Wright, a nearly forgotten philosopher of real merit, taught me when young that I must not say *necessary* about the universe, that we don't know whether anything is necessary or not. So I describe myself as a bet-abilitarian, I believe that we can *bet* on the behavior of the universe in its contact with us."

Chauncey Wright's Whitmanesque "cosmic weather" seems to pervade Holmes' thought, C. S. Peirce's "tychism," and James' nonrigid universe. Perhaps it is a democratic metaphysics of the changing pattern of law in growing society. Let us trace some of the "pragmatic" blends in Holmes.

There are two sources from which we can gather such "pragmatic" elements as Holmes' thought embodied: First, in his writings, which were, of course, in the main legal documents, treatises on law, and some printed speeches; and secondly, in his reactions, in personal letters, to the publications of pragmatic thinkers, which is to say to James' and Dewey's, for he lost touch with Peirce, gaining it briefly upon the publication of Peirce's essays in 1923 by Morris Cohen.[135]

Holmes' place in legal thinking rests largely upon his *The Common Law*, published in 1881. The book shifted theoretical legal attention in a decisive way. "The life of the law has not been logic: it has been experience."[136] "Logic" here meant "the official theory" which held that "each new decision follows syllogistically from existing precedent,"[137] and "experience" meant "the felt necessities of the time, the prevalent moral and political theories. . . . public policy . . ."[138] And the thesis as a whole meant that "the substance of the law. . . corresponds, so far as it goes, with what is then understood to be convenient . . . considerations of what is expedient for the community concerned"[139] as judges see them determine the changing law. This is the nerve of Holmes' view in *The Common Law*. If I may be permitted the use of such a vogue phrase, it seems thoroughly saturated with a pragmatic animus.

The point of view which Holmes took he held to be "scientific." In 1868 he had written to James: ". . . law as well as any other series of facts in this world may be approached in the interests of science and may be studied, yes and practiced, with the preservation of one's ideals ... they [grow] robust under the regimen ..." But what *are* the ideals? At the age of eighty-seven, when they were quite "robust," Holmes wrote: "If I were to sum up what I have learned I think I should say: faith in effort (before you see the goal or can put articulately the question to be asked)."[140] And when this point of view had been used in "the study of law" it eventuated finally in a philosophy of law which develops on practical rather than logical lines.[141]

I take this focus to be the core of what "pragmatism" may be for Holmes. It is, therefore, important to grasp what "practical" involved for Holmes. Of all the "pragmatists" of the Metaphysical Club to be considered, Holmes, the only "public official" among them, is the only one who included in his statement "practical," and in his use of pragmatic models of reasoning, the element of power. And to his mind it was central: his style of thinking is tough-minded, very shrewd and always strategic. In so far as defining "what lawyers call law," he accepts "the Austinian definition" — "a command of a political superior to a political inferior," but "philosophically" this is rejected as too narrow.[142] Law is what is *accepted* and *enforced* by the courts. It is not "the sovereign's" will, but what the judges *say* his will is. "The only question for the lawyers," writes Holmes, "is, how will the judges act?"[143] "I have," he wrote, "no belief in panaceas and almost none in sudden ruin. ..."[144] The justification of a law "must be found in some help which the law brings toward reaching a social end which the governing power of the community has made up its mind that it wants."[145] Thus did Holmes recognize the power element in "practice" and instrumentalize his position with reference to it. Of all the individuals who may be termed "pragmatist" Holmes alone has recognized the use of force and power involved in "pragmatism," as only he accepted an institutional position of power.

Richardson writes that Holmes "has been remarkable for the fact that he has enforced laws in which he did not believe, and in enforcing them has voiced his disapproval."[146]

But when decisions were more "open," it was the job of the court to make "dominant opinion" effective. This does not mean that he believed in "Equality." He asserts the contrary in a letter to his friend Wu. And writing about Laski's *Grammar of Politics,* Holmes states that it did not seem to him that "man" was "so sacred an object as Laski seems to think him . . . Malthus was right . . . Every society is founded on the death of men."[147] "The true grounds of decision," he wrote about a case concerning the right of picketing, "are considerations of policy and of social advantage, and it is vain to suppose that solutions can be attained merely by logic and the general propositions of law which nobody disputes . . . "[148] Seeking "wider common law rights for the labor organization in its encounters with the employer" we see his ingeniously liberal strategy of classifying "labor unions vs. employers" as instances of "free competition." "Malthus was right."[149]

"Judges as well as others," he believed, "'should openly discuss the legislative principles upon which their decisions must always rest in the end and should base their judgments upon broad considerations of policy . . ."[150] Such considerations might lead one into thinking about moral themes, but apparently this did not happen to Holmes. For him, in the rational study of law, "the man of the future is the man of statistics and the master of economics."[151] "Our morality," Holmes wrote, at the age of eighty-six, "seems to me only a check on the ultimate domination of force, just as our politeness is a check on the impulse of every pig to put his feet in the trough."[152]

As far as Holmes was concerned, "Life is an end in itself, and the only question as to whether it is worth living is whether you have enough of it."[153] As for the rest:

> "When men have realized that time has upset many fighting faiths, they may come to believe even more than they believe the very foundations of their own conduct that the ultimate good desired is better reached by free trade in ideas — that the best test of truth is the power of truth to get itself accepted in the competition of the market, and that truth is the only ground upon which their wishes safely can be carried out. That at any rate is the theory of our Constitution. It is an experiment, as all life is an experiment."[154]

Here, through a "legal" spectrum we see the competitive theory of truth. Holmes wants plenty of room for the fight to go on. It is in this that his "liberalism" is anchored.

Given such a position and the generally tough-minded and tentative perspective rising from it, we can well understand that Holmes replied to James' published works with "half-appreciate, half-dissenting comment."[155] About *The Will To Believe* he wrote to James in 1896:

> "With its general aim or end I sympathize deeply — I mean the justification of the idealizing impulse; in detail, I somewhat diverge. I think the demands made of the universe are too nearly the Christian demands without the scheme of salvation. I long ago made up my mind that all that one needed was a belief in the significance of the universe. And more lately it has come to seem to me that even that might be ambiguous. For all I know "significance" is an expression of finiteness and incompleteness, and the total, if there is one, is too great a swell to condescend to have a meaning. The basis of my content is precisely the denial of the possibility of that attitude of rejection and scorn for which you quote Carlyle and the City of *Dreadful Night.* Of course a man may say, "I hate it," as a mere fact of temperament, and may talk big against God while the lightning is quiet. But what warrant a sceptic can have for assuming that he is a god outside the show . . . I don't understand. This you will recognize as my ever recurring view ever since we have known each other."[156]

But to his friend in England, Holmes wrote that the "philosophical worth of its content" did not interest him as did its writing and the "essential Irishness of the writer."[157] In 1908 he wrote some lines which penetrate into the heart of James' thought and also reveal much of his own. He thought "William James's argument for free will" was "fitted to please free thinking Unitarian parsons and the ladies. I always think of a remark. . . .that the philosophers were hired by the comfortable class to prove that everything is all right. I think it *is* all right, but on very different grounds."[158]

"Pragmatism interested Holmes above James' other writings. As to what was relativistic and skeptical in James' view, Holmes felt confident; but of James' confidence, metaphysical and religious, Holmes was — skeptical.[159] Upon receiving a copy of *Pragmatism,* Holmes put his reactions to James like this: "I heartily agree with much, but I am more skeptical than you are. You would say that I am too hard or tough-minded — I think none of the philosophers sufficiently humble."[160]

In a letter to Pollock, Holmes wrote that James' death:

> "cuts a root for me that went far into the past, but of late, indeed for many years, we have seen little of each other and had little communication except as he occasionally sent me a book. Distance, other circumstances and latterly his demi-spiritualism and pragmatism, were sufficient cause. His reason made him sceptical and his wishes led him to turn down the lights so as to give miracle a chance."[161]

We shall later see how very penetrating the implications of this remark is. Apparently Holmes was much more taken by Dewey. In three separate letters written in 1928 he commented upon:

> "John Dewey's book *Experience and Nature* . . . I read . . . twice. . . .Although I could not give a summary of a chapter or a page in it, I thought it great. It seemed to me to *feel* the universe more inwardly and profoundly than any book I know, at least any book of philosophy."[162]

In 1930 he said: "Dewey's view of the universe came home to me closer than any other that I know."[163] And one year later: "So methought God would have spoken had he been inarticulate but keenly desirous to tell you how it was."[164]

From Dewey's standpoint, Holmes was much admired, indeed — and this is rare for Dewey — even quoted.[165] To this we shall return.

Such then were the members (save Peirce and James) of the Metaphysical Club — their careers in brief, and their dominant interests and ideas. By way of brief summary the following chart may be offered:

TABLE 5

OCCUPATIONAL POSITIONS OF THE MEMBERS OF THE
METAPHYSICAL CLUB AND OF THEIR FATHERS

Names of Members	Life-span	Vocation	Occupation of Father (or Guardian)
C. S. Peirce	1839-1914	Scientist & Philosopher	Professor of Mathematics
William James	1842-1910	Professor, Philosopher	Free lance writer, religionist, rentier
Joseph Warner	1800-1923	Lawyer	- - - - - - - -
Oliver W. Holmes, Jr.	1841-1935	Lawyer Lecturer	Free lance writer and physician
N. St. John Green	1830-1876	Lawyer Lecturer	- - - - - - - - - -
Chauncey Wright	1830-1875	Scientist & Philosopher	Petty official small merchant
John Fiske	1842-1901	Historian Librarian Scientific writer	Journalist
F. E. Abbot	1836-1903	Free lance Religionist & Occasional Pastor	School Teacher
John Chipman Gray	1839-1915	Lawyer, lecturer	barge merchant

If one social category were to be applied to the group as a whole, it would be "learned professional." Of them all, only Peirce and Abbot suffered serious social and economic descent during their life spans. The others either remained on a comfortable level or experienced ascension. Practically all of them were at some period engaged in some capacity at Harvard University, but none of them experienced a typical academic career. They are marginal to what was typical in the Academy, and not one could be said to have lived a "cloistered academic" life. Their fathers were scattered in vocation, ranging from school teacher to comfortable rentier; the dominant background, however, was free-professional. The members themselves were dominantly of three professions: lawyer, scientists, religionist. I say religionist rather than "clergyman" because none of them occupied a normal clergyman role, and not one of them was thoroughly orthodox. Their religious blends will be more systematically considered in connection with William

James. Here we should note that from the standpoint of what was probably typical of philosophers they were atypical in three ways. They were not sons of out-and-out clergymen (*if* we may consider that typical of philosophers — see above). They were not dominantly teachers of philosophy in colleges and universities. And they were not unashamedly, if I may use the term, religious. While only Wright and Holmes might be called irreligious, none of the members set forth religious creeds without thoroughly dressing them up in highly "scientific" drapery.

Thus, besides a general speculative interest and some connection with Harvard University — either as students or as lecturers — they possessed in common several interests which seem to have engrossed their minds and focused their attention.

The general issues of "religion and science" existing across the pervasive background of "science" itself tended to capture their attention. In Fiske, Abbot, and as we shall see, obviously in James and attenuatively in Peirce, this issue is central. On the scientific left wing, we have Wright, and on the religious side, also very much left wing, we have Abbot. In the middle we have James and Fiske; but it is a different "middle" for each of them. Peirce's position on this matter is too elaborate to be presented here; it will be presented in full context later. Not one of the members sets forth his ideas as religious, but always in the name of "science." This served as the legitimating theme for them all, in religion itself, in law, in philosophy.

The second major theme present is law. Not only did it exist in the activities of the members of the Club, but in all probability to some extent in the discussions.

But in connection with "law" and "science" we might add a third theme, which was dominant in the slant they had on law, namely, that of *logic*. It was as lecturers on law, faced with, and very intensely interested in *definition* that these lawyers were talking and thinking about law. But they were also practicing law. In this *legal* context, and specifically in the logical character of their interests in law, we find a *point of anchorage for the manner in which science and logic were approached by Peirce.* Like Abbot and James, he approached science *not* as subject matter but as method, as technique, specifically, as definitional technique. This legal slant joins neatly with certain other activities of Peirce. And it underlies the manner in which science and religion were drawn together, namely, in terms of *method*. The exception to this is John Fiske, and he is among the least pragmatic of the Club's members.

1. The precise dates and durations of these meetings are problematic. James wrote plans of them in a letter to Holmes in 1868 *Letters*, Vol. I, p. 126. James was abroad until '69 and again in '73-74. Wright died in '75. Charles Peirce was abroad in '75. It is most probable that the Club met or was most active in 1870-72; it probably continued until 1874. *See* R. B. Perry, *The Thought and Character of William James*, Vol. I, p. 536, and *The Letters of William James*, edited by Henry James, Vol. II, p. 233.

2. Charles S. Peirce, *Collected Papers*, Vol. 12 and 13.

3. The numbers of lawyers seems disproportionately high; and there is some evidence in James' 1868 letter that another lawyer, John Chipman Gray, should be included in the Club, or if not there at least in the general circle. *Letters of James*, Vol. I, pp. 151, 154, 168-69. This legal complexion will be discussed below.

4. Letter to Mrs. Franklin from C. S. Peirce, reprinted in *The Journal of Philosophy, Psychology, and Scientific Method* (Dec. 21, 1916), p. 719.

5. Ralph Barton Perry, *The Thought and Character of William James*, Vol. I, p. 537.

6. *Ibid.*, Vol. II, p. 431.

7. The facts of Abbot's life have been taken from the *Dictionary of American Biography*, Vol. I, pp. 11-12.

8. Quoted in the *Dictionary of American Biography* from *Freedom and Fellowship in Religion* (New York 1875) pp. 223-64.

9. F. E. Abbot, Ph.D., *The Syllogistic Philosophy or Prologemena to Science*, two volumes (Boston 1906) Vol. II, p. 319.

10. Abbot, *Free Church Tracts*, No. 1 (Tacoma 1895) cited in the *Dictionary of American Biography*.

11. *The Nation* (November 12, 1891) p. 372.

12. *The Nation* (November 19, 1891) p. 390.

13. *Ibid.*, (November 26, 1891) p. 408.

14. *Ibid.*, (December 3, 1891) p. 426.

15. *Ibid.*, p. 426.

16. Quoted from *The Index*, Vol. 1 (January 1870) by R. H. Gabrield, *The Course of American Democratic Thought; an Intellectual History Since 1815* (New York 1940) p. 176f.

17. F. E. Abbot, Ph.D., *Scientific Theism* (Boston 1885) p. xiii.

18. C. S. Peirce, *Collected Papers*, Vol. I, (1903) p. 6; also Vol. IV, (1898) p. 4: "Dr. Abbot in his *Scientific Theism* has so clearly and with such admirable simplicity shown that modern science is realistic that it is perhaps injudicious for me to attempt to add anything upon the subject."

19. F. E. Abbot, *op. cit.*, p. xxiii.

20. *Ibid.*, p. 3-5.

21. *Ibid.*, p. 5.

22. *Ibid.*, p. 8.

23. *Ibid.*, p. 9.

24. *Ibid.*, p. 9.

25. *Ibid.*, p. 10.

26. *Ibid.*, p. 10.

27. *Ibid.*, p. 10.

28. *Ibid.*, pp. 10-14.

29. *Ibid.*, p. 41.

30. *Ibid.*, pp. 55-56.

31. *Ibid.*, p. 59.

32. *Ibid.*, p. 67. Abbot cites Sir Wm. Hamilton's *Lectures on Method,* p. 477.

33. *Ibid.*, p. 32.

34. *Ibid.*, pp. 119-20.

35. *Ibid.*, pp. 155-56.

36. *Ibid.*, p. 157.

37. *Ibid.*, p. 163. "The fact of evolution . . . is today established beyond reasonable doubt . . ." pp. 169-70.

38. *Ibid.*, pp. 202-03.

39. *Ibid.*, p. 206.

40. *'bid.*, pp. 209-10.

41. John Spencer Clark, *John Fiske Life and Letters*, Vol. I, pp. 1-7.

42. *Ibid.*, p. 22.

43. *Ibid.*, p. 399.

44. For a revealing glimpse into the character of Fiske's intimacies with such men and his boyish delight in what was up, compare his charming letters: *e.g.*, "You ought to have heard 'em roar when I recounted . . . I thought Tyndall would have busted his diaphragm and Huxley said those were the kind . . . he liked to get pitched into by — *i.e.*, fellows who are sure to put their foot in it." *The Personal Letters of John Fiske: A Small Edition Privately Printed for Members of the Bibliophile Society* (The Roch Press, Cedar Rapids 1939) p. 139.

45. V. L. Parrington, *Main Currents in American Thought* (New York 1930) Vol. III, p. 13.

46. John Spencer Clark, *op. cit.*, p. 364.

47. Henry Holt, *Garrulities of an Octogenarian Editor* (New York 1923) p. 339.

48. John Fiske, *The Idea of God* (Boston 1902) p. xii.

49. John Fiske, *E. L. Youmans, Interpreter of Science for the People.* (New York, 1894).

50. Henry James, Editor. *Letters of William James*, Vol. II, p. 233.

51. James Bradley Thayer, *Letters of Chauncey Wright with some Account of his Life.* (Boston 1878), p. 4.

52. *Ibid.*, p. 16.

53. C. S. Peirce, *Collected Papers*, Vol. 12.

54. Letter to Mrs. Franklin, reprinted in the *Journal of Philosophy, Psy-*

chology, and Scientific Method (Dec. 21, 1916) p. 719.

55. James Bradley Thayer, *op. cit.*, p. 15.

56. *Ibid.*, pp. 11, 257.

57. *Ibid.*, p. 381. Letter from Mr. Gurney to J. B. Thayer.

58. Chauncy Wright, *Philosophical Discussions*, edited by C. E. Norton (New York 1877) pp. xi-xii.

59. James Bradley Thayer, *op. cit.*, pp. 158-59. Letter to Miss Grace Norton, January, 1870.

60. Quoted in R. B. Perry, *op. cit.*, Vol. I, p. 520.

61. *Ibid.*, p. 521.

62. *Ibid.*, p. 530. Letter to Miss Grace Norton in 1875.

63. Quoted by John Fiske, *Darwinism and Other Essays* (New York 1879) p. 96.

64. *Ibid.*, p. 97.

65. *Ibid.*, p. 102.

66. *Ibid.*, p. 107.

67. *Ibid.*, p. 96.

68. James Bradley Thayer, *op. cit.*, p. 98.

69. *Ibid.*, p. 103.

70. *Ibid.*, p. 100. July, 1867.

71. *Ibid.*, p. 103.

72. *Ibid.*, pp. 114-15.

73. *Ibid.*, p. 115.

74. *Ibid.*, p. 114. To Mr. Norton, 1867.

75. *Ibid.*, p. 117 (my italics.)

76. *Ibid.*, p. 118.

77. *Ibid.*, p. 133.

78. Chauncey Wright, *op. cit.*, p. 377.

79. James Bradley Thayer, *op. cit.*, p. 135.

80. Chauncy Wright, *op. cit.*, p. 133.

81. *Ibid.*, p. 46.

82. *See* C. S. Peirce, below.

83. *Ibid.*, p. 47.

84. *Ibid.*, p. 50.

85. *Ibid.*, p. 51. (My italics).

86. *Ibid.*, p. 376.

87. *Ibid.*, p. 52.

88. John Fiske, *op. cit.*, pp. 86-87.

89. Chauncey Wright, *op. cit.*, pp. 54-55.

90. *Ibid.*, pp. 55-56.

91. *Ibid.*, p. 282.

92. *Ibid.*, p. 56.

93. James Bradley Thayer, *op. cit.*, p. 124.

94. Chauncey Wright, *op. cit.*, p. 68.

95. Ibid., p. 96.

96. *Ibid.*, p. 383.

97. *See* below.

98. James Bradley Thayer, *op. cit.*, pp. 162-63 (My italics).

99. *Ibid.*, p. 186.

100. *Ibid.*, pp. 173-74.

101. *Ibid.*, p. 174.

102. *Ibid.*, p. 171.

103. *Ibid.*, p. 169.

104. *Ibid.*, p. 169.

105. *Ibid.*, p. 172.

106. *Ibid.*, pp. 148-52. Letter to Mr. Norton, 1869.

107. *Ibid.*, pp. 152-56.

108. *Ibid.*, pp. 163-64.

109. These facts are from *The National Cyclopedia of American Biography*, Vol. 27.

110. Written between 1869 and 1876, (published in 1933 by George Banta, Menasha, Wisconsin).

111. Pp. 6, 9 and 10.

112. *Ibid.*, p. 181.

113. *American Law Review*, Vol. 4, pp. 201-16, cited by Fisch. The following quotations are also given by Fisch.

114. Alexander Bain, *Autobiography*, (London, 1904) p. 3. Bain was born in 1818.

115. London, 1859.

116. Pp. 568 and 569.

117. *Ibid.*, p. 570.

118. *Ibid.*, p. 595.

119. R. B. Perry, *op. cit.*, Vol. 1, p. 535.

120. C. S. Peirce, *op. cit.*, Vol. 2.

121. M. H. Fisch, "Justice Holmes, The Prediction Theory of Law, and Pragmatism," *Journal of Philosophy* (Feb. 12, 1942), pp. 85-97.

122. John Chipman Gray was the son of a Boston merchant. He attended the Boston Latin School and graduated from Harvard in 1859. There he took the L.L.B. in 1861. He was a 2nd Lieutenant in the Union Army, actively serving at Harper's Ferry and the Peninsular Campaign. From 1869 until 1913 he was on the Harvard Faculty of Law. He is identified with the case method in law and he practiced law while on the faculty. He lectured at Columbia in 1908-09 as Carpentier Lecturer. These lectures are available as *The Nature and Sources of Law. See* Roland Gray, *John Chipman Gray* (New York 1917).

123. *See* Langdell's *Selection of Cases on the Law of Contracts*, preface cited by Fisch.

124. *Letters of William James*, Vol. I, p. 80

125. Letter quoted by R. B. Perry., *op. cit.*, Vol. I, p. 277.

126. *Ibid.*, pp. 293, 297, 332.

127. *Ibid.*, p. 309.

128. *Ibid.*, p. 505. Written in 1867.

129. *Ibid.*, p. 519.

130. *Ibid.*, p. 512.

131. *Ibid.*, p. 504.

132. *Ibid.*, p. 332.

133. First published in a notice of a paper by Pollock in the *American Law Review* (1871-72) Vol. 6, pp. 723-25.

134. Peirce, *Collected Papers*, Vol. II, p. 84.

135. *See Holmes-Pollock Letters* (New York, 1941) Vol. II, p. 122.

136. Justice O. W. Holmes, *The Common Law*, (Boston 1881) p. 1.

137. *Ibid.*, p. 35.

138. *Ibid.*, p. 1.

139. *Ibid.*, pp. 35-36.

140. 1928 letter to Mr. John C. H. Wu quoted in *Justice O. W. Holmes: His Booknotes and Uncollected Papers.* (New York: Central Book Co., 1936) p. 201.

141. Quoted by Dorsey Richardson, in his *Constitutional Doctrines of Justice Oliver Wendell Holmes*, Johns Hopkins University Studies, series xliii, No. 3, (Baltimore: Johns Hopkins Press, 1924) p. 11.

142. *Ibid.*, p. 11.

143. *American Law Review* (1872) p. 724, quoted by Richardson, *Ibid.*

144. *Speeches*, (New York 1913), p. 98, quoted by Richardson, *Ibid.*, p. 42.

145. "Law in Science and Science in Law," *Harvard Law Review*, pp. 433, 452.

146. Richardson, *op. cit.*, p. 20.

147. *Justice O. W. Holmes: His Booknotes and Uncollected Papers.* p. 181.

148. Dorsey Richardson, *op. cit.*, p. 29. Quoted by Richardson.

149. *See* cases examined by Richardson, *op. cit.*, pp. 30f and 36.

150. Stack vs. N.Y., N.H. & H.R.R. Co., 177 Mass, 155; quoted by Richardson, *op. cit.*, p. 25.

151. Quoted by Richardson, *op. cit.*, p. 47.

152. *Justice O. W. Holmes: His Booknotes and Uncollected Papers*, p. 187.

153. *Speeches by Oliver Wendell Holmes*, 1913, p. 86.

154. Quoted by John Dewey, *Characters and Events*, Vol. I, p. 100.

155. R. B. Perry, *op. cit.*, Vol. II, p. 457.

156. *Ibid.*, p. 458.

157. *Holmes-Pollock Letters. The Correspondence of Mr. Justice Holmes and Sir Frederick Pollock 1874-1932.* 2 Volumes. (Cambridge: The Harvard University Press, 1941) Vol. I, p. 78.

158. *Ibid.*, p. 139.

159. R. B. Perry, *op. cit.*, Vol. II, p. 458.

160. *Ibid.*, p. 462.

161. M. H. Fisch, *op. cit.*, p. 96.

162. *Justice O. W. Holmes: His Booknotes and Uncollected Papers*, p. 193.

163. *Holmes-Pollock Letters*, Vol. II, p. 272.

164. *Ibid.*, p. 287.

165. "Logical Method and Law," *Philosophical Review*, Vol. 33 (1924); "Justice Holmes and the Liberal Mind," *New Republic* (1927-28), reprinted in *Characters and Events.*

PART II

6

Charles Peirce

Benjamin Peirce, the father of C. S. Peirce, was born at Salem, Massachusetts; he was of "the purest Puritan stock."[1] He had taken the A.B. degree in 1829, having had for classmates such later notables as Oliver Wendell Holmes, Sr., James Freeman Clarke, and Benjamin R. Curtis. He dominated the mathematical situation at Harvard from 1831 until 1880. His chair was the descendant of the "first profane professorship" at Harvard.[2] He was held in awe and apparently in jealousy. An "inspiring and unconventional teacher," he was accounted the "foremost American mathematician of his day." He fulfilled an active part in the founding of the Harvard Observatory in 1843. Here, in a work which first extended his reputation, he accurately computed the general perturbations of Uranus and Neptune. Congress established the office of the *American Nautical Almanac* at Cambridge, where it could have the benefit "especially of Prof. B. Peirce."[3] He was consultant astronomer for the *Almanac* until 1867. In 1847 he was one of the five men who set up the organization of the Smithsonian Institution. From 1852 to 1867 he was director of a section of the United States Coastal Survey; from 1867 to 1874 he was superintendent of this Survey. He himself commenced the extension of the Coastal Survey to a countrywide geodetic system and is said to have persuaded Congress to make the action official.[4] Benjamin Peirce was one of the small group at the center of the fifty incorporators of the National Academy of Science in 1863. He was an associate editor of the first volume, 1878, on the *American Journal of Mathematics*, founded at Johns Hopkins University (by J. J. Sylvester). His biography reads like a listing of the professionally scientific organizations and tasks of this day.[5]

One of his sons, Benjamin Mills Peirce (1844-70) became a mining engineer; another, Herbert Henry Davis Peirce (1849-1916), became a "diplomat."[6] Another son, James Mills Peirce (1834-1906), fulfilled a conventionally successful career as an academician: attaining his B.A. degree from Harvard in 1853, he served an early apprenticeship to the Unitarian ministry and then became an "understudy" to his father in the Department of Mathematics at Cambridge.[7] He taught mathematics and was a full professor of this discipline in 1869; he was Perkins professor of Mathematics and Astronomy in 1885. He became dean of the graduate school from its foundation in 1890.[8] A colleague characterized him as "careful in dress, dignified in bearing, scrupulously polite to everyone, courteous and kindly . . . remembered . . . for his friendly greeting, his earnest speech. . ." He was not a member of the Metaphysical Club.

The second son of Benjamin Peirce was Charles S. Peirce, who was "born in Cambridge, Massachusetts, in a stone-colored wooden house in Mason Street," in 1839.[9]

C. S. Peirce studied chemistry at the ripe age of eight. At twelve he had set up his own laboratory, juggling Leibig's bottles and performing quantitative analyses. He loved puzzles. He worked out chess problems in order to amuse his playmates. He invented code languages. Not only did the young man play cards, he did tricks with them. He would sit with his father from 10:00 P.M. until sunrise playing rapid games of double dummy. During such sessions his father would criticize sharply his every error. His father also encouraged him to develop sensory discrimination. Later Peirce put himself under the tutelage of a *sommelier* to become a connoisseur of wines. From the beginning his father wanted him to be a scientist, setting up heavy expectations in this direction. In 1861 he studied techniques and classifications with Agassiz. In 1863 he took the Sci.B. from Harvard in Chemistry at the *Summa Cum Laude* level of honor. In 1861 he joined the staff of the United States Coastal Survey as an "assistant." This connection was continuous until 1884. In 1871 he was temporarily in charge of the Survey. During these twenty-three years he lived where his work took him. A sector of this Coastal Survey was directed, as we have noted, by his father at the time of his appointment.

This training and the work with the Coastal Survey by no means exhausts the active scientific career of C. S. Peirce. In 1869-72 he was an "assistant astronomer" at the Harvard Observatory at $2500 a year.[10] Again, Peirce's father had been active in the founding of this observatory in 1843. In 1871 C. S. Peirce was elected a fellow of the American Academy of Arts and Sciences and a member of the National Academy of Science, which his father had helped found in 1863. During the years 1872-75 he made the astronomical observations which were published in *Photometric Researches*.[11] Strictly speaking, this is the only book entirely of Peirce's published during his lifetime.

Wedged into the above spans of time, Peirce acted, in 1873, as an "assistant computer" for the *Nautical Almanac*, being in charge of gravity investigations. As has been noted, it was in large part due to his father's presence in Cambridge that Congress had established the *Almanac* there. Chauncey Wright had worked for the *Almanac* since 1852.

In 1875 Peirce was sent abroad by the United States government for "pendulum investigations," serving at the same time as the first American delegate to the International Geodetic Conference. He reported there that pendulum experiments were subject to a hitherto unknown inaccuracy. This report was opposed with great discussion, but was later recognized, and he was voted the approval of the Congress. His work on pendulums has been recognized by experts in this field of scientific technology.

In 1884-85 Peirce had charge of the "Weights and Measures" division of the United States Coast and Geodetic Survey. In 1888 he was a member of the Assay Commission and the International Commission of Weights and Measures. He was retained by the Survey as a "special assistant in gravity research" from 1884 to 1891. Such, in brief were his participations in scientific actions and organizations.

Peirce himself frequently notices in his writings the influences of his scientific occupations and interests upon the formation and growth of his mind. In anticipation, it should be noted that these self-observations are wedged in among *philosophical* papers and lectures.

> "I was brought up in an atmosphere of scientific inquiry, and have all my life chiefly lived among scientific men. For the last 30 years, the study which has constantly been be-

fore my mind has been upon the nature, strength, and history of methods of scientific thought . . . . My own historical studies, which have been somewhat minutely critical, have, on the whole, confirmed the views of Whewell, the only man of philosophical power conjoined with scientific training who had made a comprehensive survey of the whole course of science, that progress in science depends upon the observation of the right facts by minds *furnished with appropriate ideas.* Finally, my long investigation of the logical process of scientific reasoning . . . ."[12]

"From the moment when I could think at all, until now, about forty years, I have been diligently and incessantly occupied with the study of methods (of) inquiry, both those which have been and are pursued and those which ought to be pursued. For 10 years before this study began, I have been in training in the chemical laboratory. I was thoroughly grounded not only in all that was then known of physics and chemistry, but also in the way in which those who were successfully advancing knowledge proceeded. I have paid the most attention to the methods of the most exact sciences, have intimately communed with some of the greatest minds of our times in physical science, and have myself made positive contributions — none of them of any very great importance, perhaps — in mathematics, gravitation, optics, chemistry, astronomy, etc. I am saturated, through and through, with the spirit of physical sciences. I have been a great student of logic, having read everything of any importance on the subject, devoting a great deal of time to medieval thought, without neglecting the works of the Greeks, the English, the Germans, the French, etc., and have produced systems of my own both in deductive and in inductive logic. In metaphysics, my training has been less systematic, yet I have read and deeply pondered upon all the main systems, never being satisfied until I was able to think about them as their own advocates thought."[13]

In the following quotation, notice the tacit polarization of "laboratories" and "field" against "libraries and museums." Later we shall note how this polarization exists in other contexts:

"I should express it this way: modern students of science have been successful because they have spent their lives not in their libraries and museums but in their laboratories and in the field; and while in their laboratories and in the field they have been not gazing on nature with a vacant eye, that is, in passive perception unassisted by thought, but have been *observing* — that is, perceiving by the aid of analysis — and testing suggestions of theories."[14]

Here are four autobiographical references concerning habits of observation and sensory discrimination:

"I remember colors with unusual accuracy, because I have had much training in observing them; but my memory does not consist in any vision but in a habit by virtue of which I can recognize a newly presented color as like or unlike one I had seen before."[15]

"There are some two dozen kinds of metals well known to me. I remember to have examined lumps of those qualities. But it is only the limitation of experience which attaches that number; there is simply no end to the metallic qualities I can imagine. I can imagine an infinite variety between tin and lead, or between copper and silver, or between iron and nickel, or between magnesium and aluminum."[16]

"For example, if I and all the company are so excited that we think we see a ghost, I can try what an unimaginative kodak would say to it. (Personally, I never had anything like a hallucination except in the delirium of fever.) So Macbeth made the experiment of trying to clutch the dagger."[17]

Anticipating a more exhaustive evaluation of the influence of Peirce's father upon his mind, observe that in 1893 he wrote:

"Kepler comes very close to realizing my idea of the scientific method; and he is one of the few thinkers who have taken their readers fully into their confidence as to what their method really has been."[18]

Then he added in a footnote: "This was a remark of my father's." If in the definition of "professional philosopher" we include source of income and institutional connection with a school, Peirce was not a professional philosopher. If by the term, professional philosopher, we mean the *typical* careers and life-ways of those who lectured, wrote, and taught philosophy during the period of Peirce, he was not a professional philosopher. But he read philosophers and wrote philosophy in all its branches: aesthetics, ethics, mathematical logic, and metaphysics. And, it is not praise but a mere reporting of fact that in the minds of an increasing number of philosophers, Charles Peirce is viewed as the most original philosophical mind in the history of speculative life on the American continent.[19]

In his first years at Harvard, from 1855 to 1859, this man stood in the record as seventy-first out of the ninety-one members of his class.[20] Nevertheless, he claimed to have "more or less mastered" Whately's *Elements of Logic* (1826) at the age of thirteen. Very early, in his father's household, he had learned to read and write without the usual courses and had taken himself to encyclopedias, looking up out-of-the-way topics. However, he attended "local private schools," the Cambridge High School and filled one term at E. E. Dixwell's school in preparation for Harvard.

There are several items concerning Peirce as philosopher that must be grasped: (1) his *training*, (2) the general *slant* from which he read and evaluated philosophy, (3) his *institutional* connections with the philosophy of the day, and (4) the *public* for his philosophy and his attitude toward this public.

The training which he had in the schools of his time, which might have been an influence toward more conventional lines of reflection, was at a minimum. His mind was bent prior to training in any school. It may be asserted that such bent as his mind had taken on through the training given it by others was shaped and directed by his father. "He educated me. If I do anything it will be his work." Such theological elements as existed in the schools did not influence an unselective mind. A mathematician had written diagrams there. In his own view, his education was acquired outside the regular schools. In his writing, the experiences he mentions are seldom such as would be acquired in the regular school; they are mathematical, or rather, technical. For example, in 1906 he says in "Prolegomena to an Apology for Pragmaticism:"

> "When I was a boy, my logical bent caused me to take pleasure in tracing out upon a map of an imaginary labyrinth one path after another in hopes of finding my way to a central compartment. The operation we have just gone through is essentially of the same sort, and if we are to recognize the one as essentially performed by experimentation upon a diagram, so must we recognize that the other is performed."[21]

Peirce's reading of the classics of philosophy was direct, not being diluted by any theological waters that may have existed in the schools which he attended or the commentaries therein used. On the contrary, the guide was again a mathematician. His father taught him outside of school through discussion, criticism, and regulation. From an early time, Benjamin Peirce had presented Charles with "problems, tables or examples," never giving him the general principles; he was encouraged to work them out for himself. In 1855 and 1856 he was under his father in Harvard classrooms, and the two would have long discussions on mathematics which was well outside the ken of the brother, James Mills Peirce. In philosophy, too, Peirce's reading was "guided" by the mathematician.

> "When, in my teens, I was first reading the masterpieces of Kant, Hobbes, and other great thinkers, my father, who was a mathematician, and who, if not an analyst of thought, at least never failed to draw the correct conclusion from given premises, unless by a mere slip, would induce me to repeat to him the demonstrations of the philosophers, and in a very few words would usually rip them up and show them empty. In that way, the bad habits of thinking that would otherwise have been indelibly impressed upon me by those mighty powers, were, I hope, in some measure, overcome. Certainly, I believe the best thing for a fledgling philosopher is a close companionship with a stalwart practical reasoner."[22]
>
> "Before I came to man's estate, being greatly impressed with Kant's *Critique of Pure Reason*, my father, who was an eminent mathematician, pointed out to me lacunae in Kant's reasoning which I should probably not otherwise have discovered. From Kant, I was led to an admiring study of Locke, Berkeley, and Hume, and to that of Aristotle's *Organon, Metaphysics*, and psychological treatises, and somewhat later derived the greatest advantage from a deeply pondering perusal of some of the works of medieval thinkers, St. Augustine, Abelard, and John of Salisbury, with related fragments from St. Thomas Aquinas, most especially from John of Duns, the Scot (Duns being the name of a then not unimportant place in East Lothian), and from William of Ockham. So far as a modern man of science can share the ideas of those medieval theologians, I ultimately came to approve the opinions of Duns, although I think he inclines too much toward nominalism."[23]
>
> "The first strictly philosophical books that I read were of the classical German schools; and I became so deeply imbued with many of their ways of thinking that I have never been

able to disabuse myself of them. Yet my attitude was always
that of a dweller in a laboratory, eager only to learn what I
did not yet know, and not that of philosophers bred in theological seminaries, whose ruling impulse is to teach what
they hold to be infallibly true. I devoted two hours a day to
the study of Kant's *Critique of Pure Reason* for more than
three years, until I almost knew the whole book by heart,
and had critically examined every section of it. For about two
years, I had long and almost daily discussions with Chauncey Wright, one of the most acute of the followers of J. S.
Mill. The effect of these studies was that I came to hold the
classical German philosophy to be, upon its argumentative
side, of little weight; although I esteem it, perhaps am too
partial to it, as a rich mine of philosophical suggestions. The
English philosophy, meagre and crude, as it is, in its conceptions, proceeds by surer methods and more acute logic ...
Yet I can but pronounce English sensationalism to be entirely destitute of any solid bottom ... however antiquated and
ignorant Spencer's *First Principles* and general doctrines, yet
they are under the guidance of a great and true idea, and
are developing it by methods that are in their main features
sound and scientific. The works of Duns Scotus have strongly
influenced me. If his logic and metaphysics, not slavishly wor-
shipped, but torn away from its medievalism, be adapted to
modern culture, under continual wholesome reminders of nominalistic criticisms, I am convinced that it will go far toward
supplying the philosophy which is best to harmonize with physical science. But other conceptions have to be drawn from the
history of science and from mathematics."[24]

Why did Peirce come to this intensive study of philosophy?
What motive brought him there? We have seen that with many
students the motive pattern for the study of philosophy was basically theological. But Peirce, in 1898, wrote:

"I came to the study of philosophy not for its teaching
about God, Freedom, and Immortality, but intensely curious
about Cosmology and Psychology. In the early sixties I was
a passionate devotee of Kant, at least as regarded the Transcendental Analytic in the *Critique of Pure Reason*. I believed more implicitly in the two tables of the Functions of
Judgment and the Categories than if they have been brought
down from Sinai. Hegel, so far as I knew him through a book
by Vera, repelled me. Now Kant points out certain relations
between the categories. I detected others; but these others,
if they had any orderly relation to a system of conceptions,

at all, belonged to a larger system than that of Kant's list ...
Accordingly, I read every book I could lay hands upon on
logic, and of course Kant's essay on the *falsche Spitzfindigkeit
der vier syllogistischen Figuren;* and here I detected a fallacy
similar to that of the phlogistic chemists. For Kant argues that
the fact that all syllogisms can be reduced to Barbara shows
that they involve no logical principle that Barbara does not
involve. A chemist might as well argue, that because water
boiled with zinc dust evolves hydrogen, and the hydrogen does
not come from the zinc, therefore water is a mere form of hydrogen."[25]

The second portion of this statement is typical of all the statements made by Peirce about himself as a philosopher that have
been printed in the seven volumes of the *Collected Papers.* He
argues about philosophical issues from scientific, even laboratory,
examples. In addition we know that several of his key philosophical concerns were developed in conversational cooperation with
scientists and in particular with his father.[26] Of the latter, he
writes thus: "Sometime after my first publication, either my father
or I myself (under the instigation of my father's ideas) transformed this algebra by means..."[27]

"At the time when he [my father] thought out this definition, he, a mathematician, and I, a logician, held daily discussions about a large subject which interested us both; and he
was struck, as I was, with the contrary nature of his interest and mine in the same propositions. The logician does not
care particularly about this or that hypothesis or its consequences, except so far as these things may throw a light upon
the nature of reasoning. The mathematician is intensely interested in efficient methods of reasoning, with a view of their
possible extension to new problems, but he does not, qua
mathematician, trouble himself minutely to dissect those parts
of this method whose correctness is a matter of course."[28]

"I interested my father in the subject, and his *Linear Asso-
ciative Algebra* was issued to his friends before the printing
of my memoir was complete. We were, therefore, working
simultaneously upon closely related subjects, and continually
discussing them together; and consequently, it is impossible
to say precisely what was due to each. Of course, in mathematics, he was my master, and vastly my superior in genius;
so that, in case of doubt, it is safer to attribute any mathematical step to him."[29]

Even discounting the possible desire to link himself with the eminence of his father, which seems to have been the case, we should not fail to take into account such relations as undoubtedly existed with the mathematician.

Peirce often refers to himself as a "logician" (which to him meant a student of the methods of *science*). He seldom refers to himself as a "philosopher." Such self-references show a really supreme self-confidence:

> "I am a logical analyst by long training, you know . . ."[30]
> "I will now give over my jeering at my former inaccuracies, committed when I had been a student of logic for only about a quarter of a century, and was naturally not so well-versed in it as now, and will proceed to define probability."[31] "I often think that we logicians are the most obtuse of men, and the most devoid of common sense."[32]
>
> "I have been actively studying this subject [a point in logic], for the sake of completely satisfying my own mind about it, for 50 or 51 years. To be sure, I have, some half dozen times during the half-century, let my mind lie fallow, as to this subject, during one or two dozens of months, hoping so to rid myself of any inveterate bad habits of thinking that I may insensibly have fallen into."[33]
>
> "In 1870 I made a contribution to this subject [logic] which nobody who masters the subject can deny was the most important, except Boole's original work, that ever has been made."[34]
>
> "But the immense superiority of the Boolian method was apparent enough, and I shall never forget all there was of manliness and pathos in De Morgan's face when I pointed it out to him in 1870. I wondered whether when I was in my last days some young man would come and point out to me how much of my work must be superseded, and whether I should be able to take it with the same genuine candor . . ."[35]
>
> "The undertaking which this volume inaugurates is to make a philosophy like that of Aristotle, that is to say, to outline a theory so comprehensive that, for a long time to come, the entire work of human reason, in philosophy of every school and kind, in mathematics, in psychology, in physical science, in history, in sociology, and in whatever other department there may be, shall appear as the filling up of its details."[36]

Notice the brief, contemptuous dismissal this scientist, reading and planning enormous works in philosophy, gives to a major "philosophical" movement of his formative period:

"I was born and reared in the neighborhood of Concord — I mean in Cambridge — at the time when Emerson, Hedge, and their friends were disseminating the ideas that they had caught from Schelling, and Schelling from Plotinus, from Boehm, or from God knows what minds stricken with the monstrous mysticism of the East. But the atmosphere of Cambridge held many an antiseptic against Concord transcendentalism; and I am not conscious of having contracted any of that virus. Nevertheless, it is probable that some cultured bacilli, some benignant form of the disease was implanted in my soul, modified by now, after long incubation, it comes to the surface, modified by mathematical conceptions and by training in physical investigations."[37]

In his training in, and his manner of reading philosophy, Peirce was outside the doctrines which formed the main thread of academic diffusion, and untouched by the major non-academic movement in the philosophy of his youth, that is, transcendentalism. He read philosophy under the determinants of scientific knowledge, skill, interest, and under the personal guidance of a mathematician. There was an institutional basis lying under his alienation from the philosophy of his day.

During his entire lifetime, Peirce was given the opportunity to teach for only eight years. The major source of his income and the channels of his action were scientific. The academic connections which he had with the official institutions of philosophy were wedged between scientific pursuits and, in the main, his lectures even here were on "scientific" topics.

In 1864-65 Peirce lectured at Harvard on the philosophy of science. During the academic year of 1869-70 he gave the "university lectures" in philosophy along with a group of lecturers, including R. W. Emerson, G. P. Fisher, J. E. Cabot, John Fiske. Again, in 1870-71, he gave some "university lectures in logic." In addition to these three lecture series, he lectured three times before the Lowell Institute: in 1866 on logic, in 1892 on the history of science, and in 1903 on logic. In the last year he also lectured on pragmatism. His lectureship during the years 1879-84 in logic at Johns Hopkins was his longest academic connection, and President Gilman's *Report for 1881* shows clearly that Peirce was employed "for the benefit of these who are expecting to be engaged in scientific investigation.[38]

Too precise to be popular, Peirce could never express himself clearly to large numbers. His vocabulary was spotted with odd neologisms and with hairsplitting technical distinctions. William James found him "flashes of brilliant light relieved against Cimmerian darkness."[39] To his sister, in November of 1866, James wrote: "Your first question is, 'where have I been?' To C. S. Peirce's lectures, which I could not understand a word of, but rather enjoyed the sensation of listening to for an hour."[40] In contrasting himself to James, Peirce wrote: "I a mere table of contents, so abstract, a very snarl of twine."[41]

Yet it is known that he was eager to teach. Personal habits were against him: he was irregular in his hours, forgetful of appointments, and in his later life he was careless of personal appearance. William James wrote to Henry James in 1903: "Charles Peirce is lecturing here — a queer being...."[42] In 1869 James wrote a revealing passage to Henry P. Bowditch:

> "I have just been quit by Chas. S. Peirce, with whom I have been talking about a couple of articles in the St. Louis "Journal of Speculative Philosophy" by him, which I have just read. They are exceedingly bold, subtle and incomprehensible, and I can't say that his vocal elucidations helped me a great deal to their understanding, but they nevertheless interest me strangely. The poor cuss sees no chance of getting a professorship anywhere, and is likely to go into the observatory for good. It seems a great pity that as original a man as he is, who is willing and able to devote the powers of his life to logic and metaphysics, should be starved out of a career, when there are lots of professorships of the sort to be given in the country to 'safe,' orthodox men. He has had good reason, I know, to feel a little discouraged about the prospect, but I think he ought to hang on, as a German would do, till he grows gray . . ."[43]

In 1894, James wrote to Howison that as for Charles Peirce:

> "It's the most curious instance of talents not making a career. He dished himself at Harvard by inspiring dislike in Eliot. He is now . . . with rather fixed half-bohemian habits, and no habit of teaching, that it would be risky to appoint him . . . he is paradoxical and unsocial of intellect, and hates to *make connection* with anyone he is with . . . Anyhow he's a genius . . ."[44]

In 1903 James wrote to Schiller that Peirce was "a hopeless crank and failure in many ways, but a really extraordinary intellect... a mind of... many different kinds of spotty intensity or vigor."[45]

"In the autumn of 1875," Peirce wrote, "I went abroad in order to urge a certain truth upon the Geodetical Association."[46] From Paris, Henry James wrote to his brother, William: "Yesterday morning appeared Charles Peirce, who is wintering here. He took me up very vigorously, made me dine with him and spend the evenings at his rooms which are very charming. He seems quite a swell, has a secretary, etc."[47]

The next year Henry wrote: "... during the last two months of his stay I saw almost nothing of him... he has too little social talent... he had... a very lonely and dreary winter here..."[48] Henry was impressed by Peirce's "beautiful clothes," but found his sympathy "economical rather than intellectual"[49] Later, from the "Brevoort House, New York, 1877" C. S. Peirce wrote to James that here he was:

> "known to every waiter, etc... I insensibly put on a sort of swagger here which I hope I have nowhere else, and which is designed to say: 'You are a very good fellow in your way; who you are I don't know and I don't care, but I, you know, am Mr. Peirce, distinguished for my varied scientific acquirements, but above all for my extreme modesty in which respect I challenge the world.' I notice that if one goes into the niceties, scarcely any one is totally without swagger, and in those few the dryness is disagreeable. Required: an essay on good taste in swaggering."[50]

Peirce regretted that his father had "not taught him moral self-control." His position as an academic outsider was doubtlessly underlined by certain domestic difficulties. In 1862 he married Harriet M. Fay. This granddaughter of Bishop J. H. Hopkins was three years older than C. S. Peirce. She was very respected in Cambridge, indeed, quite distinguished as an "organizer and writer," and she joined Peirce in his early scientific work. In 1883 Charles Peirce divorced Harriet Fay. The alleged grounds consisted of Peirce's claim that she had deserted him in 1876, which happens to be just after Peirce went abroad.[51] Shortly afterward he married Mlle. Juliette Foisy of Nancy, France, with whom he lived until his death. His difficulty with his first wife seems to have been an important factor in his loss of academic standing and the partial estrangement of his friends and relatives."[52]

Continually outside academic institutions, in 1887 at the age of forty-eight Peirce went down to Milford, Pennsylvania, "The wildest country of the Northern States." In 1891 after the work in specific gravity he "retired" to Milford at the age of fifty-two from active scientific work. The conditions of his "retirement" are debated. Perhaps his experiments were too costly or his operations too leisurely or perhaps he was dissatisfied with the conduct of the survey. This loss of connection cost him $3000 a year. He had inherited "some money" around 1848 and in Milford had secured a house and a tract of land. He had, writes Weiss, a "large and select library of scientific and philosophical works," but this is a point about which Peirce continually complained: "All my life my studies have been cruelly hampered by my inability to procure necessary books..."[53] Again, in 1892, after making some historical point he says: "... or possibly in some other Renaissance writing...my library is precious small."[54] At any rate, he built an attic in the Milford place and by pulling up the ladder behind him he could "escape from his creditors" and work undisturbed.

In 1901 he had worked for J. M. Baldwin, writing articles on logic for *The Dictionary of Philosophy and Psychology* (1901-5). In 1902 he was in debt, indeed, on the edge of poverty. He did his own chores, and "dissipated his energies in small tasks in order to obtain immediate funds." So he applied to the Carnegie Fund for aid in getting some things published. He wanted to submit thirty-six memoirs on logic, "each complete in itself, forming a unitary system..." Even though eminent men wrote in his behalf, the application was rejected for the official reason that logic was outside the scope of the fund, not being a "natural science." By 1906 he had ceased his reviewing for *The Nation* and in 1907 he was really quite penniless. William James arranged a fund for him. It was "barely enough" to keep Peirce and his wife alive. In 1909 he was an ill man of seventy years of age. Each day he took a grain of morphine to stave off pain. He kept writing, hanging on "until he was gray." He said he had "the persistency of a wasp in a bottle." He died of cancer five years later. He was a "frustrated" and an "isolated" man: a writer without a publisher; a "teacher" with scarcely a disciple, largely unknown to any public. After he was dead Harvard bought his manuscripts from his wife.

The objective facts of Peirce's career spell out his position as an outsider of academic philosophy. This objective position had its counterpart in his feeling of isolation, of estrangement. In published papers he promises to send philosophical manuscripts to "any responsible person" and in others begs to receive books and papers. He well knew the minuteness of such publics as he might command: "But before all else," he wrote, in beginning to launch into another writing venture which was to come to naught, "let me make the acquaintance of my reader, and express my sincere esteem for him and the deep pleasure it is to me to address one so wise and so patient. I know his character pretty well, for both the subject and the style of this book ensure his being one out of millions."[55] He felt his isolation. Of a classmate known forty-seven years previously he wrote: "a noble-hearted, sterling-charactered young gentleman... almost the only real companion I have ever had."[56] And he, at least, felt that "critics" were either indifferent or negative toward him and his work:

> "I am a man of whom critics have never found anything good to say. When they could see no opportunity to injure me, they have held their peace. The little laudation I have had has come from such sources, that the only satisfaction I have derived from it, has been from such slices of bread and butter as it might waft my way. Only once, as far as I remember, in all my lifetime have I experienced the pleasure of praise — not for what it might bring but in itself. That pleasure was beatific; and the praise that conferred it was meant for blame. It was that a critic said of me that I did not seem to be *absolutely sure of my own conclusions*. Never, if I can help it, shall that critic's eye ever rest on what I am now writing; for I owe a great pleasure to him; and, such was his evident animus, that should he find that out, I fear the fires of hell would be fed with new fuel in his breast."[57]

Earlier, in 1875, Peirce wrote in a letter to James: "It is only when a philosopher has something very elementary to say that he seeks the great public or the great public him..."[58] Such isolation as Peirce knew doubtlessly augmented his habits of self-observation. In the absence of a concrete public he himself continually came back to his previous thought. His manuscripts are cluttered with such references and annotations, observations of the way his own ideas moved. Many of his most technical writings are liable at any point to become definitely conversational and self-referenced. For example, he footnotes in the "Improvement of Gamma Graphs" (1906):

> "Although at the time of writing that, nine and a half years ago, I was constrained against my inclinations, to make that statement, yet I never heartily embraced that view, and dismissed it from my mind, until after I had drawn up the present statement of the Conventions of Existential Graphs, I found, quite to my surprise, that I had herein taken substantially the same view."[59]

When he did find an occasional and temporary audience, he was explicitly grateful:

> "But should it happen to any of you to select for his life's explorations a region very little trodden, he will, as a matter of course, have the pleasure of making a good many discoveries of more fundamental importance than at all remain to be made in any ground that has long been highly cultivated. But on the other hand, he will find that he has condemned himself to an isolation like that of Alexander Selkirk. He must be prepared for almost a lifetime of work with scarce one greeting, and I can assure him that if, as his day is sinking, a rare good fortune should bring a dozen men of real intellect, some men of great promise, others of great achievement, together to listen to so much of what he has learned as his long habit of silence shall have lift him the power of expressing in a compass of eight lectures, he will know then an almost untasted joy and will comprehend then what gratitude I feel at this moment."[60]

That Peirce felt his position to be unjust came out clearly in preparatory notes for a Harvard lecture. He was quite bitter about the academic situation: "But suppose by some extraordinary conjunction of the planets, a really good teacher of reasoning were to be appointed..."[61] Out of frustration, and the isolation from a public arises an explicit appeal to future publics:

> "But just as there are many fogies nowadays — old and young — who with idle conservatism dispute the value of my work, so, unless the whole congregation of logicians experiences a regeneration, I expect the day will come when an-

other generation of old and young fogies will be equally in-
disposed to admit that there is any corner of the whole field
that I have not turned up, and put into the right condition.
Yet I have faithfully tried to do my share in putting an end
to all such unscientific attitudes among logicians, and am confident that the new blood that has been brought into our
house is going to insure its modicum of scientific health to the
logical stock of the next generations."[62]

He seems worried about "priorities:"

"Since my priority about the distinction of the finite and
the infinite has been pointed out in Germany, in a prominent
way, Dedekind has said that he had the same idea some years
earlier. He seems to think this an important circumstance. I
may mention that my habit has always been to record ideas
that seemed to me valuable in a certain large blank book
with the dates at which I set them down, almost always not
until I had had the ideas long enough to be quite convinced
of their value. This idea about finite and the infinite collections was thought worthy of record. But I do not see that it
has any interest for anybody but myself; and from Dedekind's conduct, I infer he would prefer I should not give it."[63]

And again:

"Mr. Schlötel has written to the London Mathematical Society, accusing me of having, in my *Algebra of Logic,* plag-
iarized from his writings. He had also written to me to inform
me that he has read the Memoir with "heitere Ironie," and
that Professor Drobisch, the Berlin Academy, and I constitute
a "liederliche Kleeblatt," with many other things of the same
sort. Up to the time of publishing my Memoir, I had never
seen any of Mr. Schlötel's writings; I have since procured his
Logik, and he has been so obliging as to send me two cut-
tings from his papers, thinking, apparently, that I might be
curious to see the passages that I have appropriated. But having examined these productions, I find no thought in them that
I ever did, or ever should be likely to put forth as my own."[64]

The frustrations of Peirce's many plans for publication indicate
a lack of a relation to any philosophical public. Articles and several full-length books, or agenda for them, were rejected. These
rejections apparently did not occasion negative attitudes toward
his own work:

". . . 1897, in which year I wrote an account of it and offered it for publication to the editor of *The Monist,* who declined it on the ground that it might later be improved upon. No changes have been found desirable since that date, although it has been under continual examination; but the exposition has been rendered more formal."[65]

Peirce's attitude toward contemporary philosophers, especially of the schools, or as he called them "seminary logicians," has been duly recorded in the midst of his technical writings and in the lectures at Harvard on "vitally important topics." He held these philosophers in low esteem. In 1906 he commented:

"I am continually obliged to make elementary explanations owing to the disgracefully unscientific state of Logic, which is quite as much behind its condition six centuries ago in some particulars as it is in advance of that state in others. As for contemporary text-books in our language, they are the merest rubbish on the whole. The very best that can be said of them is that a few have merits in particular directions. They are all amateurish and encourage amateurish views of the universe and of life. In comparison with the state of all the non-philosophical sciences, they are downright puerile; and a green scum grows over them year by year. If our people were at all aware of this blot upon our civilization, it would be possible for a scientific student of the subject of some real strength to put forth at least a primer of the science. But it is a condition of the success of any such student in penetrating to the true science that he should make himself a recluse. He is thus out of the swim, and is crowded out of all opportunities to be of much service; whereby Spencerism, Agnosticism, and other amateurisms, whose professors lose precious little time in arduous research, are able to gain the exclusive ear of the ignorant persons whom they court."[66]

"But, perhaps, on another occasion I will myself give a little essay on the subject, 'adapted to the meanest capacity,' as some of the books of my boyhood used, not too respectfully, to express it."[67]

"I hate to bore readers who are capable of exact thought with redundancies; but others often deploy such brilliant talents in not understanding the plainest statements that have no familiar jingle, that I must beg my more active-minded readers to have patience under the infliction while I exhibit in Fig. 228 the orders in 5, 8, 9, 10, and 11 piles formed by dealing 13 cards are to be taken up."[68]

"I cannot in this place enter into the elementary explanations which would be necessary to illustrate this for more than a score of readers."[69]

Around 1867 Peirce proposed to publish "one original logical paper" every month. But he had no stable public; insufficient interest was shown in the work, and Peirce soon gave up the plan. Without a philosophical public, not "connected" for any length of time with institutions of higher learning, acting occupationally as a scientist and technician, Peirce nevertheless wrote and thought philosophy. He completed an elaborate work on logic. He could not get it published. It was "too specialized" for the publishing world. Peirce was not in an academic chair; it could not be used as a textbook. Most of the things he did were never published. In 1883 he planned a twelve-volume work in philosophy. As usual, it fell through. There were not enough subscribers. In 1878 he had published his first statement of pragmatism.[70] Typically, he received no recognition for his work from the philosophical public until another, an academic man, Professor James, called attention to it.

Two major facts may be taken as outstanding in the career of C. S. Peirce. He was an *active scientist* and he was an an *outsider in philosophy*. Born in an academic family, if a slightly atypical one, living in and out of academic communities all his life, he was never strictly within the academic fold. By virtue of his shift in mates, by personal habits, by his significant trainings, by lack of academic position as a philosopher, by his consequent attitudes toward major sectors of the philosophical public, both academic and lay, he was always outside the milieu and the institutions of philosophy. By the technicist jobs he held, by his conceptions of himself, by his setting of the scientific habits of mind over against the intellectual traits of the philosophical public of the time, by the deep pieties in which he held methods which bore, according to his reckoning, the scientific brand, he was positively oriented, in action and in mind, to scientific practice.[71]

The pragmatism of Peirce is in the first instance a generalization of his awareness of the practices of his occupation. The terms of that awareness are philosophical, but its content lies in his own professional experiences as a scientist. The limited context in which he sets his statement of pragmatism and the purpose for which it was designed are, as we shall see, carefully and explicitly set forth by Peirce himself as "scientific."

I find in the records of the period no other career that matches
Peirce's: specifically, no person who knowing philosophy, its terms
and level of work, being interested in it, yet who is never for any
length of time stably within its institutions; and this taken in conjunction with actual and quite "practical" scientific work (moreover scientific technology) as the major source of income, and
making up a large content of his active working hours.

In terms of the sociology of knowledge we find (in the case of
Charles Peirce) a direct link of an abstract thinker and his concepts to his patterns of action.[72] He played an immediately active
role in scientific organizations and laboratories. He built through
direct participation a generic pattern of habit and value and vocabulary which came to constitute the background of his mind.
There are two other gross ways by which an individual's thinking
can be influenced by the mental residues of modes of action, and
Peirce was so influenced by both of them. First, he intentionally
identified himself with an *ethos* which was presumably (at least
in his own eyes) rooted in the structure of scientific action. Second, his effective audiences externally, and as he internalized them
as a generalized other, from conversations with his father, from
Chauncey Wright at the center of Peirce's Metaphysical Club,
through his denunciation of the Harvard philosophical public,
were *scientific*. Their minds were built by participation in scientific
action. It was with them that he was thinking; it was to them that
he was writing. The full *meaning* of what he thought lay in their
minds, as well as in his own. Live communication as it functioned
in his thinking, the audience as it functioned as his generalized
other, these embodied the habits of action and the meaning of acting scientists.

Not only was his reading of philosophy done from a scientific
angle of refraction, not only did his selections and evaluations of
it proceed on what he set forth as scientific grounds, but his own
pragmaticist work is a generalization from scientific *practices* into
the *discourses* of philosophy. In discussing the Metaphysical Club
he described his relation to philosophical speculation as a man "of
science rather scrutinizing the doctrines of the metaphysicians on
their scientific side than regarding them as momentous spiritually."[73] In 1897 he wrote:

> "Thus, in brief, my philosophy may be described as the attempt of a physicist to make such conjecture as to the constitution of the universe as the methods of science may permit, with the aid of all that has been done by previous philosophers ... The demonstrations of the metaphysicians are all moonshine. The best that can be done is to supply a hypothesis, not devoid of all likelihood, in the general line of growth of scientific ideas, and capable of being verified or refuted by future observers."[74]

Continually he brings into philosophical discussions, in a comparative manner, the ideals and models of science:

> "In those sciences of measurement which are the least subject to error — metrology, geodesy, and metrical astronomy — no man of self-respect ever now states his result, without affixing to it its *probable error;* and if this practice is not followed in other sciences [philosophy] it is because in those the probable errors are too vast to be estimated."[75]

Peirce's revilement of the "seminary logicians" is set by a polarization with scientific, mathematical men:

> "The seminary logicians have often seemed to think that those who study logic algebraically entertain the opinion that logic is a branch of the science of quantity. Even if they did, the error would be a trifling one; since it would be an isolated opinion, having no influence upon the main results of their studies, which are purely formal ... For my part, I consider that the business of drawing demonstrative conclusions from assumed premises, in cases so difficult as to call for the services of a specialist, is the sole business of the mathematician."[76]

The low esteem in which he holds logic is always relative to "the advance of physical science":

> "Very early in my studies of logic, before I had really been devoting myself to it more than four or five years, it became quite manifest to me that this science was in a bad condition, entirely unworthy of the general state of intellectual development of our age; and in consequence of this, every other branch of philosophy except ethics — for it was already clear that psychology was a special science and no part of philosophy — was in a similar disgraceful state .... There was no

room for it [logic] to become more degraded. It had been
sinking steadily, and relatively to the advance of physical science."[77]

The area of Peirce's thought which bears most clearly the marks
of his central occupational experiences is his theory of doubt, belief, his view of the character and function of inquiry, his pragmatism. To these items we now turn, attempting to substantiate in
some detail and further to understand the mechanics of the first
gross imputation advanced.

In his life, Peirce published about seventy-five papers and one
hundred-fifty book reviews. He published only one book, *Photo-
metric Researches,* although he did edit his students' papers in the
Johns Hopkins' *Studies in Logic.*[78] However, he left huge piles of
manuscript. The contents of this mass of writing range from geod-
esy to telepathy, astronomy to criminology, optics to metaphysics.[79] Charles Hartshorne and Paul Weiss have edited *The Collected Papers,* arranging the manuscripts in terms of the published
materials in so far as this is possible.[80]

Pragmatism "was only one phase of his work."[81] I am not *directly* concerned with any other. I do not believe that his literary
remains necessarily form a "system." I think Peirce's work is a set
of great fragments. However, pragmatism's roots and ramifications
reach into all corners of his thought.[82] And I believe it forms the
central model and technique used by Peirce's mind. Although he
never made a system, "Peirce possessed the system-making mind."[83]
The external exigencies of his life, in particular the indifference
of publishers, if nothing else, prevented his writing out a system.
However, in many fragments and in later footnotes on previous
papers he follows out digressively the ramifications of this topic,
showing a systematic mind amid unsystematic writing. Whether
or not there is a "system" implicit in these papers and manuscripts,
it "cannot be completely reconstructed; even the attempt would
mean taking indefensible liberties with the manuscripts."[84] It is
agreed by those who have competently examined *The Collected
Papers* that it will be many years before their implications will be
drawn, whatever they will be for differently oriented sectors of
future intellectual publics.

In the meantime, variously oriented thinkers have already applied and interpreted "pragmatism" in quite diverse ways. It is

with these thinkers (especially with James and Dewey) and the social angles of refraction from which they have caught "pragmatism" that I am concerned. But in order to comprehend what pragmatism meant to C. S. Peirce we have to grasp its emergence and growth within his mental and social contexts.

I have approached Peirce's "pragmatism" primarily in terms of the role of inquiry. There are several doctrines of Peirce from which we can gather what he conceived to be the generic purpose and the context of inquiry. The most important is his discussion of "doubt and belief," the next is "the pragmatic maxim." In both these contexts, the concepts of "action," or "habit" arise and are related to a theory of *meaning* and to the *end* of inquiry. In order to grasp the full meaning and orientation of these several concepts, we must examine certain of Peirce's remarks on the "practical" and the "useful" in their relation to inquiry and knowledge. It will also be necessary to examine his "realism" and the stress upon "sociality" and "sentiment" as well as his strong reactions against "individualism" and "the philosophy of greed." This is the order in which we shall proceed. And these foci will exhaust our interest in the central features of Peirce's pragmatism. In each of these modes of formulation we shall note the verification of the central imputation of Peirce: that his pragmatism arose from his occupation as a scientist in conjunction with his continual position as a philosophic outsider. For example, it is within a style of thought to be imputed to these positions, when combined, that we can locate his conceptions of "doubt," "belief" and "inquiry."

I have not hesitated to display his arguments in some detail, for in intellectual history, no matter how sociological it may be, "immanent" changes should be fully reported and understood. Also they and their logical courses, are important *sociologically*: in the case of C. S. Peirce we shall see that only very timidly does he generalize his concepts outside the context to which they are imputed. The interpretative situation surrounding Peirce at the present time is extremely confused. At least two major, and quite diverse, positions are trying to capture his prestige.[85] It is possible that both these ways of interpreting Peirce's work will be made clearer if in our statement of it we get points of support in the social facts of his career and times: persistent intellectual confusion invites the locative standpoint of the sociology of knowledge.

The modes of statement of C. S. Peirce display certain ambiguities in connection with certain concepts. These appear in all the contexts mentioned. The most important of these concepts for subsequent phases of the pragmatic movement is that of "action" or "habit." We will therefore focus especially upon this concept in Peirce, noting its ambiguity, and particularly its *ambiguity of context* or *spheres of application,* for it is precisely around changes in this connection that Dewey and James differ from Peirce most significantly. Such differences can be explained sociologically. I wish, however, to stress that I have not traced *all* the inferences made by Peirce from his presentations of the doctrine of pragmatism. It is the putatively central, the key statements of pragmatism, which are open to diverse interpretations, and they are therefore, central to my concern. More important to an understanding of the pragmatic movement than are many of Peirce's devious inferences are his key formulations. Those not so much inferred from other philosophical doctrines but rather those which have arisen from his scientific work and experience. It so happens that these are the points from which extensions of use have been made by later men in different positions thinking out different purposes.

1. *Dictionary of American Biography,* Vol. XIV, p. 394. Both for C. S. Peirce and for his father, I have drawn heavily from the *Dictionary of American Biography* accounts. Paul Weiss' account of C. S. Peirce is the only statement of his life available. Unlike many *DAB* accounts, Weiss' fully attains to the excellence of the English *National Dictionary of Biography.*

2. S. E. Morison, *Development of Harvard,* p. 248.

3. Cf. Simon Newcomb, *The Reminiscences of an Astronomer* (Boston, 1903), p. 63. Cited in the *DAB.*

4. J. E. Hilgard, *Report of Superintendent of United States Coast and Geodetic Survey,* (Wash., June, 1883), p. 3. Cited in *DAB.*

5. For evaluation and further honors *see Benjamin Peirce, 1809-1880* by Prof. R. C. Archibald (The Mathematical Association of America, 1925.)

6. *See National Cyclopedia of American Biography,* Vol. 10, p. 449; also Vol. 9, p. 539.

7. S. E. Morison, *op. cit.,* pp. 249-50.

8. *Ibid.,* p. 445.

9. C. S. Peirce, *Collected Papers,* Vol. II, Para. 663.

10. *See* James' letter in R. B. Perry, *The Thought and Character of William James,* Vol. I, p. 321.

11. *Annals of the Astronomical Observatory of Harvard College,* (Cambridge, 1878) Vol. IX.

12. C. S. Peirce, *op. cit.*, (1893) Vol. VI, p. 604.

13. *Ibid.*, (1898) Vol. I, p. 3.

14. *Ibid.*, (1909) Vol. I, p. 34.

15. *Ibid.*, (1905) Vol. I, p. 379.

16. *Ibid.*, (1895) Vol. I, p. 341.

17. *Ibid.*, Vol. II, p. 142.

18. *Ibid.*, (1893) VI, p. 604.

19. Cf. Commentaries on Peirce in *Philosophy of Science, Philosophical Review, Journal of Philosophy,* between 1936-39.

20. In contrast to the *Summa Cum Laude* in Chemistry four years later.

21. C. S. Peirce, *op. cit.*, Vol. IV, p. 533.

22. *Ibid.*, Vol. III, p. 405.

23. *Ibid.*, (1905) Vol. I, p. 560.

24. *Ibid.*, (1897) Vol. I, pp. 4-5.

25. *Ibid.* Vol. IV, p. 2.

26. Cf. the above vocational composition of the Metaphysical Club, and Wright's central place therein.

27. C. S. Peirce, *op. cit.*, (1902) Vol. IV, p. 322.

28. *Ibid.*, (1902) Vol. IV, p. 239.

29. *Ibid.*, Vol. I, pp. 244-45.

30. *Ibid.*, (1897) Vol. I, p. 160.

31. *Ibid.*, (1910) Vol. II, p. 662.

32. *Ibid.*, (1906) Vol. IV, p. 58.

33. *Ibid.*, Vol. II, p. 760.

34. *Ibid.*, Vol. III, p. 27f.

35. *Ibid.*, (1898) Vol. IV, p. 4.

36. *Ibid.*, (1898) Vol. I, p. 1. "A Guess at the Riddle."

37. *Ibid.*, (1892) Vol. VI, p. 102.

38. Report, *Johns Hopkins University* (Baltimore, 1881), pp. 47-48. *See* Ellery W. Davis, "Charles Peirce at Johns Hopkins," *The Mid-West Quarterly,* (October, 1914) Vol. 2, p.48f. This article is most unrevealing of Peirce's personal position. It concerns itself with a popular exposition of Peirce's views on science, logic, etc. Such a man as Thorstein Veblen, a student at Hopkins, was interested in Peirce's lectures and was no doubt influenced by them; such influences persisted in Veblen.

39. William James, *Pragmatism* p. 5.

40. *The Letters of William James,* edited by his son Henry James, (Boston, 1920) p. 80.

41. C. S. Peirce, *op. cit.*, Vol. VI, p. 184.

42. *The Letters of William James,* p. 191.

43. *Ibid.*, Vol. I, p. 149.

44. R. B. Perry, *op. cit.*, Vol. II, p. 117.

45. *Ibid.*, Vol. II, p. 375.

46. *Journal of Philosophy, Psychology and Scientific Method* (Dec. 21, 1916), p. 719. Letter to Mrs. Franklin.

47. R. B. Perry, *op. cit.*, Vol. I, pp. 361-62.

48. *Ibid.*, p. 367.

49. *Ibid.*, p. 536.

50. *Ibid.*, p. 538.

51. Paul Weiss, *Dictionary of American Biography*, Vol. XIV, p. 402.

52. In a psychologically technical paper of 1905, Peirce draws upon the following experience: "A lady's favorite perfume seems to me somehow to agree with that of her spiritual being. If she uses none at all her nature will lack perfume. If she wears violet she herself will have the very same delicate fineness. Of the only two I have known to use rose, one was an artistic old virgin, a *grande dame;* the other a noisy young matron and very ignorant; but they were strangely alike. As for those who use heliotrope, frangipanni, etc., I know them as well as I desire to know them. Surely there must be some subtle resemblance between the odor and the impression I get of this or that woman's nature." — *Collected Papers*, Vol. I, p. 131.

53. *Ibid.*, Vol. IV, p. 118.

54. *Ibid.*, Vol. III, p. 251f.

55. *Ibid.*, (1897) Vol. I, p. 2.

56. *Ibid*, Vol. II, p. 115.

57. *Ibid.*, (1898) Vol. I, p. 10.

58. R. B. Perry, *op. cit.*, Vol. I, p. 536.

59. C. S. Peirce, *op. cit.*, Vol. IV, p. 440f.

60. *Ibid.*, Vol. VI, p. 213.

61. *Ibid.*, Vol. I, p. 657.

62. *Ibid.*, Vol. VI, p. 319.

63. *Ibid.*, Vol. IV, p. 331. [No such record has been found. Eds.]

64. *Ibid.*, Vol. III, p. 358 [No record of this communication has been found in the official *Proceedings* of the London Mathematical Society; nor has any letter from Mr. Schlötel come to hand in a search through Peirce's correspondence. Ed.]

65. *Ibid.*, Vol. IV, p. 422.

65. *Ibid.*, (1903) Vol. IV, p. 422.

66. *Ibid.*, Vol. VI, p. 175.

67. *Ibid.*, (1908) IV, p. 593.

68. *Ibid.*, (1908) IV, p. 589.

69. *Ibid.*, (1896) III, p. 451.

70. In the *Popular Science Monthly* (January, 1878).

71. Notice how, out of his insecurity, Peirce's anxiety is focused into a positive piety toward "methods." He can write of abstruse formulae: "The genius of a man's logical method should be loved and reverenced as his bride, whom he has chosen from all the world. He need not condemn the others; on the contrary, he may honor them deeply, and in doing so he only honors her the more. But she is the one that he has chosen, and he knows that he was right in making that choice. And having made it, he will work and fight for her, and will not complain that there are blows to take, hoping that there may be as many and as hard to give, and will strive to be the worthy knight and champion of her from the blaze of

whose splendors he draws his inspiration and his courage." *Collected Papers*, Vol. V, p. 387.

72. For a systematic display and theoretical grounding of the connective mechanisms herein applied to Peirce, *see* C. Wright Mills, "Language, Logic, and Culture," *American Sociological Review* (October, 1939), p. 675.

73. C. S. Peirce, *op. cit.*, XII.

74. *Ibid.*, I, p. 7.

75. *Ibid.*, (1898) I, p. 9.

76. *Ibid.*, (1893) IV, p. 134.

77. *Ibid.*, (1903) I, p. 15.

78. In 1883. In the preface C. S. Peirce writes: "These papers, the work of my students, have been so instructive to me, that I have . . . obtained permission to publish them in one volume." The papers are by Allen Marquand, Christine Ladd, O. H. Mitchell, and B. I. Gilman.

70. *Collected Papers*, I. pp. iv-v.

80. Only 6 of the 10 volumes contemplated are published at this writing (1941-42).

81. *Ibid.*, I, p. iii.

82. "The argument of this book has been developed in the mind of the author, substantially as it is presented, as a following out of these three conceptions, in a sort of game of 'follow-my-leader' from one field of thought into another. Their importance was originally brought home to me in the study of logic, where they play so remarkable a part that I was led to look for them in psychology. Finding them there again, I could not help asking myself whether they did not enter into the physiology of the nervous system. By drawing a little on hypothesis, I succeeded in detecting them there; and then the question naturally came how they would appear in the theory of protoplasm in general. Here I seemed to break into an interesting avenue of reflection . . ." *Ibid.*, (1890) I, p. 364.

83. *Ibid.*, I, p.v.

84. *Ibid.*, I, p.v., editors of the *Collected Papers*.

85. *See* Paul Weiss, "The Essence of Peirce's System" in *The Journal of Philosophy* (May 9, 1940) and Justus Buchler, *Charles Peirce's Empiricism* (New York 1939).

7

The Laboratory Style of Inquiry

The Cartesian conception of doubt is a component of a larger conception of methodology. Descartes laid it down as a rule governing his inquiries that he should systematically and completely doubt, not only all the beliefs that he had gathered during his life and now found within himself,[1] but "all things in which the slightest trace of uncertitude can be found."[2] This Cartesian notion of doubt cannot be understood independently of Descartes' conception of mind and of the nature and locus of its operation. The mind is distinct from the body. The "sciences," says Descartes, "entirely consist in the cognitive exercise of the mind." They bear no relation whatsoever to the "arts," which depend upon an exercise and disposition of the body. Descartes identifies the "sciences taken all together" with "human wisdom," and this "universal wisdom ... always remains one and the same, however applied to different subjects, and suffers no more differentiation proceeding from them than the light of the sun experiences from the variety of things which it illuminates."[3] The end of all inquiries is contribution toward universal wisdom, hence that end is always general. Only with such a general end in view can we succeed in "seeking out truth."[4] It is mind's nature to seek out truth. The "method" by which the task is performed is intuition implemented by logical manipulation of concepts. Now just as knowledge is universal and a thing of the mind alone, so should doubt as rule of method be universal.

Cartesian doubt is *überhaupt;* it is open and unspecific. This is not to say that it is, methodologically, completely uncontrolled. For that which is opposite to this generic and immediate doubt

is the idea which presents itself to reason with illuminated clarity
and distinctness. Avowedly, upon a sea of doubt, Descartes' only
anchor is the certainty of intuition. For intuition is a technique of
mind by which universal doubt is, by a succession of flashes, replaced by certain knowledge. As a counter-symbol to Cartesian
doubt, intuition is defined in terms of it as: "the undoubting conception of an unclouded and attentive mind, and springs from the
light of reason . . . Intuition is the conception which mind gives
us so readily and distinctly that we are wholly freed from doubt."[5]

Certainty is the keynote of Descartes' system and method, and
his must be an immediate, a personal certitude — first, of self, for
out of extensive and hence chaotic doubt emerges first the crystal-
line intuition, "cogito." On this initial peg, given an elementary
logic, he hangs certitude of the world about him. And if this intuitively given and logically built web of belief is not satisfactory
on the basis of sheer indubitability, "divine veracity" guarantees
the truths only so given to human reason.[6]

Against this conception of method, doubt, intuition, and logic,
Peirce, in the 1880's, presented a set of denials, instituted a positive critique. A denial of universal doubt as a realizable method-
ologic maxim constitutes Peirce's first critique of his version of the
method of Descartes.[7] The second denial is of the notion of this
Protestant epistemology that "the ultimate test for certainty is to
be found in the individual consciousness." And third, as a corollary
to two, Peirce denied the advisability of hanging certain knowledge on a single thread of inference.[8]

The first two of these denials are not unconnected, just as the
notions denied, as features of Cartesianism, are not unconnected.
In both perspectives there is a correlativity: in Descartes, as noted,
a correlativity of doubt and a particular method of fixing belief, if
indeed, intuition may be called a "method." Peirce calls it a variation of the *a priori* method and situates it in the history of thought.[9]
In Peirce, the correlativity is of conceptions of doubt and of belief
— however fixed. In place of the scheme in which general doubt
is pierced by intuition, Peirce erects a scheme in which specific
doubt lies in a tension with belief. The framework which Peirce
projects is such that belief is a state of fact denoting a termination
of inquiry; intuition is located as one manner in which such termination is apparently achieved. Peirce has before him several

methods, *i.e.*, he empirically delineates several modes of inquiry,[10] and he locates Descartes among them. But for Descartes, intuition is the only method of attaining certain belief, *i.e.*, knowledge; for such vision is the essence of knowledge.

Peirce's refutation of the "method of intuition" with its Protestant appeal to the individual's immediate consciousness consists of three criticisms:[11]

> (a) As a methodology, it is a "mere formalism," which really amounts to saying that whatever a man is "clearly convinced of, is true." But, says Peirce, were I "really convinced, I should have done with reasoning and should require no test of certainty."[12]
>
> (b) The attendant logical requirements, that such "ideas" must be "clear and distinct" is dismissed; an idea that is "clear" is merely one with which we are "familiar,"[13] and to say that an idea is "distinct" is but to say that we can give an "abstract definition" for it.[14]
>
> (c) It makes "single individuals absolute judges of truth." This, says Peirce, is "pernicious," not in accord with the social dimension of scientific method whose generic postulates and structure Peirce would carry into philosophic — into all serious-reflective concerns.[15]

Whereas the denial of intuition is grounded mainly upon logical positions, the generic persuasion promoting Peirce's denial of Cartesian doubt as a realizable rule of method is experimental. He appeals to experience, claiming that no mind has experienced or can experience universal doubt. If a man ceases to pretend, he must recognize the existence of certain beliefs which seem indubitable to him. "Do not make-believe," writes Peirce, "if pedantry has not eaten all the reality out of you, recognize as you must, that there is much that you do not doubt, in the least."[16] Cartesian philosophy "pretended to doubt what it did not doubt," and, "why cannot men see that what we do not doubt, we do not doubt; so that it is false pretense to pretend to call it in question."[17]

For, *de facto*, you have beliefs that have not been "accepted;" you "come to recognize" that you have had them "as long as you can remember."[18] You cannot and do not *begin* with "complete doubt," or any other kind; "genuine doubt does not talk of *beginning* with doubt."[19]

There is here the recognition that the noetic has a history, an antecedent context, and that you cannot detach it from that history by acceptances of a maxim. Inquiry is not a thing in itself whose inherent traits are to be examined. Universal doubt cannot be the threshold of reflective ventures because such ventures are *de facto* conditioned by their antecedent contexts; but also because such a "state of mind" is not within the range of psychological attainability.[20] To assert the contrary is to assume the "infant's mind to be a *tabula rasa* and the adult's a school slate, on which doubts are written with a soapstone pencil to be cleaned off with the dab of a wet sponge."[21] Thus, the psychological assumptions underpinning the realizability of Cartesian doubt are unearthed and pronounced fallacious. Mind is not an independently existent insular stuff. It is situated in a conditioning context within which it functions; and it can have no complete rebirth. Is that not what Descartes would have it do? He would have us bear a new mind with only a maxim as husband and midwife. Descartes assumes that doubt can be "willed" into existence. "Supposing that one can doubt at will" is, says Peirce, another "Cartesian error."[22] You must begin your intellectual work in "the very state of mind in which you actually find yourself at the time you do begin it," and, "who knows whether if you could [divest yourself of all belief . . .] you would not have made all knowledge impossible to yourself."[23] Belief is prior to doubt and reflection: "There is every reason to suppose that belief comes first, and the power of doubting long after."[24] You are experientially aware of your mind's history by the beliefs which you recognize yourself to have. But such a history is a *fact* about mind. It is significant that Peirce here adumbrates Dewey, formally recognizes a non-cognitive context, background of mind, *i.e.*, in the existence of "acritical beliefs:" beliefs not reflectively built and "accepted," but transmitted.[25] There are beliefs there before doubt and reflection occur. They are the proximate context of reflection, and they constitute in part the mind with which we begin our intellectual adventures. Thus is mind located by Peirce within the domain of antecedent belief.

To deny doubt, Cartesian model, is not to deny something genuine for which the term may properly stand. Indeed, doubt is the origin of inquiry. Our interest focuses attention upon the locus of doubt in Peirce, for by understanding this we can more specifically locate inquiry itself. There are several statements of doubt systematizable from Peirce, but here our focus is only upon the conception of doubt insofar as it enables us to illuminate the locus and functional character of inquiry.

Doubt, writes Peirce, is "an uneasy and dissatisfied state from which we struggle to free ourselves and pass into a state of belief," which is a "calm and satisfactory state which we do not wish to avoid or to change to a belief in anything else."[26] Now such a "struggle to attain a state of belief" is inquiry. The nature of mind is not general. It is not "to know." Its function is specific. It strives to attain to a specific belief. And because doubt is of a specific belief, it cannot itself be *überhaupt*. That inquiry is a *specific* matter and that it has a *context* are two basic conceptions of Peirce. And both these contentions spring from, are intimately tied to the work on doubt. "Doubt" denotes the conditions of a juncture within experience that is itself not reflective. It focuses mind on inquiry, evokes it from smoother contexts.

Both doubt and belief are "states of mind," and that there are such states of mind is among the "variety of facts already assumed" by inquiries into logic. They are "facts which we must already know before we can have any clear conception of reasoning at all."[27] Now, doubt and belief are distinguished by a "dissimilarity between the sensation of doubting and that of believing."[28] We are "aware" of them,[29] and they are different sensations. But a complication arises: our awareness of doubt (and belief) is not clear and evident. Because "man possesses no infallible introspective power . . . to know just what he believes and what he doubts . . . the denial of such a power is one of the clauses of critical common-sensism."[30] That we do not "have an intuitive power of distinguishing between the subjective elements of different kinds of cognitions" is a clause of Peirce's anti-Cartesian program.[31]

But it is not by a "faculty" that we can distinguish belief from conception, *e.g.*, but by means of a "peculiar feeling of conviction" attendant on the former.[32] So also, it is by means of the dissimilarity between the "sensation of doubting" and that of believing that we "generally know when we wish to ask a question and when we wish to pronounce a judgment."[33] There are nuances of meaning within these notions, but generically they characterize doubt (and belief) as internal affairs, which have "positive effects upon us,"[34] *i.e.*, they are facts.[35] The first conception, then, which we systematize out of Peirce is that doubt is a factual notation of something internal; a "feeling," a "sensation," or a "state of mind."

But such is not the only characterization of doubt and of belief. "The *irritation* of doubt is the only immediate motive for the struggle to attain belief," but back of it stretches a contextual world that is not mental and in this world of behavior, sociality, and fact doubt has roots. The Cartesian isolation of mind, of inquiry, fact, and social minds from contextual antecedents, from body, is flatly denied, and inquiry is situated "naturalistically."

Doubt and belief are differentiated by a "practical difference." For our beliefs "guide our desires and shape our actions." "The feeling of believing is a more or less sure indication of there being established in our nature some habit which will determine our actions. Doubt never . . . has such an effect."[36] As belief is ultimately composed of habit, so doubt is "privation of habit" and this must be a "condition of erratic activity."[37]

The introduction of the categories of action and habit as components of belief and factors in doubt is a source of ambiguity in Peirce. These categories are not thoroughly nor consistently assimilated to his ring of working conceptions. The roots of the ambiguity involved in the relation of action and habit to doubt and belief lie in the fact that nowhere in Peirce is a clear critique for the category of action worked out. The ambiguity arises as soon as we inquire as to the *character* and *locus* of action and habit as these are involved in doubt and belief.

The conception of action implicated in belief and doubt does not seem to be that of motor behavior progressing smoothly within a physical environment or confronted with environmental obstacles. But it may be.[38] Usually, in the text, the action is described by Peirce as a kind of imaginative experimentation and, hence, within mind. "Feigned hesitancy, whether feigned for mere amusement or with a lofty purpose, plays a great part in the production of scientific inquiry."[39] And in another context, "All doubt is a state of hesitancy about an imagined state of things"[40] and again, definitively:

> "Doubt . . . is not usually hesitancy about what is to be done then and there. It is anticipated hesitancy about what I shall do hereafter, or a feigned hesitancy about a fictitious state of things. It is the power of making-believe we hesitate, togeth-

er with the pregnant fact that the decision upon the mere
make-believe dilemma goes toward forming a *bona fide* habit
that will be operative in a real emergency."[41]

The last portion of the quote deserves elaboration. It is one of
Peirce's points of stress that:

> "fancied reiterations — if well-intensified by direct effort,
> produce habits, just as do reiterations in the outer world; and
> these habits will have power to influence actual behavior in
> the outer world; especially if such reiteration be accompa-
> nied by a peculiar strong effort that is usually likened to issuing
> a command to one's future self."[42]

But this "actual behavior" which may occur in the "outer world"
is for Peirce only a *possible* consequence of reflection, and not a
generic characterization of doubt. Hence, in this conception,
inquiry need not necessarily be concerned with concrete problems
within action. Furthermore, the occurrence of actions as consequences are confined by Peirce to a certain class of beliefs,
namely, the "practical," and "religious." And these are *polarized*,
in several instances to scientific inquiry.

Indeed, it is clear that, in the main, action and habit as they enter as elements of his model of inquiry are restricted by Peirce to
imagined action, to "mental habit" and that *imagined* disrup ions
of imagined actions constitute doubt. This interpretation is supported by the kind of habit involved in belief.

Of the activity dimension of belief, Peirce has this to say:

> "The final upshot of thinking is the exercise of volition,
> and of this thought no longer forms a part; but belief is only
> a stadium of mental action, an effect upon our nature due to
> thought, which will influence future thinking."[43]

Note "future *thinking*," that is, *"mental* action." And again: "Readiness to act in a certain way under certain circumstances and
when actuated by a given motive is a habit; and a *deliberate,* or
self-controlled habit is precisely a belief."[44] A habit is not a single
act; it is a *"rule* of action." It is the application of this *"rule* for
action" which involves further doubt and further thought."[45]
A pragmatist, continues Peirce, more generically, "will hold that

everything in the substance of his beliefs can be represented in the schemata of his imagination."[46]

Belief and doubt are counter-terms. Within the conception of doubt which we are here systematizing, doubt is conceived as a "hesitancy" in action, as in some sense an interruption of "belief-habit." Now if the activity content of belief is habitual, *i.e.*, a "*rule* of action," a "*mental* action" (*ante.*), then the action which when interrupted precipitates doubt must be not concrete motor performance but rather its *character* must be in some sense mental or "cerebral"[47] and its *locus* must be the "imagination." The clearest statement of doubt in terms of interrupted action is found in the following quotation, in which we also note the relation of doubt conceived in terms of interrupted "action" to doubt conceived as internal fact noted.

> "Doubt is a state of mind marked by a feeling of uneasiness; but we cannot, from a logical, least of all from a pragmatic point of view, regard doubt as consisting in this feeling: a man in doubt is usually trying to imagine how he shall, or should, act when or if he finds himself in the imagined situation . . . His action is in imagination (or perhaps really) brought to a stop . . . His pent up activity finds vent in feeling, which becomes the more prominent from his attention being no longer absorbed in action. A true doubt is accordingly a doubt which really interferes with the smooth working of the belief-habit."[48]

In our first presentation of Peirce on doubt and belief we found them to be notations of alleged internal facts ("sensations," "feeling," "state of mind," etc.). Introduction of "habit" as component of belief and factor in habit is to Peirce not inconsistent with that conception. Smoothly-functioning-habits as belief and interrupted-habits as doubt are what lie beneath the "feelings" of doubt and belief. It is the breakdown of belief-habit within the laboratory of the imagination that "causes" the "feeling," the "irritation" of doubt. Hence these two conceptions of doubt locate the origin and task of inquiry within mind.

A third notion of doubt systematizable from Peirce contains explicit statements that are of "external origin." "Doubt, usually, perhaps always, takes its rise from surprise . . . which presupposes previous belief . . . and surprises come with novel environment."[49]

We cannot "doubt at will."[50] A novel experience, some surprise,
begins the dissolution of a belief.[51] Doubt must be "compassed
through experience."[52] For "the course of life," *i.e.*, experience,
"gives you power to doubt old beliefs."[53]

There are two aspects of this "course of life," that are relevant.
The first of these is a conception of *fact,* defined by Peirce experientially. "Some things," he says, "are *forced* upon cognition . . .
there is the element of brute force existing whether you opine it
exists or not."[54] These things are facts. Now: "as soon as it appears
that facts are against a given habit of reasoning (a belief), it at
once looses its hold" and doubt ensues.[55] Fact, in Peirce, has several critiques: it is non-general; it is "contingent, that is, the acci-
dentally actual;" it is "whatever involves an unconditional necessity; that is force, without law or reason, brute force."[56] Fact is
something that "happens;" it has "self assertion."[57] It is there, and
it cannot be avoided. Within the categories of Peirce fact is subsumed under "dyadisty" or "binarity."[58] This second category, "interaction," is objective: external, but, regardless of its origin doubt
in terms of fact remains proximately an "internal" affair. "Among
the inner shapes which binarity assumes are those of the *doubts,*
that are forced upon our minds."[59] Again relevant to the conception of doubt in terms of fact:

> "It is important for the reader to satisfy himself that genu-
> ine doubt always has an external origin, usually from surprise,
> and that it is as impossible for a man to create in himself
> genuine doubt by . . . an act of the will . . . as it would be
> for him to give himself a genuine surprise by a simple act of
> the will."[60]

Doubt, says Peirce, "has a limen, that is, it is only called into being
by a certain finite stimulus."[61] Fact is that stimulus; fact is one
factor external in origin that disrupts the smooth operations of be-
lief-habits, instituting doubt within mind. And mind or inquiry is in
some sense located within or is in interaction with the world of
physical fact. But the sharp notion is contaminated by a nascent
objective idealism. Note that the origination of inquiry is an inner form, a focus occurs within mind of dyadisty under which
"fact" is subsumed. And dyadisty runs throughout nature.

The other external factor mentioned by Peirce as involved in the origin of doubt is a social one. And by it inquiry is given a social location and its course is opened to social determinants. Experimentally known is the fact that:

> "no matter how strong and well-rooted in habit any rational conviction of ours may be, we no sooner find that another equally well-informed person doubts it, than we begin to doubt it ourselves. This is plainly shown by the anger such doubt excites in us."[62]

But the social factor is for Peirce operative at least in such a proximate manner.

In many ways Peirce's article, "The Fixation of Belief," is to be fruitfully regarded as a penetrating essay in the sociology of knowledge. In this essay are outlined the methods of fixing belief as exemplified in the history of reflection and in types of present day thinkers. Both within the methods themselves and among the factors persuading a transition from one method to the next, social factors are operative. The self-willful method of tenacity by which a man programmatically excludes all factors which might conduce him to doubt his beliefs breaks down because "the social impulse is against it."[63] In following this method a man will come to see that other men think differently than he, and he will come to doubt his method.

> "This conception," wrote Peirce, "that another man's thought or sentiment may be equivalent to one's own, is a distinctly new step, and a highly important one. . ."[64] [We] necessarily influence each other's opinions; so that the problem becomes how to fix belief, not in the individual merely, but in the community."[65]

Hence, through the "social impulse," arises the authoritarian method of fixing belief in which the "will of the state" acts, setting forth indubitable belief — indubitable by official fiat. But as soon as men are in such a "state of culture" that one opinion influences another; when they can "put two and two together," they will begin to doubt the single official opinion.[66] The authoritarian method breaks down because of cultural contacts. Access to foreign opinions, acquaintance with other "countries and ages" will drive men to see the equal status of other opinions and that the accident of the social location of their birth and maturation accounts for their ethnocentric beliefs.

So men will fall to conversing and they will appeal to individual "reason" in order to fix belief. This is an *a priori* method, or the method of "inclination" by which belief is fixed by "what men find in their minds." This method makes of inquiry "something similar to the development of taste," hence "fashion."[67] But again, the "shock of (contrary) opinions" will soon lead men to forsake this method,[68] for one which removes doubt by resting belief upon something external to man, *i.e.*, fact, and upon which all men will ultimately agree.[69] This is the method of science.

The point of this discussion relevant to our interest is (a) that each method fails. We come to doubt it, "on account of the social impulse."[70] The origin and locus of doubt is thus social. And (b) that inquiry itself is thus seen to be social in its locus and to involve "social factors" in its operation.

Logically, this social origin of doubt makes it appear to be composed of a "conflict" of two beliefs, one of which the doubter holds, and one held by another. With reference to beliefs in various methods Peirce says "the feeling which gives rise to any method of fixing belief is a dissatisfaction at two repugnant propositions."[71]

Thus, the external factor in the social origin of doubt is not an impelling, brute fact but rather the fact that a counter-belief is held by someone. Proximately, doubt occurs within mind, but its ultimate locus and thought context are not confined to individual consciousness. The roots of doubt stretch toward and lie within the world of emergent facts and within the social worlds of multitudinous opinions.

The import of the conceptions of doubt as involving confrontation with emergent fact and contradictory opinion held by others is that they give to reflection a wider context than individual consciousness. They arise from a very new conception of the character and task of inquiry, and this conception involves the notion that inquiry has a context, that it is specific. Inquiry is related to and has its origin within something not cognitive. It is related to the world of brute fact and to the beliefs of others that are not of its own making. And timidly, thought at both ends, in origin and outcome, is nascently related to a world of action which is smoothly durational or which is interrupted and troubled. Inquiry is given a context first by the recognition of belief and second by recognition of the focus of doubt. In Peirce these conceptions are not sharply drawn. To make them appear as clear to Peirce would be not only a historical distortion but it would be an indication of slothfulness in the face of difficulties. To Peirce, the notion that one can "doubt at will" is a Cartesian eidolon. Opposing it are the several conceptions of doubt systematized above. Opposing it also is the Peircian insistence that doubt is not completely characterized by an experimental account of its origin and effects; for doubt must be conceived in relation to a technique that is involved in its attainment. Doubting "is not a thing you can do in a minute as soon as [you] decide what [you] want to doubt."[72] Nor does "the mere putting of a proposition into the interrogative form . . . stimulate the mind to . . . [inquiry]"[73] Peirce regards no belief as indubitable "without a systematic and arduous endeavor to attain a doubt of it;" but "the pragmatist knows that doubt is an art which has to be acquired with difficulty."[74] He is not "content to ask himself whether he does not doubt, but he invents a plan for attaining to doubt, elaborates it in detail, and then puts it into practice, although this may involve a solid month of hard work."[75] And, adds Peirce elsewhere, having learned the "difficult art" of doubting, "his genuine doubts will go much further than those of any Cartesian."[76]

Motivating these statements is the generic revolt against the notion that doubt can be willed into being. Constructively, but standing squarely opposed to the Cartesian assumption, there is the insistence that doubt as experience of whatever character, origin, and location is the end of an artful search for it, that it may be programmatically instituted. But exactly in what the "difficult art" of attaining to the experience of doubt consists, Peirce nowhere directly informs us. The Peircian insistence that doubt must be programmatically instituted has led us to search textually for a connection of doubt with larger methodological patterns. I have found implicit in Peirce the conception that doubt is an element within the structure of a certain methodology, that doubt is a juncture in experience that is normatively guided, that the experience of genuine doubt occurs only within the continuum of a type of inquiry.

The method in which doubt is programmatically included,

whose rules contain exhortation to doubt and techniques for critically attaining it, is the method of laboratory science as seen by Peirce. This is the method whose structure and generic postulates Peirce wishes to generalize and ubiquitously to apply.[77] Such generalization occurs in Peirce by means of "analogical extensions" from scientific practices. He is viewing mind or imagination *as* laboratory. Under his guidance a student at Johns Hopkins University made a *logical machine.* Peirce is exploring the implications and suggestions of this fruitful metaphor. "Thought," for a key-instance, is not to be "taken in that narrow sense in which silence and darkness are favorable to thought. It should rather be understood as governing all rational life, so that an experiment shall be an operation of thought."[78] Whoever would understand the minutely varied conceptions of doubt in Peirce must view them against this persistently pervasive attempt to extend the methods of laboratory science to all serious intellectual concerns.

We have seen that Peirce conceives doubt as: (a) proximately composed of certain sensations existent in mind and noted as psychologic fact; (b) as due to a breakdown in deliberate imagination (or "real") action; (c) as due to an impelling, surprising fact forcing a challenge to belief;[79] (d) as due to the recognition of counter-beliefs held by other persons whose experience is honored; and (e) as an experience that must be searched out, programmatically instituted.

These conceptions can be ordered and accounted for only by locating them within the structure of "scientific method." I do not find such a locational linkage explicit anywhere in Peirce's published writings. But it is consonant with his conceptions of himself and what he was trying to do in philosophy. This locational interpretation is not, however, without some positive textual grounds, and Peirce makes no explicit statement which contradicts it.

(a) Only by keeping in mind the fact that Peirce is attempting to extend his laboratory practices, as he was aware of them, into all inquiry can we understand his reformulating and going behind, beneath, doubt as an experience. We can understand his inclusion of *fact* and *action* as elements involved in the precipitation of doubt.

In the laboratory, experimental-action is actually arrested by emergent, exceptional fact; and the experimenter is forced to revise or reject the hypothesis or belief upon which the experimental-action was predicated. Experimentation is the "difficult art," the technique of seeking out emergent exceptions, for this "difficult art" of instituting doubt can, from the Peircian perspective, be nothing other than experimentation, during the course of which factual items arise, "surprising" the investigator precisely because they cannot be subsumed within the belief-habit or hypothesis whose experimental actuation they interrupted. The "habit" which Peirce elevates as the essential component of belief is a "deliberate," a "controlled" habit, *i.e.*, as an experimental action.[80] The "rule of action" content of belief is the continuous experimental exemplification of a theoretically erected meaning or universal, *i.e.*, as the meaning and testing of scientific assertion or hypothesis. The inclusion of *social* factors springs *negatively* from the polemic with Cartesianism; but it grows *positively* from the belief that in science the seat of intellectual authority is within the community of scientists.[81] As in the "logic of science," so also is the "social principle . . . rooted intrinsically in [all] logic"[82]

Challenging the dominant epistemological traditions which he largely subsumes under the spirit of Cartesianism, Peirce analogically translates the component elements of experimental science into a formulation of the general structure of the processes of inquiry. His conceptions of doubt arise readily from within this program, from within the metaphor: mind as laboratory. For mind genuinely at work with meanings, theories, and with words, exemplifies to Peirce the form of experimental inquiry. The structure of each inquiry is carried over into mind. It is, synoptically, then, the "laboratory habit of mind" which is the central thought-model for Peirce. *And it is only within the structure of this thought-model that all the conceptions of doubt lie in consistent and integrated fashion to be understood.*

(b) That not all "methodologies" conduct their bearers consciously to strive for doubt is attested to by the existence of the methods of tenacity and of authority. In the former, *i.e.*, a man, ostrich-like, "goes through life systematically keeping out of view all that might cause a change in his opinions."[83] These methods consist in programmatically excluding any conditions or perceptions which might stimulate doubt.

That the kind of situation or experience which precipitates or constitutes doubt is relative to the normative persuasions of a method is certified by the rise of doubt within the *a priori* method. For here the seat of doubt and conviction is confined to the conceptual level. "It is hard to convince a follower of the *a priori* method by adducing facts; but show him that an opinion he is defending is inconsistent with what he has laid down elsewhere, and he will be apt to retract it."[84]

(c) That Peircian doubt is a formulation in connection with the scientific style of thought is further evidenced by the incipiently present and incomplete contention that if doubt be genuine, evidence or "reasons" for it must be given. "A person . . . in the course of his studies, find[s] reason to doubt . . . but in that case he doubts because he has a positive reason for it."[85]

Examining Peirce on doubt, we find that his anti-Cartesianism carries the implication that the experience of doubt is not a self-warrant for its genuineness, for its being the "weighty and noble metal itself."[86] The implication is that a description of doubt and of its origins do not adequately conclude discussion of it. For it to be genuinely a factor of inquiry, there must be *grounds* for doubt.

But exactly what the objective general or logical grounds for doubt may be, Peirce nowhere informs us. Again, his adducing the point, emphasis upon it in connection with his distinction between "genuine" and paper-doubt[87] can be accounted for only by understanding the generic character of his projection of laboratory methods. For within physical science, as he perceived it, the grounds of doubt are clear: one must institute a factual-complex which cannot be taken into account by the current hypothesis, and if one cannot do this, doubt will be inconsequential. It will not be a pivot around which new discovery and new theory can rotate.

(d) A further ground supporting the contention that Peircian doubt takes its form from his occupational practices and views is the stress upon the specificity of doubt. Belief is prior to doubt, and doubt is of a specific belief, *i.e.*, of an hypothesis. An hypothesis (a prag matically formulated belief) is a necessary condition for the experience of doubt. One of the essentials of a scientific experiment, says Peirce, is "a verifiable hypothesis"[88] and a "sincere doubt in the experimenter's mind as to the truth of that hypothesis."[89] So also in "thought," the belief which we doubt must be clearly formulated, for "so long as we cannot put our fingers on our erroneous opinions, they remain our opinions, still."[90] "Vagueness" attending experiential doubt can do what "precise reasoning" about it cannot do: vagueness can destroy doubt.[91]

The locational framework of Peircian doubt is thus seen to be the style of thought derived from the methodological structure of physical or laboratory science. The imputation (if it has been substantiated) that Peirce's various conceptions of doubt can be put together and understood only within the framework of a laboratory model of thought seems to be "evidence" that his work in laboratories entered significantly into the perspective from which this concept was seen and elaborated. From this perspective the different modulations of the concept make sense.

---

1. "... as regards all the opinions which up to this time I had embraced, I thought I could do nothing better than endeavor once and for all to sweep them away ..." *Discourse on Method*, G.R.T. Ross and E.S. Haldane, editors of *The Philosophical Works of Descartes* (Cambridge 1912) Vol. I, p. 89.

2. *Principles*, Ross and Haldane, ed. Part I, p. 219

3. *Scribner's Selections From Descartes*, Edited by R. M. Eaton (New York 1927) p. 38.

4. *Ibid.*, p. 39.

5. *Rules for Direction of the Mind*, Ross and Haldane Edition, *op. cit.*, Part I p. 7.

6. Cf. Storck, *The Method of Descartes in the Natural Sciences* (Jamaica, New York 1931) Ph.D. Thesis, Columbia University, pp. 11-12.

7. C. S. Peirce, *Collected Papers*, V, p. 264.

8. C. S. Peirce, *Collected Works*, V, p. 264.

9. *Ibid.*, V, p. 382.

10. Cf. "Methods of Fixing Belief," V, pp. 233-48.

11. These three grounds are not to be regarded as adequately representative of Peirce's position at this point. *E.g.*, I have omitted as not pertinent to our present concern the denial of immediate experience or knowledge of the self and of cognitions. (Cf. V, pp. 135-55.)

12. *Ibid.*, V, p. 265.
13. *Ibid.*, V, p. 389.
14. *Ibid.*, V, p. 391; V, p. 392.
15. *Ibid.*, V, p. 265; V, p. 411; V, p. 412.
16. *Ibid.*, V, p. 416.
17. *Ibid.*, II, p. 192.
18. *Ibid.*, V, p. 523.
19. *Ibid.*, V, p. 264; VI, p. 498.
20. *Ibid.*, V, p. 523; V, p. 410.
21. *Ibid.*, V, p. 519.
22. *Ibid.*, V, p. 524.
23. *Ibid.*, V, p. 416.
24. *Ibid.*, V, p. 512.
25. *Ibid.*, V, p. 523.
26. *Ibid.*, V, p. 372.
27. *Ibid.*, V, p. 369.
28. *Ibid.*, V, p. 370.
29. *Ibid.*, V, p. 396.
30. *Ibid.*, V, p. 499. A doctrine regarded by Peirce as "involved" in "pragmaticism."
31. *Ibid.*, V, p. 237.
32. *Ibid.*, V, p. 242.
33. *Ibid.*, V, p. 370.
34. *Ibid.*, V, p. 315.
35. *Ibid.*, Cf. II, p. 110.
36. *Ibid.*, V, p. 371.
37. *Ibid.*, V, p. 417.
38. *Ibid.*, V, p. 394.
39. *Ibid.*, V, p. 394.
40. *Ibid.*, V, p. 231f.
41. *Ibid.*, V, p. 231f.
42. *Ibid.*, V, p. 487.
43. *Ibid.*, V, p. 397.
44. *Ibid.*, V, p. 480.
45. *Ibid.*, V, p. 397.
46. *Ibid.*, V, p. 517.
47. *Ibid.*, III, p. 160.
48. *Ibid.*, V, p. 510.
49. *Ibid.*, V, p. 512.
50. *Ibid.*, V, p. 524.
51. *Ibid.*, V, p. 417.
52. *Ibid.*, V, p. 498.
53. *Ibid.*, V, p. 416.
54. *Ibid.*, II, p. 138.
55. *Ibid.*, II, p. 160.
56. *Ibid.*, I, p. 427.
57. *Ibid.*, I, p. 434.

58. Cf. "A New List of Categories." Also, Vol. V., Book I, Lecture II. "The Universal Categories."
59. *Ibid.*, II, p. 85.
60. *Ibid.*, V, p. 433.
61. *Ibid.*, V, p. 416.
62. *Ibid.*, II, p. 168.
63. *Ibid.*, V, p. 378.
64. *Ibid.*, V, p. 378.
65. *Ibid.*, V, p. 378.
66. *Ibid.*, V, p. 381.
67. *Ibid.*, V, p. 239f.
68. *Ibid.*, V, p. 382.
69. *Ibid.*, V, p. 384.
70. *Ibid.*, II, p. 665.
71. *Ibid.*, V, p. 384.
72. *Ibid.*, VI, p. 498.
73. *Ibid.*, V, p. 376.
74. *Ibid.*, VI, p. 498.
75. *Ibid.*, V, p. 451.
76. *Ibid.*, VI, p. 498.
77. *See* above section.
78. *Ibid.*, V, p. 420.
79. It is this meaning that is later taken up by Mead as the "novel fact" around which problems emerge and new hypotheses come into vision.
80. *Ibid.*, V, pp. 480, 425, 427.
81. *Ibid.*, V, pp. 351f, 384, 407.
82. *Ibid.*, V, pp. 354, 265.
83. *Ibid.*, V, p. 377.
84. *Ibid.*, V, p. 406.
85. *Ibid.*, V, p. 265.
86. *Ibid.*, V, p. 451.
87. *Ibid.*, V, pp. 445, 451.
88. "This is a proposition relating to the universe environing the experimenter . . . and affirming or denying of this only some experimental possibility or impossibility." *Ibid.*, V, p. 424.
89. *Ibid.*, V, p. 424.
90. *Ibid.*, V, pp. 232-33f.
91. *Ibid.*, V, p. 515.

8

The Practical in Peirce

Using autobiographic statements, methodological self-reflections, and, more specifically, the general conception of inquiry and the constructed model within which the Peircian conception of "doubt" may be most readily understood, we have been led to build up a picture of his style of thought as basically informed by scientific practices. It is not, however, to be *supposed* that this style has complete dominance in the total field of his thinking. It is not a central working principle in terms of which his *entire* effort and structure of concepts and opinions are directed and self-judged. Indeed, it is carefully and explicitly restricted in its applications. In particular, this model of thought which he has built from scientific procedures is vigorously insulated from the domain of "practice," from analyses of what he called "vital affairs."

In depicting Peirce's view of science we have used the concept of "doubt." We have also used it as an important instance or key to his style of thinking. Therefore, it is well to continue with "doubt" in depicting his restriction of the scientific model. It is all the more useful for his purpose in that it is "doubt" which initiates the working of the scientific mind.

It is within the perspective of the laboratory that Peirce's conceptions of "doubt" are to be seen and understood. It is only in connection with scientifically formulated beliefs that "genuine doubt" can, in his view, arise. And the conceptions of "doubt" and "inquiry" are very cautiously generalized by Peirce. Their legitimate context remains restricted. These conceptions are thoroughly insulated from the sphere of "practice." Genuine doubt is methodologically encouraged only in connection with those beliefs which take the form of experimental science. For Peirce sets forth differentials of the likelihood of doubt occurring in scientific inquiry as against "religious and practical" ideology, in "practice."

In the former, the scientist "ardently desires to have his present provisional beliefs . . . swept away and will work hard to accomplish that object." For a scientific belief "is something you take up provisionally as being the proper hypothesis to try first and endeavor to refute."[1] Precisely opposite such a state of affairs stand "religious" beliefs. "Religion is a practical matter. Its beliefs are formulae you will go on." We *believe* them to be correct. Doubt of practical beliefs seldom, if ever, are programmatically instituted. The lingual form often attendant to practical action is the answer. No question lives easily there. There is necessarily dogma inherent in practical, religious, or social belief and action.

Science is useless. Under the title, "Science as a guide to conduct," (1896) Peirce writes:

> "But what is worse, from our point of view, they begin to look upon science as a guide to conduct, that is, no longer as pure science but as an instrument for a practical end. One result of this is that all probable reasoning is despised. If a proposition is to be applied to action, it has to be embraced, or believed without reservation. There is no room for doubt, which can only paralyze action. But the scientific spirit requires a man to be at all times ready to dump his whole cartload of beliefs, the moment experience is against them. The desire to learn forbids him to be perfectly cocksure that he knows already. Besides positive science can only rest on experience; and experience can never result in absolute certainty, exactitude, necessity, or universality. But it is precisely with the universal and necessary, that is, with Law, that science can concern itself. Thus the real character of science is destroyed as soon as it is made an adjunct to conduct; and especially all progress in the inductive sciences is brought to a standstill."[2]

The practical is far from being the test of a true belief. On the contrary, ". . . it is perfectly true," writes Peirce, "that the belief which I shall do well to embrace in my practical affairs, such as my religion, may not accord with the proposition which a sound scientific method requires me provisionally to adopt." In the very midst of a tremendous application of science to industry, Peirce

stands opposed to any attempt to mingle philosophy, which is to
him a science, with practice. He limits the connective of theory
and practice by relating it to one period, the Hellenic.[3] "Gentlemen, it behooves me to confess to you that I stand before you a
scientific man, condemning with the whole strength of conviction
the Hellenic tendency to mingle philosophy and practice. Do you
think that the physiologist who cuts up a dog reflects, while doing
so, that he may be saving a human life? Nonsense. If he did, it
would spoil him for a scientific man; and then the vivisection
would become a crime."[4]

Indeed, he equates "useless inquiry" with "scientific inquiry:"

> "A useless inquiry, provided it is a systematic one, is pretty
> much the same thing as a scientific inquiry. Or at any rate if
> a scientific inquiry becomes by any mischance useful, that as-
> pect of it has to be kept sedulously out of sight during the
> investigation, [or] its hopes of success are fatally cursed."[5]

Polarizing and completely compartmentalizing "practice" and "philosophy," he lays the defects which he sees in the latter squarely
upon the philosopher's attention to "practice." Notice that "practice," to Peirce, is synonymous with "vital affairs" and that together they are almost surrogates for "religious" activities. This is true
in most of his writings:

> ". . . In my opinion, the present infantile condition of phi-
> losophy . . . is due to the fact that during this century it has
> chiefly been pursued by men who have not been nurtured
> in dissecting-rooms and other laboratories, and who conse-
> quently have not been animated by the true scientific *Eros;*
> but who have on the contrary come from theological sem-
> inaries, and have consequently been inflamed with a desire
> to amend the lives of themselves and others, a spirit no doubt
> more important than the love of science, for men in average
> situations, but radically unfitting them for the task of scien-
> tific investigation."[6]

As with "doubt," conversely with the ordinary meaning of "belief"
and "action." They are rigidly excluded from "science."

> "Hence, I hold that what is properly and usually called *be-
> lief* . . . has no place in science at all. We *believe* the prop-

osition we are ready to act upon. *Full belief* is willingness to act upon the proposition in vital crises, *opinion* is willingness to act upon it in relatively insignificant affairs. But pure science has nothing at all to do with *action*. The propositions it accepts, it merely writes in the list of premisses it proposes to use. Nothing is *vital* for science; nothing can be. Its accepted propositions, therefore, are but opinions at most; and the whole list is provisional. The scientific man is not in the least wedded to his conclusions. He risks nothing upon them . . . But in vital matters, it is quite otherwise. We must act in such matters; and the principle upon which we are willing to act is a *belief*."[7]

"Thus, pure theoretical knowledge, or science, has nothing directly to say concerning practical matters, and nothing even applicable at all to vital crises. Theory is applicable to minor practical affairs; but matters of vital importance must be left to sentiment, that is, to instinct."[8]

Writing a chapter, "The Centuries' Great Men in Science," in the *Annual Report of the Smithsonian Institution* for 1900, Peirce explicitly denies the Protestant ethic of Franklin as a force in nineteenth century science: "The glory of the Nineteenth Century has been its . . . scientific great men . . . Their distinctive characteristic throughout the century . . . has been devotion to the pursuit of truth for truth's sake. In this century we have not heard a Franklin saying, 'What signifies a philosophy which does not apply itself to some use?' [That is of the] Eighteenth Century science."[9]

This insulation of science and philosophy from conduct in Peirce's perspective is again evidenced in his discussion of the role of reason in:

"The conduct of life [in which] we have to distinguish everyday affairs and great crises. In the great decisions, I do not believe it is safe to trust to individual reason. In everyday business, reasoning is tolerably successful; but I am inclined to think that it is done as well without the aid of theory as with it."[10]

Not only does he fail to give reason a role in conduct but he blesses "conservative sentimentalism" as a guide in conduct with such adjectives as "formal," "manly," "sane and wholesome."

"The opinion prevalent among radicals that conservatives, and sentimentalists generally, are fools is only a cropping-out

of the tendency of men to conceited exaggeration of their
reasoning powers. Uncompromising radical though I be upon
some questions, inhabiting all my life an atmosphere of science, and not reckoned as particularly credulous, I must confess that the conservative sentimentalism I have defined rec-
ommends itself to my mind as eminently sane and wholesome.
Commendable as it undoubtedly is to reason out matters of
detail, yet to allow mere reasonings and reason's self-conceit
to over-awe the normal and manly sentimentalism which
ought to lie at the cornerstone of all our conduct seems to me
to be foolish and despicable."[11]

This "sentimentalism" is related by Peirce to "instinct" and to the
lives of animals. "But in practical affairs, in matters of vital importance, it is very easy to exaggerate the importance of ratiocination.
Those whom we are so fond of referring to as the "lower animals"
reason very little. Now I beg you to observe that those beings very
rarely commit a *mistake,* while we-----!"[12]
It is to "instinct," and not to any of the types of reasoning, that
we must go for guidance in vitally important matters.

> "Reasoning is of three kinds — The first is necessary, but it
> only professes to give us information concerning the matter
> of our own hypotheses and distinctly declares that, if we want
> to know anything else, we must go elsewhere. The second de-
> pends upon probabilities. The only cases in which it pretends
> to be of value is where we have, like an insurance company,
> an endless multitude of insignificant risks. Wherever a vital
> interest is at stake, it clearly says, 'Don't ask me.' The third
> kind of reasoning tries what *il lume naturale,* which lit the
> footsteps of Galileo, can do. It is really an appeal to instinct.
> Thus reason, for all the frills it customarily wears, in vital
> crises, comes down upon its marrow-bones to beg the succour
> of instinct."[13]

"Invariably follow the dictates of Instinct in preference to those of
Reason when such conduct will answer your purpose: that is the
prescription of Reason herself."[14]

> "Were I willing to . . . admit that there was one study
> which was at once scientific and yet vitally important, I should
> make that exception in favor of logic; for the reason that if
> we fall into the error of believing that vitally important ques-
> tions are to be decided by reasoning, the only hope of salva-

tion lies in formal logic, which demonstrates in the clearest manner that reasoning itself testifies to its own ultimate subordination to sentiment."[15] Do not harbor any expectation that the study of logic can improve your judgment in matters of business, family, or other departments of ordinary life. Clear as it seems to me that certain *dicta* of my conscience are unreasonable, and though I know it may very well be wrong, yet I trust to its authority emphatically rather than to any rationalistic morality. This is the only rational course."[16]

Indeed, what comes from reasoning about practical affairs is set forth as "most contemptible:"

"The mental qualities we most admire in all human beings except our several selves are the maiden's delicacy, the mother's devotion, manly courage, and other inheritances that have come to us from the biped who did not yet speak; while the characters that are most contemptible take their origin in reasoning."[17]

Conversely to the motif dominating the above quotations, philosophy cannot succeed if "morals" interfere or are in any way mixed with it.

"It may very easily happen that the over-development of man's moral conception should interfere with his progress in philosophy. The protoplasm of philosophy has to be in a liquid state in order that the operations of metabolism may go on. Now morality is a hardening agent. It is astonishing how many abominable scoundrels there are among sincerely moral people. The difficulty is that morality chokes its own stream. Like any other field, more than any other, it needs improvement, advance. Moral ideas must be a rising tide, or with the ebb foulness will be cast up. But morality, doctrinaire conservatist that it is, destroys its own vitality by resisting change, and positively insisting: This is eternally right. That is eternally wrong. The tendency of philosophers has always been to make their assertions too absolute. Nothing stands more in the way of a comprehension of the universe and of the mind. But in morals this tendency acquires a triple strength. The practical side of ethics is its most obviously important side; and in practical matters, the first maxim is that everything may be exaggerated. That is the substance of Aristotle's *Ethics*."[18]

And again, he writes:

> "Having thus shown how much less vitally important rea-
> soning is than instinct, I next desire to point out how exceed-
> ingly desirable, not to say indispensable, it is for the success-
> ful march of discovery in philosophy and in science generally
> that practical utilities, whether low or high, should be *put
> out of sight* by the investigator. The point of view of utility
> is always a narrow point of view."[19]
> "I would not allow to sentiment or instinct any weight what-
> soever in theoretical matters, not the slightest. Right senti-
> ment does not demand any such weight; and right reason
> would emphatically repudiate the claim if it were made."[20]

The severely restricted application which Peirce gives to "science" and "reasoning"[21] stands somewhat in disharmony, if not in
contradiction, with the conception of action or habit and belief as
the outcome of inquiry in the discussion of doubt and belief. This
disharmony is to be explained, in part, in terms of the immediate
public which he was addressing with the remarks quoted above
and his attitude toward this public. They occurred in a lecture at
Harvard at the turn of the century. He took this occasion to revile
the academicians, apparently grasping at anything he could fling
in their faces. He was:

> "bound honestly to declare that I do not hold forth the
> slightest promise that I have any philosophical wares to offer
> you which will make you either better men or more success-
> ful men. It is particularly needful that I should say this owing
> to a singular hybrid character which you will detect in these
> lectures. I was asked in December to prepare a course of lec-
> tures upon my views of philosophy. I accordingly set to work
> to draw up in eight lectures an outline of one branch of phi-
> losophy, namely, Objective Logic. But just as I was finishing
> one lecture word came that you would expect to be addressed
> on topics of vital importance, and that it would be as well
> to make the lectures detached. I thereupon threw aside what
> I had written and began again to prepare the same number
> of homilies on intellectual ethics and economics. They were
> wretched things; and I was glad enough to learn, when three-
> quarters of my task was done, that it would be desirable that
> as much as possible should be said of certain philosophical
> questions, other subjects being put in the background. At that
> time, however, it was too late to write a course which should
> set before you what I should have greatly desired to submit

to your judgment. I could only patch up some fragments partly philosophical and partly practical. Thus, you will find me
part of the time offering you detached ideas upon topics of
vital importance, while part of the time I shall be presenting
philosophical considerations, in which you will be able to feel
an undercurrent toward that logic of things concerning which
I shall have an opportunity to interject scarce one overt
word."[22] "To sum it up, all sensible talk about vitally important topics must be commonplace, all reasoning about them
unsound, and all study of them narrow and sordid."[23]

His attitude toward this audience was such that in apparent contradiction to his repeated assertions that the practical and useful
have no place in science nor philosophy, he wishes to flay them:

"I repeat that I know nothing about the Harvard of today,
but one of the things which I hope to learn during my stay
in Cambridge is the answer to this question, whether the
Commonwealth of Massachusetts has set up this university to
the end that such young men as can come here may receive
a fine education and may thus be able to earn handsome incomes, and have a canvas-back and a bottle of Clos de Vou-
geot for dinner — whether this is what she is driving at —
or whether it is that, knowing that all America looks largely
to sons of Massachusetts for the solutions of the most urgent
problems of each generation, she hopes that in this place
something may be studied out which shall be of service in
the solutions of those problems. In short, I hope to find out
whether Harvard is an educational establishment or whether
it is an institution for learning what is not yet thoroughly
known, whether it is for the benefit of the individual students or whether it is for the good of the country and for
the speedier elevation of man into that rational animal of
[which] he is the embryonic form."[24]

Peirce might be speaking of himself and the universities in the
following:

"The first thing that the Will to Learn supposes is a dissatisfaction with one's present state of opinion. There lies the
secret of why it is that our American universities are so mis-
erably insignificant. What have they done for the advance of
civilization? What is the great idea or where is [the] single
great man who can truly be said to be the product of an
American university? The English universities, rotting with

sloth as they always have, have nevertheless in the past giv-
en birth to Locke and to Newton, and in our time to Cayley,
Sylvester, and Clifford. The German universities have been
the light of the whole world. The medieval University of Bol-
ogna gave Europe its system of law. The University of Paris
and that despised scholasticism took Abelard and made him
into Descartes. The reason was that they were institutions of
learning while ours are institutions for teaching. In order that
a man's whole heart may be in teaching he must be thoroughly imbued with the vital importance and absolute truth of
what he has to teach; while in order that he may have any
measure of success in learning he must be permeated with
a sense of the unsatisfactoriness of his present condition of
knowledge. The two attitudes are almost irreconcilable."[25]

On the negative side, such a view might well come from his own
position as a philosophical and academic outsider; on the positive side, from science. Or it may be said, on a psychological level
of imputation, that not being able but wanting to enter the academic ranks, his reaction against the universities was reflected in
the polarization of *learning* and *teaching,* and on a higher level of
abstraction as *laboratory* versus *seminary* minds. In the latter polarization, "science" is the positive acceptance, the strategy used
against the schools. Some of the strong *animus* against "the practical" is no doubt conditioned by this same life-situation. Certainly
we would not expect this man, with his high conception of his
own reasoning powers and his failure as an academician, to equate
"success" with intelligence. His life and his conception of himself
make comprehensible this statement: "What is the significance of
that? Is it not a plain sign that the faculty of reasoning is not of
the first importance to success in life?"[26]

It is precisely at this point that Peirce's humanistic "sentimentalism" stands opposed to a Protestant ethic. The following passage reveals this opposition in the most explicit form in which it
appears in Peirce's published writings:

"To pursue 'topics of vital importance' as the first and best
can lead only to one or other of two terminations — either
on the one hand what is called, I hope not justly, Americanism, the worship of business, the life in which the fertilizing
stream of genial sentiment dries up or shrinks to a rill of comic
tit-bits, or else on the other hand, to monasticism, sleepwalk-

ing in this world with no eye nor heart except for the other. Take for the lantern of your footsteps the cold light of reason and regard your business, your duty, as the highest thing, and you can only rest in one of those goals or the other. But suppose you embrace, on the contrary, a conservative sentimentalism, modestly rate your own reasoning powers at the very mediocre price they would fetch if put up at auction, and then what do you come to? Why, then, the very first command that is laid upon you, your quite highest business and duty, becomes, as everybody knows, to recognize a higher business than your business, *not* merely an avocation after the daily task of your vocation is performed, but a generalized conception of duty which completes your personality by melting it into the neighboring parts of the universal cosmos. If this sounds unintelligible, just take for comparison the first good mother of a family that meets your eye, and ask whether she is not a sentimentalist, whether you would wish her to be otherwise, and lastly whether you can find a better formula in which to outline the universal features of her portrait than that I have just given."[27]

This same polarity underlies, with other reasons also operating, his opposition to the schools wherein a Scottish realism legitimated this ethic of Protestantism. It operates in his opposition to the "creed of greed" and to "individualism," in his *tychism* and antipracticalism. Before examining these contexts, however, we must present and discuss some ambiguities in his statements and versions of the pragmatic maxim. Another context in which such concepts as *action, habit, practical* arise is in connection with "the pragmatic maxim" which is generally considered to be the *locus classicus* of Peirce's pragmatism. The first written statement of what later becomes the pragmatic maxim was set forth by Peirce within a review of Frazer's edition of the *Works of Berkeley* in the *North American Review* of 1871. In this context it is more or less a marginal note:

"A better rule [than Berkeley's] for avoiding the deceits of language is this: Do things fulfill the same function practically? Then let them be signified by the same word. Do they not? Then let them be distinguished. If I have learned a formula in gibberish which in any way jogs my memory so as to enable me in each single case to act as though I had a general idea, what possible utility is there in distinguishing between

such a gibberish and a formula and an idea? Why use the
term *a general idea* in such a sense as to separate things
which, for all experiential purposes, are the same?"[28]

We have noted that the explicit formulation of pragmatism arose
in the Metaphysical Club in the early seventies, but it was first
proposed explicitly in writing in the January issue, 1878, of the
Popular Science Monthly. The title was "How to Make our Ideas
Clear."[29] The maxim reads:

> "It appears, then, that the rule for attaining the third grade
> of clearness of apprehension is as follows: Consider what ef-
> fects, that might conceivably have practical bearings, we con-
> ceive the object of our conception to have. Then, our concep-
> tion of these effects is the whole of our conception of the ob-
> ject."[30]

In 1905, Peirce restated the "purpose" of pragmatism.

> "In order to ascertain the meaning of an intellectual con-
> ception one should consider what practical consequences
> might conceivably result by necessity from the truth of that
> conception; and the sum of these consequences will consti-
> tute the entire meaning of the conception. Pragmatism does
> not undertake to say in what the meanings of all signs consist,
> but merely to lay down a method of determining the mean-
> ings of intellectual concepts, that is, of those upon which rea-
> sonings may turn."[31]

The pragmatic maxim embodies a *technique of definition* and
a *theory of meaning*. Within each of these ways of approaching it
there are two conceptions of meaning. Let us examine the 1878
statement:

(a) The term "effects" in conjunction with "conceivable," on
the one hand, and in conjunction with "practical bearings" and
"sensible," on the other, sets the critical reader on two lines of interpretation: just what sort of "effects" are meant? In the context
in which the maxim is enunciated and in Peirce's explanation first
by extensions and examples of it these two directions stand out
clearly: Let us examine what we shall call *technological* meaning.
In giving the meaning of "wine" according to this axiom, it is stated
that: "We can mean nothing by wine but what has certain effects

direct or indirect, upon our senses. I only desire to point out how impossible it is that we should have an idea ... which relates to anything but conceived sensible effects of things. Our idea of anything *is* our idea of its sensible effects."[32]

Illustrating the maxim by the meaning of *"hard,"* he says: "let us ask what we mean by hard. Evidently, that it will not be scratched by many other substances. The whole conception of this quality, as of every other, lies in its conceived effects."[33] But why "conceived" before "effects" here? The meaning of hard, as of wine, is, in the example, in terms of its interactional relationships with, or its "effects" upon, certain other substances. Peirce himself says: "There is absolutely no difference between a hard thing and a soft thing so long as they are not brought to the test."[34] "Test" here can only mean whether or not the object in question is scratched by or scratches "many other objects."[35]

Again, in an application of the maxim: "To say that a body is heavy means simply that, in the absence of opposing force, it will fall. This (neglecting certain specifications of how it will fall, etc., which exist in the mind of the physicist who uses the word) is evidently the whole conception of weight."[36]

All the above quoted texts seem capable of generic translation as follows. In them "effects" mean two things: (1) the "effect" of one object upon another, *i.e.*, their interaction, or of a tool object on another; (2) the effect of their interaction upon the senses of the observer. This interpretation is reinforced by Peirce's notion of reality as something "whose characters are independent of what anybody may think them to be,"[37] something outside us, an "external permanency ... something upon which our thinking has no effect ... But which ... unceasingly tends to influence thought."[38]

This *technological* meaning of the maxim corresponds with the laboratorial analogy within which Peirce worked. It is quite similar to the positivist view enunciated by Chauncey Wright.

But there is another line of interpretation which centers around the terms "conceivable" and "conception" and occurs in the maxim five times.

(b) We shall call this *conceptual* meaning. In a footnote to the maxim, "written ten years earlier," Peirce comments on his use of the term "conceivable." There were, he tells us, two reasons for his usage: to show that he was speaking of meaning "in no other sense than that of *intellectual purpose* ... to avoid all danger of being understood as attempting to explain a concept by percepts, images, schemata, or by anything but concepts."[39]

It is at this point that we must shift our consideration of the maxim from a *technique of definition* over to *a theory of meaning*. More precisely, we must consider Peirce's theory of concepts, which, of course, is, in his view, part and parcel of pragmatism itself.

Peirce defines pragmatism as a "method of ascertaining the meaning of hard words and of abstract concepts."[40] This method is drawn from his occupational awareness of the procedures of experimental sciences. The method is to be applied only to those concepts "upon the structure of which arguments concerning objective fact may hinge." He accepts the qualities of feelings to be just what they seem of themselves in raw experiences. But intellectual concepts carry not merely the feeling, not merely the existential fact but also the "would-acts of habitual behavior," an implication concerning general behavior of the data. Thus, such concepts lean to a future in prediction of behavior relative to stated conditions, and the kernel of pragmatism is this: that "the *whole* meaning of an intellectual predicate is that certain kinds of events would happen, in the course of experience, under certain kinds of existential conditions."

The first moment for the argument for pragmatism is "the valency of concepts." Every concept has a valency: on the basis of a logical analysis of forms of expression we can classify indissoluble concepts and corresponding predicates or characters into three main groups: "Thus, the predicate is *blue* is univalent." This *"firstness"* "refers to positive internal characters of the subject in itself." The predicate *kills* is bivalent. Its correspondent is *"secondness,"* or brute actions of one subject or substance on another." In like manner, the predicate *gives* is *trivalent* (A gives B to C) and corresponds with *"thirdness"* — the mental or quasimental influence of one subject on another relative to a third. These statements are not logically verified by Peirce but are left for subsequent observation to affirm. His concept of thirdness as being in *nature,* also his *habits in nature,* connotes a sort of disjointed teleology. Evidently in some sense platonic universals are having earth shoveled upon them. However, these points are not germane to our present interest.

Dyadic action is exemplified by a brute force, A, producing an Event B. Event B may produce C, but no matter how long the chain is, the action is only dyadic. It concerns only a pair of objects. Now that triadic action in which we are here interested is exemplified in situations involving a sign. In the first passages of Peirce concerning the triadic action we note that a future enters the discussion. That is the fact that Event C, which is about to be produced by B, has an influence on the production of B by A. ("The action of B in producing C is a contingent future event at the time B is produced.")[41] The heart of the discussion is suggested by an inadequately explained example given by Peirce: an officer orders a platoon to "ground arms." This order is the *sign*. The existent *object*, which causes the sign, is represented by it, and is in a type of correspondence with it, as the will of the officer. Now the action of his will upon the sign is not simply dyadic. For there is produced a sort of counterpart to the *existent object* in the form of a "mental representation" and this Peirce calls the "immediate object of the sign." Now it is this object which "triadically produces the intended or proper effect of the sign strictly by another mental sign . . . for the proper significant outcome of a sign, I propose the name, the *interpretant* of the sign." This interpretant need not be a mental mode of being. The interpretant, says Peirce, is "all that is implicit in the sign itself apart from its context and circumstances of utterance."

The problem of what the meaning of a concept is for Peirce can only be solved "by the study of the interpretants of signs." The first two of the three general cases into which interpretants are divided need not detain us long: (1) the feeling produced by sign is the "emotional interpretant" and usually results in no more than a recognition; (2) when more effort is present, the effect is the "energetic interpretant." The effort may be muscular, but "is more usually an exertion upon the "inner world," a discussion of which in general terms yields nothing. The meaning of a *general* or intellectual concept can never be this, for it cannot be gained in a single act. It is of a general nature. The third effect is that of the *logical interpretant*. Now if this effect is a mental sign (or a

thought), this mental sign need itself have a logical interpretant
so that such an effect cannot be ultimate. The mental effect that
is the ultimate logical interpretant of a concept is a habit change.
A habit change is a "modification of a person's tendencies toward
action" resulting from previous experiences or from previous exertions of his will or acts, or from both. Events causative of habit
changes may not be acts of the given mind but experiences enforced upon it. These experiences, however, if they be effective, are
not involuntary. The event that causes a habit cannot be a muscular effort alone. Nothing like a concept can be acquired by muscular effort alone. Such muscular action must be accompanied by
inward efforts, imaginative acts, if they are to produce habits.

> "*Here is the point* — every man exercises more or less con-
> trol over himself by means of modifying his own habits; and
> the way in which he goes to work to bring this effect about in
> those cases in which circumstances will not permit him to
> practice reiterations of the desired kind of conduct in the
> outer world shows that he is virtually well-acquainted with
> the important principle that *reiterations in the inner world —
> fancied reiterations — if well-intensified by direct effort, pro-
> duce habits,* just as do reiteration in the outer world; *and
> these habits will have power to influence actual behaviour in
> the outer world;* especially, if each reiteration be accompa-
> nied by a peculiar strong effort that is usually likened to is-
> suing a command to one's future self."[42]

After establishing the notion that logical interpretants are of a future conditional mood and that to predicate a "concept of a real
or imaginary object is equivalent to declaring that a certain operation, corresponding to the concept, if performed upon that object, would be followed by a result of a definite general description," we are in a position to ask again: What is the nature of the
effect upon the interpreter of what Peirce called the logical interpretant? We do not explain its nature by stating that it is a concept
or a desire or an expectation.[43] The essence of the logical interpretant is *habit.* What sort of habit is it and how is it produced?
To this question there is no answer in this context.

> "In every case . . . the activity takes the form of experi-
> mentation in the inner world; and the conclusion . . . is that

under given conditions, the interpreter will have formed the habit of acting in a given way whenever he may desire a given kind of result. The real and living logical conclusion *is* that habit; the verbal formulation merely expresses it. I do not deny that a concept, proposition, or argument may be a logical interpretant. I only insist that it cannot be the final logical interpretant, for the reason that it is itself a sign of that very kind that has itself a logical interpretant . . . Action cannot be the logical interpretant because it lacks generality . . . The deliberately formed, self-analyzing . . . self-analyzing because formed by the aid of analysis of the exercises that nourished it — is the living definition, the veritable and final interpretant. Consequently . . . account of a concept [if it be good, will be] a description of the habit which that concept is calculated to produce . . . It does not seem that we can describe a habit in manner other than by stating the kind of action it gives rise to and by indicating the motive and the condition of that action."[44]

This conclusion is, on the one hand, a generalization from a description of laboratory technique; and, on the other hand, melts into a metaphysical view of nature, a nature which is conceived to have "habits." It is not here necessary to examine this. We are interested in the meaning of the concepts "action" or "habit" and "practical" as a component of pragmatic statements of intelligence, thinking, of mind.

An examination of the "activity" and "practicality" content of the pragmatic axiom and of the theory of meaning indicates that there are two themes for interpretation.

One we have called technological. It is to be understood as an element within Peirce's contextually restricted laboratorial vision. Here "action" and "practical" mean, in the first instance, the *physical* interaction, or inter-effects of objects, or the effects of them positivistically recorded upon the human senses.

The other theme is to be understood, in part, as a syntactical extension of the laboratorial perspective within a different focus and with two additional constructions added: "scholastic realism" and the phenomenological "categories." It may be called "conceptual" meaning. At one point in its statement it seems to contradict the technological mode. Pierce here did not believe that a "concept" could be explained "by percepts, images, schemata, or by anything but concepts." But then when *concepts* are examined, "action" on the human side comes into the context. But rather than "action," "habit" is the term stressed. It is preferred because of its *generality* as over against action. The particularity of meaning is not dyadic, it participates in triadicity. Concepts cannot be their own ultimate interpreters. The logical and ultimate interpretant is a change in "habit." These changes are not merely muscular but involve "imaginative action." It requires "experimentation in the inner world." Thus we see that Peirce's position on these matters is kept carefully within the laboratory perspective. All generalizations from this context are kept within it *by enlargement of the context itself.* For *nature* has "habits" and man is a "sign." Mind becomes *not* (as in Mead) "a forum", but an "experimental laboratory." And so does the universe.

This distinction between the technological and the conceptual theories of *meaning* is very important in the entire movement of pragmatism and of its criticism. In a sense, it is one of the major vehicles with which the structure of "scientific thought" is generalized. It appears in Dewey's "denotative," "objective meaning," and "social-action as rule" meaning. And, as we shall see, it is the frequent ambiguity in the use of this distinction, which is implicit in pragmatic literature, that forms the bases of Veblen's attack on Dewey from a *strictly* technologic viewpoint. In a sense it is around this abstruse problem that the extension of the analysis of "science" into a pragmatic view of social and practical action is pivoted. In order to interpret the ambiguities of the pragmatic theory of inquiry and of the maxim, especially in connection with terms like habit and practical which they incorporate, it is necessary, as in the case of the concept "doubt," to reconstruct the several contexts in which these terms are presented by Peirce. This is the only way to get a generic grasp of his position. These contexts include ethics to which he came from his doctrine of logic.

> "The fundamental problem of ethics is not . . . What is right, but, What am I prepared deliberately to accept as the statement of what I want to do, what am I to aim at, what am I after? To what is the force of my will to be directed? Now logic is a study of the means of attaining the end of thought. It cannot solve that problem until it clearly knows what that end is. Life can have but one end. It is Ethics which defines that end. It is, therefore, impossible to be thoroughly and rationally logical except upon an ethical basis."[45]

But just at this point we must carefully ascertain what Peirce means by "ethical." To begin with, "the science of ethics" is for him completely "useless."[46] It does not mean reasoning out the basis of morality."

> "Now what's the *use* of prying into the philosophical basis of morality? We all know what morality is: it is behaving as you were brought up to behave; that is, to think you ought to be punished for not behaving. But to believe in thinking as you have been brought up to think defines *conservatism*. It needs no reasoning to perceive that morality is conservatism. But conservatism again means, as you will surely agree, not trusting to one's reasoning powers. To be a moral man is to obey the traditional maxims of your community without hesitation or discussion. Hence, ethics, which is reasoning out an explanation of morality is — I will not say immoral, [for] that would be going too far — composed of the very substance of immorality."[47]

Notice how some consequences of his view of reasoning are insulated, namely, those which touch "conservative sentimentalism." This is true throughout Peirce's writings. Nevertheless, since reasoning involves approving and disapproving of certain lines of thought, Peirce must and does ask: "What is it that may properly be approved or disapproved?" And he answers:

> "We approve of means of bringing about purposes which we embrace, assuming it to be in our power to adopt or to reject those means. As to the purposes themselves, every man must decide for himself, though others may offer suggestions. A physiological operation takes place under nature's laws, and is beyond our control. It is, therefore, idle to approve or to disapprove of it. But in this essential respect reasoning is not a physiological operation; being a method, perfectly under our control, of attaining a definite end, that of ascertaining how future phenomena will appear. As to the purpose of a physiological operation, we know nothing, unless we may presume that it is designed to perform the function which it does in fact perform."[48]

Here the end of reasoning is to ascertain how future phenomena will appear. The laboratory style and analogy is again operating. This statement is underlined elsewhere. For instance:

"Facts are hard things which do not consist in my thinking so and so, but stand unmoved by whatever you or I or any man or generations of men may opine about them. It is those facts that I want to know, so that I may avoid disappointments and disasters. Since they are bound to press upon me at last, let me know them as soon as possible, and prepare for them. This is, in the last analysis, my whole motive in reasoning. Plainly, then, I wish to reason in such way that the facts shall not, and cannot, disappoint the promises of my reasoning. Whether such reasoning is agreeable to my intellectual impulses is a matter of no sort of consequence. I do reason not for the sake of my delight in reasoning, but solely to avoid disappointment and surprise. Consequently, I ought to plan out my reasoning so that I evidently shall avoid those surprises. That is the *rationale* of the English doctrine. It is as perfect as it is simple."[49]

But this is not all, although this is where Dewey is to stop and to elaborate. In Peirce's writing, this is only one termination of the quest for the end of inquiry and of action. Another approach is taken which, in Peirce's view, goes deeper.

The pragmatic maxim is a maxim of logic. But logic, for Peirce, entails ethical considerations, since both logic and ethics, as well as esthetics, are "normative sciences."

In 1903, Peirce addressed himself to the question of the "ideals of conduct." This topic intersects with the "purposes of inquiry" because of the normative character of both logic and ethics, because reasoning is purposive, deliberate, and because "right reasoning . . . consists in such reasoning as shall be conducive to our ultimate aim." Therefore, it must be asked: "What, then, is our ultimate aim?"[50] It seemed to Peirce that the "logician ought to recognize what our ultimate aim is." Going to the "moralists," he receives the answer, according to Peirce, that "we have a power of self-control, that no narrow or selfish aim can prove satisfactory." Then he goes to "the esthetician, whose business it is to say what is the state of things which is most admirable in itself . . ." He answers, "Beauty." "Yes," says Peirce, "such is the name that you give it, but what *is it?*" And Peirce offers an answer.

"Reason," says Peirce, "is something that never can have been completely embodied." Then he brings into the discussion the pragmatic maxim, using again the same example that he used in the 1878 paper!

> "I say of a stone that it is *hard*. That means that so long
> as the stone remains hard, every essay to scratch it by the
> moderate pressure of a knife will surely fail. To call the stone
> *hard* is to predict that no matter how often you try the experi-
> ment, it will fail every time. That innumerable series of con-
> ditional predictions is involved in the meaning of this lowly
> adjective. Whatever may have been done will not begin to
> exhaust its meaning. At the same time, the very being of the
> General, of Reason, is of such a mode that this being consists
> in the Reason's actual governing events . . . The essence of
> Reason is such that its being never can have been completely
> perfected. It always must be in a state of incipiency, of growth.
> It is like the character of a man which consists in the ideas
> that he will conceive and in the efforts that he will make, and
> which only develops as the occasions actually arise."[51]

In terms of this example of "reason," of "meaning," Peirce asserts
an answer to the question: "What is our ultimate aim?"

> "This development of Reason consists, you will observe, in
> embodiment, that is, in manifestation. The creation of the
> universe, which did not take place during a certain busy
> week, in the year 4004 B.C., but is going on today and never
> will be done, is this very development of Reason. I do not
> see how one can have a more satisfying ideal of the admir-
> able than the development of Reason so understood. The one
> thing whose admirableness is not due to an ulterior reason
> is Reason itself comprehended in all its fullness, so far as we
> can comprehend it. Under this conception, the ideal of con-
> duct will be to execute our little function in the operation of
> the creation by giving a hand toward rendering the world
> more reasonable whenever, as the slang is, it is 'up to us' to
> do so. In logic, it will be observed that knowledge is reason-
> ableness; and the ideal of reasoning will be to follow such
> methods as must develop knowledge the most speedily . . ."[52]

This passage is probably the best single keystone of Peirce's philosophy, if we must select one. In it, his epistemology, his logic,
are comprehended within his ethics. And his ethic is anchored
ontologically.

"Action" is not the end of inquiry nor of man for Peirce. It was
precisely this interpretation of the pragmatic doctrine that he imputed to James' 1896 statement and which he refuted. He wrote
in 1902 that this was a "stoical axiom which, to the present writer

at the age of sixty, does not recommend itself . . ."[53] In another, a more general context, he writes: " . . . those whose sentiments I share abhor certain doctrines of certain writers upon Ethics — say, for example, those who make action the ultimate end of man."[54] Peirce goes on to say that the "only ultimate good which the practical facts to which it [the pragmatic maxim] directs attention can subserve is to further the development of concrete reasonableness . . ."[55] Three years later he wrote that:

> " . . . the pragmaticist does not make the *summum bonum* to consist in action, but makes it to consist in that process of evolution whereby the existent comes more and more to embody those generals which were just now said to be *destined*, which is what we strive to express in calling them reasonable."[56]

It is in connection with this line of argument that we can see the basis of the difference between Peirce and James. Writing to James in 1897, Peirce stated the meaning of "practical results" in his work and mind:

> "That everything is to be tested by its practical results was the great text of my early papers . . . In my later papers, I have seen more thoroughly than I used to do that it is not mere action as brute exercise of strength that is the pu: pose of all, but, say, generalization, — such action as tends towards regularization, and the actualization of the thought which without action remains unthought."[57]

It is Peirce's wish to ontologize the conceptual aspect of meaning which underlies the ambiguity of his statements on the pragmatic maxim. He set forth the pragmatic axiom, etc., letting his thought dip into a radical theory of the relation of thought and practice. Others drew the radical conclusions which can be inferred from his ambiguities. But Peirce closed the possibility to himself. Admitting purpose into a statement of inquiry, he recaptured his glimpse at practice by making the aim Reason *itself* ontologized, read via *a theory of meaning* into the structure of a universe of growing events. This ontologizing of the purpose and action component of reason is but the other side of his anti-practicalism. He does this in three contexts:

(1) In the pragmatic maxim, a technique of definition which might involve action contains an ambiguity between "technological" and "conceptual" meaning. This maxim ramifies and finds its completion in the theory of meaning. In this theory the ultimate interpretant of meaning is not action but habits, and those are general and get ontologized in a sophisticated but nevertheless idealistic manner.

(2) In the more general statement of inquiry, a *purposive* element is introduced which raises the question of the end of inquiry. Tracing this out into the context which it ramifies, we find that it crosses ethics. Both the general statement of *inquiry* and the *ethics* are anti-practical. Both of them intersect in "concrete reasonableness," which again is an end of man but which is read into the structure of the universe in an idealistic manner.

(3) In the statement of *agapism*, or "evolutionary love," which will be discussed in the following chapter.

We shall see that it is precisely the sloughing off of such ontological anchors from ethics and inquiry that permits Dewey to give human reason an active practical role in remaking everyday events. That this Deweyan line of inference from Peirce, if indeed, one can state Dewey's assertions as inferred from Peirce, is only one, the current arguments over Peirce show. Not all those who "agree" with Peirce "agree" with Dewey. But *this* full blown consequence in one direction is the one which has become identified with pragmatic modes of thought. Peirce's contribution to it is only in connection with the abstracted sphere of "logic." He resuscitated and opened the door. He did it by a wholesale de-ontologization of education, psychology, and social interpretation.

1. *Ibid.*, VI, p. 216.
2. *Ibid.*, I, p. 55.
3. Later we shall see Veblen using this same strategy against Dewey.
4. *Ibid.*, I, pp. 618, 619. (1898)
5. *Ibid.*, I, p. 668 (1898)
6. *Ibid.*, p. 620.
7. *Ibid.*, I, p. 635.
8. *Ibid.*, I, p. 637.
9. *Ibid.*, p. 694.
10. *Ibid.*, I, p. 623.
11. *Ibid.*, (1898) I, p. 662

12. *Ibid.*, I, p. 626.
13. *Ibid.*, I, p. 630.
14. *Ibid.*, II, p. 177.
15. *Ibid.*, I, p. 672.
16. *Ibid.*, II, p. 177.
17. *Ibid.*, I, p. 627.
18. *Ibid.*, II, p. 198.
19. *Ibid.*, I, p. 640.
20. *Ibid.*, I, p. 634.
21. Reproduced above in quotation.
22. *Ibid.*, I, pp. 621, 622.
23. *Ibid.*, I, p. 677.
24. *Ibid.*, V, p. 585.
25. *Ibid.*, V, p. 583.
26. *Ibid.*, I, p. 657.
27. *Ibid.*, I, p. 673.
28. *Ibid.*, V, p.v.
29. It was the first printed in the *Revue Philosophique*, VII. Cf. V, p. 18.
30. *Ibid.*, V, p. 402.
31. *Ibid.*, V, p. 8.
32. *Ibid.*, V, p. 401.
33. *Ibid.*, V, p. 403.
34. *Ibid.*, V. 403.
35. *Ibid.*, Cf. V, p. 225.
36. *Ibid.*, V, p. 403.
37. *Ibid.*, V, p. 405.
38. *Ibid.*, V, p. 384.
39. *Ibid.*, V, p. 402, Footnote 3.
40. *Ibid.*, V, pp. 317-46.
41. *Ibid.*, V, p. 472.
42. *Ibid.*, V, p. 487.
43. *Ibid.*, V, p. 333.
44. *Ibid.*, V, p. 491.
45. *Ibid.*, II, p. 198.
46. *Ibid.*, I, p. 666.
47. *Ibid.*, I, p. 666.
48. *Ibid.*, II, p. 165.
49. *Ibid.*, II, p. 173.
50. *Ibid.*, I, p. 611.
51. *Ibid.*, I, p. 615.
52. *Ibid.*, I, p. 615.
53. *Ibid.*, V, p. 3.
54. *Ibid.*, p. 151.
55. *Ibid.*, V, p. 3.
56. *Ibid.*, V, p. 433.
57. Ralph Barton Perry, *The Thought and Character of William James*, Vol., II, p. 222.

9

The Realist Definition of Society

There are several uses to which Peirce puts the notion of "social" or of "public". In all these uses it is an accepted concept to him. It is an essential part of "scientific method," for it is upon the "social principle" that all the methods of escaping doubt break down, except science, Peircian model.[1]

The term "secular" or "public" is used by Peirce in the Kantian sense of *cosmicus,* as an important element in the building of philosophy. In the parallel which Kant draws between "a philosophical doctrine and a piece of architecture" the term "cosmic" is used, But Peirce thinks *"secular* or *public* would have approached nearer to the expression of his meaning."[2]

> "... a great building," writes Peirce, "such as alone can call out the depths of the architect's soul, is meant for the whole people, and is erected by the exertions of an army representative of the whole people. It is the message with which an age is charged, and which it delivers to posterity. Consequently, thought characteristic of an individual — the piquant, the nice, the clever — is too little to play any but the most subordinate *role* in architecture . . . This [is] equally true of philosophy . . ."[3]

Another usage makes logicality depend upon a social principle. Among the "lower animals" instincts suffice. But for man, the "discourse of reason is requisite because men are so intensely individualistic and original that the instincts, which are racial ideas, become smothered in them." A "logical faculty" has to take their place, and "the sole function of this logical deliberation is to grind off the arbitrary and individualistic character of thought."[4]

In the middle of a rather abstracted discussion of the "Doctrine of Chances," with which we need not be here concerned, Peirce asserts that:

> "logicality inexorably requires that our interests shall not be limited ... most not stop at our own fate. ... must embrace the whole community ... [which] must extend to all races of being with whom we can come into immediate or mediate intellectual relation ... He who would not sacrifice his own soul to save the whole world, is, it seems to me, illogical in all his inferences, collectively. Logic is rooted in the social principle."[5]

To be logical, men should not be selfish. Nor are men as selfish "as they are thought," wrote Peirce referring to the constant habit of "speaking of *our* possessions in the Pacific, and of *our* destiny as a republic."[6] Logicality ... "requires a conceived identification of one's interest with those of an unlimited community."[7]

> "It may seem strange that I should put forward three sentiments, namely, interest in an indefinite community, recognition of the possibility of this interest being made supreme, and hope in the unlimited continuance of intellectual activity, as indispensable requirements of logic. Yet, when we consider that logic depends on a mere struggle to escape doubt, which, as it terminates in action, must begin in emotion, and that, furthermore, the only cause of our planting ourselves on reason is that other methods of escaping doubt fail on account of the social impulse, why should we wonder to find social sentiment presupposed in reasoning? As for the other two sentiments which I find necessary, they are so only as supports and accessories of that. It interests me to notice that these three sentiments seem to be pretty much the same as that famous trio of Charity, Faith, and Hope, which, in the estimation of St. Paul, are the finest and greatest of spiritual gifts. Neither Old nor New Testament is a textbook of the logic of science, but the latter is certainly the highest existing authority in regard to the dispositions of heart which a man ought to have."[8]

Notice that in such contexts Peirce, a man without a public, does not mean by social, "any ... existing person or collection or persons." His point is that "no man can be logical whose supreme desire is the well-being of himself or of any other existing person or collections of persons."[9] His own lack of a public, along with the hope of one sometime, somewhere in the future, plus his own supreme confidence in his work may well be a complex of situations making for a stress upon the *future* when he speaks of social. Peirce's concept of *social* is frequently polarized against *gregariousness,* which he does not like at all. He wrote that:

> "One thing which helps to make me feel that we are developing a living science, and not a dead doctrine, is the healthy mental independence it fosters, as evidenced, for example, in the divergence between Professor Shröder's opinions and mine. There is no bovine nor ovine gregariousness here. But Professor Schröder and I have a common method which we shall ultimately succeed in applying to our differences, and we shall settle them to our common satisfaction; and when that method is pouring in upon us new and incontrovertible positively valuable results, it will be as nothing to either of us to confess that where he had not yet been able to apply that method he has fallen into error."[10]

It is true that man is "essentially a social animal:" but "to be social is one thing, to be gregarious is another. I decline to serve as bellwether. My book is meant for people who *want to find out;* and people who want philosophy ladled out to them can go elsewhere. There are philosophical soup shops at every corner, thank God!"[11]

> ". . . as regards the verdict of German *university professors,* which, excepting at epochs of transition, has always presented a tolerable approach to unanimity upon the greater part of fundamental questions, it has always been made up as nearly as possible in the same way that the verdict of a jury is made up . . . Psychical forces, such as the spirit of the age, early inculcations, the spirit of loyal discipline in the general body, and that power by virtue of which one man bears down another in a negotiation, together with such physical forces as those of hunger and cold, are the forces which are mainly operative in bringing these philosophers into line; and none of these forces have any direct relation to reason."[12]

Again, by social Peirce emphatically does not mean what Justice Holmes apparently came to mean by it: "The free trade in ideas

— that the best test of truth is its power ... to get accepted in the competition of the market."[13] Of *such* conceptions Peirce wrote:

> "Some persons fancy that bias and counter-bias are favorable to the extraction of truth — that hot and partisan debate is the way to investigate. This is the theory of our atrocious legal procedure. But Logic puts its heel upon this suggestion. It irrefragably demonstrates that knowledge can only be furthered by the real desire for it, and that the methods of obstinacy, of authority, and every mode of trying to reach a foregone conclusion, are absolutely of no value. These things are proved. The reader is at liberty to think so or not as long as the proof is not set forth, or as long as he refrains from examining it. Just so, he can preserve, if he likes, his freedom of opinion in regard to the propositions of geometry; only, in that case, if he takes a fancy to read Euclid, he will do well to skip whatever he finds with A, B, C. etc., for, if he reads attentively that disagreeable matter, the freedom of his opinion about geometry may unhappily be lost forever."[14]

Peirce uses the social, as we have seen, in refuting Descartes' Protestant epistemology, which is too "individualistic." Now the Scottish philosophy, widely prevalent at the time, was in this connection an embodiment of the Cartesianism which Peirce presented the better to demolish.

The positive core of Peirce's social and political views is his doctrine of "sentimentalism", of "love", which he squarely and at every point and on every occasion opposes to "the use of reason in vital affairs and to the philosophy of greed." It was precisely this philosophy of greed that Scottish philosophy legitimized.

The only explicit statement of Peirce's social and political orientation is his heavy reaction against "the greed philosophy." This corresponds with his attack upon "individualism" in epistemology, which, during the time of his early formative philosophizing, was a component of the official common sense philosophy which justified both orthodox Protestantism and the regnant individualism of a growing capitalism and the ideology of wealth.

Before displaying the article on "evolutionary love," let us present and interpret several typical passages from Peirce's writings which explicitly discuss social and political matters.[15] He did not have a worked-out view of his politics. His opinions come out in several of his reviews for *The Nation* and in infrequent illustrations in papers on logic. The essay on "the greed philosophy" was the only article directly concerned with such matters.

Reviewing a set of biographies of "worthies of all ages," he notes that the "pious frauds" who "infest" biography have their "origin in that deep faith in mendacity, as the only thing to be trusted to excite a desire to be good and to keep society straight . . . which was pervading and powerful in this country up to thirty years ago!"[16] He protests that Jesus was not considered by Comte among his great men. He thinks "a large majority of the world's powerful thinkers are either crushed by circumstances or forced into the pursuit of wealth, and so lost to the world's uses."[17] Then, later, he adds: "Perhaps among our sixty millions there may just now live such a mind; certainly, nobody is on the lookout for him."

Reviewing A. B. Buckley's *Moral Teaching of Science,* he writes:

> " . . . the prosecution of scientific research necessarily requires and strengthens certain moral qualities. . . and [they] must undeniably be so good so far as they go, although they may be one-sided . . . Many great scientists go to church, and are there very unlike what they are in their laboratories. At one time they are studying one aspect of truth, at another time another. To regard either aspect fairly and honestly, the other must for the time be excluded. If they conflict, the presumption, the faith of the scientific man, is that it is because the last word has not been said, on one side or on the other; at any rate, it must at least be hoped that there is an ultimate resting place which will be satisfactory from both points of view."[18]

In reviewing some essays by Huxley in *The Nation,* January 11, 1894, Peirce mentions that Huxley had discussed Individualism (*laissez-faire*) and Socialism. Huxley had said that "neither can be admitted as an absolute principle." Peirce thinks it "obvious" that:

> "evolutionism supplies a third political maxim, perhaps superior to either of the others . . . . Government must be considered as one of those adaptive characters of the genus homo which results from development . . . . Now, since the characters of races are generally highly adaptive, and are also un-

changeable, except under the operation of those almost cosmical changes which gradually bring about changes in races,
the evolutionary philosopher will not attempt to do more than
deflect very slightly the actions of these forces; whence. . . .a
maxim of political conduct . . . . aid only such changes as are
either inevitable or else both natural and beneficial; and so
act that those changes may be brought about with the least
total harm. If we were to write *integral* in place of *total,* it
would . . . . sound more mathematical; and sound is almost
everything in matters like this."[19]

In a review of A. R. Wallace's *Studies, Scientific and Social*
(1900), which is quite long, over three big columns of *The Nation,*[20] Peirce concludes abruptly: "We do not mean to discuss Mr.
Wallace's socialistic doctrines. We only note that he holds . . . . such
as the state owning all the land, issuing paper money, etc."

In 1893 Peirce wrote that the *New York Evening Post* was "incontestably one of the very best newspapers in the world, and especially remarkable for the sagacity of its judgments upon all questions of public policy." But he took it to task when it maintained
that "reasoning like that of the differential calculus ought to be
struck out of political economy because that science is of no service unless everybody, or the great majority of voters. individually
comprehend it and assent to its reasonings. No doubt the reasoning
was too sound for the convenience of those who maintain the consumer pays the whole duty."[21]

In the same year, Peirce gives a detailed statement of Ricardo's
reasoning on rent, saying that "the whole reasoning of political
economy proceeds in this fashion."[22] The whole affair was for Peirce
merely a proof that "there is no possible way of establishing the
true doctrines of political economy except by reasoning about *lim-
its* . . . that is, reasoning essentially the same as that of the differential calculus."[23] The entire affair seemed to Peirce merely an
incidental example of a logical matter. In his mind, it had little
direct connection with Ricardo, or the *Evening Post,* or with political economy.

The same cannot be said for Peirce's essay, written in 1893, entitled "Evolutionary Love." It is the only publication in which he
is *explicitly* concerned with political and social affairs. To be sure
it is enmeshed in a context of technical philosophy. For this reason, the article will be reviewed in some detail.

An idea "is a little person." A man makes his circle of ideas grow "not by dealing out cold justice" to them, but by "cherishing and tending them." That is "the way mind develops." Love is "the ardent impulse to fulfill another's highest impulse." Now only in so far as "the cosmos" is "mind" and so has life is it capable of further evolution. This view is entailed by synechism.[24]

The characterizing feature of the nineteenth century is that it is:

> "the economical century." For "political economy has more direct relations with all the branches of its activity than has any other science. Well, political economy has its formula of redemption, too. It is this: Intelligence in the service of greed ensures the justest prices, the fairest contracts, and the most enlightened conduct of all the dealings between men, and leads to the *summum bonum,* food in plenty and perfect comfort. Food for whom? Why, for the greedy master of intelligence.[25] The great attention paid to economical questions during our century has induced an exaggeration of the beneficial effects of greed and of the unfortunate results of sentiment, until there has resulted a philosophy which comes unwittingly to this, that greed is the great agent in the elevation of the human race . . ."[26]

And then Peirce imputes that this doctrine has been projected: that "greed" is considered the great agent "in the evolution of the universe."

Taking up Simon Newcomb's *Principles of Political Economy* which he considered a "typical and middling one," he thinks it is full of "trappings which serve to hide from author and reader alike the ugly nakedness of the greed-god."[27] He refutes two of the three motives to human action which Newcomb sets forth: First, "love of self" and, second, "of mankind at large," which Peirce translates as "merely public spirit, perhaps little more than a fidget about pushing ideas."[28] "Love of self" is the motive upon which the economists depend; they think that the "motives which animate men in the pursuit of wealth . . . are in the highest degree beneficent." Peirce believes that such statements show a disrespect for science. They only confound "scientific propositions, which have nothing to say concerning what is 'beneficent' ", with "brummagem[29] generalizations."[30]

Against the political economists, Peirce "confesses" to "sentimentalism," which is "a doctrine that great respect should be paid to the natural judgments of the sensible heart."[31] He denies that a miser is a beneficent power in a community," writes very strongly about "Wall Street sharps," comments negatively upon Mandeville's *Fable of the Bees,* and is indignant at the view that "all acts of charity and benevolence, private and public, go seriously to degrade the human race."[32] He then imputes Darwinism as an extension of:

> "politico-economical views of progress to the entire realm of animal and vegetable life ... Among animals, the mere mechanical individualism is vastly reenforced as a power making for good by the animal's ruthless greed. As Darwin puts it on his title-page, it is the struggle for existence; and he should have added for his motto: Every individual for himself, and the Devil take the hindmost! Jesus, in his sermon on the Mount, expressed a different opinion."[33]

And then he defines "the issue":

> "The gospel of Christ says that progress comes from every individual merging his individuality in sympathy with his neighbors. On the other side, the conviction of the nineteenth century is that progress takes place by virtue of every individual's striving for himself with all his might and trampling his neighbor under foot whenever he gets a chance to do so. This may accurately be called the Gospel of Greed."[34]

In the second portion of his paper, Peirce first set forth the conditions of the reception of Darwin's work. Intellectually, they included Quetelet's work, John Herapath, the English chemist, the memoirs of Clausius and Krönig Maxwell. Peirce regarded the theory, on the logical side, as an application of statistics, as "evolution by chance." But two other factors were important to the reception of Darwinism, which was not "at all near to being proved."[35]

> (1) " .... anaesthetics had been in use for thirteen years. Already, people's acquaintance with suffering had dropped off very much; and as a consequence, that unlovely hardness, by which our times are so contrasted with those that immediately preceded them, had already set in, and inclined people to relish a ruthless theory."[36]

(2) ". . . the extraordinarily favorable reception it met with was plainly owing, in large measure, to its ideas being those toward which the age was favorably disposed, especially, because of the encouragement it gave to the greed-philosophy."[37]

This Darwinian mode of "evolution by fortuitous variations," which Peirce calls "tychism," is only one of three modes. There is also "anaclastic evolution," "evolution by mechanical necessity," and "agapastic evolution" or "evolution by creative love." This last is Peirce's choice. It is not necessary here to trace the manner in which Peirce discusses these three ways of development of (1) the universe and (2) of mind, the history of thought. He does employ them in connection with *both* matters, for to him in this context "all matter is really mind."[38]

This adherence to *agapism* is, of course, correspondent with his position as a "conservative sentimentalist." If we understand "traditional dogmas" to embrace this "conservative sentimentalism" and "the doctrine of love," Peirce's political views verify one of his own self-depictions as "an individual whose unbiased study of scientific logic has led him to conclusions not discordant with traditional dogmas."[39]

Similar to John Fiske's interpretation of Christianity as having at its center a spirit of love and altruism, so for Peirce does creation itself proceed by love. The difference between those two on this point is that Peirce had been much more deeply bitten by the scientific ethos and had to work harder and go deeper than Fiske to reconcile the two. For Peirce had to include his religious sentiment within his statement of reasoning, and to do this he had to so interpret reasoning as first, to restrict its range of legitimate application, and second to insist upon an architectonic of thought. In almost every context of Peirce's thought that we have examined there is an extremely insistent exposition of *logical realism*. Such insistence invites our close attention, and we must weigh its significance. Belief in Realism covers large portions of Peirce's work, and it has both positive and negative linkages. If we would understand it, we must trace these linkages: surrogates of logical realism.

Historically, for Nominalism reality is a series of sensory things. Nominalism looks at these things in their individuality. It is the individual that is vital and real. The general is a collection of these individuals. Realism's world is a rich bloom of ideas. Concepts hang over things, and these individual things are their thin shadows. Several thinkers, including Chauncey Wright and C. S. Peirce, have imputed political motives and social correspondences to those who have held Nominalist doctrines. C. G. Jung has pointed out that the skepticism of the Cynic and Megaran critics of Plato's traditionalist respectability and realism was advanced under the sign of concepts as "mere" nomina. He imputes this doctrine to the peripheral position of these schools, to "proletarian" strata (presumably in the sense of the Ancient World), and to "envy."[40]

The Platonism of the *universalia ante rem* with its antagonism to *universalia post rem* was taken up by medieval thinkers, and between them stood Aristotle's *universalia in re*. Throughout the medieval period, positions were taken around these points with Abelard's "conceptualism" as an ameliorating doctrine. Edward Cronze has contended that in the modern era Nominalism has corresponded from the fourteenth century with a "capitalist economic system," and was held in the seventeen and eighteenth by precisely "those thinkers who most ardently and clearly fought for the realization of a bourgeois conception of society."[41]

Peirce made a similar imputation:

> "Notwithstanding a great outburst of nominalism in the fourteenth century which was connected with politics, the nominalists being generally opposed to the excessive powers of the pope and in favor of civil government, a connection that lent to the philosophical doctrine a factitious following, the Scotists, who were realists, were in most places the predominant party, and retained possession of the universities.[42]

And again: "as matters went Ockhamism derived its chief strength from its political alliance."[43]

Peirce himself defines the issue of Nominalism and Realism as follows: the question of Nominalism and Realism was "whether *laws* and general *types* are figments of the mind or are real."[44] He restates it later as "the question of which is the best, the laws or the fact under these."[45] The Nominalist looked upon "the general element in cognition to be merely a convenience for understanding this and that fact." The Realist, "roughly speaking, looked upon the general, not only as the end and aim of knowledge, but also as the most important element of being. Such was and is the question."[46]

His own allegiance is uniformly given to Realism: "I am myself a scholastic realist of a somewhat extreme stripe."[47] "Never, during the thirty years [of philosophical writing] have I failed in my allegiance to realistic opinions and to certain Scotistic ideals."[48]

Peirce probably could not have accepted any doctrine, and in particular have accepted it so emphatically as he did Realism, unless it was compatible with what he understood by science and scientific method. Not only is Realism held by him to be compatible with scientific method, it is said to "underlie" scientific method. Undoubtedly, it is significant that this view was strongly impressed upon Peirce precisely by F. E. Abbot's *Scientific Theism*,[49] in which Realism was used for the purpose of mediating science and religion and was polarized against "petty" individualism; it stood for the "social" as against the individual.

A contextual understanding of Peirce's realism indicates that the acceptance of Realism is linked positively to "scientific method," with "sociality," with a *social* and *agapistic* theory of reality; and that, negatively, it stands opposed to "individualism," both metaphysical individualism (nominalism *per se*) and, the individualism and "selfishness" of the political economists' "philosophy of greed." Realism's link to the idealized model of scientific method is clear from the character of Peirce's references to Abbot[50] in which he agrees "that a realism is implied in modern science.[51] It is also explicitly made by Peirce thus: "Ockhamistic thought [Nominalism] . . . is anti-scientific in essence."[52] It is sustained by "political alliance." But "had the conception of modern science been present to the minds of the disputants, the victory of the Scotists would have been more overwhelming than it was."[53] "Scientific method," then, involves the acceptance of Realism and the denial of Nominalism.

It is the Nominalists who are skeptical of God. The acceptance of Realism, for Peirce, entails a removal of such skepticism.

> ". . . as to God, open your eyes — and your heart, which is also a perceptive organ — and you see him . . . I cannot think a thing is black if there is no such thing to be seen as black. Neither can I think that a certain action is self-sacri-

ficing, if no such thing as self-sacrifice exists, although it may be very rare. It is the nominalists, and the nominalists alone, who indulge in such scepticism, which the scientific method utterly condemns."[54]

Thus Realism seems to link "scientific method" with "religious belief." In Abbot this is very clear. In Peirce the linkage is fainter and much more intricate. But the enthusiastic manner in which Peirce accepts Abbot's work confirms this interpretation of the function of Realism in the psychic economy of Peirce.

References to Realism and Nominalism are also made in ontological discussions in which a "social" theory of reality and an *agapistic* view were advanced. " ... general principles are really operative in nature. That is the doctrine of scholastic realism."[55] Again, he states the general question as "how far real facts are analogous to logical relations and why."[56] Discussion of:

> "socialistic, or as I prefer to term it, agapistic ontology [is a] natural path by which the nominalist may be led into the realistic ways of thought."[57] "My social theory of reality, namely, that the real is the idea in which the community ultimately settles down ... "[58] "The one intelligible theory of the universe is that of objective idealism, that matter is effete mind, inveterate habits becoming physical laws."[59]

Realism, as the denial of nominalism, seems to involve for Peirce the notion that "every general idea has the unified living feeling of a person."[60] "Individualistic nominalism" and "nominalistic metaphysics" involve the denial of "intellectual relations in the universe."[61]

Despite Realism's connection with "Idealism", and Peirce's acceptance of "Idealism," he rejects Hegel. He thinks Hegelianism is essentially nominalistic. In the same paragraph he remarks how the followers of Hegel think philosophy is a "practical science and the best of guides in the formation of what they take to be Religious Beliefs." The nominalistic *weltanschauung* is part of "the very flesh and blood of the average modern mind," and is not confined to "modern philosophers,"[62] *i.e.*, in its name, the political economists uphold individualism and greed.

In "Notation for a Logic of Relatives" Peirce asserts that:

"the absolute individual cannot only be realized in sense or thought, but cannot exist, properly speaking. For whatever lasts for any time, however short, is capable of logical division, because in that time it will undergo some change in its relations. But what does not exist for any time, however short, does not exist at all. All, therefore, that we perceive or think, or that exists, is general. So far there is truth in the doctrine of scholastic realism."[63]

Here Realism is opposed to logical individualism. That this opposition to individualism goes beyond the sphere of logic is clear when we read that to Peirce "... the most balsamic of all the sweets of sweet philosophy is the lesson that personal existence is an illusion and a practical joke."[64] Peirce's heavy insistence upon Realism and his equally strong opposition to individualism come out clearly in his polemic with the Scottish Common Sense Philosophy. In a dialogue with "common-sensism," under a section on "individualism," he calls his opponent "Doctor X," and a "general type". The pragmaticist he asserts; would be "nowhere less at home" than "in the ranks of individualists, whether metaphysical (and so denying scholastic Realism), or epistemological (and so denying innate ideas)."[65] It is the Nominalism and consequent individuality in "common-sensisms" that Peirce denies.

By a belief in "innate ideas" Peirce means the existence of *acritical* and *indubitable beliefs.* The acceptance of this is what makes Peirce call himself a "critical common-sensist." His leaning upon "the natural sentiments of the heart" in vital matters and his view of conservative sentiment as a guide to practice[66] are also linked to his calling himself a "critical common-sensist." Thus, positively he accepts *critical* Common-sensism for its leaving open the guidance in practical affairs of the sentiments of the heart. This is logically consistent and valuatively compatible with his anti-reason in practical affairs. But, negatively, he rejects Common-sensism for its individualistic emphasis. This emphasis is subordinated to its Nominalism. Peirce's relation with Common-sensism has these two aspects. It is especially in the latter that Nominalism is clearly a surrogate for individualism. This line of surrogateship extends further. Common-sensism was a doctrine held by certain academic schools, and they used reason in practical affairs in the support of the individualistic philosophy of greed.[67]

Thus, the second aspect of Peirce's relation to Common-sensism curves around to tie in with the first. By denying its Nominalism (as well as the Nominalism he saw in Hegelianism) Peirce fights against individualism, the use of reason in practical affairs, and the philosophy of greed. At the same time, by accepting Common-sensism's "acritical and indubitable beliefs," he negates the use of reason in practical affairs and lets in the "natural judgments of the human heart" as the guide for the "vital affairs" within the realm of conduct.

1. Cf. Above.
2. *Ibid.,* I, p. 176.
3. *Ibid.,* I, p. 176.
4. *Ibid.,* I, p. 178.
5. *Ibid.,* II, p. 654. This last statement is repeated in V, p. 354.
6. *Ibid.,* II, p. 654.
7. *Ibid.,* II, p. 654.
8. *Ibid.,* II, p. 655.
9. *Ibid.,* II, p. 661.
10. *Ibid.,* (1896) III, p. 455.
11. *Ibid.,* (1897) I, xi.
12. *Ibid.,* (1896) III, p. 425.
13. Quoted by John Dewey, *Character and Events,* p. 100.
14. *Ibid.,* II, p. 635.
15. A later volume in the *Collected Papers* is to contain Peirce's social views, but through the kindness of Professor Paul Weiss, I have learned that it will not contain anything beyond what is now available in scattered but extant materials.
16. *The Nation,* (1892) 54, p. 54.
17. *Ibid.,* p. 55.
18. *Ibid.,* (June 2, 1892) p. 417.
19. *Ibid.,* Vol. 58, p. 35.
20. *Ibid.,* (January 10, 1901) Vol. 72, pp. 36-37.
21. *Collected Papers,* IV, p. 114.
22. *Ibid.,* IV, p. 115.
23. *Ibid.,* IV, p. 114.
24. *Ibid.,* VI, p. 289.
25. *Ibid.,* VI, p. 290.
26. *Ibid.,* VI, p. 290.
27. *Ibid.,* VI, p. 291.
28. *Ibid.,* VI, p. 291.
29. "gaudy but worthless; sham. Slang . . . counterfeit . . . a nickname applied to supporters of the Exclusion Bill in 1860 . . ." *Webster International Dictionary,* 1930 ed., pp. 282-83.

30. *Ibid.*, VI, p. 291.
31. *Ibid.*, VI, p. 292.
32. *Ibid.*, VI, p. 292.
33. *Ibid.*, VI, p. 293.
34. *Ibid.*, VI, p. 294.
35. *Ibid.*, VI, p. 298.
36. *Ibid.*, VI, p. 297.
37. *Ibid.*, VI, p. 297.
38. *Ibid.*, VI, p. 301.
39. Quoted in *Ethics* (July, 1939).
40. *Psychological Types* (New York 1926) pp. 38-41, 47.
41. "Social Origins of Nominalism," *Marxist Quarterly*, Vol. I, no. 1, pp. 115-24. (January-February, 1937)
42. *Collected Works*, I, p. 17.
43. *Ibid.*, II, 167. *See* also IV, pp. 22-25.
44. *Ibid.*, I. 16.
45. *Ibid.*, VI, p. 1.
46. *Ibid.*, VI, p. 1.
47. *Ibid.*, V, p. 470.
48. *Ibid.*, VI, p. 605.
49. *See* above section on Abbot and his use of realism.
50. *See* above and IV, p. 1.
51. *Ibid.*, IV, p. 50.
52. *Ibid*, II. 166.
53. *Ibid*, II. 167
54. *Ibid.*, (1910) V, p. 493.
55. *Ibid.*, V, p. 101.
56. *Ibid.*, IV, p. 68.
57. *Ibid.*, VI, p. 610.
58. *Ibid.*, VI, p. 610.
59. *Ibid.*, VI, pp. 25, 605.
60. *Ibid.*, VI, p. 270. Cf. also IV, p. 551 where "signs" as the instances of thought are taken to live in the purely "physical world."
61. *Ibid.*, VI, p. 393.
62. *Ibid.*, V, p. 61.
63. *Ibid.*, (1870), III, p. 93f.
64. *Ibid.*, (1893), IV, p. 68.
65. *Ibid.*, V, p. 504.
66. *Ibid.*, V, p. 522f.
67. *Ibid.*, Cf. V, p. 522. "Just how and why Scottish philosophy lent itself so well to the exigencies of religion I cannot say; probably the causes were more extrinsic than intrinsic; but at all events there was firm alliance established between religion and the cause of "intuition." John Dewey, "From Absolutism to Experimentalism" *Contemporary American Philosophy*, Vol. II, p. 15.

10

Social Components of Peirce's Perspective

Positively, Peirce's pragmatism flows from his professional connections with and intellectual pieties for scientific practices. Such conceptions as "doubt" and "belief," and such theories as the central one of "meaning," are to be understood as elements in a perspective to be imputed to Peirce's dominant profession. But, negatively, the restrictions placed by Peirce upon this style and upon its elements cannot be so explained. Such restrictions involve the exclusion of action, practice, religion, and "rational" consideration of "vital affairs" from the statement and the legitimate domain of the scientific technique.

These exclusions can be only very partially explained in terms of technical, syntactical considerations such as the possible locus of doubt and the necessary conditions of an objectively fixed belief. Certainly, the intention to exclude "science" from "ethics" and from "practice" cannot be explained as due to factors logically necessary to the syntactical expansion of any system Peirce may have had in mind. However, the conceptions set forth above are more readily understood by bringing to the fore two broad social facts: first, Peirce's position as an academic outsider, and second, the social bearings of the academic ideology from which Peirce was excluded throughout his life.

It so happens that the perhaps dominant academic philosophy of the period consisted precisely of those elements against which Peirce revolted and from which he isolated his own positive statement. It is little else than historical polemic for Dewey, for example, to say that the pragmatists joined action and thought. What the pragmatists after Peirce did was to execute a rationale for a type of action different from the prevailing one. But that prevailing action had its rationale also. On more obvious levels the individualism of Cartesianism was incorporated in Scottish Common Sensism. For the Scottish school, as carried forth by the academics in the United States operated as a sanction, first of all, of Protestantism;[1] and, second, both directly and indirectly through its Protestantism, of the routines and necessities of the rising capitalist, middle class order of society. Not only does Peirce's position as an academic outsider place him in a position for such revolt, but it leads him to see any "practical" contact on the part of philosophy or science as just *this* kind of practice. Thus, he is against *any* contamination of theory by practice. Later Dewey, more hopeful and fully in the midst of educational institutions and the progressive political movement, is to be in a position to envision a Utopian mode of practice and to see a type of thought as intrinsically involved in it.

This same opposition to "the greed philosophy" and "selfishness" is displayed upon another level in the opposition to Nominalism, which is seen as sanctioning individualism. The polarities in Peirce may be systematized:

(1a) reasoning about "vital affairs" and practice	(1b) Anti-reasoning about practice and the rise of "sentimentalism" and "instinct" in everyday life.
(2a) "the philosophy of greed" and "selfishness"	(2b) "evolutionary love."[2]
(3a) the Calvinist determination	(3b) "tychism"[3]
(4a) "individualism"	(4b) "sociality."

In the dialogue between Common-sense Scottism, he calls the defender of this doctrine with its involvement of (5a), "nominalism," "Doctor X," thus, identifying it with the academies. Against this stands the strongly defended (5b), "realism."

Two further features of Peirce's generic perspective are set by these polarizations which rest upon his outsider position:

(1) The statement of scientific inquiry, the concepts of doubt, belief, and the theory of meaning — these positive features of his

thought which arose from preoccupation and personal identification with "science" and scientific technology are rigorously restricted in their very statement and in all their details so as to exclude or bypass all of the negative ends of the poles.

(2) So strong and urgent are the pieties for "science," a strength no doubt augmented by his academic isolation and opposition to prevailing academic legitimations, that all of the positive elements in the panel of polarizations, 1b - 5b, are so stated as to be indispensable features of scientific inquiry *itself*. Thus, to be *logical* one must *not* be selfish; thus "realism" is involved in science. The statement of scientific inquiry is also so constituted as to *exclude* 1a - 5a. Thus, science is successful because it in no way involves "practice." In a social and economic structure which was increasingly assimilating the results of the laboratory into industrial practices, this exclusion of "science" from "practice" was difficult.[4]

This organized Peirce's opposition to all "practice" and its affiliations with any intellectual life. For, again, focused negatively upon the academic legitimations of dominant social organizations and practices, Peirce could see only *this*, the existent, the mode of practice and thought relationship. He was too far out of line with the dominant practices of his context, too out of sympathy with their intellectual rationale to give assent, much less aid, to either. He stood socially isolated within a view of science which perceived it as pure and uncontaminated by these practices and the intellectualized justifications by the schools. To tie thought to practice, or: "to pursue topics of vital importance [can lead] only to one of two terminations. Either to what is called Americanism, the worship of business, the life in which the fertilizing stream of genial sentiment dries up or shrinks to a rill of comic tit-bits, or else to monasticism, sleepwalking in this world with no eye nor heart except for the other."[5]

This is what tying thought and life-practice together meant for C. S. Peirce. As against both these he places "a conservative sentimentalism" which leads to a "melting" of your personality into the neighboring parts of the universal cosmos.[6]

That the academies were linked in his mind to that which would obviate scientific thought is amply shown by his shrewd discussion of "the gentleman":

"In more ways than one an exaggerated regard for morality is unfavorable to scientific progress . . . Morality consists in the folklore of right conduct. A man is brought up to behave in certain ways. If he behaves otherwise, he is uncomfortable . . . If a man cuts loose from it, he will become the victim of his passions. It is not safe for him to reason about it, except in a purely speculative way. Hence, morality is essentially conservative . . . The gentleman is imbued with conservation . . . conservatism about morals leads . . . conservative about opinions of a speculative kind . . . This tendency is necessarily greatly exaggerated in a country where the 'gentleman,' or recognized exponent of good manners, is appointed . . . as the most learned man."[7]

That he is here again tilting at the universities is clear: "Wherever there is a large class of academic professors. . . .provided with good incomes and looked up to as gentlemen, scientific inquiry must languish."

The set of polarizations given serves as a frame of allegiances restricting the sphere of scientific application. But more than this occurs in the conceptual mechanics of Peirce's mind. *Purpose* has been let into the statement of scientific inquiry, and therefore, the end of inquiry is a question which the "logician" must answer. Peirce drastically restricts his answer in terms of the limiting pieties, but he anchors his answer in reality itself. It is to avoid forever the "use" of inquiry in the dominant "practices," against which he stands, that he insists so urgently upon Realism and upon the necessities for a metaphysical rationale of the place of inquiry.

In his statement on inquiry the "restrictions" which he would place upon it react to inform it. He has defined his inquiry in such a way as to include, *not* merely involve or entail, his humanistic or sentimental pieties. He does not want such pieties external to the statement of inquiry. He does not want it assumed that they are involved. That is why he reacts against the obviousness of the popular James.[8] He wants his statement of the operation of scientific mind intrinsically to include the humanistic pieties which he calls sentimental or love, and he wants this to be anchored in the stuff of reality.

His strategy is similar in connection with the "social" versus "individualism." He does not directly exhort for sociality. He makes his statement of thinking include it. He does not merely rant against "selfishness." He denies that anyone can be logical unless he is non-selfish, and the reaction against the philosophy of greed of the political economists is linked with the positive belief that true science is the study of "utterly useless things."[9]

We find in Peirce only the slightest of beginnings of that "pan-logism" which is to be much more prominent in James and especially so in Dewey. I mean by "pan-logism" the attempt to state a method so as to include some value. The *methods* set forth by pragmatists are by no means socially, politically, or morally neutral.[10]

The difficulty of solving what turns out to be moral questions with a scientific technique is stated more popularly as getting the heart and the head together in the face of intellectual publics which believe in "science." William James cannot get his heart within his head's scientific commands. For him *believing* creates what can then be seen as scientifically justified,[11] thus making the true the good. Peirce goes about the matter much more circumspectly. He tries to unite his heart, the humanistic pieties, and his head, scientific inquiry in several ways: (1) Methodologically, by making the conditions of successful scientific inquiry exclude selfishness. (2) Ontologically, by making the theory of meaning involve, and the purpose of inquiry result in, an increasing rationality of reality itself. Being outside and against the prevailing ends of "inquiry," he so states inquiry as to avoid these ends and he anchors other humanistic ends in the stuff of reality: concrete reasonableness. (3) If this does not do the job, there is available an *ontology* of love, which sees the determination and the evolution of the universe as involving sociality and evolutionary love.

The extremely high level of abstraction upon which the bulk of Peirce's work rests is a condition favorable to the thesis that his brand of pragmatism is, as he avows, very largely due to syntactical developments from Kant.[12] But this is not an all-sufficient explanation, for the *direction* of inferences and the fact of settling to work upon a highly abstracted level cannot be explained on the level of syntax, *i.e.*, in terms of "mere" philosophical tradition and "pure deduction" from it. The underside of the perspective can only be understood in terms of his scientific occupations and the character of such audiences as he had. It has been shown above that several of the various statements of his key concepts and central ideas can be fitted together only in terms of a model of inquiry which is to be imputed to scientific practice. To be sure, given his isolated and outsider position as a philosopher, his frequent academic frustrations, it is not at all unlikely that his affirmative extolling of "science" along with what he took to be its corollaries, performed a bolstering function for his psychic economy. What he wished to do was to include within it and its entailments certain pieties and to exclude others. These exclusions and inclusions have been presented in a series of key polarizations which "set" them. These polarizations, in turn, are to be understood in terms of Peirce's continual outsider positions in the academies. In opposing the legitimating ideologies which they carried, he came to oppose the practices they legitimated. These were the dominant practices of a rising capitalist society; individuality and calculating greed were seen at their center. Since this was both the practice and thought of his milieu, and since he was deeply against it, he came to be against all mingling of "practice" and "theory" and to join action and thought on an ontological level with the underlying sentiment which he called love.

The reader will note that in the case of Peirce we have proceeded on a social-psychological level, and very cautiously: we have been perhaps overly careful in presenting immanent changes and full intellectual contexts. This is quite deliberate and mindful of the confused intellectual condition of Peirce's posthumously published papers and the diverse ways they can be stylized. In such a situation, a sociological basis offers a chance to reconstruct the broad determinants of Peirce's work. It cannot be done on a purely logical level of analysis. The interpretation which has been offered may be mistaken in broad outline as well as in details, but it is only by some such procedure that "the Peirce question" will be solved.

In James, the situation is otherwise. In his case we may think in larger terms and to derive certain leads from the composition of the social structure within which he thought.

1. *See* quotation in last section from Dewey.

2. Cf. Abbot's "social gospel."

3. Cf. Chauncey Wright's letters above, concerning types of "law."

4. As witness, *e.g.*, the ambiguities in the statement of the pragmatic maxim and the theory of meaning, above. Here is displayed the difficulty of keeping the statement within the polarizations and their social bases.

5. *Collected Papers*, I, p. 673.

6. *Ibid.*, I, p. 673.

7. *Ibid.*, I, pp. 50, 51.

8. Although notice that Peirce agrees with sentiments and values for which James strove, writing that *The Varieties of Religious Experience* was "the best of his books" and that "His penetrating into the hearts of people was most wonderful." Perry, *op. cit.*, Vol. II, p. 286.

9. *Collected Papers*, I, p. 75.

10. This will be most fully discussed in connection with Dewey.

11. *See Will to Believe*, pp. 23-24. This is of course a sloganized simplification. *See* the full presentation below in the sections on James.

12. C. E. Witter, *Pragmatic Elements in Kant's Philosophy* (Chicago 1913) Ph.D. Thesis, University of Chicago, 1912.

PART III

11

William James

William James lived in the center of many of the literary and intellectual ways of his time. Openly sensitive to quite diverse influences, he felt the import of their particularity, and things around him quickly became part of his flights of mind. He wanted to live with them all in a Whitmanesque manner and mood. But he was also sensitive to the rules of study and was compelled to think according to such rules — or to make up and justify new ones. These simple facts of his life and mind, if fully understood, go quite a way in explaining his philosophy and especially the pragmatic style of reasoning as he employed it.

It is possible to classify James' training and influences in several ways. The most useful and revealing for our present purposes happens to be the most empirically precise. In the many contexts of his writings, in his biography, in training, reading, and in personal contacts, he was caught between both the temper and the letter of "religion" and "science." Much of his philosophy can be understood under the sign of this major polemic.

William James, the eldest son of Reverend Henry James was born in New York City in 1842, three years before the birth of Charles Peirce and seventeen years before John Dewey.[1] William James died in 1911. Thus, the curve of his life is thrust into the nineteenth century. His boyhood and many of his feelings are touched heavily by the pre-Civil War era, and reaches forward to receive transitional experiences into the twentieth century.

His activities and experiences within his father's circle, which included Emerson's group, links James with a religious sect, however radical it may have been. His training and close associations with such men as Louis Agassiz, and later Peirce and Chauncey Wright, link him with some of the most rigorous scientific workers of his time and place.

Beginning as a merchant and moving out into commerce and banking, William James' grandfather had accumulated $3,000,000. He had died in 1832, leaving a Calvinistically oriented will, arranging the inheritance so as "to discourage prodigality and vice, and furnish an incentive to economy and usefulness." Whoever led a "grossly immoral, idle, or dishonorable life" was to receive a small annuity, but his portion was to be withheld.[2] But such "piety and acquisition" as the elder James sought to transmit was not embodied by the father of William James. Gross Calvinism and money-grabbing came to a family end with William James' father and for two generations no one was "guilty of a stroke of 'business.' "[3] At one time the stern grandfather thought James' father would end in prison.[4] But Henry James completed college in 1830 and became a theological student at the Presbyterian's Princeton in 1835. He probably had little to do with his fellow students, for to him religion "was an original and personal revelation."[5] He had the "habit of spiritualizing secular things and secularizing sacred things."[6] By 1838 he was "permanently alienated from the church, being 'disaffected both by temper and culture to ritual or ceremonial views' of religion, and believing that the Church promoted self-righteousness by segregating a class as the alleged recipients of God's special favor."[7]

The ministerial career was closed to him and he became, in his own words to his children: ". . . a philosopher, say I am a seeker for truth, say I am a lover of my kind, say I'm an author of books if you like; or, best of all, just say I'm a Student."[8]

The father of William James had no occupational routines nor office. He lived in his home the more to mold the early lives of his children. He wrote and read and studied "in the plain sight of his household." Occasionally he gave public lectures, the attention to which usually disappointed him.

He had among the center of his intimates the Brook Farm group, had written for *The Harbinger*,[9] was a devoted Fourierist and Swedenborgian. With these conceptual devices he melted himself into the "social community;" fraternity was the spiritual bond of each to all within the good. In proper Swedenborgian manner the material and the mental, the natural and the spiritual, the beings of the terrestrial world and of the spiritual were seen as one. Man can know religious truths directly and from his knowing a purified Christianity is to arise.

The same year in which William James was born, 1842, his father met Ralph Waldo Emerson, with whom he later became intimate.[10] A little later he met Thoreau, and they enjoyed one another immensely. Letters and visits passed between Emerson, Thoreau, and Henry James, Sr., as well as others as the circle of friends grew. However, after mid-century the "intellectual and moral intimacy of James and Emerson . . . steadily declined."[11] In 1866, after voyages abroad, Henry James moved from Boston to Cambridge[12] at which place he lived for fifteen years. The father of William James died there in 1882, still "enthusiastic and eccentric."[13]

E. L. Godkin frequently visited at "the Jameses" from 1875-81. It was this editor of *The Nation* who gave William James his political education. In his father's house James was exposed during his boyhood to personal representatives of many of the leading "literary" movements and enterprises of the times. His father was a talker with a feeling for words and with immense energy and much temperament. But "as we pass from temperament and personal traits to ideas, the influence of Henry James upon his son William becomes attenuated."[14] Nevertheless, we find at least slender points of transmission. Henry James "*believed* in believing: 'For he is far likelier to prove a wise man in the long run, whose negations are fed by his beliefs, than he whose beliefs are starved upon his negations' . . . the deepest truth has to be lived and can never be adequately thought."[15] In one of his first letters to Emerson, Henry James had written: "Now my conviction at present is that my intelligence is the necessary digestive apparatus for my life . . . Is it not so in truth with you?"[16] And Thoreau wrote to Emerson apropos of James: "He wants an expression of your faith, or to be sure that it is faith, and confesses that his own treads fast upon the neck of his understanding."[17]

William James' own words concerning his inheritance runs as follows: "For me, the humor, the good spirits, the humanity, the faith in the divine, and the sense of his right to have a say about the deepest reasons of the universe, are what will stay by me."[18] In 1883 William James wrote that his "Father's cry was the single one that religion is real."[19] Writes Perry:

> "In short, the father testified most eloquently and memorably to the *reality of religion*, and the son was supremely interested in religion. How was he interested? Not merely as a collector and describer . . . No — he was interested in the *justification* of religion . . . He wanted to save a place for his own generalized religious feelings, but above all did he want to save a place for the more concrete beliefs of those more intensely pious fellow creatures with whom he sympathized."[20]

"Father would find in me today," wrote James in 1891, "a much more receptive listener — all *that* philosophy has got to be brought in."[21] And nine years before, James had written to his wife, a former teacher in a Boston private school, concerning the "value and meaning of religion in Father's sense, in the mental life and destiny of man. It is not the *one* thing needful, as he said. But is needful with the rest. My friends leave it altogether out."

With his father, William had begun his travels at the age of two years and five months — to Europe.[22] He was privately tutored, at first by a series of "educative ladies," later by males.[23] He went to school in New York, then to school and to be tutored in England and France. Then to Switzerland and Germany. In 1860-61 he painted in Newport with W. M. Hunt. Again a pivot: in 1861 he entered the Lawrence Scientific School at Harvard, thus beginning a twelve-year tentativeness as to precisely what kind of "sciencing" he would do. Three years later he entered Harvard Medical School, after which he went to Brazil with Agassiz on the Thayer Scientific Expedition.[24] The next few years he was studying and sojourning in Europe, mainly in Germany. In 1869 he attained the M.D. from Harvard. After entering the Scientific School in 1861 his contacts were with a literary or "humanistic" group, including Boston and Cambridge's "literary cosmopolitans"[25] and with such personages as Lowell, Godkin, Hawthorne, Longfellow, Mrs. Stowe, *et al.* The other circle in which he moved and learned was "scientific." It included Asa Gray, Peirce's father, and Jeffries Wyman.[26] His interest in science was eager but impatient.[27] In 1863 he shifted from chemistry to anatomy and physiology, studying with Wyman. He was given to "unsystematic excursions," as Eliot wrote.[28] Hours with Agassiz gave him a yearning to live in the "world's concrete fullness," the desire not to become an "abstractionist."[29] From the width of his social life, from his father's heavy influence and Transcendental and Swedenborgian friends, from the Humanist group of the 1860's, William James developed the taste for literary and artistic skill and the deep feeling and yearning for personalist religion that were to persist to inform his philosophy.

From his training with Wyman and Agassiz and perhaps more importantly from his contacts with Charles Peirce and also Chauncey Wright, William James developed a scientific conscience. "Conscience" is the right word. When he was on the Brazilian expedition he wrote: ". . . I don't enjoy it so much."[30] But with these contacts and trainings he learned that you should talk and think according to rules, logically. Chauncey Wright and Charles Peirce, along with Wyman, represented for James, positively, the model of scientific excellence of mind, while negatively, "it was . . . Chauncey Wright and Charles S. Peirce that during his formative period steeled James against the transcendentalism which dominated the Cambridge of his day."[31] That he was personally implicated with these men,[32] especially with Peirce, given James' character, made this influence more effective as a model for a style of thinking and its contents.

Wright was an intimate in the James household. William James considered him a "redoubtable champion whom to overthrow in argument was peculiarly sweet."[33] He was to James "a master in the field of scientific thought," accepted "as an authoritative exponent of scientific arms and methods," represented "the ideal scientific temper — restrained, impersonal, and scrupulous."[34] He confirmed the tendency to "experimental philosophy in James." But philosophically, Wright, with his "anti-religious teaching," was an adversary to James and to James' father.[35]

In 1861 James wrote: In last year's class "there is a son of Professor Peirce, whom I suspect to be a very 'smart' fellow with a great deal of character, pretty independent and violent though. . . ."[36] In some notebooks in 1862 James preserved some of the "sayings of Charles Peirce."[37] His "unintelligibilities fascinated" James, who was to carry Peirce's professional career as a "responsibility" on his conscience for forty years.[38] In 1869, after Peirce had become an intimate of the family, James thought he possessed "a capacity for arbitrariness that makes one distrust him."[39] But in the same letter he wrote that he "never saw a man go into things so intensely and thoroughly."[40] As a friend of James, like Chauncey Wright, Peirce represented "not only the scientific *approach* to philosophy, but the carrying over of the scientific method *into* philosophy — interested in method for its own sake."[41] James' view of Peirce was "one of puzzled and intermittent admiration."[42]

We have the authority of Royce that "James listened . . . to those aspects of Peirce's philosophy with an interest which . . . did not follow Peirce's thought into precisely those regions which Peirce himself most valued."[43] And we have James' confirmation of this: he "could not understand a word" in 1869, but he "enjoyed the sensation of listening" to him.[44]

In later years of their relationship, in 1909, to be precise, Peirce wrote: "I thought your *Will to Believe* was a very exaggerated utterance, such as injures a serious man very much, but to say what you now do is far more suicidal. I have lain awake several nights in succession in grief that you should be so careless of what you say. . ."[45]

And in 1907 he wrote a postscript that brings out a highly illuminating aspect of their relation, one that shows how personal feelings suffused into the "scientific" piety of Peirce and how he tried to impress it upon James:

> ". . . the day is past when I wanted *anything* for my personal satisfaction . . . I just have one lingering wish, for your sake and that oᶠ the countless minds that, directly or indirectly, you influence. It is that you, if you are not too old, would try to learn to think with more exactitude. If you had a fortnight to spare I believe I could do something for you, and through you to the world; but perhaps I do not sufficiently take account of other physical conditions than purely rational ones . . . "[46]

What "laboratory content" there was in James, and it is not much, judged by Peirce's rigorous standards, James did not build directly by his own impatient laboratory practices; he acquired it by sharing in a personal manner the ethos and judgments of Peirce's mind. Peirce was a scientific gadfly to James. He represented "science" and its implications, and he had to be included in James' statement of what the world was like and how men know it. But there were many other blends to which James was personally sensitive and they had also to be included in his sensitively pluralistic mind.

I do not wish to impute to James' pragmatism one single feature, but had I to do so, it might be his *popularization* and all that it implies. That is the role he seems to fill in pragmatism considered as an intellectual *movement*. This seems to offer a key to understanding his variations on the pragmatic style of reasoning enunciated by Peirce.

James was definitely concerned with getting his "message out."[47]

> "His popular hold is not at all due, I think, simply to his charm of style. His readers instinctively feel that here is a man who believes something and whose belief is not professional and acquired, but personal and native; a man who believes so deeply in the importance of what he sees and reports that he is not satisfied until his readers also see and have their tone of belief and life modified accordingly. He was, especially in his later writings, an apostle seeking the conversion of souls."[48]

During the early years of this century, when pragmatism was focusing in his mind, he was in a tension between the "desire to round out his system" and a "weakness for public lecturing."[49] And always the weakness won out.

> "I have found by experience," he wrote in 1899, "that what my hearers seem least to relish is analytical technicality, and what they most care for is concrete practical application. So I have gradually weeded out the former, and left the latter unreduced ... Some of my colleagues may possibly shake their heads at this; but in taking my cue from what has seemed to me to be the feeling of the audiences I believe that I am shaping my books so as to satisfy the more genuine public need."[50]

It was in orientation to popular publics that he gave such "system" as exists in his thinking. He wanted to speak "the exact word that opens the center [of pragmatic vision] to everyone, mediating between it and the old categories and prejudices."[51] In 1905, he gave a successful lecture series at Wellesley, Chicago, and Glenmore, and read a paper at Rome.

James wrote President Eliot apropos of Chicago: "I felt them pulling on my line like one fish."[52] He lectured evangelically during this period. He wanted to "communicate his latest ideas to others without waiting to give them technical or systematic form" and he was eager to get "social reactions to his thoughts."[53]

In these lectures he was developing *Pragmatism*. In 1906 he gave *Pragmatism* as the Lowell lectures. Then he repeated it at Columbia University in 1907 before an audience of over 1,000, and he felt that the lectures composed "the high tide of my existence, so far as *energizing* and being 'recognized' were concerned."[54] Ralph B. Perry soberly asserts that the lectures and volumes "were dictated by personal and by strategic reasons rather than by the logic of his philosophical development."[55]

Of his pronunciamento of pragmatism in 1898 in California James had written that his topic was selected with a desire to speak of "something sufficiently popular and practical from his existing arsenal of ideas."[56] He begins the lectures with: "An occasion like the present would seem to call for an absolutely untechnical discourse... something connected with life... a message with a practical outcome."[57]

It should not be thought, however, that James' pragmatism is merely enlarged from some technical system. His books, with the clear exception of *The Principles of Psychology*, are largely composed of essays spoken before audiences. Many of them were given before "clubs formed by the students [who invite] some maturer scholar to address them, the occasion often being made a public one."[58]

The publics for which James formulated many of his essays include the following representative list: The Philosophical Clubs of Yale, Brown, and Harvard,[59] Harvard Young Men's Christian Association,[60] Unitarian Ministers' Institute at Princeton,[61] Harvard Divinity Students,[62] and Harvard National History Society.[63]

I have already indicated the semi-popular lecture basis of *Pragmatism*. *A Pluralistic Universe* was given as the Hibbert Lectures at Manchester College and were "meant to be public;" James assumed that "some topic of general interest" was "required."[64]

The publics for whom he wrote were heterogeneous and popular. He was sensitive to their pull and to their worries. In his psychic economy pragmatism was "a mediating way of thinking"[65] which allowed him to live with the many ideas and moods he had personally experienced and to address the wider troubles of popular publics. "His profession brought him . . . a continuous stream of appreciative audiences."[66] But such an assertion must be carefully handled in terms of what kind of audiences they were. Apparently they were not technical academic philosophers. Dewey has remembered "the contrast between the attitude of professional colleagues toward him while he was doing his work and his established position to-day. Well do I remember the tone of thirty years ago. A great psychologist, certainly, but as to his ill-advised forays into philosophy, there was an amused and pitying condescension."[67]

In Peirce, an academic outsider, pragmatism was the slogan for a sect. It was a concentrated reaction against several intellectual fronts and when it became somewhat diffuse, Peirce called it "Pragmaticism," a name that was so ugly that no one would kidnap it. The "sect" attracted another member. For James, "the beloved Harvard professor," living in the midst of many social and intellectual currents, pragmatism was to serve as a "church" for everyone, and not even a collection was to be taken up. He inclines toward naming individuals pragmatic if he can find something in their work that seems to suggest the *mood* or "temperament" that he has in mind.[68]

Peirce's precision, his many fine distinctions painstakingly made to limit misinterpretation is overrun by James, who cannot anywhere in his writing about pragmatism be termed overly precise.

James is gossiping with these audiences about what the philosophers are up to: he is letting them in on things. He lets them, as he said, "taste the milk in the cocoanut." He asks them what are *their* problems, what they want and before you know it, these are *his* problems. It is what *he* wants. The breadth and consequent popular level of his effective audience reaffirms his problems and the milk in the cocoanut is the real thing for him, too.[69] In terms of such a view we can understand the two major foci of James:

(1) the moral questions as they bear upon personal life.

(2) the reconciliation of science and religion, which is placed for solution within the moral questions.

In short, James focuses directly and at all times upon what the isolated Peirce had termed "vital matters," and about which Peirce said, "all reasoning is sterile." He could not compartmentalize as did Peirce (although Peirce also "mediated" an unintelligible level). He wanted to mediate directly, for a popular public. This drive toward mediation is a third chief element in his thinking. After we briefly chronicle James' connection with "pragmatism," we shall turn to this.

Although "James' philosophical thinking, both his ethics and his metaphysics, abounds in ideas which are irrelevant, if not alien, to his pragmatism,"[70] it is nevertheless true that in *Pragmatism*, published in 1907, his philosophical thinking comes to a kind of focus. *Pragmatism* embraces ideas which he had been working out for thirty years; it is a name, an emphasis, a formulation and a banner under which he himself felt that he and his total apparatus of ideas could be most "effective."[71] And he was right: it is fit, as we shall see, for the competition of ideas.

Briefly, the chronological sequence of James' pronunciamentos of pragmatism and his use of a pragmatic method are as follows: In *Pragmatism* he writes that pragmatism "lay entirely unnoticed by anyone for twenty years, until I, in an address before Professor Howison's union at the University of California [1898], brought it forward again and made a special application of it to religion."[72] Maurice Baum has definitely disproved the historical truth of this assertion, and Perry has gathered the earlier uses of a pragmatic method made by James himself.[73]

In 1878 James had quite clearly stated the method as he interpreted it:

> "Every question has sense and imposes itself unmistakably, when it produces a clear practical alternative, in such wise that according as one answers the question one way or the other, one is obliged to adopt one or the other of two lines of conduct."[74]

In "Reflex Action and Theism" (1881) we find:

> "Indeed, it may be said that if two apparently different definitions of the reality before us should have identical consequences those two definitions would be really identical definitions, made delusively to appear different merely by the different verbiage in which they are expressed."

There is footnoted here a reference to Peirce's 1878 article. Indeed, according to Baum, James was using the criterion of meaning in November, 1877,[75] before Peirce's article, but, of course, James had heard it from Peirce in the Metaphysical Club, and Peirce's paper had been written in the early seventies.[76]

In 1885 James again used pragmatism in "On the Function Cognition."[77] James looked upon the essay as "the *fons et origo* of all *my* pragmatism." This essay is pivotal for the history of pragmatism and James in that it identifies "truth" with "the success of ideas." And with this notion of truth it links the theoretical with the practical situation.[78] It should also be noted that components of James' pragmatism were entailed and even somewhat explicit in previous writings. For instance, *The Principles of Psychology* contains a general teleological view of mind[79] as does the 1879 "The Sentiment of Rationality." Roots of "pragmatism" have been found by Perry in James' notes that go back to 1873,[80] and traces are found in marginal annotations, written perhaps in 1876, on James' copy of Locke's *Essay*.

There are several ways in which one may locate a doctrine. In the case of James' pragmatism, the most apt way is to ask what pragmatism does for James, that is, in what condition is he and what does pragmatism do for him in this condition, what function does it fill in the economy of his mind. In the case of James the answer is not buried very deep between his explicit lines. Pragmatism is his seat upon a number of fences. He begins *Pragmatism* with the distinction between tender minded and tough minded.[81] But we must remember quickly that James draws the distinction only to get its parts immediately together again. "Pragmatism [is] their mediator."[82] In a very real sense this dichotomy is a slightly elaborated surrogate for what he understands "religion" and "science" to embody, and again, on another level, for "rationalism" and "empiricism." The "cash-value" of pragmatism for James is its openness, its mediative character. It is a set of bridges which enables him to link the many experiential values which he holds, and which his two dominant types of circles held. He is a very sentient being exposed to all the blends of thought and feeling of his day, and he wants to get them together. The pragmatic perspective enables him to catch all of them from one angle. And this angle functions for James as mediation. This mediatory element is so pervasive in his thinking, flowering principally in his pragmatic utterances, that it may be made a typical component of his "pragmatic" style of thought. He says to his popular audiences, and it becomes *his* problem, too:

> "You want a system that will combine both things, the scientific loyalty to facts and willingness to take account of them, the spirit of adaptation and accommodation, in short, but also the old confidence in human values and resultant spontaneity, whether of the religious or of the romantic type. And this is then your dilemma; you find the two parts of your *quaesitum* hopelessly separated. You find empiricism with inhumanism and irreligion; or else you find a rationalistic philosophy that indeed may call itself religious, but that keeps out of all definite touch with concrete facts and joys and sorrows."[83]

Every time in his text his "own solution begins to appear,"[84] mediation is advanced and typically it is a *mediation* of the horns of some popular or widespread dilemma. In his time this means the doubting about and longing for religion amidst the esteem given to science. He is trying to define what his doctrine will do for the public's worry. He says, "I offer the oddly-named thing pragmatism as a philosophy that can satisfy both kinds of demand."[85] This drive towards mediation enters into James' concepts through the concept of "truth." There is more than one notion of truth in James, but there is a dimension or way of taking the term that is common to all of them. "New truth is a go-between, a smoother-over of transitions." Here is "the old opinion" and there is the "new fact" and he does not want to be jolted about such matters. In short, he does not want scientific discoveries to upset our religious opinions. "We hold a theory true just in proportion to its success in solving this 'problem of maxima and minima.' "[86]

> "Purely objective truth, truth in whose establishment the function of giving human satisfaction in marrying previous parts of experience with newer parts played no role whatever, is nowhere to be found. The reasons why we call things true is the reason why they *are* true, for 'to be true' *means* only to perform this marriage-function."[87]

"You see already," writes James, "how democratic" pragmatism is. She is "various and flexible," "rich and endless" in "resources" and very "friendly" in her conclusions.[88] "Let us hope," he bursts out in discussing various truths, "that they shall find a *modus vivendi!*"[89]

Specific metaphysical issues are handled by this style. Where, for example, does pragmatism stand on the question "the one and the many"? It "must equally adjure absolute monism and absolute pluralism. The world is One just so far as its parts hang together by any definite connection. It is many just so far as any definite connection fails to obtain."[90]

Just as we would expect, "pending the final empirical ascertainment of just what the balance . . . may be" pragmatism "must obviously range herself upon the pluralistic side."[91] And "this leaves us with the common sense world, in which we find things partly joined and partly disjoined."[92] Shall we then accept and develop some philosophy of "common sense" and call it "true"?

By no means. For there is also "philosophy" and there is "science." And these vary from one another. They compete; we mediate between them. "Common sense is *better* for one sphere of life," says James, "science for another, philosophic criticism for a third; but whether either be *truer* absolutely, Heaven only knows."[93] Here we see that the common ground on which James stands and in terms of which he accepts or rejects various ways of looking at the world and living in it is moral. The conflict of "common sense" (to James, an Aristotelian affair, but de-eternalized) and "philosophy" and "science", obliges one to overhaul the very idea of truth.[94] And then there occurs what seems the most penetrating and revealing passage in his *Pragmatism:*

> "Ought not the existence of the various types of thinking which we have reviewed, each so splendid for certain purposes, yet all conflicting still, and neither one of them able to support a claim of absolute veracity, to awaken a presumption favorable to the pragmatistic view that all our theories are *instrumental*, are mental modes of *adaptation* to reality, rather than revelations or gnostic answers to some divinely instituted world-enigma? I expressed this view as clearly as I could in the second of these lectures. Certainly the restlessness of the actual theoretic situation, the value for some purposes of each thought level, and the inability of either to expel the others decisively, suggest this pragmatistic view . . ."[95]

There are several lines of thought in James which come to a focus in this passage.

We see here the drive for mediation with pragmatism as its spearhead. It arises from his desire to retain and intellectually to exploit various phases of his poly-sided experience, to reconcile the divisive intellectual tensions which have developed between these diverse modes of experience and thought. Pragmatism is his answer to this generic dilemma. Back of this technical solution on a technical sphere lies his sensitivity to many publics and thinkers. It is precisely at the hands of an individual, who, by virtue of his cosmopolitan mobility and sensitivity to a variety of *persons*, representing different views, focusing on diverse perspectives, that the category of "instrumentality" or "purpose" could arise and be given central status.

But on what level does this instrumental mediation occur? Into what terms may diversities be reduced? That the mediation does *not*, cannot occur for him upon a sheerly syntactical level, that it is not a "logical" reconciliation, is a mark of his penetration. Such, for James, would have been only "mere talk." The mediation of diversities is performed by means of relativizing each mode of experience and style of thinking to its purpose, and to the scope of its legitimate area of application. This leads to the pragmatistic view of all doctrines: they are instrumental. But this is a highly *formal* solution.

So we must ask again: into precisely what one sphere does James translate the contending positions that make up the "restlessness of the actual theoretic situation"? Here we enter into his "practicalism," his commercial vocabulary, his "expediency." The meaning of these in terms of James' pragmatism will be shown.

---

1. Factual account of James' life is taken from the biographies in the *Dictionary of American Biography* and *National Cyclopedia of American Biography*. Especially from R. B. Perry, *The Thought and Character of William James as Revealed in his Unpublished Correspondence and Notes, Together with his Published Writings* (Boston 1935). This is the definitive biography of James.

2. C. H. Gratten, *The Three Jameses*, quoted by R. B. Perry, *op. cit.*, Vol. I, p. 6.

3. Henry James, *A Small Boy and Others* (New York 1918) pp. 18-19. Quoted in Perry, *op. cit.*, Vol. I, p. 6.

4. Perry, *Ibid.*, p. 9.

5. Perry, *Ibid.*, p. 11.

6. Quoted by Perry, *Ibid.*, p. 11.

7. Perry, *Ibid.*, pp. 11-12.

8. Henry James, *Notes of a Son and Brother* (New York 1914). Quoted in Perry, *Ibid.*, p. 12.

9. *See* Perry, *Ibid.*, Chapter II.

10. Perry, *Ibid.*, p. 39.

11. Perry, *Ibid.*, p. 101.

12. Perry, *Ibid.*, p. 104.

13. Perry, *Ibid.*, p. 104.

14. Perry, *Ibid.*, p. 146.

15. Perry, *Ibid.*, p. 146.

16. Perry, *Ibid.*, p. 42.

17. Perry, *Ibid.*, p. 49.

18. Henry James, Ed. *Letters of William James,* Vol. 1, p. 221, quoted by Perry, *Ibid.*, p. 152.

19. Perry, *Ibid.*, p. 165.

20. Perry, *Ibid.*, pp 165-66.

21. Perry, *Ibid.*, p. 166.

22. Perry, *Ibid.*, p. 178.

23. Perry, *Ibid.*, p. 180.

24. Perry, *Ibid.*, Chapter XII.

25. Perry, *Ibid.*, pp. 204-5

26. Perry, *Ibid.*, p. 205.

27. Perry, *Ibid.*, p. 206.

28. Perry, *Ibid.*, p. 207.

29. Perry, *Ibid.*, p. 209.

30. Perry, *Ibid.*, p. 221.

31. Morris Cohen, *Journal of Philosophy, Psychology and Scientific Method*, (December 21, 1916), p. 728.

32. In connection with the "tragic futility" which the Jameses saw in Wright's life, as well as for William James' piety for Wright, *see* his notice in *The Nation*, 1875, pp. 21, 194.

33. Perry, *op. cit.*, Vol. I, p. 520.

34. *Ibid.*, p. 521.

35. *Ibid.*, p. 522.

36. *Ibid.*, p. 211.

37. *Ibid.*, p. 215.

38. *Ibid.*, p. 289.

39. *Ibid.*, p. 296.

40. *Ibid.*, p. 321.

41. *Ibid.*, p. 229.

42. *Ibid.*, p. 534.

43. *Journal of Philosophy, Psychology, and Scientific Method* (December 21, 1916), p. 703.

44. *Ibid.*, p. 703.

45. Perry, *op. cit.*, Vol. II, p. 438.

46. *Ibid.*, p. 437.

47. R. B. Perry, *op. cit.*, Vol. II, p. 44.

48. John Dewey, *Character and Events* (New York 1929) Vol. I, pp. 110-11.

49. R. B. Perry, *op. cit.*, Vol. II, p. 441.

50. William James, *Talks to Teachers on Psychology* (New York 1899), Preface, p. ix.

51. Letter to Dewey, August, 1908. *Letters of William James*, Vol. II, p. 310.

52. R. B. Perry, *op. cit.*, Vol. II, p. 441.

53. *Ibid.*, p. 441.

54. *Ibid.*, p. 447.

55. *Ibid.*, p. 447.

56. Letter quoted by Perry, *ibid.*, p. 449.

57. "Philosophical Conceptions and Practical Results," reprinted in *Collected Essays and Reviews*, (New York, 1920), p. 406.

58. *Will to Believe*, (N.Y. 1923), p. vii.

59. *Ibid.*, pp. 1, 63, and 184.

60. *Ibid.*, p. 32.

61. *Ibid.*, p. 111.

62. *Ibid.*, p. 145.

63. *Ibid.*, p. 216.

64. *A Pluralistic Universe*, (N.Y. 1909), p. 3.

65. *Pragmatism*, (N.Y. 1907), p. 40.

66. R. B. Perry, *op. cit.*, Vol. I, p. 446.

67. John Dewey, *Characters and Events*, Vol. I, p. 118. From *The New Republic*, June 30, 1926, published under the title, "William James in Nineteen Twenty-Six."

68. *E.g.*: "It gives me pleasure to welcome Professor Carveth Read into the Pragmatistic church . . ." *The Meaning of Truth*, (N.J. 1909), p. xvii. One cannot imagine Peirce writing such a sentence.

69. Later, I shall reconstruct the probable religious compositions of James' publics.

70. R. B. Perry, *op. cit.*, Vol. II, p. 515.

71. *Ibid.*, Vol. II, p. 452.

72. *Pragmatism*, p. 47.

73. Gwendolyne Tubb, in an M.A. thesis at the University of Texas has briefly reviewed this matter, "The Relationship between William James and Charles Saunders Peirce," 1938. Drawn in the main from the data printed in Perry, this thesis is a useful compilation of letter-contacts of James and Peirce.

74. Perry, *op. cit.*, Vol. II, p. 449.

76. *See* above section.

77. Reprinted as the first essay in *The Meaning of Truth.*

78. R. B. Perry, *op. cit.*, Vol. II, pp. 450-51.

79. It is from the psychology of James, and not from the "pragmatism" that Dewey derives his philosophy.

80. R. B. Perry, *op. cit.*, Vol. II, p. 448.

81. Chapter I.
82. *Ibid.*, p. 273.
83. *Pragmatism*, p. 20.
84. *Ibid.*, pp. 32-33.
85. *Ibid.*, p. 33.
86. *Ibid.*, p. 61.
87. *Ibid.*, p. 64.
88. *Ibid.*, p. 81.
89. *Ibid.*, p. 109.
90. *Ibid.*, p. 156.
91. *Ibid.*, p. 161.
92. *Ibid.*, p. 161.
93. *Ibid.*, p. 190.
94. *Ibid.*, p. 192.
95. *Ibid.*, pp. 193-94.

12

Three Vocabularies of Social Practice

"Are not all our theories just remedies and places of escape... " asked James; and he answered, "Yes: Temperaments ... do determine men in their philosophies, and always will."[1] What more is James' pragmatism than the view that all philosophy is "really" in the realm of "philosophies of life"? Philosophies arise out of different personal temperaments, and the correct method of philosophizing, which is pragmatism, would state all philosophic questions in terms of their function in the economy, mood, and promises of somebody's life. "On pragmatic principles we cannot reject any hypothesis if consequences useful to life flow from it."[2] If we observe the pragmatic style of thought at work through James' pages, this is what we shall find it constantly accomplishing. It is into this sphere of life-ways with its set of questions and answers that he typically translates "philosophical questions." And it seems that this is the meaning of Dewey's trenchant assertion that "William James did not need to write a separate treatise on ethics, because in its larger sense he was everywhere and always the moralist."[3]

There are three facets involved here: one is "individualism" or, even better, "personalism." Another is "practicalism," but practicalism may mean several things. To James it means that which has to do with a way-of-life. Thirdly, his applications are *prospective*: philosophy asks the question "what does the world promise?"[4]

The common element in these applications of the pragmatic style of reasoning is the pointing of all doctrines and philosophical issues at their meanings for ways-of-life. There are two steps in this translation: first, James puts "metaphysical issue" into the domain of the "practical," then, almost inevitably, he moves it again by

232

translating "practical" as "moral," as "personal," as mood and manner of a life-way. On the more strictly metaphysical level, "practical" means "the individual,"[5] but more usually it means for James a significant life-style. After citing "the principle of Peirce" he elaborates its meaning.[6] First, he mentions several laboratory difficulties that had been cleared up by its tacit usage. Then *without any transitional explanatory* link he continues:

> "The whole function of philosophy ought to be to find out what definite difference it will make to you and me, at definite instants of our life, if this world-formula or that world-formula be the true one."[7] "In every genuine metaphysical debate some practical issue, however conjectural and remote, is involved."[8]

In the issue between "theism" and "materialism" each points "to wholly different outlooks of experience." And then:

> "Materialism means simply the denial that the moral order is eternal, and the cutting off of ultimate hopes; spiritualism means the affirmation of an eternal moral order and the letting loose of hope. Surely here is an issue genuine enough, for any one who feels it; and, as long as men are men, it will yield matter for a serious philosophical debate."[9]

In this case the real issue for James is whether men shall be optimistic or pessimistic: "The issues of fact at stake in the debate are of course vaguely enough conceived by us at present. But spiritualistic faith in all its forms deals with a world of *promise,* while materialism's sun sets in a sea of disappointment."[10] Then he introduced, and in the very same paragraph in fact, the personal element of the issue: "I myself believe that the evidence for God lies primarily in inner personal experiences."[11]

There are other ways in which this personal-way-of-life interpretation of philosophical doctrines is used by James. In his evaluative statements, one might say his "appreciation," of other philosophers, for example, Herbert Spencer. James states his work in terms of how people "feel" about it:[12] It is a "dry school master temperament, a hurdygurdy monotony his system is wooden." But we feel his heart to be in the right place philosophically for the reason that "his books try to mold themselves upon the particular shape of this particular world's carcass."[13]

This personalist and moral style informs James' treatment of the most formidably abstract concepts. Take the category of "cause." He discusses its origin and meaning in "common sense." The search for "causal influences seems to have started in the question: "Who, or what, is to blame?" "From this center the search for causal influences has spread."[14] Or, again he discusses "rationality and of reasons for things":

> "Talk of logic and necessity and categories and the absolute and the contents of the whole philosophical machine-shop as you will," he writes, "the only *real* reason I can think of why anything should ever come is that *some one wishes it to be here*. It is *demanded*, — demanded, it may be, to give relief to no matter how small a fraction of the world's mass. This is *living reason*, and compared with it material causes and logical necessities are spectral things."[15]

This perspective is also used by James in his evaluations of philosophies. For example, rationalism: it spells out an "airy optimism." In criticizing it he takes several pages for quotations from an anarchist's account of a suicide of a clerk, and a Cleveland worker's killing of his children and himself. He confronts the "thorough fed thinkers," Royce and Bradley, with this account of tragic lives. Then he says:

> "What these people experience *is* Reality. It gives us an absolute phase of the universe. It is the personal experience of those best qualified in our circle of knowledge to *have* experience, to tell us *what is*. Now what does *thinking* about the experience of these persons come to, compared to directly and personally feeling it as they feel it?"[16]

Thus again, the level, the sphere of reality, the domain of the practical are made up of personal lives. It is directly within various life-ways that James would point philosophical doctrines. Experience gives one Reality. It is in terms of *their* meaning and consequences for *them* that he would grasp a doctrine's meaning *and* evaluate it.

> ". . . the philosophy of evolution (as distinguished from our special information about particular cases of change) is a metaphysical creed, and nothing else. It is a mood of contemplation,

> an emotional attitude, rather than a system of thought, — a
> mood which is old as the world, and which no refutation of any
> one incarnation of it (such as the Spencerian philosophy) will
> dispel; the mood of fatalistic pantheism, with its intuition of the
> One and All, which was, and is, and ever shall be, and from
> whose womb each single thing proceeds."[17]

It should be emphasized that the "practical," in terms of which
James' pragmatism would trace meaning and define issues, means
to James the "personal" and "moral." In this connection four other
elements may be considered.

(a) The category of *"action"* in James.

(b) His elevating *"common sense"* to the status of the philosophically considered.

(c) The place of *"expediency"* in James' work.

(d) His use of a *"commercial vocabulary."*

Crudely put, "pragmatism" denotes a doctrine and mood which
looks to "the practical," to "consequences," which elevates the "actions" which come out of given ideas to the status of a philosophical category. But we must ask: What do such terms mean for different thinkers? We have seen how Peirce brings this "action" into
those of his discussions which are "controlled" by laboratory context. Peirce only flirts with downright motor behavior. For "action"
becomes "habit." This term, with the aid of realism and a theory
of meaning, ends up, on the one hand, in an objective idealism in
which "nature" possesses "habits." On the other hand, there is
"mental action," an "inner" form. "Action" for Peirce ultimately
ends up cosmologically.

Now in James, no matter in what context, action is very broadly
conceived, but philosophically it is kept within the human locus,
within a human individual. We would not expect a man as intensely centered upon religious issues as James and who believed that
"inner personal experience" supplies "evidence for God" to develop a philosophy involving "action" in which the concept signified
only motor behavior. At the turn of the century he said:

> "You must remember that, when I talk of action here, I mean
> action in the widest sense. I mean speech, I mean writing, I
> mean yeses and nos, and tendencies 'from' things and tenden-
> cies 'toward' things, and emotional determinations; and I mean
> them in the future as well as in the immediate present."[18]

Writing against critics, who had charged him with "practicality" he wrote:

> "Ideas do work ... in the physical world ... of course, immediately or remotely; but they work infinitely inside of the mental world also. Not crediting us with this rudimentary insight, our critics treat our view as offering itself exclusively to engineers, doctors, financiers, and men of action generally, who need some sort of a rough and ready *Weltanschauung*, but have no time or wit to study genuine philosophy. — It is usually described as ... a sort of bobtailed scheme of thought, excellently fitted for the man on the street, who naturally hates theory and wants cash returns immediately."[19]

This passage occurs among James' list of "misunderstandings" of pragmatism.

James "admits" that pragmatism is a wide window opening out upon human action. But, it is a window in a "prior epistemological edifice" and critics (here the polemic is against technical philosophical groups) should not ignore this "primary step." The "relation to action" is to James "our secondary achievement."[20] Such is his own evaluation in which he displays the character of "action" to be "internal," not merely "motor." Such is the meaning for James. I am not here concerned with the role of other interpretations of "action" in the diffusion and acceptance of his work.

On the "common sense level of matters of fact"[21] the "truth of a state of mind means this function of *a leading that is worth while*"[22] In general, pragmatism finds truth to be "bound up with the way in which one movement in our experience may lead us toward other movements which it will be worth while to have been led to."[23]

> "When a moment in our experience, of any kind whatever, inspires us with a thought that is true, that means that sooner or later we dip by that thought's guidance into the particulars of experience again and make advantageous connexion with them."[24]

To have "true thoughts means everywhere the possession of invaluable instruments of action." We have a "duty to gain truth" not as "a blank command from the blue" nor as "a stunt self-imposed by our intellect" but rather for "practical reasons." The "world of realities" can be "useful" or "harmful."[25] And "ideas that tell us which of them to expect count as true ideas in all this primary sphere of verification." That is why the pursuit of such ideas "is a primary human duty."[26] To possess truth is not a terminal point, but is "only a preliminary means towards other vital satisfactions." He then chooses the example of an individual "lost in the woods."[27]

> "You can say of [truth] then either that 'it is useful because it is true' or that 'it is true because it is useful.' Both these phrases mean exactly the same thing, namely that here is an idea that gets fulfilled and can be verified. True is the name for whatever idea starts the verification-process, useful is the name for its completed function in experience."[28]

Here we have truth defined as it functions in "common sense." What is important and significant here is the tacit assumption that whatever it leads to will be *worthwhile*. Nowhere in James is this assumption examined. It operates everywhere as a tacit persuasion. It is only under this assumption that he elevates common sense to a high place. In doing so we get a slight plebian contempt for "minds debauched by learning" who suspect common sense.[29]

Correspondingly we get the view that common sense has developed just like *science and philosophy*. Notice here, again, the individualistic interpretation.

> "But when we look back, and speculate as to how the common-sense categories may have achieved their wonderful supremacy, no reason appears why it may not have been by a process just like that by which the conceptions due to Democritus, Berkeley, or Darwin, achieved their similar triumphs in more recent times. In other words, they may have been successfully *discovered* by prehistoric geniuses whose names the night of antiquity has covered up; they may have been verified by the immediate facts of experience which they first fitted; and then from fact to fact and from man to man they may have *spread*, until all language rested on them and we are now incapable of thinking naturally in any other terms."[30]

It is not, however, to be supposed that James blots out science and philosophy by common sense. As we have seen, he relativizes each to its purpose and sphere, again mediating between them. Indeed, common sense has "exceedingly dubious limits ... [of] application today,"[31] which is to say (a) that he would not accept the peripatetic eternalization of common sense categories[32] and (b) he would allow "a merely curious or speculative way of thinking." As we have seen, if common sense means personal life-ways, as "practical" does, then all abstractions and philosophical issues must find their import and test there. Such leanings toward the "plebianization" of criteria rest upon James' intense desire to make philosophy mean something to his audiences, and upon the academic situation and his desire to break down the isolation of the philosophical classroom from "life." He cites one of his students, "a graduate of some Western college,"[33] as remarking upon this separation of classroom and street, and then he attempts to bring the street perspective into the classroom, or to find a *modus vivendi* for it.

In this connection, the fact of the elective system and the consequent competitive curricula, both facts resting upon and reflecting the social character and occupational chances of students, should be recalled. Also, the heterogeneity of the philosophical staff at Harvard during William James' maturer period.[34] In his position, it was necessary for him to take account in some manner of his many-faceted set of colleagues.

We might possibly interpret James' practicalism, not in the moral terms of personal life-ways, but as an "expediency"; and, moreover, as a commercial expediency. I do not think that this would be correct. I believe that those passages upon which such interpretations would presumably rest can be better fitted into other explanatory schemes and imputations. But, nevertheless, we should examine such passages in full context.

The most extreme instance of the connection of "expediency" with "truth" and with the more customary moral value, "rightness," is the following:

> " 'The true,' to put it very briefly, is only the expedient in the way of thinking, just as 'the right' is only the expedient in the way of our behaving. Expedient in almost any fashion; and expedient in the long run and on the whole of course; for what meets expediently all the experience in sight won't necessarily meet all farther experiences equally satisfactorily."[35]

In the same context we see how this "expedient" is always assumed to be "good" by James: "As summary names for the concrete reasons why thinking in true ways is overwhelmingly expedient and good for mortal men, it is all right to talk of claims on reality."[36]

What we witness is the instrumentalizing of the truth of ideas and then always the tacit assumption that this instrumental value (which ideally might be expected to be morally neutral) is always put to good, to beneficent use. Both "truth" and the "expedient" are moralized, made *ipso facto* "good." This underlying assumption crops up explicitly, occasionally, as when he writes:

> "In the case of truth, untrue beliefs work as perniciously in the long run as true beliefs work beneficially. Talking abstractly, the quality 'true' may thus be said to grow absolutely precious and the quality 'untrue' absolutely damnable: the one may be called good, the other bad, unconditionally. We ought to think the true, we ought to shun the false, imperatively."[37]

Again, the true, the expedient, as well as the good, get their final statement as guides for life-ways. "The essential thing," writes James, "is the process of being guided."[38]

In the lectures on pragmatism, James employs a commercial vocabulary rather extensively. Typical examples are:

> "Our account of truth is an account of truths in the plural, of processes of leading, realized *in rebus*, and having only this quality in common, that they *pay* . . . Truth for us is simply a collective name for verification-processes, just as health, wealth, strength, etc., are names for other processes connected with life, and also pursued because it pays to pursue them."[39]
>
> ". . . if you follow the pragmatic method . . . You must bring out of each word its practical cash-value, set it at work within the stream of your experience. It appears less as a solution, then, than as a program for more work, and more particularly as an indication of the ways in which existing realities may be changed."[40]
>
> ". . . any idea that will carry us prosperously from any one part of our experience to any other part, linking things satisfactorily, working securely, simplifying, saving labor; is true for just so much, true in so far, true *instrumentally*." [41]
>
> "It pays for our ideas to be validated. Our obligation to seek truth is part of our general obligation to do what pays. The payments true ideas bring are the sole why of our duty to follow them. Identical whys exist in the case of wealth and

health. Truth makes no other kind of claim and imposes no
other kind of ought than health and wealth do."[42]

I do not believe that such passages are open to the charge of
making philosophy a servant of "commercial success." Rather I
should evoke in explanation for such vocabulary choices James'
sensitivity to his popular audiences and his intense desire to communicate with them. For the same reason he speaks of "a live op-
tion" in a context quite removed from those above upon which the
imputation has rested.[43] Such usages are to be explained in terms
of audience-sensitivity and not as evidence that "pragmatism" is a
philosophical articulation for middle class entrepreneurs. By "success" and "prosperously" he does not mean business success. All the
context in which the terms are used show this clearly. For example,
negatively, he speaks of the "Bitch goddess, success" and, positively, he writes:

> "Give us a matter that promises success, that is bound by its
> laws to lead our world ever nearer to perfection, and any ra-
> tional man will worship that matter as readily as Mr. Spencer
> worships his own so-called unknowable power."[44]

Nevertheless, quite apart from what James meant, and the function of such commercial terms in his psychic economy, and connections with audiences, it is undoubtedly true that such usages served
as vehicles of diffusion for his utterances. They were implements
of the success of his ideas in competition. This commercial vocabulary is for James another way of referring to individual, to personal
life-ways, as the ultimate meaning and test for ideas.

> "Pragmatism, on the other hand, asks its usual question.
> 'Grant an idea or belief to be true,' it says, 'what concrete dif-
> ference will its being true make in any one's actual life? How
> will the truth be realized? What experiences will be different
> from those which would obtain if the belief were false? What,
> in short, is the truth's cash-value in experiential terms?' "[45]

It is the "value" of ideas "for concrete life" in which he is inter-
ested.[46] And this life is the life of an individual. It is his moral life.
"An idea is 'true' so long as to believe it is profitable *to our lives*."[47]
In continuing these passages he comes as near (as he ever

does) to the brink of admitting that the instrumentally true may not be automatically good:

> "That it is *good,* for as much as it profits, you will gladly admit. If what we do by its aid is good, you will allow the idea itself to be good in so far forth, for we are the better for possessing it."[48]
>
> "The whole function of philosophy ought to be to find out what definite difference it will make to you and me, at definite instants of our life, if this world-formula or that world formula be the true one."[49]

I want to underline that the practical, the expedient, the true, the good, the satisfactory — that all these equivalent terms are laid in an *individual* life-way. Pragmatism solves the key "problem of maxima and minima:"

> "on the whole more satisfactorily than [before]. That means more satisfactorily to ourselves, and individuals will emphasize their points of satisfaction differently."[50]
>
> And again, "A new opinion counts as 'true' just in proportion as it gratifies the individual's desire to assimilate the novel in his experience to his beliefs in stock. It must both lean on old truth and grasp new fact; and its success (as I said a moment ago) in doing this, is a matter for the individual's appreciation."[51]

It is through the *individual,* that James' *pluralism* intersects his *pragmatism.* The character of this individual, or more precisely, of his lifeway in which the pluralist metaphysics and the pragmatist epistemology covering, results in "a militant moralism and a theistic faith."[52]

In the latter half of the nineteenth century and early twentieth, men, confronted with "science"[53] and living in an industrial order in which science was deeply implicated, had three paths open to them.[54] They could cling tenaciously to the old religion. They could attempt any one of several compromises, the subtlety and ingenuity of which would vary with verbal skill, or they could become merely indifferent to the whole intention, program, and paraphernalia of religion. It is this third path that was a major factor in the secularization of the schools. In general, native American industrial workers have trodden it. The "decline" of religion is more properly stated as the decline of a feeling of its relevance. It is only the middle class professionals and intellectuals who have really been worried into taking the second path of harmonization. It has been these who have wanted a *scientific* justification of religion or a rapprochement of religion and "science." It was particularly among them that William James recruited his audiences and publics.

The liberal religious development of the latter nineteenth century rejected old doctrines but also set forth new items and new grounds for their acceptance. In general, wide areas of the intellectual, professional, and urban middle classes rejected Calvinism, at least in its older statement. And God changed his face. To anticipate our conclusion, James represents the "modern liberal." His type may be contrasted with Weber's classic account of the Puritan. Generally, the attitude toward the present order, on the part of the Puritan was defiance and an attempt to remake it. The modern liberal accepts it with some discrimination and makes an effort to "better" it. The representative groups of Puritanism were members of the old middle-class; whereas the public of modern religious liberalism is made up of professionals and intellectuals situated, in the main, among the larger middle groupings of the cities. The source of religious authority for Puritanism is the individually interpreted Bible, whereas the modern liberal will admit "tested experience." In James "experience" becomes the keystone to religious reality. The end of life for both the Puritan and the religious liberal of James' variety is individual salvation. Modern liberalism has replaced the trinitarian Puritan God with a Unitarian and then with a nebulous notion. In James, He is, from the older standpoint, extremely nebulous. The heaven and hell of the Puritan becomes for the liberal a general belief in immortality. Both reduce magical elements to a minimum. Both place great faith in education; both are quite commensurate with a far flung business enterprise and direct religious zeal into the work of this world.

Using a romantic immanence theme, the all-embracing John Fiske eased the shock of the acceptance of evolution. But there were those intellectuals who rejected the old and did not accept the new religious patterns. Such a man was Chauncey Wright. These were likely to have a very deep piety to "science." Peirce had such a piety. But Peirce also, along with Abbot, worked very tenuously, from the standpoint of the wider religious publics (had they known of this work) to get "religious" conceptions back into the picture on the basis of science itself; on the basis not of dramatic and known scientific discoveries reinterpreted (such as Fiske with evolution) but on the basis of scientific method itself. Peirce found no public. Abbot wrangled and fell out with everyone. The best single index of Peirce's effort to see God from within scientific method is "realism" and the manner and context in which Abbot, from whom Peirce derived his statement of realism, handles the doctrine. For Fiske, Abbot, Wright, and Peirce the tension and difficulties of science and religion arose and were solved in several ways on an ontological plane. This is not the case with James. His genius in relieving the religious worries of men in those trying times of Huxley and Ingersoll consisted in throwing the entire argument directly upon a human and moral plane. But he set forth no "social gospel." It was on the level of the human *individual*. And it was ethical. Everywhere James was moral. This feature of James' level of statement and solution of the religious worries increased its competitive efficiency among scholars and laymen alike, for among reading publics, religious texts had been, in effect, debunked by the "higher criticism" of the historically minded theologies. The seat of this movement was Germany in the eighteenth and nineteenth centuries. As we have seen, it was precisely to German universities that those who were to man the American academic scene went to study. Now one positive effect of this higher or historical criticism was to shift attention from the content of the Bible to *ethical* ideals contained therein. The criterion for its "specialness" becomes its ethical worth. It was not to scriptures (religious or "scientific") that James appealed in his religious discussions. It was to experience. And "experience" to him, "experience" in his pragmatic vision, is ethically charged. Thus the influence of the "higher criticism" worked in such a way as further to make fit for competitive survival the religious perspective and strategy of James. Dewey has seen this religious function of James. "As far as I can judge, popular response to pragmatic philosophy was moved by two quite different considerations. By some it was thought to provide a new species of sanctions, a new mode of apologetics, for certain religious ideas whose standing has been threatened."[55]

The combination of theology with evolution, proceeded with

the aid of the *romantic* theory of the immanence of God. The fuller force of the big idealisms of Germany was received in America and England in the eighties and nineties, and served therein as a legitimation of religion in confrontation with philosophies reflecting science. On such an immanence interpretation the romantics and the absolute idealists could unite in a monistic view — the world is shot through with a Being that holds within all parts of the cosmos and holds all parts of the cosmos together. The universe of the gross materalist and the universe of the absolute idealist, however they differed, were on the same ground in this "blocklike and fixed universe." The "absolute," against which James most persistently directs his heaviest blows, stands for both sides of the polemic as it was most usually stated. He does not argue for one or the other. Both had defects and corollaries that left them unfit for the competition of ideas in James' mind and in the mind of his public. He goes further than either of the standpoints, striving to pick up positivistic materialism erected on science and the romantic-idealist absolutist justification of religion within his own terms. These terms were not, in the first instance ontological (as are both the above positions) but rather humanist, psychological. If God lies back of the universe, it is in man's personal experience that the divine spark is available for inspection and it is there that James inspects it and thereby justifies it.

As a psychologist, it is through the soul of man and his inner experiences that James approached religion. In this way he could follow "religious interest" as a scientist, that is, as a psychologist. As a philosophy, James does not, in the first instance, approach God through Nature via the eighteenth century, but rather through human experience. Such ontological bases for religious faith as can be gotten from James' texts are wholly secondary. One would have to get at them through a psychological spectrum. And if his approach is not ontological, neither is it theological or even "philosophical" in any narrow sense. Max Weber has commented that "The content of the ideas of a religion is....far more important than William James is inclined to admit."[56]

The humanist approach, finding divinity within men, receives in James a highly individualistic flavor commensurate with broader American traditions and practices in many spheres, including as we shall see, some surrogates of Puritanism. The divine is within the soul or the experiences of *an individual man.*

Even within the context of the evolution discussion, James can enter from this individualistic and ethical angle. Within theologized evolutionism, the old God that is both power and goodness permeates the universe and comes to a focus in men. Man thus may be the individuation of universal power. In the "Energies of Men" he speaks of a "second wind" which taps a "level of new energy." "The problem is . . . how men can be trained up to their most useful pitch of energy?. . .Everyone feels that his total *power* rises when he passes to a higher *qualitative* level of life." And he goes through discussions including Christian Science, Yoga, pledges, prayer — "ideas which unlock our hidden energies."[57] From many sides and in all the major religious discussions of his day James could relate his point of view. And this standpoint satisfies religious worries, attempts to live logically with the source of that worry, "science", and certain areas of religious criticism (such as the historical critique of scripture) and it is commensurate with general individualistic traditions. His was a stratagem, which at that time was very able in ideational and emotional competition.

1. *Pragmatism,* pp. 34-35.
2. *Ibid.,* p. 273.
3. *The Independent* (September 8, 1910), "William James," reprinted in John Dewey, *Character and Events,* Vol. I, p. 112f.
4. *Pragmatism,* p. 102.
5. ". . . by practical one often means the distinctively concrete, the individual, particular, and effective as opposed to the abstract, general and inert. To speak for myself, whenever I have emphasized the practical notions of truth, this is mainly what has been in my mind." *The Meaning of Truth,* pp. 209-10.
6. *Pragmatism,* p. 46.
7. *Ibid.,* p. 50.
8. *Ibid.,* p. 100.
9. *Ibid.,* p. 107.
10. *Ibid.,* p. 108.
11. *Ibid.,* p. 109.
12. *Ibid.,* p. 39.
13. *Ibid.,* pp. 39-40.
14. *Ibid,* p. 180. The manner in which the pragmatistic style of thought is a method which can be used by different thinkers in entirely different

directions is clearly brought out in connection with the origin of "cause."
James handles its origin in moral terms: "Who is to blame?" Peirce and
Mead and Dewey handle it *technologically:* cause originates in the *pushing*
of physical objects.

15. *Ibid.,* pp. 288-89.
16. *Ibid.,* p. 30.
17. *The Will to Believe,* p. 253: "Great Men and Their Environment."
18. *Talks to Teachers on Psychology.* By William James (New York
1899), p. 27.
19. *The Meaning of Truth,* p. 185.
20. *Ibid.,* p. 186.
21. *Pragmatism,* p. 209.
22. *Ibid.,* p. 205.
23. *Ibid.,* p. 204.
24. *Ibid.,* p. 205.
25. *Ibid.,* p. 202.
26. *Ibid.,* p. 203.
27. *Ibid.,* p. 203.
28. *Ibid.,* p. 204.
29. It suffices for all the necessary practical ends of life; and, among
our race even, it is only the highly sophisticated specimens, the minds debauched by learning, as Berkeley calls them, who have ever even sus-
pected common sense of not being absolutely true." — *Pragmatism,* p. 182.
30. *Ibid.,* pp. 182-83.
31. *Ibid.,* p. 183.
32. *Ibid.,* p. 184.
33. *Ibid.,* p. 21.
34. Cf. Above.
35. *Pragmatism,* p. 222.
36. *Ibid.,* p. 228.
37. *Ibid.,* p. 231.
38. *Ibid.,* p. 213.
39. *Ibid.,* p. 218.
40. *Ibid.,* p. 53.
41. *Ibid.,* p. 58.
42. *Ibid.,* p. 230.
43. *The Will to Believe,* p. 3f.
44. *Pragmatism,* p. 102.
45. *Pragmatism,* p. 200.
46. *Ibid.,* p. 73.
47. *Ibid.,* p. 75. My italics.
48. *Ibid.,* p. 75.
49. *Ibid.,* p. 50.
59. *Ibid.,* p. 61.
51. *Ibid.,* p. 63.
52. Cf. R. B. Perry, *Philosophy of the Recent Past* (New York 1926),
p. 194.

53. I put science in quotes because it is, of course, less "operative science" than philosophies allegedly "drawn from" science that have figured in the religious versus "science" controversies.

54. *See* J. H. Randall, Jr., *The Making of the Modern Mind*, (Boston, 1926), p. 521.

55. *Creative Intelligence: Essays in the Pragmatic Attitude* (New York 1917), "The Need For a Recovery of Philosophy" by Dewey, pp. 59-60.

56. Max Weber, *The Protestant Ethic and the Spirit of Capitalism*, p. 232. See *Varieties of Religious Experience*, p. 444f.

57. "Energies of Men", *Religion and Medicine*, Publication No. 3 (Moffot, Yard & Co. 1908).

13

The Polarization of Science and Religion

Unlike Peirce, James was not interested in "science" because of its technique; unlike Chauncey Wright, he was not at all "interested in the nugatory implication which could be drawn from it. What he liked about "science" was its "fidelity to fact," its welter of empirical matter. He distrusted "logical form." He possessed an "inaptitude for mathematics and laboratory experimentation."[1] What drew him to science and forced him to include "it" in his philosophy was the desire for "firsthand acquaintance with the raw materials of nature,"[2] and the inclusion of Peirce and his kind into the operative other of James' mind. That James' mind was not informed by his own participation in scientific practice is confirmed by the facts concerning his activities and by the character of his relation and attitude toward Wright and Peirce.[3]

James' "science" was not "a reaction against the excesses of an adolescent religion" nor was his religion "a reaction against the rigors of a scientific schooling." "In the liberal and tolerant atmosphere of his early environment it was possible for him to be both religious and scientific at the same time, and both in moderation."[4] Always he wished to include the *positive affirmations* of both science and religion, to reject both their negations.[5] That is the surface tactic in his polarization; it is a portion of his grander strategy of a mediatory style of thinking. Or better: it is the polarization of religion and science and his answers to it that sets his answers to other issues and manner of thinking them through. It works down at the center of his thinking. Other terms and views are its surrogates. Other dichotomies are arranged around religion and science in his mind. That is the key polarization in William James.

This imputation is born out from two sides of his series of positions: on the one side, his experience and training and circles of associations, such as his father and Charles Peirce; and on the other, by his larger publics and their problems to which he was responsive. I have already indicated that James was sensitized to his audiences, was in effective contact with them, that they were popular audiences. Most of his essays were written for direct vocal presentation to such audiences. Peirce's were for small groups, such as the Metaphysical Club, or for technical journals; or, more probably, they ended up in his own files. On the very surface of James' thought is the major tension of the broad intellectual publics of his day: religion and science. His first paper on pragmatism in 1898 was directed at this "problem," *not* technically redefined but addressed on the level and in the terms of which it was popularly formulated. Nowhere is this matter more clearly documented and extended than in *Pragmatism*.

In the course on Metaphysics at Harvard in 1905-6 James developed ideas which were to appear in *Pragmatism:* "The aim of the course was 'to unite empiricism with spiritualism.' "[6] That "empiricism" operates as a surrogate for "science," and "spiritualism" for "religion" is readily seen upon examination of the book. And a consideration of James' publics makes clear that the mediative outcome, "empiricism," was a shock absorber for these middle class professionals. In the first chapter, he lines up various terms under the generalized heading of tender and tough-minded. Notice that the *headings* for these polarized series are terms for qualities determining outlooks on "life."[7]

> "And now I come to the first positively important point which I wish to make. Never were as many men of a decidedly empiricist proclivity in existence as there are at the present day . . . But our esteem for facts has not neutralized in us all religiousness. It is itself almost religious. Our scientific temper is devout. Now take a man of this type, and let him be also a philosophic amateur, unwilling to mix a hodge-podge system after the fashion of a common layman, and what does he find his situation to be, in this blessed year of our Lord 1906? He wants facts; he wants science; but he also wants a religion. . . . A very large number of you here present, possibly a majority of you, are . . . of just this sort . . . You find an empirical philosophy that is not religious enough, and a religious philosophy that is not empirical for your purpose."[8]

That is what James wanted. And pragmatism is his answer. It underlies his mediating style and, seeing it beneath other polarizations, it prepares him for their reconciliation. These polarizations run as follows:[9]

"The Tender-Minded	The Tough-Minded
Rationalistic (going by 'principles'),	Empiricist (going by ('facts'),
Intellectualistic,	Sensationalistic,
Idealistic,	Materialistic,
	Pessimistic,
Religious,	Irreligious
Free-willist,	Fatalistic,
Monistic,	Pluralistic,
Dogmatical.	Skeptical."

In each case he (a) *gets them together* by a "free-will determinism," a "practical pessimism combined with metaphysical optimism," a "pluralistic monism," neither "optimism" nor "pessimism" but "meliorism,"[10] or (b) he *chooses the most affirmative* and the least "noble" side of the dilemma, or (c) he becomes *pluralistic.* He would be an empiricist, would wallow in a wealth of sensationalistic items, but he would be free in his will. Pragmatism means a *modus vivendi,* it "may be a happy harmonizer of empiricist ways of thinking with the more religious demands of human beings."[11]

> "Since pragmatism [is] a mediator and reconciler and . . . 'unstiffens our theories . . . she is completely genial . . . It follows that in the religious field she is at a great advantage both over positivisitic empiricism, with its anti-theological bias, and over religious rationalism, with its exclusive interest in the remote, the noble, the simple, and the abstract in the way of conception."[12]

And "she" can do this because:

> "her only test of probable truth is what works best in the way of leading us, what fits every part of life best and combines with the collectivity of experience's demands, nothing being omitted. If theological ideas should do this, if the nothing of God, in particular, should prove to do it, how could pragmatism possibly deny God's existence?"[13]

Let us turn in more detail to James' statement and beliefs on re-

ligion and to the role of pragmatism in their formation and reconciliation with "science." Then we shall take up his "empiricism," the
"scientific" pole of his dilemma.

First, in *Pragmatism* itself we find the following incomplete keys:
"On pragmatistic principles, if the hypothesis of God works satisfactorily in the widest sense of the word, it is true."[14] The
full meaning of this assertion, and especially "works satisfactorily'"
will be realized a little later:

> "Between the two extremes of crude naturalism on the one
> hand and transcendental absolutism on the other, you may
> find that what I take the liberty of calling the pragmatistic or
> melioristic type of theism is exactly what you require."[15]

Here, again, in the last words of *Pragmatism,* we see the drive
for an *affirmative mediation* of forms of religion and implications
of science. And then, with reference to religion as such:

> "When I tell you that I have written a book on men's re-
> ligious experience, which on the whole has been regarded as
> making for the reality of God, you will perhaps exempt my
> own pragmatism from the charge of being an atheistic system.
> I firmly disbelieve, myself, that our human experience is the
> highest form of experience extant in the universe."[16]

James had first thought of organizing his Gifford Lectures in two
parts: (1) "Man's Religious Appetites," and (2) "Their Satisfaction through Philosophy."[17] Although he did not follow this plan,
such philosophical matter as *The Varieties of Religious Experience*
contains is consonant with such an intent. He wants to "sift out from
the ... discrepancies" of religion "a common body of doctrine"
which would be formulated "in terms to which physical science
need not object."[18] This would be the "reconciling hypothesis"
which could be recommended "for general belief."[19]

James also wants his "hypothesis" to be "fair" to all religions, so
he searched for "mediating terms," finding it in "the subconscious
self." This is "a well-accredited psychological entity." And by using
it we see that there is "more life in our total soul than we are at
any time aware of."[20] Each person is so much of an individual that
no self gets fully "manifested."[21] What is "unmanifested" makes up
the "more" in contact with which we feel in religious experi-

ences.[22] This doorway into the subject, writes James, "seems to me the best one; for it mediates between a number of different points of view"[23] And again, he gives his acceptance a "quantitative" twist which we shall witness again in Mead's theory of value. He believes that his "piece-meal supernaturalism" is a doctrine or view "by which the largest number of legitimate requirements are met."[24]

Especially "Religion" and "Science." He "can, of course, put" himself "into the sectarian scientist's attitude and imagine. . . .that the world of sensations and of scientific laws and objects may be all." But whenever he did this, he heard some "inward monitor. . . whispering the word 'Bosh!' "[25]

James' thought about religion focuses like his other pragmatic applications upon "experiences which have a meaning for our life."[26] In the first place, he selects the diverse religious experiences of *individuals* as matter for his religious speculations. And secondly, he is not content to have religion mean only an "illumination of facts already elsewhere given," it is also "a postulator of new *facts* as well." He does not want it to be a mere interpretation of the material world — which makes this world divine by viewing it as an "expression of absolute spirit."[27] The "thoroughly 'pragmatic' view of religion," which "has usually been taken as a matter of course by common men," must be "such that different events can be expected in it, different conduct must be required."[28] Its meaning is for individual ways of life. By faithfulness to his "own over-belief" he seemed "to keep more sane and true."[29]

The existence of God, if so, *must* make some alteration in some "concrete particular of experience."[30] But what sort of experience on what level? *Personal* experience on the level of an *individual* way, attitude, and mood of life:

> "If asked just where the differences in fact which are due to God's existence come in, I should have to say that in general I have no hypothesis to offer beyond what the phenomenon of 'prayerful communion,' especially when certain kinds of incursion from the subconscious region take part in it, immediately suggests."[31]

"The appearance" of such a state "raises our center of personal energy."[32]

Another "difference in natural 'fact' which ... the existence of a God ought to make" is "personal immortality."[33] To James this seemed a "secondary point." He leaves it an open question, leaning a little toward affirmation in the name of the psychical research experiments.[34]

Both from the standpoint of (1) the selection of personal experiences as vehicles for his lectures on religion, (2) the pragmatic meaning and test of religion, and (3) his statement as to what religious experience can and cannot "support," James lay the matter within the individual's life and the moral quality it renders thereto. As for (3) he states unequivocally that religious experience cannot support "the infinitist belief."

> "The only thing that it unequivocally testifies to is that we can experience union with *something* larger than ourselves and in that union find our greatest peace ... the practical needs and experiences of religion seem to me sufficiently met by the belief that beyond each man and in a fashion continuous with him there exists a larger power which is friendly to him and to his ideals."[35]
>
> *"If theological ideas prove to have a value for concrete life, they will be true, for pragmatism, in the sense of being good for so much."*[36]

He applies the pragmatic technique to the metaphysical attributes of God, and concludes: "From the point of view of practical religion, the metaphysical monster which they offer to our worship is an absolutely worthless invention of the scholarly mind."[37]

But as for the *moral* attributes, that is another matter. It is here that James finds something "great" in "significance". "Pragmatically, they stand on an entirely different footing. They positively determine fear and hope and expectation, and are foundations for the saintly life."[38]

These attributes interpreted pragmatically spell out a God that does good and can secure triumph, can see us in the dark, and punish us for what he sees, or pardon us: "These qualities enter into connection with our lives" and it is in personal life-ways that William James finds the *meaning* of God's moral attitudes. Despite Max Weber's comment that "James' pragmatic valuation of the significance of religious ideas according to their influence on life is incidently a true child of the world of ideas of the Puritan home of that eminent scholar."[39]

This God is not for him. In spite of the general directive he derives from this source, I think James senses the illiberal Calvinism against which his father revolted. In a footnote he remarks: "Pragmatically, the most important attribute of God is his punitive justice."[40] Notice the moral equivalence and use of the term, "pragmatically." But such results even of the pragmatic maxim are excluded. He will not *reason* about God even pragmatically. We recall Peirce's compartmentalization of reason and practice as we read:

> "Ratiocination is a relatively superficial and unreal path to the deity 'I will lay mine hand upon my mouth; I have heard of Thee by the hearing of the ear, but now mine eye seeth Thee.' An intellect perplexed and baffled, yet a trustful sense of presence — such is the situation of the man who is sincere with himself and with the facts, but who remains religious still."[41]

Neither the metaphysical attributes of God (which are pragmatically meaningless) nor the moral attributes, which go against James' sentiments, nor the attributions and interpretations of the idealist philosophers can give a firmer foundation to God than "the sphere of feeling and of the direct experience of the individual"[42] can lend it. Religion is a private faith. James' philosophy carefully and on all sides allows it, but "we must conclude that the attempt to demonstrate by purely intellectual processes the truth of the deliverances of direct religious experience is absolutely hopeless."[43] However, philosophy can "offer mediation between different believers, and help to bring about consensus of opinion."[44]

Turning to the other side of James' key polarization, "science," we see that he states it as "empiricism" and in such a way as to have its elements, norms, and implications allow his religious demands and affirmations. There were in James' day, as now, many ways of absorbing science into a way of thinking; and James "took" it as "empiricism." "The empiricist tendency," he writes, "has largely prevailed in science ..."[45] I have already shown the persons with whom James studied science, his manner of incorporating it into his experience and thought, the men whose scientific experience he used vicariously, and whose "temper" he incorporated as a gadfly. It now remains to ascertain the meaning of empiricism and what it is made to include.

Precisely as he affirmatively *mediated* the various other positions[46] so does he in the case of religion and science: with a "philosophy of experience."[47] But his "philosophy of experience" embraces: (a) "experimentalism," (b) "voluntarism," and (c) "experientialism" or the immediately sensationalist "intuitive theory of reality."[48]

Each of these three elements are caught up in one manner or another in his variation of the pragmatic style of thinking, and "science" for James is taken into account by them, or at least allows them to be held.

Pragmatism is the technique of experimentalism, a philosophical implication of scientific practices. Experimentalism holds that concepts must be "subordinate to the direct perception of fact,"[49] and pragmatism is the way of getting this accomplished. I have already indicated that in James, pragmatism operates as a switch throwing the experience of these "facts" from the laboratory of science to personal experiences encountered in life-ways.

Pragmatism, in looking into the future for tests of meaning, involves voluntarism, which holds that believing exceeds the immediately and already known. Voluntarism would justify believing which exceeds "the limits of experimental verification and must, in so far as this is the case, proceed on moral grounds."[50] In James the real locus of pragmatic testing turns out to be a personal and moral sphere.

The voluntarism of James is consistent with his empiricism, with his "experimental science." For, as Perry points out, the experimentalist operates with "proposals" contrived by "an act of will." They are united by the "voluntary activity of the knowing mind"[51] which is part of "scientific method."

But there still is an edge of belief to the "intellectual rigorism" of strictly following *perceptual* confirmation of beliefs. If this is so, James would jump from *perceptual* verification to moral evidence, and as has been indicated, the "practical" testing of pragmatism is for James *moral* and has its significance realized in terms of outlooks on "life."

This voluntaristic component of James' "empiricism" forms the peak, or the focus, so to speak, of his attempt to include "science" in such a way as to have religious sensitivities satisfied. He was talking in "The Will to Believe" to that part of himself incorporated from "academic audiences, fed . . . on science . . ." who had suffered "paralysis of their native capacity for faith. . ." and who had succumbed to "the notion, carefully instilled, that there is something called scientific evidence by waiting upon which they shall escape all danger of shipwreck in regard to truth."[52]

> "In this age of toleration, no scientist will ever try actively to interfere with our religious faith, provided we enjoy it quietly with our friends and do not make a public nuisance of it in the market-place. But it is just on this matter of the market-place that I think the utility of such essays as mine may turn. If religious hypotheses about the universe be in order at all, then the active faiths of individuals in them, freely expressing themselves in life, are the experimental tests by which they are verified, and the only means by which their truth or falsehood can be wrought out. The truest scientific hypothesis is that which, as we say, 'works' best; and it can be no otherwise with religious hypotheses."[53]

It is precisely the Jamesian *variety* of pragmatism which links it to the experiential element in his empiricism.[54] Experimentalism is slightly contemptuous of "concepts," biased strongly in favor of *particular* items of experiences: they are the more real; thought and concepts are second-best.[55] "Nothing happens," he wrote, "in the realm of concepts."[56]

Throughout his pragmatic utterances James was set apart from Peirce by stressing and insisting upon interpreting the pragmatic maxim as forcing thought to have *particular* consequences. And it was the sensationalism of "science," its adherence to first-hand experience of nature, that was for James so attractive.

Further confirmations of this line of interpretation are found in those contexts in which "empiricism," which we have seen is James' way of taking into account "science," is directly and tacitly equated with the "fruits for life." The following passage occurs in connection with a discussion of conversion:

> "Our spiritual judgment, I said, our opinion of the significance and value of a human event or condition, must be decided on empirical grounds exclusively. If the *fruits for life* of the state of conversion are good, we ought to idealize and ven-

erate it, even though it be a piece of natural psychology; if not, we ought to make short work with it, no matter what supernatural being may have infused it."[57]

And in a letter to Santayana in 1888 he illustrates the moral grounds of his experientialism:

> "Neither do I expect absolute illumination from human philosophizing. At most you can get arguments either to reinforce or to protect certain emotional impulses. In any minute of moral action where the path is difficult, I believe a man has deeper dealings with life than he could have in libraries of philosophizing."[58]

And in the following we see how *"empirical,"* like *"pragmatism"* and *"religion"* adds up in its usage to "uses to the individual."

> "We have wound our way back, after our excursion. . . .to where we were before: the uses of religion, its uses to the individual who has it, and the uses of the individual himself to the world, are the best arguments that truth is in it. We return to the empirical philosophy: the true is what works well, even though the qualification 'on the whole' may have to be added."[59]

So from many segregated corridors through James' thought we are led to his conception of "individualism" and his mystique of "life." It is convenient now to approach it in connection with his social-political views.

1. R. B. Perry, *op. cit.*, Vol. I, p. 450.
2. *Ibid.*, Vol. I, p. 450.
3. *See* above.
4. R. B. Perry, *op. cit.*, Vol. I, p. 449.
5. *Ibid.*, Vol. I, p. 450.
6. *Ibid.*, Vol. II, p. 443.
7. And not as C. G. Jung asserts "thinking qualities." *Psychological Types.* (New York, 1926), p. 397.
8. *Pragmatism*, pp. 14-15.
9. *Ibid.*, p. 12.
10. *Ibid.*, p. 285. *See* section above on mediationalism, and pragmatism's origination and role in the reconciling of these polar terms by relating them to their meanings for life-ways.

11. *Ibid.*, p. 69.
12. *Ibid.*, pp. 79-80.
13. *Ibid.*, p. 80. C. G. Jung's views on pragmatism in *Psychological Types* are limited to acquaintance with *Pragmatism*. Otherwise, his remarks are simply uninformed. (*See* p. 398 where he states that pragmatism "originated" with F. C. S. Schiller! and p. 399 of pragmatism's presupposal of "resignation.") Jung's aim in approaching James is to line him up with Jung's "types." Hence he treats pragmatism almost solely as an attempted reconciliation of his two types, not seeing that they are elaborated surrogates for religion and science, both of which are stated in terms of their value for lifeways. Because Jung's types are supposed to be suprahistorical he can conceive of James' pragmatism as a reenactment of the medieval drama of nominalism vs. realism and of their reconciliation, William James being a sort of Abelard of the nineteenth century. *See* p. 398.
14. *Pragmatism*, p. 299.
15. *Ibid.*, p. 301.
16. *Ibid.*, pp. 299-300.
17. *Varieties of Religious Experience*, preface, xvii, (Modern Library Edition).
18. *Ibid.*, pp. 500-01.
19. *Ibid.*, p. 501.
20. *Ibid.*, p. 501.
21. *Ibid.*, p. 502.
22. *Ibid.*, p. 502.
23. *Ibid.*, p. 503.
24. *Ibid.*, p. 513.
25. *Ibid.*, p. 509.
26. *Ibid.*, p. 509.
27. *Ibid.*, pp. 508-09.
28. *Ibid.*, p. 508.
29. *Ibid.*, p. 509.
30. *Ibid.*, p. 512.
31. *Ibid.*, p. 513.
32. *Ibid.*, p. 513.
33. *Ibid.*, p. 514.
34. The character of James' attitude toward "Psychical Research" is illuminative of my interpretation. "Thousands of sensitive organizations in the United States to-day live as steadily in the light of these experiences, and are as indifferent to modern science, as if they lived in Bohemia in the 12th Century. They are indifferent to science, because science is so callously indifferent to their experiences. Although in its essence science only stands for a method and for no fixed belief, yet as habitually taken, both by its votaries and outsiders, it is identified with a certain fixed belief — the belief that the hidden order of nature is mechanical exclusively, and that non-mechanical categories are irrational ways of conceiving and explaining even such things as human life ... The spirit and principles of

science are mere affairs of method; there is nothing in them that need hinder science from dealing successfully with a world in which personal forces are the starting-point of new effects. The only form of thing that we directly encounter, the only experience that we concretely have, is our own personal life." *The Will to Believe, etc.*, pp. 323-24, 327: "Psychical Research" This view of James may be revealingly compared with the attitudes of C. S. Peirce: "I declined to join the American Psychical Research Society when it was started; I thought that to do so would be to sanction a probable great waste of time, together with the placing of some men in a compromising position." *Collected Papers*, Vol. II, p. 63.

35. *The Varieties of Religious Experience*, p. 515.
36. *Pragmatism*, p. 73.
37. *The Varieties of Religious Experience*, p. 437.
38. *Ibid.*, p. 437.
39. *The Protestant Ethic and the Spirit of Capitalism*, Translated by Talcott Parsons (New York 1930) p. 232.
40. *The Varieties of Religious Experience* (New York 1925) p. 438.
41. *Ibid.*, p. 438.
42. *Ibid.*, p. 443.
43. *Ibid.*, p. 445.
44. *Ibid.*, p. 446.
45. *The Will to Believe and Other Essays*, 12.
46. *See* sections above.
47. Perry, *op. cit.*, Vol. I, p. 451.
48. *Ibid.*, pp. 453-54.
49. *Ibid.*, p. 454.
50. *Ibid.*, p. 454.
51. *Ibid.*, p. 455.
52. *The Will to Believe*, pp. x-xi.
53. *Ibid.*, pp. xi-xii. The essays "Sentiment of Rationality" and "Reflex Action and Theism" are also to be understood as statements of "science" and "rationality" in such a way as to allow "faith" and "religious" sentiments.
54. *See* Perry, *op. cit.*, Vol. I, p. 458.
55. *Ibid.*, p. 457.
56. *The Pluralistic Universe*, p. 340.
57. *The Varieties of Religious Experience*, p. 232.
58. Quoted in Perry, *op. cit.*, Vol. I, p. 403.
59. *The Varieties of Religious Experience*, p. 448.

14

Psychological Liberalism

William James never fully articulated, much less systematized, his social and political opinions. They are more properly called "sentiments."[1] Like so many of his views, they frankly rested upon feelings and values which lie upon the very surface of his statements. His "sentiment of humanity" sat squarely upon "the sufferers' sensitiveness to the suffering of others."[2] Many of James' views, seem directly underpinned by his personal sensitiveness. We must recall that when he confronts the Absolutism of Royce, the empirical case he calls upon for his support is an individual suicide and murder induced by poverty and consequent despair. He always took the side of the "underdog," of "The Boers and the Irish," of "The Filipinos against the United States."[3] He tried to get publishers to handle books for people whom he knew to be incompetent and whose books were "hopeless."[4]

Now "the generalization of James' tender-heartedness into a humanitarian sentiment and creed"[5] proceeded within the ideas and orientation of the editor of *The Nation*, E. L. Godkin. As I have mentioned, Godkin was an intimate of the James household during the late seventies. At the age of twenty-five, from Tepliz, Bohemia, James wrote: "Pray engineer a *Nation* to me frequently. You can't imagine what a treat they are."[6] Frequent postscripts to James' letters from Europe contain such requests. He wrote to Godkin himself in 1889: "In the earlier years I may say that my whole political education was due to the *Nation*. You have the most curious way of always being right, so I never dare to trust myself now when you're agin me."[7] Later he wrote to a friend: "You see the *Nation* took me at the age of 22." Six years later he pledged his support to Godkin's "campaign" apropos "the Venezuela incident."[8] Godkin died in 1902 and James wrote:

> "to my generation his was certainly the towering influence in all thought concerning public affairs, and indirectly his influence has certainly been more pervasive than that of any other writer of the generation, for he influenced other writers who never quoted him, and determined the whole current of discussion."[9]

Founded in 1865, *The Nation* gained 5,000 paid circulation in the third issue, reached a peak of 38,000 in 1920. The circulation has fluctuated: in 1900 it was 9,498; in 1910, 6,500; in 1928 it was down from the 1920 peak to 30,000.[10] In 1926, its circulation was 29,113 distributed demographically as follows: thirty-nine per cent in cities over 300,000; fourteen per cent in urban places 100,000 to 300,000 in population; twenty-one per cent in places below 10,-000.[11] So far as I can determine, *The Nation* has circulated among professional people and in university circles. Although the meaning of the term has, of course, changed it has remained generally "liberal" in viewpoint. In 1881 its ownership passed to the *New York Evening Post*.[12]

The political cant "mugwump" became widely used during the campaign of 1884. It designated those individuals who bolted from the Republican Party during that campaign. More generally, it designates an "independent" in politics. The mugwumps of the 1884 campaign were charged with regarding themselves as superior in character and intelligence to the Republican Party. The Republican Party leader, J. G. Blaine, had been accused of "using his powers in Congress to favor high tariffs and railroad corporations in return for monetary considerations."[13] He was officially examined by a Congressional Committee and acquitted but his conduct was "not conspicuous for candor and nicety."[14]

One of James' few "political friends" was one F. G. Bromberg, a member of Congress from Alabama. James knew him, not directly as a politician but as a former classmate. To Bromberg, James wrote apropos Blaine, agreeing that Blaine was not to be "confounded with the grosser pecuniary corruptionists," that his "slips" were "relatively venial in that line," but he wanted, and thought it "right to make the very most . . . of them — for what does Blaine stand for in any other line?" He objected strongly to Blaine's earlier arousal of "sectional animosities."[15]

James would side with the Democrats to oust the Republicans and then he would oust the Democrats "in the name of a new national party with something of an intellectual character in purposes, which will devote itself to civil service and economical reform, and perhaps ultimately to certain constitutional changes of which we are in pressing need."[16] So, James was a mugwump "both in the historical and in the generalized sense."[17] He was not as much interested in negating the "immediate motive of gain" as he was in the "underlying ethical principles of the broad human purpose of social institutions." He apparently looked upon politics as an arena of personal struggles: "the strongest force in politics is human scheming, and the schemers will capture every machinery that you can set up against them."[18] But positively he believed "that the party of critical intelligence might offset their lack of heat by their greater steadiness."[19]

We feel frequently that his positive model for society was along the lines of the ethics of a profession and are therefore gratified to find that there is a confirming basis for this impression. The only model for his political views which was derived from personal experience was apparently one drawn from his brief contact with the medical profession. After completing the medical course he wrote:

> "So there is one epoch of my life closed, and a pretty important one, I feel it, both in its scientific 'yield' and in its general educational value as enabling me to see a little the inside workings of an important profession and to learn from it, as an average example, how all the work of human society is performed."[20]

The role for his "party of critical intelligence," mentioned above, was, again, mediative and balancing:

> "So far, then, as the mission of the educated intellect in society is not to find or invent reasons for the demands of passion, it reduces itself to this small but incessant criticizing, or equalizing function. It reestablishes, because it never forgets, the normal perspective of interests, and keeps things in their proper places in the scale of values."[21] It is to take a "judicial and neutral attitude. The intellectual critic as such knows of

so many interests, that to the ardent partisan he seems to have none."[22]

He was willing to admit that "often" the "only audience" of such a party "is posterity."[23] He "broadly" polarizes all political parties into "the party of animal instinct, jingoism, fun, excitement, bigness; and that of reason, forecast, order gained by growth, and spiritual methods — briefly put, the party of force and that of education."[24]

He rests his faith with the latter, with an individualist qualification, only if it be led by a "magnetic leader." Liberalism "will be between the upper and the nether millstone if it have no magnetic leader ... The chronic fault of liberalism is its lack of speed and passion."[25] Again, in "Great Men and their Environment" he asks: "What are the causes that make communities change from generation to generation?" And he answers: "The difference is due to the accumulated influences of individuals, of their examples, their initiatives, and their decisions."[26] The "social philosophy ... must simply accept geniuses as data, just as Darwin accepts his spontaneous variations" although environment may "reject, preserve or destroy ..."[27]

In letter-writing action, too, James opposed passionate outbursts. "Three days of fighting mob-hysteria at Washington can at any time undo peace habits of a hundred years."[28] "It was a political crime, James felt, to take any steps which would arouse these passions."[29] Rather than passion and surprise, he wrote in *The Harvard Crimson* in 1896, "Let us consult our reason as to what is best, and then exert ourselves as citizens with all our might."[30] He continually looked out for and morally condemned the:

> "aboriginal capacity for murderous excitement which lies sleeping even in his ['the average church-going civilizee'] own bosom ... The watertight compartment in which the carnivore within us is confined is artificial and not organic. It never will be organic ... It is where the impulse is collective, and the murder is regarded as a punitive or protective duty, that the peril to civilization is greatest."[31]

Notice in the following quotation the tacit identification of "shrewdness" with "principles," both terms standing in a moral opposition to "excitement."

"Our American people used to be supposed to have a certain hardheaded shrewdness. Nowadays they seem smitten with utter silliness. Their professed principles mean nothing to them, and any phrase or sensational excitement captivates them."[32]

During the muckraking era, writing in one of its leading magazines, *McClures,* he stated that the "college bred" should:

"guard the 'tone' of society, to promote the 'critical sensibilities' or 'admiration of the really admirable,' and to 'divine the worthier and better leaders': we ought to have our own class-consciousness. *'Les Intellectuels!'* what prouder club-name could there be than this one, used ironically by the party of 'redblood,' the party of every stupid prejudice and passion, during the anti-Dreyfus craze, to satirize the men in France who still retained some critical sense and judgment!."[33]

Such was his most mature view of the political role of those among whom he placed himself and for whom he intended to write.

As a "reformer" James took several moral stands. As we have seen, he desired civil service reforms; he was antipathetical to the use of alcohol, but he would not "join" any temperance organizations.[34] He supported, in the main, Eliot's educational policies.[35] Being interested in "the new mental therapy," and in the "scandal" of his "colleagues in the medical school," he "used his influence against bills before the Massachusetts Legislature" requiring "the examination and licensing of medical practitioners."[36] Later, in 1906-09, he wrote in behalf of and gave $1,000 to the National Committee for Mental Hygiene.[37]

But the central political issue for James was occasioned by the Spanish-American War. He spent "time and effort" on the question of imperialism. In his reactions to this event and its issues he reveals again two central modes of his political thinking: the polarization of "passion" with mediative "reason" and the personalizing of causes of political history. He tends to explain them almost entirely on the psychological level, where *ideals* and *passions* could operate. For example, he does not focus upon the American investment in Cuba, but states the *entire* issue in psychological and moral terms. He could not think economically or historically; in all contexts, even in social and political matters, his metier was biographical.

James had written in 1896 to an English friend: "the latest anglophobia . . . is most of it directly traceable to the diabolic machinations of the party of protection for the past twenty years."[38] Two years later:

> "this whole business has thrown a most instructive light on the way in which history is made, and has illustrated to perfection the *psychologie des foules!* The basis of it all is, or rather was, perfectly honest humanitarianism, and an absolutely disinterested desire on the part of our people to set the Cubans free . . . One this, various interests worked for their purposes in favor of war. The explosion of the *Maine* and the diplomatic negotiations ensued, together with the preparations for possible defense and attack; and by that time Congress was entirely mad, supposing that the people was in the same condition, as it probably was, in less degree. Congress, unfortunately, by our constitution, has the right to declare war, and in the psychological condition in which it was, that was the only possible direction of discharge."[39]
>
> And again: ". . . after all, hasn't the spirit of the life of all the great generals and rulers and aristocracies always been the spirit of sport carried to its supreme expression? Civilization, properly so-called, might well be termed the organization of all those functions that resist the mere excitement of sport. But *excitement!* Shall we not worship excitement? And after all, what is life for, except for opportunities of excitement?! It makes all humdrum moralizing seem terribly dead and tame! And it beautifully corroborates the 'chance' theory of history, to find that the critical turning-points in these great movements are purely accidental."[40]

But when the United States "benevolently coerced the Filipinos," James became less detached and wrote of those who justified the act as being educative, and as philanthropic, that such feeling of:

> "*possibilities* . . . consist . . . in absolutely nothing but the uplift of mere *excitement,* — empire and war being the great excitements of peoples, in the face of which all ordinary prudential talk (such as individuals would carry on their affairs with) is deemed base, if not treasonable. These excitements and ambitions are of course the forces that make nations great (when they do not ruin them), and it may be that war is to be the only force that can hammer us into decency, as it is the great force that has hammered the European states."[41]

And still on the psychological level, he continues to explain "imperialism" as "an outlet for blind passion masked by a profession of benevolence."[42]

"... those old-fashioned animal ambitions for mastery and mere success which seem now to be sweeping away the world, and us at the wake. This is the real and concrete spring of action, it seems to me, that is exciting us; and raising and educating inferior races, is mere hollow pretext and unreality ..."[43]

Positively, his position was individualisic and moral: it was the idea of forcing the Filipinos that was "impossible." Leaning upon this deep respect for individuals, he wrote to a newspaper:

"It is obvious that for our rulers at Washington the Filipinos have not existed as psychological quantities at all ... We have treated [them] as if they were a painted picture, an amount of mere matter in our ways. They are too remote from us ever to be realized as they exist in their inwardness."[44]

James thought that Roosevelt's "Strenuous Life" was "abstractness."[45]

"Of all the naked abstractions that were ever applied to human affairs, the outpourings of Governor Roosevelt's soul in this speech would seem the very nakedest. Although in middle life ... and in a situation of responsibility concrete enough, he is still mentally in the *Sturm und Drang* period of early adolescence ..."[46]

When Roosevelt fought for ideals, James was with him, but James found his "roughness of method ... profoundly offensive."[47] James did not mind "robustness" but he cared very deeply what one was robust about. There was always a prior condition of "legitimate belligerency — namely, the purity of one's cause."[48] For the same reasons James had dissented from Holmes' statement that "life is action, the use of one's powers." Of this James said: "Mere excitement is an immature ideal, unworthy of the Supreme Court's official endorsement."[49]

James' essay, "The Moral Equivalent of War,"[50] was probably written in response to Roosevelt's assertion that an occasional war was good for "the moral fiber of the nation." The balanced statement, the strategy, and the level upon which James placed his essay is worthy of display. The first reason that the "war against war" is difficult is that "the military feelings" are "deeply grounded" among our "ideals."[51] The locus of the causes of war are throughout the essay assumed to be "public opinion." It is in James' view quite directly a "plebian imperialism." "Let public opinion once reach a certain fighting pitch and no ruler can withstand it." He interprets the Boer War in terms of "the military tension" being too much for the governments concerned.[52] James tries to find a "promising line of conciliation"[53] between "the militarist imagination" and "the pacifistic." It is "asserted" by James that "militarism" preserves "our ideals of hardihood, and human life with no use for hardihood would be contemptible. Without risks or prizes for the darer, history would be insipid indeed."[54] The state must continue to be built upon such stays. "The war party is . . . right in affirming and reaffirming that the martial virtues . . . are absolute and permanent human goods."[55] So rechannel what makes for them. Conscript the "whole youthful population to form for a certain number of years a part of the army enlisted against *Nature* . . ."[56] Thus, by sublimating the struggle of man against man into a battle of man against nature, he would preserve "the manly virtues" in the midst of "a pacific civilization."[57]

In his last pronouncement on "imperialism," an address to the Anti-Imperialist League, James' central polarization comes in:

> "Political virtue does not follow geographical divisions. It follows the eternal division inside of each country between the more animal and the more intellectual kind of men, between the tory and the liberal tendencies, the jingoism and animal instinct that would run things by main force and brute possession, and the critical conscience that believes in educational methods and in rational rules of right . . ."[58]

Whatever other factors entered into James' views and feelings about international relations and politics, his individualism certainly figures largely in it. Perry holds that "James' standard of international politics was an application of his individualism: tolerate differences, and enjoy them. To this he added the usual corollary, that intolerance is intolerable."[59] That there is close correspondence and interaction between his social-political views and his epistemological, metaphysical, and psychological opinions is clear.

> "Damn great Empires! including that of the Absolute . . . Give me individuals and their spheres of activity . . . I am against bigness and greatness in all their forms, and with the invisible molecular moral forces that work from individual to individual, stealing in through the crannies of the world like so many soft rootlets, or like the capillary oozing of water, and yet rending the hardest monuments of man's pride, if you give them time. The bigger the unit you deal with, the hollower, the more brutal, the more mendacious is the life displayed. So I am against all big successes and big results; and in favor of the eternal forces of truth which always work in the individual . . ."[60]

"James," writes Perry, "sensed the inwardness of the great nations with as much relish as that of the small. But he believed that the great empire was blind to the essence of nationality in others, and at the same time in danger of losing its own soul through attention to mere quantity."[61] "We 'intellectuals' in America must all work to keep our previous birthright of individualism, and freedom from these institutions."[62]

This was the same individualism which made James refrain from joining temperance organizations, underpinned his reaction against "professionalization" in the case of the legislation, and propelled his reaction against the borrowing of "individual talent" by the requirement of the Ph.D. degree.[63]

What I wish to indicate is that it was not James' reactions to and knowledge gained through political incidents that set his general style of thinking or even the content of his views about other things. I have indicated that Peirce and Wright acted as *scientific* gadflies to James, representing a point of view which had to be included in his views, determining that inclusion. But Godkin was the only individual who acted as a *political* gadfly to James, and Godkin was not a professional public figure. Holmes was, but his views were not pressing into the *personal* composition of James' viewpoint.[64] James' thinking was not informed by Holmes' mature life and thought. Examples drawn from a jurist's experience and reflection do not enter his pages as pivots and anchors for his thinking as do the scientific work and ideals of Wright and especially Peirce. The instances about which James' thought revolved were not political. His political experience was meager and he did not use the experiences of men in public affairs. The political was peripheral to James' major foci, incidental to his major interests. One might almost say that his political reactions, on the one hand, were derived syntactically from other domains of his mind, which had been otherwise *set*; and on the other hand, that they derived from his general sympathetic quality. Intellectually, he leaned upon *The Nation*, it being the closest to what he felt. He did not innovate nor think in any original or distinctive way about political and social affairs.

I would not attempt to derive, logically or psychologically, James' general style of thinking and the content of his thought in non-political spheres from his political orientation. Nevertheless, there are in general three twists or opinions that run throughout his general style of thinking, whether it is concerned with politics, psychology, epistemology, religion, or the doctrine known as pragmatism.

His thinking is "rationalistic" in the non-technical, broad sense of this term. Or better than "rationalistic," he tends to use the positive model of society as a professional organization, to set opposite "personal scheming" and overturnings of passion and animality. Yet such a view is restrained from fuller expression in James by his personalism so that he rests his political faith and hope in the substantive rationality of an individual, and even upon this leader's "magnetism." The political leader which James sought would be legitimated substantively by his intellect, his foresight, as well as by his magnetic appeal. Such latent contradictions as might be buried in this balance are left buried by James.

As a counterpart to such hopes for a leader, his answer to the question implicit in the title, "The Social Value of the College-Bred," is one that runs as a refrain through this essay: it is that a college education "should *help you to know a good man when you see him.*"[65] Despite the primacy of the will, the emotion, the moral stuffing in the face of the demands of intellect, James occasionally puts the moral act itself in terms of a substantive rationality of the individual:

"*In what does a moral act consist* when reduced to its simplest and most elementary form? You can make only one reply. You can say that *it consists in the effort of attention by which we hold fast to an idea* which but for that effort of attention would be driven out of the mind by the other psychological tendencies that are there. *To think,* in short, is the secret of will, just as it is the secret of memory." And then he gives the example of "an habitual drunkard under temptation" whose "moral triumph or failure literally consists in his finding the right *name* for the case."[66]

Gradual and in the middle-of-the-road. This is basic to all of James' thinking. I have already isolated and discussed pragmatism as a *mediatory* affair, but in the following passages the matter is spread and we see that this element characterizes for James the practical, social world. "Our difficulties and our ideals are all piece meal affairs."[67]

His meliorism, which in his view is entailed by pragmatism, also consists largely in a "piece meal" middle-of-the-road attitude:

> "Nevertheless there are unhappy men who think the salvation of the world impossible. Theirs is the doctrine known as pessimism. Optimism in turn would be the doctrine that thinks the world's salvation inevitable. Midway between the two there stands what may be called the doctrine of meliorism, though it has hitherto figured less as a doctrine than as an attitude in human affairs . . . Meliorism treats salvation as neither necessary nor impossible. It treats it as a possibility, which becomes more and more of a probability the more numerous the actual conditions of salvation become."[68]

The same attitude underlies the pragmatic handling of concepts; for example, in the following he is discussing the central conception of "truth."

> "Yet in the choice of these man-made formulas we can not be capricious with impunity any more than we can be capricious on the common-sense practical level. We must find a theory that will *work;* and that means something extremely difficult; for our theory must mediate between all previous truths and certain new experiences. It must derange common sense and previous belief as little as possible, and it must lead to some sensible terminus or other that can be verified exactly. '[69]

In the penultimate paragraph of "The Will to Believe," James writes an informative passage which shows the blend of individualism, tolerance, empiricism and live-and-let-live:

> "No one of us ought to issue vetoes to the other, nor should we bandy words of abuse. We ought, on the contrary, delicately and profoundly to respect one another's mental freedom; then only shall we bring about the intellectual republic; then only shall we have that spirit of inner tolerance without which all our outer tolerance is soulless, and which is empiricism's glory; then only shall we live and let live, in speculative as well as in practical things."[70]

The third element in James' style which is exhibited in all spheres of his thinking is individualistic piety. This blend is a durable link of James to a center of American intellectual and political traditions. Both Puritanism *and* the Enlightenment were individualistic in incidence, temper, and in theory. Immediately prior to the opening of the nineteenth century American schools, as we have seen, were heavily impregnated by the canny Scottish answer to the skepticism of Hume. Thomas Reid's ideas were transplanted to the United States by Witherspoon and, later, McCosh of Princeton. Whatever other usages and tones the philosophy of common sense embodied, it was certainly individualistic. For Reid a "being and an individual being mean the same thing."[71] Romanticism as it flowered in America in the Transcendentalist movement, one of James' circles, not only stressed the individual but conceived of him as "the vehicle of the all creative spirit."[72] Emerson, as Perry remarks, may have spiritualized the individual, but he was still left an individual. Institutions were still *men's* shadows. It is only in the face of immense opposition that thinkers on this continent have advanced against individualism and only by some polemic leverage of note. The lonely Peirce did. The cantankerous and constantly frustrated Abbot did. James did not. Through him flowed urgently the individualism that has been a very central current in American life and thought.

As a theory of knowledge, James' pragmatism is built upon a psychological view which stresses intention and action — of individuals. Applied to concepts, it spells out their meaning and tests them in the lives of individuals. The "radical empiricism" of James tried to state all individual transcendent items in terms of continuities of sense experiences. And they would differ for individuals. His pluralistic universe is a world composed of individuals and individual things. When he spoke of "humanity" it was, as Perry says, merely out of sensitiveness to individuals other than himself. "The individual, the person in the singular number, is the more fundamental phenomenon, and the social institution, of whatever grade, is but secondary and ministerial. The best commonwealth will always be the one [that cherishes and] leaves the largest scope to [the] peculiarities [of individual men]."[73]

Naturally, James leaned strongly to Nominalism. Such hesitancy and lapses as his Nominalism displays can be imputed to Peirce's insistence rather than to any element indigenous to James' own style and temper.[74]

Definitely against Peirce, James' stress upon individuality and substantive rationality come together into a "first fact": "The first fact for us, then, as psychologists, is that thinking of some sort goes on." Thinking is, of course, spread to embrace "consciousness", which, against the associationalists, is not viewed as chopped into bits, but rather as a "stream."[75] This "thinking" with which we must begin, is "owned" by a person; it is a personal, an individual thing.[76] For James, individuality is the central point. Society is based on the "enormous fly wheel" of "habit."[77] Although habit is acquired through education, it is *of* the individual. It is grafted upon the instincts of the animal individual. The rationalistic assumptions of James' psychology come out even in his famous definition of the concept of instinct. Instinct is "faculty of acting in such a way as to produce certain ends, without foresight of the ends and without previous education . . ."[78] Now because of "memory," "reflection," and "inference," man can and does connect the ends of instincts with the present by means of "foresight," so that after it is once performed, "instincts" themselves lose their original "blindness."[79] As is later the case with Dewey, James sees that not absence of instinct but the existence of conflicting impulses make for a use of experience and the rise of rational reflection.[80] A little later,[81] there comes this priceless quotation which foreshadows the orientation to be elaborated upon in larger ways by Dewey:

> "In a perfectly-rounded development, every one of these instincts would start a habit toward certain objects and inhibit a habit toward certain others. Usually, this is the case; but, in the

one-sided development of civilized life, it happens that the timely age goes by in a sort of starvation of objects, and the individual then grows up with gaps in his psychic constitution which future experiences can never fill. Compare the accomplished gentleman with the poor artisan or tradesman of the city: during the adolescence of the former, objects appropriate to his growing interests, bodily and mental, were offered as fast as the interests awoke, and, as a consequence, he is armed and equipped at every angle to meet the world. Sport came to the rescue and completed his education where real things were lacking. He has tasted of the essence of every side of human life, being sailor, hunter, athlete, scholar, fighter, talker, dandy, man of affairs, etc., all in one. Over the city poor boy's youth no such golden opportunities were hung, and in his manhood no desires for most of them exist. Fortunate it is for him if gaps are the only anomalies his instinctive life presents; perversions are too often the fruit of his unnatural bringing up."

Individualism deeply informs James' strictly philosophical thought. And it is also evident in his political sentiment — in his own position as an intellectual mugwump, the psychological level upon which he keeps political and social explanation and hopes in his appeal and search for an individual leader, and in his distaste and political fear of crowds that are seen as bearers of passionate animality.

In his many contexts James was at bottom conservative. In his pronouncements on morals, family life, and temperance this is true. In religion, the only thing not conservative about his view, the only thing original is his explanation, the grounds on which he justified theism. In political matters we have seen that his individualism was bound to place his weight with the regnant *laissez-faire* attitude. On economic and political questions he was usually in the classic liberal position. He wrote to the dainty Henry that the Chicago anarchists were bound to be foreigners, for no native American would act like that. In a time when the muckrake pack were at a high frenzy he could write that the only motive which "socialistic literature" reckons with is "the fear of poverty if one is lazy."[82] And in one of his most widely read books he roots property in the fundamental constitution of man:

"The next instinct which I shall mention is that of *Ownership,* also one of the radical endowments of the race ... The sense of ownership begins in the second year of life. Among the first words which an infant learns to utter are the words 'my' and 'mine' ... The depth and primitiveness of this instinct would seem to cast a sort of psychological discredit in advance upon all radical forms of communistic utopia. Private proprietorship cannot be practically abolished until human nature is changed ... In education, the instinct of ownership is funda mental, and can be appealed to in many ways."[83]

1. Following Perry., *op. cit.*, Vol. II, Chapter LXVII.

2. *Ibid.*, p. 280.

3. *Ibid.*, p. 281.

4. *See* letter to Holt, *Ibid.*, p. 288.

5. *Ibid.*, p. 282.

6. R. B. Perry, *op. cit.*, Vol. I, p. 243.

7. *Letters of William James,* Vol. I, p. 284, quoted by Perry, *op. cit.*, Vol. II, p. 291.

8. *Ibid.*, p. 291.

9. R. B. Perry, *op. cit.*, Vol. II, pp. 294-95.

10. *American Newspaper Annual and Directory,* N. W. Ayer and Son, Philadelphia, yearly statements.

11. "Publishers Statement" for period ending July 30, 1926; A.B.C. *Blue Book,* pp. 105-06.

12. *Fifty Years of American Idealism: The New York Nation, 1865-1915.* Selections and Comments by Gustav Pollak. (New York, 1915).

13. Charles A. and Mary R. Beard, *The Rise of American Civilization,* Vol. II, p. 306.

14. *Ibid.*, p. 306.

15. R. B. Perry, *op. cit.*, Vol. II, p. 296.

16. *Ibid.*, p. 297.

17. *Ibid.*, p. 296.

18. *Ibid.*, p. 298.

19. *Ibid.*, p. 298.

20. *Ibid.*, Vol. I, pp. 300-01, quoted from *Letters of William James,* Vol. I, p. 154.

21. *Ibid.*, Vol. II, p. 298.

22. *Ibid.*, Vol. II, p. 298.

23. *Ibid.*, Vol. II, p. 299.

24. *Ibid.*, Vol. II, p. 299.

25. *Ibid.*, Vol. II, p. 299.

26. *The Will to Believe,* p. 218.

27. *Ibid.*, pp. 225-26.

28. R. B. Perry, *op. cit.*, Vol. II, pp. 28-29, quoted from *Letters of William James.*

29. *Ibid.*, p. 304.

30. *Ibid.*, p. 304.

31. *Ibid.*, p. 317.

32. Letter, July 27, 1903, to Dr. Samuel Delano, quoted by Perry, *ibid.*, p. 318.

33. *McClures Magazine*, February, 1908, "The Social Value of the College Bred," reprinted in *Memories and Studies* (New York, 1911).

34. R. B. Perry, *op. cit.*, Vol. II, pp. 300-01.

35. *Ibid.*, p. 302.

36. *Ibid.*, p. 303.

37. *Ibid.*, pp. 318-19.

38. *Ibid.*, p. 305. Quoted from Letters of William James, Vol. II, pp. 30-32.

39. Letter quoted in Perry, Vol. II, p. 307.

40. Letter, quoted in Perry, Vol. II, p. 308.

41. Letter, quoted in Perry, Vol. II, p. 309.

42. R. B. Perry, *op. cit.*, Vol. II, p. 310.

43. Letter quoted in Perry, Vol. II, p. 310.

44. Letter to *Boston Evening Transcript*, March 4, 1899, quoted in Perry, Vol. II, p. 311.

45. R. B. Perry, *op. cit.*, Vol. II, p. 311.

46. Letter to *Boston Evening Transcript*, Apr. 15, 1899, quoted in Perry, Vol. II, pp. 311-12.

47. R. B. Perry, *op. cit.*, Vol. II, p. 314.

48. *Ibid.*, pp. 314-15.

49. *Letters of William James*, pp. 124-29, quoted in Perry, Vol. II, p. 251. *See* also James' pleas for American leisure and recreation against "Strenuousness" in *The Nation* and again in *The Atlantic Monthly*, both of 1873.

50. *McClures Magazine*, August, 1910, reprinted in *Memories and Studies*, (New York 1910) p. 267f.

51. It is interesting to observe that this general position is upheld by James, Dewey and Mead. In the latter two it sometimes operates as a pervasive assumption in addition to an explicit ideal.

52. *Ibid.*, p. 272.

53. *Ibid.*, p. 275.

54. *Ibid.*, p. 276.

55. *Ibid.*, p. 288.

56. *Ibid.*, p. 290.

57. Interestingly, this general position is upheld by James, Dewey and Mead. In the literature it sometimes operates indelicately as a pervasive assumption in addition to an explicit ideal.

58. Report of Fifth Annual Meeting of the New England Anti-Imperialist League, November 28, 1903, quoted in Perry, Vol. II, p. 313.

59. R. B. Perry, *op. cit.*, Vol. II, p. 315.

60. *Ibid.*, Vol. II, p. 315.

61. *Ibid.*, Vol. II, p. 316.

62. *Letters of William James*, Vol. II, pp. 100-01, cited in Perry *ibid.*, Vol. II, p. 316.

63. "The Ph.D. Octopus," *Harvard Monthly*, (March, 1903).

64. *See* above, on Holmes.

65. *Memories and Studies* p. 309.

66. *Talks to Teachers on Psychology* (New York 1899), pp. 186-88.

67. *The Varieties of Religious Experience*, p. 512.

68. *Pragmatism*, pp. 285-86.

69. *Ibid.*, p. 216.

70. *The Will to Believe*, p. 30.

71. Quoted by R. B. Perry in *Shall Not Perish from the Earth*, (New York 1940), p. 44.

72. *Ibid.*, p. 45.

73. *Memories and Studies*, pp. 102-03, quoted in Perry, Vol. II, pp. 286-87.

74. "In one way or another he always found a way to provide for universals, generals, and concepts, however much he might disparage them. This persistent retention of a modicum of Platonic realism, despite the general tendency of his thought to the contrary, was largely due to Perice's insistence on the rights of thought as opposed to sensation." Perry, Vol. II, pp. 406-07.

75. *Principles of Psychology*, Vol. I, p. 225

76. *Ibid.*, p. 125.

77. *Ibid.*, p. 121.

78. *Ibid.*, Vol. II, p. 383.

79. *Ibid.*, p. 390.

80. *Ibid.*, p. 440f.

81. *Ibid.*, p. 393.

82. *Memories and Studies*, p. 284.

83. *Talks to Teachers on Psychology*, pp. 55-56.

PART IV

15

John Dewey

John Dewey was born in Vermont, in the town of Burlington, in the year 1859. His father, Archibald Sprague Dewey, had also been born in Vermont; he was the son of a farmer come to town and turned groceryman.[1] Above his store he placed a sign "Hams and cigars, smoked and unsmoked" and urged the sale of cigars with a Yankee moral twinge: "a good excuse for a bad habit." Practically without formal schooling, he was far from illiterate. He read the great English dramatists, quoted Milton, Burns, enjoyed Lamb, Thackeray, held a regard for conventional theology. He was "easy going." He sold more goods than he collected bills for. He hoped that at "least one of his four boys would become a mechanic."

Lucina Artemesia Rich, John Dewey's mother, was almost twenty years younger than Archibald Sprague Dewey. She derived from a more prosperous family than he; she possessed a grandfather in Congress, brothers who went to college and a father who was a lay judge, had property, and was called "squire." After a visit to the "revivalizing" West, Lucina Rich broke the Universalist tradition to become a member of the Congregationalist church. She wanted her sons to go to college.

John's close friends were sons of the president of the University of Vermont, which was located in Burlington. He spent a few summers on "Squire" Rich's farm and on "fishing trips" on Lake Champlain. From an early age John was "bashful," "self-conscious," and somewhat of a "bookworm." The Dewey boys had a newspaper route and tallied lumber in from Canada. The money so earned was spent for books: an encyclopedia, the Waverley novels. Like the bulk of Burlington's young, and unlike the men of the previous generation who had come together in the Metaphysical Club, John Dewey attended a local public school.

Back in 1827 the legislature of Vermont had provided for the examination and licensing of teachers. Schools were sponsored by "town committees." This arrangement was changed several times.[2] About the year Dewey finished high school, there was a change in the arrangement. But the tradition of a free and public system through high school was rather steady in Vermont. Dewey finished high school in 1874 at the age of fifteen. Peirce was then thirty-five, James was thirty-two, the Metaphysical Club was coming to an end.

During the last half of the nineteenth century New England states in general were industrialized. But Vermont tended strongly to remain agricultural; even in 1913 more of the population derived support from agriculture than from any other industry.[3] Only one-seventh of the farms were in this year let out to tenants. In very few states has the general body of citizens been so free from want.[4] Vermont has been "conservative, rural, individualistic; in all respects it is moderate. There is little extreme poverty and no great wealth."[5]

Burlington has been and remains the largest town in the state. In 1913 it contained 20,468 persons.[6] In 1937 its population numbered around 25,000.[7] Between 1860 and '75 the lumber industry boomed and "foreigners" came in: French Canadians, Irishmen, a few Germans, and some Italians to dig sewers.[8] Nevertheless, such industries as lumber moved West with the population, leaving Vermont, and Burlington, predominantly agricultural. Despite the fact that many of its sons moved out of the state, the population has been rather stationary. In 1850, thirty-eight per cent of those born in Vermont had emigrated.[9] From the Civil War to the nineties represented a period during which very many farmers became suddenly quite wealthy from the doubling or trebling of land value and the increased price of farm products.[10] There was money made on sheep, which was perhaps the central industry of the state. New England, a land of small holdings and home industries was a land of "chores;" there was work for all, and they did it.

The religion of Vermont was, of course, Protestant. As for Dewey's early contacts with religious institutions and view, not much need be directly said. There was some "moralistic emotional pressure" exerted by "the religious atmosphere" which was "evangelical rather than puritanic."[11] But, "more broadening influences were not lacking," *i.e.*, "escape into the outdoors." However this may be, Dewey only "nominally accepted the religious teachings" of his period and place. At an early age he had "joined the White Street Congregational Church in Burlington." This organization did not apparently satisfy his "emotional need," and "his belief was never whole-hearted."[12] Not until his contact with the Idealism of Hegel during late adolescence did he attain to a "fusion of emotions and intellect." He reserved the "private judgment," so dear to and typical of Congregational "independence."

After uneventfully completing high school Dewey entered the University of Vermont, which was situated near his home, and graduated Phi Beta Kappa. With him in the class were his brother, Davis, and sixteen other men. The year was 1879.

The University of Vermont (under various names) was chartered in 1791, 1800, and again in 1834; it was finally given its public legal status in 1865 in connection with the United States Act of 1862 covering land.[13] No figures are readily available on graduates during the period of Dewey's attendance. But some indication of the scale of things is shown by the fact that 333 students (not including the medical school) graduated between 1891-1900. A breakdown of their eventual occupations is interesting: fifty-five per cent became businessmen; thirty-three per cent, teachers; twenty-three per cent, engineers; nine per cent, physicians; four per cent, clergymen; four per cent, agriculturalists. Even taking into account the agricultural school the number of agriculturalists seems quite low; these figures probably should be viewed in conjunction with the emigration indicated.[14]

In Dewey's time the curriculum of the university was rather fixed, but by no means was it particularly "narrow." Fortunately, in recollection, Dewey has singled out for comment certain instructors, courses, and publications from his college years. A Professor G. H. Perkins taught geology and zoology. He was a member of the Congregational Church, but he used Dana's text, did not hold to a seven-day creation, indeed, he "ordered his material on the theory of evolution." This procedure "aroused little, if any, visible resentment."[15] There was a course which Dewey took in physiology; the text used was written by T. H. Huxley. From this course, Dewey obtained "an impressive picture of the unity of the living creature."

> "I have an impression [he writes] that there was derived from that study a sense of interdependence and interrelated unity that gave form to intellectual stirrings that had been previously inchoate, and created a kind of type or model of a view of things to which material in any field ought to conform. Subconsciously, at least, I was led to desire a world and a life that would have the same properties as had the human organism in the picture of it derived from study of Huxley's treatment. At all events, I got great stimulation from the study, more than from anything I had had contact with before . . ."[16]

The library of the university subscribed to certain English periodicals. There was the *Fortnightly*, "a radical wing of scientific thought." In this sheet, Frederick Harrison's articles were appearing and then Comte's *Positive Philosophy*. Of the latter, in undergraduate days, Dewey writes:

> "I had run across, in the college library, Harriet Martineau's exposition of Comte. I cannot remember that his law of 'the three stages' affected me particularly; but his idea of the disorganized character of Western modern culture, due to a disintegrative 'individualism,' and his idea of a synthesis of science that should be a regulative method of an organized social life, impressed me deeply."[17]

Dewey also states that this was a lead into later contact with Hegel, and:

> "I did not, in those days when I read Francis Bacon, detect the origin of the Comtean idea in him, and I had not made acquaintance with Condorcet, the connecting link."[18]

Other English periodicals available and read were the *Contemporary Review*, "a moderate organ of more traditional views" and the *Nineteenth Century*, which took the "middle course" via symposia. In all these magazines evolution, Tyndall and Huxley, and science in general, were central topics of discussion. They formed the "chief stimulus of John Dewey at this time and affected him more deeply than his regular courses in philosophy."[19]

On the other hand, President Buckham, who gave little moral "pep talks," was "Socratic" rather than "dogmatic" in his theme, and such moral and religious content as there was made "little permanent impression on the future philosopher." H. A. P. Torrey taught psychology. "Like most philosophy taught in American Colleges at this time," his lectures were based upon the Scottish school.[20] "Insistence upon intuitions" formed "the chief intellectual bulwark of moral and religious beliefs against the dissolving effect of English empiricism."[21] Later "German spiritualistic idealism" performed this role. There was some mediation of Marsh and his Transcendental tradition via Torrey.[22] Other books indicated by Dewey are Noah Porter's *Intellectual Philosophy*, Butler's *Analogy*, Plato's *Republic* and Bain's *Rhetoric*, which Dewey terms "relatively innocuous."

After graduating from the University of Vermont, Dewey was anxious and uncertain about a career. "Like many other young graduates" in the same position, Dewey "wanted a teaching position." He was twenty. Apparently he was not out for money.[23] He needed a job. His appointment to a high school in South Oil City, Pennsylvania, for the next two years, 1879-80, seems to have been connected with his cousin, Clara Wilson, being principal of the school; when she "resigned to marry" Dewey left South Oil City. He had taught the usual round of high school subjects, including "latin, algebra, natural science."

Back in Vermont, he taught during part of the winter in "a village school" in Charlotte, a town neighboring Burlington. He started reading some classics in philosophy "under the direction of Professor Torrey." Dewey and Torrey took walks together, had long talks. Dewey remembers Torrey's comment that:

> "undoubtedly pantheism is the most satisfactory form of metaphysics intellectually, but it goes counter to religious faith." Dewey comments: "I fancy that remark told of an inner conflict that prevented his native capacity from coming to full fruition. His interest in philosophy, however, was genuine, not perfunctory; he was an excellent teacher, and I owe to him a double debt, that of turning my thoughts definitely to the study of philosophy as a life-pursuit, and of a generous gift of time to me during a year devoted privately under his direction to a reading of classics in the history of philosophy and learning to read philosophic German. In our walks and talks during this

year, after 3 years on my part of high-school teaching, he let
his mind go much more freely than in the class-room . . ."[24]

The university library subscribed to *The Journal of Speculative
Philosophy;* to its editor, W. T. Harris, Dewey sent "in fear and
trembling" an essay, and asked Harris for career advice.

> ". . . .a few articles which I sent to Dr. W. T. Harris, the well-
> known Hegelian, and the editor of the *Journal of Speculative
> Philosophy,* the only philosophic journal in the country at that
> time, as he and his group formed almost the only group of lay-
> men devoted to philosophy for non-theological reasons. . .His
> reply was so encouraging that it was a distinct factor in decid-
> ing me to try philosophy as a professional career."[25]

These articles show no influence of Hegel. Indeed, as Dewey has
written, "of Hegel I was then ignorant."[26] The articles are quite
formal in treatment and intuitively put. It is safe to pass them over,
as Dewey does, writing: "My deepest interests had not as yet been
met."[27] It is interesting, however, to note that "The Metaphysical
Assumptions of Materialism" ends with his:

> ". . . as a philosophical theory materialism has proved it-
> self a complete felo-de-se. To afford itself a thinkable basis, it
> assumes things which thoroughly destroy the theory."[28]

At any rate, encouraging word finally came and Harris published
three essays. It was due, then, to Torrey and to Harris that Dewey
was led into philosophy as a profession. In 1882 John Dewey bor-
rowed $500 from an aunt and enrolled in Johns Hopkins at Balti-
more, Maryland. His second year at Hopkins was financed by a
fellowship. His reasons for selection of schools are not available.
A year later his brother, Davis, came to Baltimore; upon gradua-
tion he went to the Massachusetts Institute of Technology to teach
economics and statistics, to organize a course in "engineering administration."[29] Another brother, whom Dewey had not seen
much, became a businessman in California.

Of course, the place to go for a downright statement that Dewey's mode of thought is explainable in Green Mountain terms is to
Green Mountain. Going there, we are not disappointed, for we
find a most interesting little book, *The Yankee Tradition,*[30] in

which Dewey is viewed as the Philosopher of Chittenden County. On page four we read: "We are not here so much concerned with the fact that Vermont became a part of the U.S.A.; we are very much more concerned with what Vermont *brought* to the Union!" Which reminds one of what the Vermont farmer told the New Yorker who said that if there was war, he'd just come to Vermont and settle down until it was over. To which the Yankee replied: "The trouble with that, mister, is that if the U.S. went to war it wouldn't be long before Vermont would also."

"It is clear," asserts the address, "that Dewey gave philosophical statement to ways of Yankee culture."[31] And again, "John Dewey's brand of instrumental philosophy is nothing other than the Yankee's common sense practical way of looking at everyday situations and problems in terms of getting things done."[32] And then, mounting in pitch: "John Dewey wedded philosophy to practical life and related Yankee folkways so powerfully to modern living that through him the Yankee tradition has become the single greatest influence in the mind and character of the Twentieth Century!"

This is a rather strong statement. It attributes an enormous influence to John Dewey and this power is to be imputed to "the Yankee tradition." Despite the Vermont Historical Society, we shall have to reserve judgment on both points until evidence is brought to bear.[33] But now two things should be noted. One is, of course, "practicality" and the other is emphasis upon "the primary community." Both of these items are to receive detailed attention. Here it must only be remarked (1) that large areas of America (and not only Vermont) in the latter nineteenth century displayed both facts socially; (2) that other boys from Chittenden County, Vermont, came away to become intellectuals, businessmen, or statisticians without displaying in any marked intellectual manner either of the two traits;[34] (3) that Dewey had a few experiences beyond the Green Mountains and they have to be given some independent weight. One cannot proceed so genetically as to make unnecessary a biography beyond age twenty. The point is that we have to seek out, if there are such, factors in the post-Vermont career of Dewey that implemented what he felt and thought within the confines of Vermont.

By the fall of 1882, when Dewey entered Johns Hopkins, this

graduate center had been in operation for six years, had a staff of forty-three men.[35] Apparently three of them taught philosophy.[36] Dewey was one of the eight hundred or so persons who, during the early eighties, worked on the Ph.D. degree in America.[37] It would be nineteen years before the American Philosophical Society would be formed. Even at Hopkins, President Gilman told the bookish Dewey to shift fields, apparently on the grounds that the professional chances were low for anyone not a clergyman. But it was not to be expected that a young man who had published three articles in philosophy would now shift career prospects. Dewey took a minor in history and political science under Herbert Adams.

The generally scientific atmosphere of Hopkins has been detailed in Part I above. Concretely, those individuals who are singled out as Dewey's circle at Hopkins were predominantly concerned with the several divisions of scientific work. In addition to his brother, there was an individual who later became a governor of Puerto Rico; the others were being trained in science: one becoming a professor of physics; another (Dewey's room mate for a while) a biologist; another a physiologist; and two, noted psychologists.

The philosophical situation at Hopkins was handled by "one of the few teachers in philosophy in the United States who was not a clergyman," one George S. Morris.[38] Apparently at no time in his incubative period was Dewey exposed to active religious denunciations of science. Indeed, quite the reverse. Hopkins was the very center of academic, scientific influence at the time, and this general atmosphere was concretely implemented by the fellow students and teachers with whom Dewey was in closest contact. G. Stanley Hall, recently returned from Germany, also handled philosophy. From him Dewey was infected with the new "experimental psychology" and with the belief that psychology and philosophy were intimates.[39] But, seemingly, it was neither Hall nor Peirce but Morris to whom Dewey was then most drawn and who "left a deep impress" upon his mind. Morris had "reacted strongly against the religious orthodoxy of a puritanic New England upbringing," had passed through a discipleship of the latter British empiricists.[40] More importantly, he had received Hegel directly from German hands in Germany and was in correspondence with Oxford Hegelians of the day.[41]

Since Dewey was, as we shall see, constantly and deeply influenced by G. S. Morris, it is worthwhile briefly to examine Morris' career. He was of the generation of Peirce and James, was born in 1840 in, significantly, Dewey's native state of Vermont. His father was a preacher, who was also "interested in several . . . modest manufacturing industries."[42] Wenley, his biographer, has aptly indicated the Puritanical traces on his thought and has written that he was among "the last, or almost the last incarnation of a race of thinkers whose theological beliefs determined their political aspirations."[43] Concerning these theological beliefs, it is interesting and symbolic to note, in view of the above statement made under Dewey's own direction of Morris' insurgency from religious beliefs, that Morris, like James' father, James himself (and also Tufts, an associate to be presented below) was concerned with the overthrow of "the barrier between the sacred and the secular."

> "He hardly saw [writes Wenley] that the dangerous foe of idealism is, not materialism, but dualism. For, disciplines to account Christianity a thing apart, it was more than difficult for him to replace this tradition with a conception of experience dependent upon a view of unity that overthrew every artificial barrier between *the* sacred and *the* secular. No doubt, he came to realize that a denial of the possibility of knowledge of the infinite struck at the foundations alike of thought and morals. Nevertheless, he scarcely arrived at the point where this unity became fatal to the last form of exclusiveness — the separate self. Odd reminiscences of the 'relation between faith and works,' survivals of Puritan modes, maintained a separation between self and the Ultimate."[44]

An excerpt from a letter from Joshua L. Chamberlain of Bowdoin College to Professor Smith in 1872 about Morris is significant in this general respect:

> "Some of our watchmen on the walls think Professor Morris may have tendencies to Rationalism, or at all events may not be in strict accordance with the 'orthodox' faith.
> "I regard the chair of Philosophy as of more importance than the Presidency. We need a strong, sound man.
> "May I venture to ask for a word in confidence as to Professor Morris?"[45]

Relative to political orientation, the following is very revealing and interesting; it is written from a conservative point of view:

"... the single recorded attack upon Morris ... February, 1884 ... The ground of criticism reflected the callow *Aufklarung* fashionable then with some undergraduates, whose thinking lay altogether ahead. Indeed, it was a survival of eighteenth century *Weltweisheit* which, thanks in large measure to their preoccupation with middle-class politics and commerce, continued to pass for philosophy among the English-speaking peoples, for nigh a century after the *Critique of Pure Reason*. The valiant spokesman charged, briefly, that Morris and Howison were 'totally out of sympathy with that thought which is admitted to be most characteristic of our own race and time'; and at much greater length, that their political teaching was 'fundamentally opposed to the spirit of our own institutions as well as of every other good government.' The eagle screams here, striking the note that was to dominate the symphony of Mc-Kinleyism ... Dr. Angell told me that the incident caused some amusement, at the expense of the writer; and an alumnus who belongs to this period writes, 'I doubt if students in general took much interest in the matter.' Nevertheless, it intimates something as a symptom. For, as my correspondent adds, the critic 'was the most aggressive of a group of men who took pride in advanced ideas on philosophy, politics and religion, and were ardent followers of Herbert Spencer.' "[46]

Morris had gone to Hopkins in 1878-84, retaining his connection with The University of Michigan.[47]

It was at Hopkins under Morris that Dewey began an intensive learning of Hegel. And it is Hegel that formed Dewey's first, late adolescent orientation, the first categorical ground plan of his mind. Fortunately, we know from his own remarks what Hegel meant to him at this time and also what some of the personal and social factors were which led him so quickly to acceptance. There was undoubtedly the appeal of the enthusiasm of Professor Morris, who believed in the "demonstrated truth of the substance of German idealism and of belief in its competency to give direction to a life of aspiring thought, emotion and action." At the age of seventy-one Dewey could look back and say of Morris:

"I have never known a more single-hearted and whole-souled man — a man of a single piece all the way through; while I long since deviated from his philosophical faith, I should be happy to believe that the influence of the spirit of his teaching has been an enduring influence."[48]

Morris' enthusiastic devotion in presenting his material served as a focus close at hand of the wide influence which Hegelianism was exerting in English and American thought in the eighties and nineties. It was a reaction against the British sensationalism and affiliated individualistic blends which we have seen drew James. But Dewey took to the reaction and became a Hegelian. This movement, which was ascendent in much philosophical literature[49] which Dewey apparently read:

> "naturally . . . fell in with and reinforced that of Professor Morris. There was but one marked difference, and that, I think, was in favour of Mr. Morris. He came to Kant through Hegel himself. Moreover, he retained something of his early Scotch philosophical training in a common-sense belief in the existence of the external world. He used to make merry over those who thought the *existence* of this world and of matter were things to be proved by philosophy. To him the only philosophical question was as to the *meaning* of this existence; his idealism was wholly of the objective type."[50]

But perhaps the simple fact of the ascendency of Hegelian writing and of its espousal at the hands of Dewey's teacher would not have been sufficient to have swung Dewey so well into its ambit without the factors of his previous social and intellectual maturation which also led him to embrace it. The only self-statement of such factors was what Dewey wrote in 1930, that Hegel's thought had:

> "supplied a demand for unification that was doubtless an intense emotional craving, and yet was a hunger that only an intellectualized subject-matter could satisfy . . . the sense of divisions and separations that were, I suppose, born in upon me as a consequence of a heritage of New England culture, divisions by way of isolating of self from the world, of soul from body, of nature from God, brought a painful oppression — or, rather, they were an inward laceration."[51]

Dewey's earlier reading of philosophy under the guidance of Torrey "had been an intellectual gymnastic. Hegel's synthesis of subject and object, matter and spirit, the divine and the human, was, however, no mere intellectual formula; it operated as an immense release, a liberation."[52]

It has already been indicated that Dewey failed to achieve an early orientation within the religious doctrines of Congregationalism. It was not until the assimiliation of Hegel that such an orientation was achieved. As for the strictly "religious problem" and the way in which it functioned in the formation and direction of Dewey's mind, it seemed to remain largely on the personal sphere. It was not thrown up *directly* into his intellectual focus. Of this Dewey writes: ". . . while the conflict of traditional religious beliefs with opinions that I could myself honestly entertain was the source of a trying personal crisis, it did not at any time constitute a leading philosophical problem."[53] It should be kept in mind that the continuation of this passage, which follows, was written in 1930:

> "This might look as if the two things were kept apart; in reality it was due to a feeling that any genuinely sound religious experience could and should adapt itself to whatever beliefs one found oneself intellectually entitled to hold — a half unconscious sense at first, but one which ensuing years have deepened into a fundamental conviction."[54]

The statement indicates and implies (a) that "religious questions" were on the personal plane and, more importantly, (b) that what one decided about them was thought to be a function of the solution of "intellectual" matters. "Religion" as such is not given cognitive status. This statement, even though it is retrospective, is given support by several other items in the career of Dewey. It is possible, Dewey thinks, that the "cold logic and acute analysis" of Butler's *Analogy*, which Dewey studied in Vermont, "in a reversed way" might have implemented a "skepticism."[55] He has also stated in this connection:

> "I was brought up in a conventionally evangelical atmosphere of the more 'liberal' sort; and the struggles that later arose between acceptance of that faith and the discarding of traditional and institutional creeds came from personal experiences and not from the effects of philosophical teaching. It was not, in other words, in this respect that philosophy either appealed to me or influenced me."[56]

The keeping of the "religious issues" on the plane of "personal experiences" seems to hang together with the influence of Dewey's wife as this influence has been stated by their daughter. Dewey's wife, who "never accepted any church dogma" seems to have been a catalytic agent upon the "young man from conservative Burlington."

Dewey's acceptance of Hegel, whose works were available to him in current literature and through a teacher representative, can then be looked upon as filling such personal religious emptiness as existed; but this filling took its own forms, which were not directly religious. That is, in no sense did Dewey take to Hegel in order to justify conventional religious beliefs which troubled him. The troubles, such as they were, at least on the surface, were kept to himself.[57]

We have considered briefly factors in the acceptance of Hegel, his availability and the function he filled in Dewey's psychic economy. We shall now set forth the character and focus which made up the "permanent deposit" left by Hegelian thought in Dewey.[58] They seem to be twofold.

On the one side, Hegelianism filled in, reinforced, gave respectable and public sanction to the bent toward logical schematization, so deeply impressed upon the reader of Dewey's writings, especially the earlier publications. Detailed attention will be given to this categorical imprint upon his logic. It should perhaps here be mentioned that Dewey's interest in logic was itself fed greatly by Morris. "The influence of Professor Morris was undoubtedly one source of Dewey's later interest in logical theory."[59]

More important in our present context, Hegel seems to have performed a service in Dewey's development in focusing his attention upon social and psychological affairs. This focus on "social interests and problems," in Dewey's own words, "from an early period had to me the intellectual appeal and provided the intellectual sustenance that may seem to have been found primarily in religious questions."[60]

We have already indicated Dewey's contact with Comte's view of science as having a "regulative" role in society. And now Dewey found in Hegel, he writes, a similar type of criterion of "individualism" "combined with a deeper and more far reaching interpretation in Hegel,"[61] that is, an interpretation of personal and social experiences involving dissatisfaction with conventional religion.

Apart from the personal "religious function" of Hegel upon Dewey and the sanctioning he derived of schematic thinking, there was another function of Hegel which is even more important for Dewey's future mental development: it was Hegelian thought, on the strictly intellectual side, which channelled the "displacement" of religious matters by the social and psychological. "Hegel's treatment of human culture," writes Dewey, "of institutions and the arts, involved the same dissolution of hard-and-fast dividing walls, and had a special attraction for me."[62] And, in 1939, Dewey made more precise the character of this function of Hegel: "Hegel's idea of cultural institutions as an 'objective mind' upon which individuals were dependent in the formation of their mental life fell in with the influence of Comte..."[63] The very central influence of this notion not only upon Dewey's social psychology but upon the full statement of his logic will be seen later. His face was turned toward the social contents, but it was later at Michigan where he first taught courses that he looked quite closely at them.

The summer of 1884 was for Dewey an uncertain one until Professor Morris returned to his regular position at the University of Michigan and offered him $900 a year and an instructorship. The acceptance of this position led to social experiences that were to operate decisively upon the direction of his intellectual attention. Given his eastern background, he felt at Ann Arbor the full force of the liberal state institution under President Angell. Among state universities, Michigan in the eighties and nineties was one of the most progressive, that is, it maintained close contacts with other institutions and social affairs in the state.[64] It encouraged instructor participation at faculty meetings; it was coeducational; its curricula contained a heavy emphasis on the sciences and technologies.

The following passage in appreciation of Morris is indicative not only of Morris' style but of his appeal to Dewey as a reinforcement of what Hegel *did for* Dewey, as discussed above. It also links with the mood of a state or public university:

> "... before the time of Dr. Morris and his able assistant, Dr. Dewey, the Department of Philosophy occupied a vague and dusty corner, set apart for those isolated metaphysical discussions that seem out of relation to everything. But it gradually

began to dawn upon us as we listened to his lectures that what we called philosophy was really an explanation of life itself in all its relations and import. It was a recognition of the 'spiritual yearning' that comes even to the least thoughtful that underlay all of Dr. Morris' teaching. His lectures were not simply to tell us what Kant and Hegel taught, and what were the missing links in Berkeley and Hume, but to give us sane conceptions of thinking and acting."[65]

In 1888, there were 1,882 students and 100 faculty members at the University of Michigan. In this community at Ann Arbor, Dewey was for the first time fully accepted as an adult with a responsible task. And this situation at Michigan "made a deep impression on Dewey, starting the chain of ideas which later comprised his educational theory."[66]

It was in a boarding house, where Dewey roomed with another young instructor, that he met Miss Alice Chipman, whom he was to marry two years later, in July 1886. She had taught school "for several years to earn the money to complete her education" and was in 1884 a "coed." Those who would like to see Dewey's thought interpreted as having some intrinsic and direct connection with the life of pioneers on the frontier will be happy to find that Miss Chipman was of "pioneer" background. She is the only member of the pragmatic retinue we have found who was directly so linked. Her father had moved from Vermont to Michigan as a boy and followed the trade of a "cabinet maker." Being orphaned young, Alice Chipman was reared by maternal grandparents, the Riggs. Mr. Riggs was an agent for the Hudson Bay Company, "a very early settler . . ." he had surveyed, "managed Indian trading posts," knew well the Chippewa Indian tongue, and "later took up farming in the wilderness."[67] He apparently exerted little dogmatic moral pressure on his grandchildren, was "a free thinker" who encouraged "intellectual independence and self-reliance."

Alice Chipman's influence on Dewey was "stimulating and exciting." Apart from such purely personal influences there seems to have been two points of contact with her at which Dewey was directly influenced:

(1) "She had a deeply religious nature but had never accepted any church dogma. Her husband acquired from her the belief that a religious attitude was indigenous in natural experience, and that

theology and ecclesiastic institutions had benumbed rather than promoted it."[68]

(2) She had been "awakened by her grandparents to a critical attitude toward social conditions and injustices." Mr. Riggs, for example, was a Democrat, had opposed war, and out of his rather meager accumulations bought "substitutes" for "friends and relatives who were drafted."[69] He had also championed the "vanishing rights" of the Indian. These patterns were part of Alice Chipman and:

> "she was undoubtedly largely responsible for the widening of Dewey's philosophic interests from the commentative and classical to the field of contemporary life. Above all, things which had previously been matters of theory acquired through his contact with her a vital and direct human significance."[70]

Besides the marriage to Miss Chipman, there was a feature of the state of Michigan and its institutions which focused Dewey upon social contents, or more precisely upon educational affairs. There was, first, a chair of education at Michigan, it being one of the very few in the country at that time. Second, there was the practice of the University faculty of visiting the high schools of the state, which was an aid to decisions concerning preparation for college and perhaps an encouragement to high school students to ascend the educational ladder. In addition, there was an organization, "The Schoolmasters Club of Michigan," which by conferences and committees attempted to bring the high schools and university closer together. Dewey visited the high schools, was a member of the Club. Having professionally been thrown into psychological discussions, these institutional connections focused him upon "the learning process" and "in his later years at Ann Arbor he spoke frequently at Teachers' Institutes and Conventions on such topics as " 'attention,' 'memory,' 'imagination,' and 'thinking,' all in relation to teaching and study."[71] While at Ann Arbor he published two books "for teachers in training."[72]

In addition to these affiliations and interests, at Michigan the size of the Department of Philosophy (two and then three men) "permitted" him to teach courses dealing with a rather wide range. They included "political philosophy" and "ethics." In the case of the latter, courses "were assigned to him to teach." These courses are a very important occasion in the development of Dewey's pragmatism. For, as we shall see when we examine his two outlines of ethical theory which he produced for his classes, it is in this sphere of thought that certain categories which are later central to his total style of thinking emerge.

At Ann Arbor also Dewey first began giving courses in political philosophy.

> "In these lectures, he discussed, largely from the historical point of view, theories of 'natural right,' utilitarianism, the British school of jurisprudence, and the idealistic school. The most noteworthy feature of the course was that in the department of philosophy the topics of sovereignty, the nature of legal and political rights and duties, and the history of political thought, in terms of Hobbes, Locke, and Rousseau, were discussed."[73]

During this time, it is stated, "Dewey's political philosophy developed as a line of thought independent of his technical philosophical interests."[74] So, through courses and, in the case of education, institutional affiliation, Dewey's first explicit orientation in ethics, education, and political philosophy came into shape in the atmosphere of Ann Arbor. That changes had come about in his attitudes are indicated in that his father and mother, who came to live with the Deweys during their last years at Michigan were "hurt" at the "son's recreance to the Republican Party" and his "defection from the religious teachings of his boyhood."[75]

There remains to be indicated several of the men with whom Dewey was associated at the University of Michigan. There was first, George S. Morris, about whom we previously commented. The Morrises and the Deweys were in close contact, both intellectually and socially. It was at this time that Dewey was "closest to German objective idealism." One year Dewey went to the University of Minnesota and during this year "his revered teacher" died. At the end of the year Dewey returned to Michigan as head of the department. That same year James Hayden Tufts came to Michigan.

Son of a Yankee, who had been trained at Yale and Andover Theological Seminary, sustaining an interest in discussing theology, principal of a "New England Academy," James Tufts had oscillated between the ministry and college teaching of philoso-

phy, and finally took a doctorate at Frieburg.[76] Very quickly he
and Dewey formed a "personal and intellectual friendship." Later
at Chicago they collaborated on the *Ethics*.[77]

Later to Michigan came A. H. Lloyd and G. H. Mead. Both had
studied at Harvard. Mead was "called from Berlin." With both
men and their families the Deweys formed close bonds, but "the
Meads remained the closest friends of the Deweys . . . until their
deaths."[78] "From the nineties on, the influence of Mead" on Dewey
"ranked with that of James." The character of this influence at that
time is put as follows by Jane Dewey under John Dewey's direction:[79]

> "Mead's scholarship, especially in the natural sciences, was
> much greater than Dewey's. In the years of his association with
> Dewey, Mead's principal interest was the bearing of biological
> theories upon scientific psychology . . . Mead . . . started from
> the idea of the organism acting and reacting in an environment;
> in this view the nervous system, brain included, is an organ for
> regulating the relations of the organism as a whole with objec-
> tive conditions of life. Psychological phenomena, including
> processes of thought and knowledge, must then be described
> from this point of view. Mead had also developed an original
> theory of the *psychical* as the state occurring when previously
> established relations of organism and environment break down
> and new relations have not yet been built up; and, through in-
> clusion of relations of human beings with one another, a the-
> ory of the origin and nature of selves. Dewey did not attempt
> a development of these special ideas, but he took them over
> from Mead and made them a part of his subsequent philoso-
> phy . . ."[80]

The last contact we must mention as occurring during these
early years was with James' writings. Dewey has repeatedly stated
that the influence of James was not exerted by *Pragmatism*:

> "which appeared after Dewey's theory had been formed,
> but by chapters in the *Principles of Psychology* dealing with
> conception, discrimination and comparison, and reasoning.
> Dewey has frequently recommended these chapters to students
> as a better introduction to the essentials of a pragmatic theory
> of knowledge than the *Pragmatism*."[81]

Dewey's mind had, of course, been "prepared" for such conceptions by G. S. Hall at Baltimore. "William James' *Principles of Psychology* was much the greatest single influence in changing the direction of Dewey's philosophical thinking."[82] It is the strain in James which emphasizes the biological bases of an objective psychology which fell in with Dewey's focus. It was similar to such independent development as Mead was then displaying and which held Dewey's attention. This "biologic conception of the *psyche*... worked its way more and more into all" of Dewey's "ideas and acted as a ferment to transform old beliefs."[83]

Dewey was then in letter contact with James. In 1891 he wrote to him, relating that he was going through the *Psychology* with his students and then, referring to the philosophical situation, asserts: "The hope seems to be with the rising generation ... many of my students, I find, are fairly hungering. They almost jump at the opportunity to get out from under the load and to believe in their own lives."[84] This close orientation at Michigan and then later at Chicago to a student body composed of the sons of farmers and businessmen and rising into professional occupations is a feature of Dewey's situation and consequent experience which should not be minimized.

An impression of Dewey in his last years at Michigan from the standpoint of one who was his student runs as follows:

> "John Dewey, whose lectures on political philosophy I attended in 1893-94, certainly left a lasting mark, but rather by his personality, I think, than by his lectures. I had already known him some ten years, as he had come and gone from Michigan as a young instructor in the early eighties when I was an undergraduate. In the group to which I belonged his character was deeply admired, for its simplicity, perhaps, and for a fine gallantry, which, one felt sure, would never compromise the high purpose by which he was visibly animated. We believed that there was something highly original and significant in his philosophy, but had no definite ideas as to what it was. The chief thing I now recall from his lectures is a criticism of Spencer, in which Dewey maintained that society was an organism in a deeper sense than Spencer had perceived, and that language was its 'sensorium'."[85]

When Harper's university opened, James Tufts went to Chicago. "This led to Dewey's being called to Chicago in 1894."[86] There seems to have been at least three generic circles in which Dewey moved during his ten years of residence in the lake city. (1) There was the continuation of educational work which both broadened and deepened his activities in the circles professionally interested in new educational endeavor; this domain also afforded a radical departure for Dewey and for educational theory and practice. (2) For perhaps the first time, he got an intimate glimpse of that area of social affairs conventionally called "social problems" or social conditions. (3) And, of course, there were the professional contacts, the work with the students and the Staff of the University of Chicago and neighboring places.

One of the reasons for John Dewey's acceptance of the offer to come to the University of Chicago was that Pedagogy was included in the courses of the Department he was to head along with Philosophy and Psychology.[87] The leadership of such a Department by no means exhausted his participation in educational affairs. Within a few years, Dewey had organized a group of parents who allowed their children to be educated in ways not available in the Chicago system. Under Dewey's Department an elementary school was begun. "the most widely read and influential of Dewey's writings, *School and Society* . . . consisted of talks given to raise money for the laboratory school."[88] The organization and participation in this school on the part of Dewey is important to us for several reasons:

(a) Through it Dewey was now definitely thrown into contact not only with a full gamut of problems of education, but it enabled him to attempt to put into practice, rather freely it would seem, his theories. Here, in fact, theory and practice (of certain kinds) could interpenetrate. The reasons for this possibility lay in the institutional character of the school. It was not a public school. Dewey and his associates must have had almost complete autonomy. When Dewey left Chicago, the school was promptly terminated. Its connection with the University was through Dewey. Financially it was always in trouble. Its upkeep came from three sources: The University of Chicago gave $1,000; tuition was paid by the parents with rates kept low "for the sake of the parents."[89] For a child of from four to six years of age the rate was $75 a year; for older children it was $90. The third source was gifts. Mrs. C. R. Linn gave $1,200 in 1896, and the deficit was covered by "parents and friends."[90] Regarding the social position of the children's

parents, all we find is the statement that the children came "mainly from professional families."[91] And this is only a guess — that
they were alumni of the University, rising into the professions from
business and farming. At any rate, "The entire history of the school
was marked by an unusual degree of cooperation among parents,
teachers, and pupils."[92]

Due to this institutional arrangement Dewey had a relatively
free hand. This, of course, would not have been the case had the
school been a member of a city or a state system — nor if it had
been larger. The number of pupils at all times seems to have been
below 100.

(b) The experimental school formed perhaps the central experience and activity from which the leading ideas in at least the "educational" publications of Dewey are correspondent. We have indicated the first social use of *School and Society; How We Think*
and *Democracy and Education* are direct fruits of his Chicago experience."[93] Elsewhere Dewey has stated that the latter book
"was for many years that in which my philosophy . . . was most
fully expounded."[94]

That the school was not merely an "administrative" matter to
Dewey is quite clear; it was a domain into which he translated
ideas for "test."

> "John Dewey, when called to be the head of the department
> in 1894, had arrived at certain philosophical and psychological
> ideas which he desired to test in practical application. This de-
> sire was not merely personal, but flowed from the very nature
> of the ideas themselves. For it was part of the philosophical and
> psychological theory he entertained that ideas, even as ideas,
> are incomplete and tentative until they are employed in appli-
> cation to objects in action and are thus developed, corrected,
> and tested. The need of a laboratory was indicated . . . A school
> was the answer to the need. During the years at Chicago, Mr.
> Dewey's thought along these lines was greatly stimulated and
> enriched."[95]

Dewey translated philosophical or general problems into the
context of the school.[96] For example, here is a central concern of
Dewey's so translated:

> ". . . there is still one unsolved problem in elementary and

secondary education. That is the question of duly adapting to each other the practical and utilitarian, the executive and the abstract, the tool and the book, the head and the hand. This is a problem of such vast scope that any systematic attempt to deal with it must have great influence upon the whole course of education everywhere. The School of Education, both in its elementary and secondary departments, is trying to make its contribution to this vexed question."[97]

In facing concrete situations and having no tradition of routines to guide procedure, the "experimental" character of the school was underlined by the situation in which it existed. In another connection, the entire school set-up in America was expanding and in such a situation, the "experimental", as against the traditional, had its chance. Dewey states:

"The concrete circumstances of school life introduce many factors that are not foreseen and taken account of in theory. This is as formal and static as the life of teachers and children in school is moving and vital . . . not merely the concrete material, the subject matter of the pupils' studies, but the methods of teaching were developed in the course of the school's own operations. This development signifies, of course, that the experience of one year taught something about what was to be done the next year and how it was to be better done."[98]

And again:

"It involved departure from the conception that, in the main, the proper materials and methods of education are already well-known and need only to be furthered, refined, and extended. It implied continual experimentation to discover the conditions under which educative growth actually occurs. It implied also much more attention to present conditions in the life of individuals, children, and contemporary society than was current in schools based chiefly upon the attainments of the past. It involved the substitution of an active attitude of work and play and of inquiry for the processes of imposition and passive absorption of readymade knowledge and performed skills that largely dominated the traditional school. It implied a much larger degree of opportunity for initiative, discovery, and independent communication of intellectual freedom than was characteristic of the traditional school."[99]

As far as the central ideas governing the operation and plan of the school are concerned two are stressed. In terms of conceptions, they are "action" and the "social":

> ". . . two cardinal principles were held in mind. First, in all educative relationships the starting point is the impulse of the child to action, his desire responding to the surrounding stimuli and seeking its expression in concrete form. Second, the educational process is to supply the materials and the positive and negative conditions — the let and hindrance — so that his expression, intellectually controlled, may take a normal direction that is social in both form and feeling. These principles determined the entire school's operation and organization, as a whole and in detail."[100]

And Dewey writes in the *University Record* of May 21, 1897:

> "As regards the spirit of the school, the chief object is to secure a free and informal community life in which each child will feel that he has a share and his own work to do. This is made the chief motive towards what are ordinarily termed order and discipline. It is believed that the only *genuine* order and discipline are those which proceed from the child's own respect for the work which he has to do and his consciousness of the rights of others who are, with himself, taking part in this work. As already suggested, the emphasis in the school upon various forms of practical and constructive activity gives ample opportunity for appealing to the child's social sense and to his regard for thorough and honest work."[101]

Throughout, one underlying aim was to utilize the child's "original impulses to express himself." But what impulses? Four are given by Dewey:[102]

> (a) "The social impulse . . . share . . . experiences . . ."
> (b) "The constructive impulse . . . shaping raw materials"
> (c) "The impulse to investigate and experiment . . ."
> (d) "The expressive impulse . . . utensils and materials necessary to express ideas were . . . at hand . . ."

It would seem that a sort of *artisan community* in microcosm was being reconstructed. It should not, however, be assumed that this was utilitarian — for Dewey asserts that because of the professional families from which the children came "there was little prospect of any utility of this sort."[103]

(c) It is responsibly asserted that "contacts formed through the school are among the most important of the many formed in Chicago."[104] That is, this endeavor and organization circumscribed to some extent the area of Dewey's social experience in a quite formative episode of his career. As to what the organization meant to Dewey personally we can infer from the fact that it was directly because of President Harper's "indifference or hostility to the unendowed school" that Dewey resigned his position at Chicago in 1904. The range of contact made available by the Laboratory School included "the parents and friends who had given the school its financial support" who were "organized into what was probably the first active Parents and Teachers Association in the country."[105] This group was "for Dewey" in the controversy over the abandonment of the organization. The school also threw Dewey into contact with "a group of educationalists of the State of Illinois,"[106] and with Ella Flagg Young, who had risen to a Superintendence of Chicago City schools from a grade school teacher. To her and to his wife Dewey "attributes the greatest influence in educational matters in those years." More especially, through contact with Ella Young, Dewey filled a gap in his experience "in matters of practical administration, crystallizing his ideas of democracy in the school, and by extension, in life."[107] Yet this by no means exhausts the meaning and consequences of contact with Mrs. Young.

Ella Flagg Young — born in New York, 1845, daughter of a sheetmetal "mechanic"[108] — entered Dewey's seminar in 1895, continued it for four years, seems to have been a central student,[109] then for five years she was his colleague in the Department at the University of Chicago. Dewey wrote in a letter anent his "relations to Mrs. Young" that it was:

> "hard for me to be specific, because they were so continuous and so detailed . . . I was constantly getting ideas from her . . . She gave me credit for seeing all the bearings and implications which *she* with her experience and outlook got out of what I said . . . She had by temperament and training the gist of a . . . pragmatism with reference to philosophical conceptions before the doctrine was ever formulated . . . What I chiefly got from Mrs. Young was just the translation of philosophical conceptions into their empirical equivalents."[110]

It should be noted that it was in large part through the departures of "The Dewey School" that Dewey rose among professional educators throughout the country at this time of wide educational ferment and growth.

1. Unless otherwise cited, details of Dewey's life herein contained are drawn from "Biography of John Dewey," written by his daughter, Jane, from material supplied by himself: p. 3f in *The Philosophy of John Dewey*. edited by P. A. Schilpp; or "From Absolutism to Experimentalism" by John Dewey, *Contemporary American Philosophy*. Any *interpretations or imputations* drawn from these sources will be quoted; otherwise I shall make only this general acknowledgement. The first sketch cited above is the most detailed and authoritative extant account of Dewey's life.

2. Rowland E. Robinson, *American Commonwealths: Vermont*. (Boston, 1892). *See* p. 310f.

3. *A Study in Education in Vermont*, Carnegie Foundation for the Advancement of Teaching: Bull. No. 7 (New York, 1913).

4. *A Study in Education in Vermont*, p. 32.

5. Elin L. Anderson, *We Americans*, (Cambridge, 1937) p. 12.

6. *A Study in Education in Vermont*, p. 20.

7. Elin L. Anderson, *op. cit.*, p. 9.

8. *Ibid.*, p. 9f.

9. *A Study in Education in Vermont*, p. 20.

10. Rowland E. Robinson, *op. cit.*, p. 354.

11. Jane Dewey, p. 7.

12. Jane Dewey, p. 17.

13. *A Study in Education in Vermont*, pp. 154-55.

14. Figures from *A Study in Education in Vermont*, p. 162.

15. *Contemporary American Philosophy*, p. 10.

16. *Ibid.*, p. 13.

17. *Ibid.*, p. 20.

18. *Ibid.*, p. 20.

19. Jane Dewey, p. 10.

20. *Ibid.*, p. 11.

21. *Ibid.*, p. 12.

22. *Ibid.*, p. 12. On Marsh *see: Philosophical Review* 34 (1925) pp. 28-50. M. H. Nicolson, "James Marsh and the Vermont Transcendentalists"; and Dewey himself: *Journal of History of Ideas* (April, 1941) on philosophy in early Vermont.

23. Even in 1912-13 no high school teacher in Vermont made more than $844 with an average of $650. *A Study in Education in Vermont*, p. 231.

24. *Contemporary American Philosophy*, pp. 14-15.

25. *Ibid.*, p. 16.

26. *Contemporary American Philosophy*, Vol. II, p. 16.

27. *Ibid.*, p. 16.

28. *Journal of Speculative Philosophy* 16 (1882), pp. 208-13.

29. Rather conservative in political and social opinion, Davis Rich Dewey has by no means been unsuccessful. He was president of the *Economic Association* in 1909, for many years was managing editor of the *American Economic Review*, a trustee of two smaller colleges, he has advised on the US Census and chaired several Boards of Investigation for Mass. *See Leaders In American Education* XX, p. 263, 80. By P. F. Douglas and J. B. Abbott, (Free Press Printing Co., Burlington, Vt. 1941) The substance of this document was "delivered as the address at the annual meeting of the Vermont Historical Society."

30. *Ibid.*, p. 84.

31. *Ibid.*, p. 74.

32. *Ibid.*, p. 23.

33. As it will be, below.

34. *See* figures above on careers of Vermont University graduates and remember that Dewey's brothers became an engineer-statistician-economist and the other, a businessman.

35. *See* Part I above.

36. "Professor G. S. Morris, Professor G. Stanley Hall, and Mr. C. S. Peirce" *see* the brief announcement, "Philosophy at Johns Hopkins University," *Journal of Speculative Philosophy*, 16 (1882) pp. 431-32.

37. Part I above.

38. *See* R. M. Wenley, *Life and Work of G. S. Morris.*

39. Jane Dewey, in *The Philosophy of John Dewey*, p. 22.

40. *See* the *Journal of Speculative Philosophy*, XIII (1879), p. 398 for an announcement of courses in philosophy at Hopkins. They include a heavy emphasis upon "British Thinkers."

41. Jane Dewey, *op. cit.*, pp. 16-17.

42. Wenley, *Life and Work of G. S. Morris*, p. 17.

43. *Ibid.*, p. 17.

44. *Ibid.*, pp. 287-88.

45. *Ibid.*, p. 132.

46. Wenley, *op. cit.*, pp. 162-63.

47. *Ibid.*, pp. 138-42. Also E. F. Farrand, *History of University of Michigan*, (Ann Arbor, 1885) p. 262.

48. Dewey in *Contemporary American Philosophy*, Vol. II, p. 18. *See* also Dewey's review of Wenley's book on Morris, *op. cit.*, in the *Philosophical Review* (March, 1919).

49. Dewey mentions the symposium *Essays in Philosophical Criticism* by younger thinkers under Lord Haldane, the writings of T. H. Green, the Cairds, and of Wallace.

50. *Contemporary American Philosophy*, pp. 18-19.

51. *Ibid.*, p. 19.

52. *Ibid.*, p. 19.

53. *Ibid.*, p. 19.

54. *Ibid.*, pp. 19-20.

55. *Ibid.*, p. 16.

56. *Contemporary American Philosophy*, pp. 15-16. If this is an adequate statement, and I believe it is if taken with other items interpreted in this section, then Dewey and Peirce seem to have at least disavowed similar reasons for entering upon philosophy.

57. We shall enter certain qualifications of this statement later, when we come to consider his early writings. Here I am concerned (1) to give as much weight to Dewey's own self-assertions as possible and (2) to give free play to syntactical change, *i.e.*, what he took from other thinkers.

58. *Contemporary American Philosophy*, p. 21.

59. Jane Dewey, p. 18.

60. *Contemporary American Philosophy*, p. 20.

61. *Ibid.*, p. 20.

62. *Ibid.*, p. 19.

63. Jane Dewey, *op. cit.*, p. 17.

64. It should be mentioned in this connection that philosophy at Johns Hopkins had been linked to a public beyond the student body. In an announcement of "Philosophy at Johns Hopkins" (*J. of Speculative Philosophy*, XIII, 1879, p. 398) it is stated that philosophic programme includes (a) "a course of public lectures; (b) critical and expository lectures for students of the university; and (c) private readings and examinations."

65. Wenley, *op. cit.*, p. 304. Quoted from a former student of Morris.

66. Jane Dewey, *op. cit.*, p. 19.

67. Jane Dewey, p. 20.

68. *Ibid.*, p. 21.

69. *Ibid.*, p. 20.

70. *Ibid.*, p. 21.

71. *Ibid.*, p. 27.

72. *Ibid.*, p. 27.

73. *Ibid.*, p. 38.

74. *Ibid.*, p. 39.

75. *Ibid.*, p. 26.

76. *See* J. H. Tufts, "What I Believe," *Contemporary American Philosophy*, Vol. II, p. 333f.

77. Jane Dewey, p. 24.

78. *Ibid.*, p. 25.

79. "In the philosophical portions" this statement "may be regarded as an autobiography." *Ibid.*, p. 3f.

80. *Ibid.*, pp. 25-26.

81. *Ibid.*, p. 23.

82. *Ibid.*, p. 23.

83. *Ibid.*, p. 23 and *Contemporary American Philosophy*, p. 24.

84. Perry, Vol. II, p. 516.

85. Charles H. Cooley, "History of Department of Sociology at Michigan," *Sociological Theory and Social Research* (New York 1930) p. 6.

86. Jane Dewey, *op. cit.*, p. 24.

87. *Ibid.*, p. 27.

88. *Ibid.*, p. 28.

89. K. C. Mayhew and A. C. Edwards, *The Dewey School: The Laboratory School of The University of Chicago*, 1896-1903. (NY, 1936), p. 12. Both authors were teachers in the school; John Dewey has given his complete approval of the contents of this account, indeed, he guided its realization.

90. *Ibid.*, p. 12.

91. Ibid., In appendix Vol. II, 473, written by Dewey.

92. *Ibid.*, Dewey's Introduction, p. xv.

93. Jane Dewey, *op. cit.*, p. 33.

94. *Contemporary American Philosophers*, Vol. II, pp. 22-23.

95. Mayhew and Edwards, *op. cit.*, pp. 3-4.

96. And was definitely aided in such translation by such personnel as E. F. Young; *see* below.

97. *Ibid.*, p. 16.

98. *Ibid.*, pp. 11-12.

99. *Ibid.*, pp. 6-7.

100. *Ibid.*, p. 23.

101. *Ibid.*, p. 32.

102. *Ibid.*, pp. 40-41.

103. *Ibid.*, p. 473.

104. Jane Dewey, *op. cit.*, p. 28.

105. *Ibid.*, p. 34.

106. *Ibid.*, p. 28.

107. *Ibid.*, p. 29.

108. J. T. McManis, *Ella Flagg Young*, (Chicago, 1916), p. 15.

109. *Ibid.*, pp. 102-03, Cf. 1.

110. *Ibid.*, pp. 119-21.

16

Hull House and Consequent Writings

In Chicago, in the late 'nineties, John Dewey met Jane Addams of the Hull House social settlement. In this contact, Dewey saw at first hand an area of social life and reform method rather different from his laboratory but nevertheless one with definite limits. "The Deweys were regular visitors and formed warm personal friendships with its residents, especially with Jane Addams."[1] One of his daughters, born in Chicago, Dewey named Jane Mary, "after Jane Addams and her close friend, Mary Smith... the Deweys found contact with many types of persons there the most interesting and stimulating part of their non-professional life."[2]

When the House was incorporated Dewey was among the trustees; his "faith in democracy as a guiding force in education took on shape and a deeper meaning because of Hull House and Jane Addams."[3] The character of this deeper meaning insofar as it reflected the standpoint of Hull House may be grasped in terms of the social situation and animating perspectives of the House itself.

The importance of cooperative association with an individual and institution like Jane Addams and Hull House lies in the at least vicarious participation in the perspective in which the personnel of such an institution views "social conditions". The perspective of the settlements around the turn of the century, when Dewey cooperated with Hull House, was actuated by several motives. It was, of course, molded by the desire for a "more exigent standard in philanthropic activities," and it stood for the amassing of "facts" prior to the undertakings in aid of the underprivileged.[4]

Daughter of a Sunday-School teaching, mill-owning state Senator, born in a small town, an Illinois Quaker, Jane Addams opened

Hull House in 1889. Its theory was rather embracive: "Hull House was soberly opened on the theory that the dependence of classes on each other is reciprocal; and that as the social relation is essentially a reciprocal relation, it gives a form of expression that has peculiar value."[5] Jane Dewey, commenting upon John Dewey, has asserted an understanding of the standpoint of Hull-House: Miss Addams viewed and tried to run the settlement as a manner "of learning how to live together" regardless of economic and social position, of "learning especially that democracy is a way of life, the truly moral and human way of life, not a political institutional device."[6] And into the Charter was inscribed the aim: "To provide a center for a higher civic and social life; to institute and maintain educational and philanthropic enterprises, and to investigate and improve the conditions in the industrial districts of Chicago."[7] Set down in the middle of industrial Chicago's slums, it focused upon "the poor,"[8] the negatively privileged immigrants. These immigrants, wrote Miss Addams, had only "a dim kinship" with "the pioneers."[9] The settlement had programs with which to de-isolate such groups, to improve their social and "cultural" conditions. Readings, kindergartens, and clubs were operated. Two years before Dewey had come to Chicago Miss Addams had read a paper, "The Subjective Necessity for Social Settlements," before a group of earnest young people interested in settlements. It views settlements as an "outlet" for (a) "that sentiment of universal brotherhood, which the best spirit of our times is forcing from an emotion into a motive." For the "educated young people" with such motives, settlements save them from being:

> "cultivated into unnourished, oversensitive lives. They have been shut off from the common labor by which they live which is a great source of moral and physical health. They feel a fatal want of harmony between their theory and their lives, a lack of coordination between thought and action. I think it is hard for us to realize how seriously many of them are taking to the notion of human brotherhood, how eagerly they long to give tangible expression to the democratic ideal."

And then:

> "you may remember," she said, "the forlorn feeling which occasionally seizes you when you arrive early in the morning a

stranger in a great city: the stream of laboring people goes past you as you gaze through the plate-glass window of your hotel; you see hard working men lifting great burdens; you hear the driving and jostling of huge carts and your heart sinks with a sudden sense of futility. The door opens behind you and you turn to the man who brings you in your breakfast with a quick sense of human fellowship. You turn helplessly to the waiter and feel that it would be almost grotesque to claim from him the sympathy you crave because civilization has placed you apart, but you resent your position with a sudden sense of snobbery."[10]

"It is true that there is nothing after disease, indigence and a sense of guilt, so fatal to health and to life itself as the want of a proper outlet for active faculties."

Both the positions of the personnel involved, the estrangement of certain members of an upper status group, and the character of the "activity" intended by them are clear from these passages. The middle and upper class "girls ... after they leave school ... accept and long to perpetuate ... a heritage of noble obligation." But this new and religiously underlaid *noblesse oblige* of Chicago results in "the desire for action, the wish to right wrong and alleviate suffering which haunts them daily." "We have," said Miss Addams, "in America a fast-growing number of cultivated young people who have no recognized outlet for their active faculties ... their uselessness hangs about them heavily." And, before knowing Dewey, the finger of science is wagged:

"Huxley declares that the sense of uselessness is the severest shock which the human system can sustain, and that if persistently sustained, it results in atrophy of function. These young people had had advantages of college, of European travel, and of economic study, but they are sustaining this shock of inaction."[11]

Such "young people feel nervously the need of putting theory into action, and respond quickly to the Settlement form of activity."[12]

Such are the compound motives and positions of the personnel participants[13] in the "renaissance of the early Christian humanitarianism" which is "an experimental effort to aid in the solution of the social and industrial problems which are engendered by the modern conditions of life in a great city."[14] Significantly:

"It insists that these problems are not confined to any one portion of a city. It is an attempt to relieve, at the same time, the over-accumulation at one end of society and the destitution at the other, but it assumes that this over-accumulation and destitution is most sorely felt in the things that pertain to social and educational advantages. From its very nature it can stand for *no political or social propaganda* ... The one thing to be dreaded in the Settlement is that it lose its *flexibility*, its power of *quick adaptation*, its *readiness to change its methods as its environment may demand.*"[15]

" ... the residents in the early Settlements were in many cases young persons, who had sought relief from the consciousness of social maladjustment in the 'anodyne of work' afforded by philanthropic and civic activities; their former experiences had not thrown them into company with radicals. The decade between 1890-1900 was, in Chicago, a period of propaganda as over against constructive social effort; the moment for marching and carrying banners, for stating general principles and making a demonstration, rather than the time for uncovering the situation and for providing the legal measures and the civic organization through which new social hopes might make themselves felt."[16]

This was the situation and perspective of the institution through which Dewey had his first close look at "social conditions."

The character of Dewey's contact was not only that of a trustee but as a "warm friend" and a "regular visitor." The records show that he participated at least twice as a speaker. The background of the first occasion is very interesting. One of the problems that occurs among immigrants is an estrangement of second generation from the culture and, indeed, the persons of the older generation. So Miss Addams reflected:

"Could we not interest the young people working in the neighboring factories, in these older forms of industry, so that, through their own parents and grandparents, they would find a dramatic representation of the inherited resources of their daily occupation. If these young people could actually see that the complicated machinery of the factory evolved from simple tools, they might at least make a beginning towards that education which Dr. Dewey defines as 'a continuing reconstruction of experience.' They might also lay a foundation for reverence of the past which Goethe declares to be the basis of all sound progress."[17]

About this she had "many talks with Dr. Dewey and with one of the teachers in his school who was a resident at Hull House." And "within a month a room was fitted up to which we might invite those of our neighbors who were possessed of old crafts and who were eager to use them."[18] Later, there was:

> "an audience who listened to a series of lectures by Dr. John Dewey on 'Social Psychology' as genuine intellectual groups consisting largely of people from the immediate neighborhood, who were willing to make 'that effort from which we all shrink, the effort of thought.' "[19]

It is not probable that to such a group, the morally sensitive Dewey would stress the instinct of ownership (as James) and innateness of intelligence. Miss Addams wrote: "During those first years on Halsted Street nothing was more painfully clear than the fact that pliable human nature is relentlessly pressed upon by its physical environment."[20] It cannot be said that Dewey explicitly shared this perspective, but there would seem little question that it shaped his views, at least in this period.[21] At least there is no evidence that he flirted with perspectives towards Settlements that were exemplified by certain other intellectuals residing in Chicago at the time, for instance, Thorstein Veblen, who was then on the staff at the University of Chicago. Of Settlements, Veblen wrote in 1899 under a chapter heading "Survivals of Non-Invidious Interest":

> "The tendency to some other than an invidious purpose in life has worked out in a multitude of organizations, the purpose of which is some work of charity or of social amelioration. These organizations are often of a quasi-religious or pseudo-religious character, and are participated in by both men and women . . . The solicitude of 'settlements,' for example, is in part directed to enhance the industrial efficiency of the poor and to teach them the more adequate utilization of the means at hand; but it is also no less consistently directed to the inculcation, by precept and example, of certain punctilios of upper-class propriety in manners and customs . . . Those good people who go out to humanise the poor are commonly, and advisedly, extremely scrupulous and silently insistent in matters of decorum and the decencies of life. They are commonly persons of an exemplary life and gifted with a tenacious insistence on ceremonial cleanness in the various items of their daily consumption. The cul-

tural or civilising efficacy of this inculcation of correct habits of thought with respect to the consumption of time and commodities is scarcely to be overrated; nor is its economic value to the individual who acquires these higher and more reputable ideals inconsiderable."[22]

We are not concerned here with the truth or value of Veblen's characterization. Needless to say, Dewey's continued and intimate participation in Hull House's activities would seem to assure us that he did not see the matter in Veblen's way, indeed, that his view was close to Miss Addams. During the Chicago residence, Dewey spent his summer vacations in the Adirondacks where he had a cottage. He was associated with professional philosophers from several universities, with Thomas Davidson, who had a summer school there, and here he first met William James in person. But perhaps the more decisive contacts were on the campus of the University of Chicago. And of these, "the closest and most influential contacts" were with G. H. Mead and James Tufts. Of the students, Addison Moore seems to have been outstanding; he continued, after graduate work, on the instructing staff.[23] Another student of Dewey's from Michigan days, Angell, was in the Psychology Department, working out, in opposition to Titchener, a *functional* standpoint.

Dewey managed a pre-doctoral seminar in logic. It dealt at various times with Bradley, Bosanquet, as well as with Mill, Venn, and Jevons.[24] In one seminar Lotze's logic was chosen for analysis "because of the importance attached by its author to empirical and scientific theories." Out of this seminar grew the significant *Studies in Logical Theory* of 1903. Dewey feels that this monograph would not have gained attention had not William James celebrated it in a review hailing "the Chicago Schools." It was about that time that James spotted Dewey; their subsequent correspondence is revealing.

In 1903 and 1904 James was "much interested of late in the philosophy of John Dewey of Chicago."[25] Of course, "Dewey is obscure," yet his "stuff" is "splendid" and "noble" and he is a "hero."[26] But "Dewey's primary appeal is to those who like their philosophy difficult and technical, and will respect nothing that is not obscure."[27] In 1903 Dewey wrote to James: "...I see how far I moved along when I find how much I get out of Peirce this year, and how easily I understand him, when a few years ago he was mostly a sealed book to me . . ."[28] Again there is a mention of the students: "as for the whole point of view, it needs working out in all . . . directions . . . But one thing that makes me believe in it is that students, graduates and some of the undergraduates, get hold of it and make it a working method . . ."[29] I have already indicated the class and occupational composition of Chicago's student body. As for his connection with the university, Dewey occupied a position precisely within a major vehicle of vertical mobility. He helped build and worked within the increased spread of ascent chances for the sons of farmers and businessmen into professional careers.

We have arrived at the point in John Dewey's career at which it ceases to be necessary, convenient, or fruitful to trace chronologically his life as a whole. Now we shall begin to examine his publications, trace various lines of publication. It should be stressed that this "break" in mode of presentation is *not* based on any theory of the career which assumes that social experience is influential only in early stages of the career. It is merely for the purpose of expediency and due to the fact that intellectually, by 1904, a surprising number of his leading ideas were at least nascently put in writing.

Dewey's life after Chicago was realized mainly in New York City at Columbia, his appointment to which was engineered by a classmate of Johns Hopkins days, J. McKeen Cattell. Here Dewey taught and wrote intermittently since 1904. In 1930, he became "emeritus." From 1904 until the war his contacts were on the whole absorbed by technical philosophical issues which were carried by the circles of academic philosophers in and around the city. From within and working out of New York, during and after the first World War, Dewey participated in "committees" and "leagues" and wrote articles on social and political affairs. His travels during the twenties, as we shall see, are important in terms of the development of his political views. He met A. C. Barnes in 1915, and much later lectured out *Art as Experience*. He joined teachers' unions. Most of the books he published after 1903 were developments "from lectures given on various foundations"[30] and at such universities as Yale, Hopkins, and Harvard. He had been president of the *American Psychological Association* in 1899; in 1905-06 he was president of the *American Philosophical Association*. He has received honor-

ary degrees from at least nine universities, beginning with one from
the University of Wisconsin in 1904, with one from Harvard finally
in 1932. In short, he was a highly successful wide-ranging university professor, doing a lot of travelling, a lot of lecturing, working
very hard at his writing, carrying a huge load of the "extra-curricu-
lum activities" that liberal professors carried at the time. Dewey,
however, carried more than the usual.

Observation of Dewey's bibliography shows that there are many
articles which, without violating their content, could have been entitled "X *and* Y": philosophy and education; ethics and anthropology; education and democracy, and so forth. In the earlier writings,
to the extent that he thinks across hitherto isolated fields we get
specifically Deweyan formulations. This is one of the chief characteristics of Dewey's strategy, and from it he has derived much of
his intellectual power and influence. He does not merely "relate"
topics. He does not simply shift the meanings and shapes of two
opinions so that he can "live" with both, as tends to be the rather
patent case with much of William James. Dewey takes a point of
sight and builds a conceptual structure within which he can grasp
both the points which were being argued over; this structure is different from either of the conflicting or isolated doctrines which it
"combines." It is Deweyan. A logic of certain central conceptions
enables him to perform this operation. Some of these concepts are
new, at least to the American scene and in the way that they are
used. In later sections we shall catalogue such *central conceptions*,
interrelate them, tag them in their nascent contexts, and trace their
evolution. Here we merely wish grossly to indicate the cross-field
and combination style of thought indicated by observation of
Dewey's total bibliography. It has accomplished much. With it he
has materially aided in the growth of a social psychology, in carrying over social considerations into ethical theory, political considerations into education, psychology and sociology, and, importantly,
ethics into logic. These are surface observations, but these com-
binational concepts are at the center of Dewey's working habits
of thought. They, and the generic style of approach underlying
them, have not only operated across "fields" but in solving any
polarized and contending "positions" which he has addressed.

In anticipation, and to illustrate this style, we may take the central conception of "action" as it mediates "interest" and "effort."

This concept of action also mediates other polarized notions, such as value and science,[31] but we only wish to illustrate the mechanics or form of the style here. This style consists in the "establishment of continuity between contrasted concepts or competing hypotheses."[32] Separation of viewpoint and concept is condemned in the essay ninety-five times, whereas there are forty-five cases of emphasis upon continuity. It is significant for us that in this essay the concept of "activity" performs the function of a mediating term. The tenable point about "interest" in educational theory is translated into an adverb modifying "action": "Wherever there is life, there is ... an activity having some ... direction of its own ... total lack of interest ... is [therefore] ... mythical ..." And on the other side, what is valid about "effort" is also adverbial of "activity": it is "persistency, consecutiveness of activity ... a demand for *continuity* in the face of difficulties."

However much New England Puritan culture loved to dwell upon extremes, John Dewey revolted from this completely. It was Hegel for him, with a plunge into unity. He would not split vice and virtue. Refusing to think man a creature of wrath, he refused to let all days be Sundays — thus his secularization. And logically, the form of his thinking (as against the manner in which he might *state* the "act of thought") is combination strategy which builds a third construction and sees opposites playing integrated roles within it. We shall see that such central categories as "practice" and "scientific method" and "intelligence" act out the parts of a synthesizing construction.

On the sheerly chronological basis of our data, it would appear that in general "epistemology and logic" were a first focus, with "ethics" closely following. "Education" comes a good while later, and "political and social affairs" begin to draw sizable attention a great while later. "Art" and "religion" come latest of all, and they come very late indeed. Judged by bibliographical distribution, they have been incidental to Dewey's main drives and foci.

The focus that begins earliest, that is most continuous and, as we shall subsequently see, is perhaps the most pervasive in "philosophy," that is, *logic*, including in the term as Dewey does, epistemology. In the only self-explanation of this kind extant, Dewey has written of the interaction of his interest in social-political affairs and technical philosophy:

"I have usually, if not always, held an idea first in its abstract form, often as a matter chiefly of logical or dialectic con-
sistency or of the power of words to suggest ideas. Some personal experience, through contact with individuals, groups, or
(as in visits to foreign countries) peoples, was necessary to give
the idea concrete significance . . . My ideas tend, because of
my temperament, to take a schematic form in which logical con-
sistency is a dominant consideration, but I have been fortunate
in a variety of contacts that has put substance into these
forms."[33]

This statement is supported (1) by the temporal order of his publications in different topic fields. It is also born out (2) by content,
and especially abstraction-level analyses of each of the topic
columns, as well as (3) by a study of the character of the concepts
which "bridge" one topic to another.

Two of the most obvious things about the distribution of Dewey's
attention and effort, as indicated by publications, consist in the fact
that the beginning of the writing-interest in education and in
political and social topics, in art and religion, began later than the
philosophy, ethics, and psychology, and each of them is an accom-
paniment to *definite career happenings.* He began to produce educational reading upon appointment to the University of Chicago's
Department of Philosophy, Psychology and Pedagogy. The years
at Chicago, from 1894-1904, show a concentration upon educational
articles, and three books on education. Upon going to Columbia in
1905, the educational interest drops off and heavier attention is
given to "philosophy" (logic, epistemology). This is to be accounted for, in part at least, by a competitive though friendly situation
within the Columbia faculty of philosophy and the handling of
graduate students unaccustomed to the Deweyan point of view.
This situation led to a rethinking of many of his philosophical
ideas.[34]

Up until the advent of World War I, when he was fifty-seven
and thirty-four years had elapsed since his first article, Dewey did
not write, to any noticeable extent, *explicitly* on social and political
affairs. It was the war that precipitated his production for political
publics *per se.* And his political public was possibly already recruited to some extent by his educational work. Many of the "political
articles" are slanted educationally. It seems that at this time attention previously given to education moved into the social and

political sphere, or more accurately stated, that the focus during the second decade of the twentieth century became *even more* concerned with education *and the social order* than was the case prior to this period. Notice that the focus directly upon the more formal "ethics," although fairly constant throughout the career, dropped off somewhat and became intermittent when the heavy attention was placed upon social and political affairs. It may be ventured that time and effort were here transferred.

It was World War I which drew Dewey, along with many other liberals, into the social-political arena, and his discussions here were sustained, in addition to education, with two other sub-areas of political and social affairs: First, "post-war reconstruction problems," The League of Nations and "outlawing of war"; and second, with articles on China, Japan, Russia, Turkey, and Mexico. Trips to these countries definitely influenced his writing on social and political matters. Publications about these countries made up a large portion of his social and political publications in the decade following the First World War. Notice the selection of countries; they are all "backward countries" on the move to industrialization. They are all setting up educational systems with which to anchor new regimes. They are moving away from a theocratic orientation. There are "liberal" movements in all but Russia and when he began writing on Russia, American liberals were decisively split. But there was a general opinion that what was happening there was experimental on a grand scale and that one had better keep his hopeful eye on it. Throughout all writings on social and political affairs, irrespective of proximate topic, there was, of course, a faith, a contention, an explanation of "liberal democracy." In this field, more of his writings are published in *The New Republic* than in any other one periodical.

Dewey's political attention and mind have worked during three periods: (a) the postwar, (b) the somewhat stifling prosperity of the twenties, and (c) the "pink" thirties. During (b) he refracted for liberals the enthusiasm and hope of certain "new countries." During (c) his general liberalism was challenged for the first time seriously from the left. One of his students, Sidney Hook, rose to intellectual attention by blending pragmatism with Marxism.

Consider his work on "Religion." It indicates that no explicit attention was given until very late in Dewey's writing career. No long polemics against it; certainly no explicit justifications of it. If he had been "fighting religion," he really used a roundabout strategy. On the surface and at first, it would seem that such "religious content" as his publications had and such religious elements as figured in his recruitment of a public lay in that sphere we have designated above as indifference and ignoring, shooting to the side of religious contents. On the other hand, the reasons for such negations of "religion" as he later renders are, in the main, clearly social and political, such as the discussion of the secularization of Turkey or of the church in Mexico. The 1903 and 1908 articles are both upon "religion" in connection with education. The 1917 article is on "H. G. Wells, Theological Assembler." It is a rather sardonic examination of Wells' search for the "extraordinary" ending up in "supernaturalism." Positively it speaks for "the humble of all ages." It seems to be the first explicit, written negation, and it is definitely an incidental piece.

Nothing explicit on "Art" emerges until 1925. The article of 1891 is a "review" of "Matthew Arnold and Robert Browning;" the piece published in 1897 dealt with topics congenial to the National Education Association before which it was read. Dewey met Albert C. Barnes in 1915 in his seminar at Columbia. Barnes had a collection of modern paintings and wanted to use them for educational ends. The 1925 article, "adopted from *Experience and Nature*," appeared in the *Journal of The Barnes Foundation*, October, 1925. The *Art as Experience* of 1934 is dedicated to Barnes; Dewey's contact with the Barnes Foundation "gave definite philosophical form to his previously scattered ideas of the arts."[35]

These notes on career points and foci of attention have served crudely to sketch the scope and contours of Dewey's work. But what kind of publics were back of these foci on different "subjects"? And what is the relation between one focus and another? "Relation" here means: (a) the overlap and interaction of different publics, and (b) the transferral and modifications of conceptions used in two or more foci.

> "The most elaborate philosophies are founded on a few simple ideas. For the generation in which the philosophy is developed these fundamental ideas are most often obscured by the *abstruse and technical aspects* of the system; but in the course of time they rarely ever fail to disengage themselves

from the superstructure they support and to become part of the common· intellectual coin which circulates in the realm of mind."[36] [My italics]

The distinction here drawn between (a) "simple" yet "fundamental ideas" and (b) "the abstruse and technical aspects of the system" may be interpreted sociologically. The "simple" and "fundamental" ideas (a) of which Ratner speaks are ideas as they are stated in the context of political and periodical discussions; whereas "the abstruse and technical aspect" (b) is made up of the meanings of ideas in a context of professional philosophic readers and shaped by the more technical polemics of this context. Secondarily, and by definition, as well as by inspection, the presentation in (a) context is upon a lower level of abstraction than that in (b) context. The differences consist in topic, context, including publics, and level of abstraction.[37]

Dewey has written and thought with reference to both types of context (as well as to others). If we would fully interpret his meaning, we must observe the career of his conceptions in both contexts and chart the relations of given ideas and concepts as they operate in these two contexts. We cannot, however, accept *a priori* as definitive the statement of Ratner that in respect to the diffusion of Dewey's work in context (a), instrumentalism's "basic ideas have been rapidly appropriated, if not completely assimilated, by contemporary thought."[38] "Contemporary thought" is a very large phrase. C. E. Ayres, a competent observer of such matters, has also commented on the quick and wide translation of Dewey's ideas, but he sees no logical connection between ideas, as "pragmatism" in the sphere of logic and social and political analyses.

To account for what he speaks of as the "easy naturalization" of Dewey's ideas, ("their" translation from b to a) Ratner suggests the following:

> "This easy 'naturalization' is partly due — to employ Mr. Dewey's own criterion — [1] to the fact that instrumentalism is grounded in the pervasive interests of life and is concerned with the values that all men cherish; but it is also [2] in significant measure due to the fact that Mr. Dewey has constantly used his philosophy as a basis for analyzing and interpreting current social and political affairs. To be able effectively to develop,

in popular essays, the social and political implications of instrumentalism, he had to divest philosophic principles of their technical garments and dress them in the fashion of common speech and circumstance; as a result, large audiences have had, through these essays, ready access to the essentials of his teaching . . . It is hardly just a sheer accident of Mr. Dewey's interest or versatility that made him apply instrumentalism to the criticism of current events. Such application is a natural consequence of his central doctrine concerning the nature of reason or intelligence. According to instrumentalism, reason or intelligence does not reside in some transcendental sphere where it concerns itself primarily with observing its own precious states, and from where, when it is so inclined, it views as a pale spectator what goes on below; the proper home of intelligence is the world, and its true function is to act as a critic and regulator of the forces operative within it. This doctrine, which is the philosophic *raison d'être* of these essays, is also one of their fundamental unifying principles."[39]

In connection with [1] it may be remarked that it is nonsense. If Dewey has been "concerned with the values that all men cherish," limiting the case to America, then he would have been concerned with what the *American Magazine* and the *Saturday Evening Post* have been concerned with. And then the circulation figures of the journals in which Dewey's articles have appeared are a *tiny* fraction of the magazines with really wide appeal. Point [2] is complicated. In particular, it assumes that there is some intrinsic logical connection between the logical theory and the social political analyses of Dewey. This is a moot point, about which a decision will be reached later on the basis of analysis of specific concepts. C. E. Ayres has asked: "What is the secret of Mr. Dewey's power?" and answers that (with Mr. Ratner) he supposes Mr. Dewey has "used his philosophy" to analyze "current social and political affairs," but it seems to him "a great deal more conspicuous that he has constantly used his mind."[40] And then, speaking of of a selected set of Dewey's social-political essays:

"A considerable number of these essays contain no clue whatever, perceptible to me, to the 'instrumental logic' which is thus supposed to be the mainspring of all Mr. Dewey's thought. This is true of by far the majority of the essays . . . [which] contain either no trace of the underlying logic and metaphysics or traces so dilute as to be perceptible only to the most sensitive and practiced eye, certainly not to the 'large audiences' invoked by Dr. Ratner."[41]

He then cites cases of Dewey's analytic ability, which he admires, and asks his question again:

"Of what is this evidence? I should say, quite simply, of intellectual power, that, and nothing else. I see no more evidence of pragmatic bias in this superb feat of intellectual clarification than I do of anarchistic bias, or Bolshevism, or pro-Germanism. It is a case of brains, pure and simple."[42]

I have picked up Ratner and Ayres (instead of others who could have been just as readily used) because their differences not only serve briefly to indicate the level, so far, or attempts to "explain" Dewey's "power" and "influence" and "assimilation" but because they stand quite at odds with one another. And this fact, granting, as I certainly do, that both of them understand Dewey's thought very well indeed, suggest that the many questions underlying their contentions have not been stated in such a way as to permit empirically based answers. Indeed, these assertions are not answers at all. They are "questions" which are badly stated because they miscellaneously absorb very many specific problems.

Ayres' point is no explanation: a lot of people were "using their minds." But all minds were not the same. The questions here are:

(a) Precisely *what kind* or style of thinking, and what kind of opinion did Dewey exemplify?

(b) *Whom* did it appeal to as "powerful?" (certainly not to all reading publics, nor even all readers of the publics of Dewey's mediums), and

(c) *Why* did it appeal to those to whom it did?[43]

Another of the simple questions which such comments and contentions raise is just how many persons have John Dewey's words reached? The extent of his influence, but not necessarily its character, is indicated by his success in recruiting publics. It would be possible to ascertain the answer to this question, with certain permissable limits of error, by compiling a list of the number of subscribers to journals in which he has published, of the number of copies of his books that have been sold, and by counting two or three and so on readers for each copy sent to libraries and the number of readers in terms of the size of the probable clientele of the type and and size of library in question. Such a compilation would take several men at least a year's work, it would be shot through with guesses, and fortunately it is not necessary. Much more important and pertinent to our concern is the question of the characteristics of the selected publics which Dewey has contacted. It is not as important to know *how many* in total as it is to know *why* they were responsive and what their positions in the social structure were. For example, a bulk of Dewey's social-political articles were published in the *New Republic*. By reconstructing the social composition and position of the *New Republic's* readership from its beginning in 1918 through the twenties and knowing its total circulation, we may be in a position to speak of the character of his influence and the reasons for his appeal in connection with social-political publics. One thing is sure: we have to do better than talk in general terms of Dewey's "influence" and "power."

In the problems of accounting for the "assimilation" of Dewey into the context of public discussion, the gross *extent* of this diffusion is less important than the selectivities of it; and to estimate this we must have some knowledge of those types of publication in which he was printed and the composition and situations of their publics, whom he presumably influenced.

1. Jane Dewey, p. 29.
2. *Ibid.*, p. 34.
3. *Ibid.*, p. 30.
4. Jane Addams, *Twenty Years at Hull House, With Autobiographical Notes* (New York, MacMillan Co., 1910) p. 129.
5. *Ibid.*, p. 91.
6. *Ibid.*, p. 29.
7. *Ibid.*, p. 108.
8. *Ibid.* p. 111.
9. *Ibid.*, p. 108.
10. *Ibid.*, pp. 115-18.
11. *Ibid.*, p. 120.
12. *Ibid.*, pp. 121-22.
13. That is, of the personnel. The guilt feelings of upper classes were not, however, the whole story. Why did capitalists and merchants contribute hard cash? Perhaps, like those in England who gave to the Salvation Army, they gave because settlements channeled energies into less politically harmful outlets. It is not our aim here to render an account of Settlements,

nor even of Hull House. Hence, we need not either deny or even attempt to document the imputation suggested of the motives of those who gave money. What is important here is that the Settlements focused upon "immigrants" and not upon "classes." It so happened that in the cities many of the lower classes were foreign born. Hence the problem, the effort, the solution, could be and was put in terms of "assimilation," "Americanization" or "democratization." *Thus, the "immigrant problem," their "adjustment" or "assimilation" to American milieux obscured the class problem.* On this problem, *see* my ms., "The Professional Ideology of Social Pathologists."

14. *Ibid.*, p. 125.

15. *Ibid.*, pp. 125-26.

16. *Ibid.*, p. 127.

17. *Ibid.*, pp. 236-37.

18. *Ibid.*, p. 237.

19. *Ibid.*, p. 435.

20. *Ibid.*, p. 196

21. It should be noted that Dewey continued a settlement contact in New York City. *See* M. Simkovitch, *Neighborhood* (New York 1938) p. 150.

22. Thorstein Veblen, *Theory of the Leisure Class*, pp. 399, 344-45.

23. "Moore" wrote Dewey to James in 1903, "has taught here since about '95 . . . The flexibility and freedom of his mental operations I needn't speak of — his articles do that. He hasn't had fair play, he has been so loaded with 'section' . . . but probably has gained maturity from his enforced inhibitions . . . I am tremendously glad that you liked his article, and very appreciative of the fact that, liking it, you expressed your satisfaction so generously." R. B. Perry, Vol. II, p. 520.

24. Jane Dewey, p. 32.

25. Perry, Vol. II, pp. 345-46.

26. *Ibid.*, Vol. II, pp. 479, 501.

27. *Ibid.*, Vol. II, p. 508.

28. *Ibid.*, Vol. II, p. 523.

29. *Ibid.*, Vol. II, p. 525.

30. Jane Dewey, *op. cit.*, p. 36.

31. *See* below.

32. This illustration is taken from B. B. Bogoslovksy's unique and excellent *Technique of Controversy.* (N.Y. 1913), which analyzes in great detail John Dewey's essay, "Interest and effort in Education". *See* pp. 13, 88.

33. Jane Dewey, *The Philosophy of John Dewey op. cit.* pp. 44-45.

34. *See* Jane Dewey, p. 36.

35. Jane Dewey, *The Philosophy of John Dewey, op. cit.*, p. 37.

36. Joseph Ratner, *Preface to Characters and Events*, Vol. I, p. v.

37. It is interesting to note that Joseph Ratner, a former student and a consistently faithful disciple of Dewey, labels the "few simple ideas" in the more public context "fundamental." It may indicate the public or political orientation in the *development* of Dewey's thought, or more probably an evaluative bias of Ratner for the democratic "use" of ideas, the assumption

that they should be open, shared by a public, a bias which Dewey undoubtedly shares.

38. *Ibid.*, p. v.

39. *Ibid.*, pp. v-vi.

40. *International Journal of Ethics* (Jan., 1930), p. 264.

41. *Ibid.*, pp. 264-65.

42. *Ibid.*, p. 266.

43. Ayres finds the answer to such questions in the Deweyan antagonism to the *occult*, the mysterious, and extraordinary ["Dewey: Master of the Commonplace," *New Republic,* January 18, 1929] as polarized against the "commonplace" and everyday. I think this not only too simplistic, but probably mistaken, for it rests the case in a surrogate of the religious vs. science polemic; this is not so central in Dewey as other matters. Also the Ayres' point is too reminiscent, too localized: it represents a phase of thought of the twenties, and could not hold of the entire career and periods through which Dewey has moved.

17

John Dewey's Reading Public

In what specific journals did Dewey publish? What were the social and economic positions of their publics? What was their circulation when he published in them? But first, what spheres must we consider in order adequately to graph Dewey's total set of publics? We shall consider four and for each of them we must answer the above questions. First, there is the *social* and *political*, then, *technical philosophy*, then *education* and finally, running through these, his *student-public*. There are perhaps other publics not caught by consideration of these, but they are not so central as to vitiate assertions based upon knowledge concerning these four. Dewey has never written for mass publics. He has written for, *i.e.*, been read by more definitely *selected* publics.

Let us take the "social and political" first. These are the periodicals in which the bulk of his essays in this sphere have appeared:[1]

The New Republic	The Independent
Asia	The Nation
The Atlantic Monthly	Common Sense
The Christian Century	The Survey
The Current History Magazine	The World Tomorrow
The Dial	The Andover Review
Foreign Affairs	The Seven Arts Magazine
The Hibbert Journal	Forum

I shall take as roughly representative of this group of magazines the *New Republic*. The choice is based not only upon its resemblance in policy and probably (quite roughly again) in publics to many of the others, but also upon the fact that during the late 'teens and then the twenties, when Dewey was writing on social and political affairs, it was the *New Republic* that published more of his essays than any other magazine. Indeed, it may be said that the two organs of pragmatic opinion in the social and political sphere have been the older *Nation* and *The New Republic*. James, who was not so politically informed nor as interested in political affairs as Dewey was, called *The Nation* "right". Even Peirce reviewed for *The Nation*. And most of Dewey's utterances about public affairs, prior to the middle thirties, have, as has been stated, been written for *The New Republic*. It may also be presumed that his effective public for the books dealing with political and social affairs, has been similar to, and has doubtless overlapped with, the publics of these two.

The first issue of *The New Republic: A Journal of Opinion* is dated "Saturday, 7th, November, 1914." In this Volume I, no. 1, the six editors did not make any speeches. They began immediately. They ran one paragraph which said that the *New Republic* is an experiment, an attempt to find a national audience for a journal of interpretation and opinion; we are setting out with faith. Then the columns plunged into the political arena.

The editors of the early *New Republic* included Herbert Croly, Walter E. Weyl, Walter Lippmann and Francis Hackett.[2] Starting from nothing but "angels" in 1914 (Mr. and Mrs. Willard Straight), the circulation of the *New Republic* rose to around 15,000 by 1915. It circulated at a peak in 1920 of 37,000 as an average. During the twenties it dropped; in 1928 it printed 20,000; in 1930, only 12,000.[3]

In 1931 the occupational composition of 828 subscribers to the *New Republic* in percentage terms are:[4]

Occupation	Per cent
1. Educators, professors, teachers	34.5
2. Lawyers, doctors, engineers, scientists, clergymen	18.5
3. Businessmen and executives	17.0
4. Housewives, social workers, students, clerks, secretaries	13.5
5. Artists, journalists, editors, librarians, writers	7.5
6. Public officials	1.0
7. Farmers and ranchers	1.5
8. Miscellaneous	4.5

All the *individual* occupations below groups 1 and 2 contain 5-1/2 percent or under.

The average income was $5700 a year, distributed as follows:

$10,000 or over	20.0
5,000 - 9,999	26.5
2,500 - 4,999	40.0
Under $2,500	12.5

It is interesting to note that eighty-one percent of the readers were, in 1931, over thirty years of age, that sixty-seven percent were male, that on the average the subscribers bought 23.8 books per year per reader. Quite interesting are the classes or books the subscribers most often read: forty-seven percent of them read Biography; thirty-eight percent, philosophy; whereas down the line, "politics and economics" were read by eight percent!

If this sample is at all representative[5] we have in this readership a group highly selected in income, occupation, and judging from these items, in education. They are successful upper middle class professionals.

His first article is interesting, in view of certain broad imputations we shall advance later of "American progressivism" or "liberalism" for, politically, this was of course, the movement in which the *New Republic,* and also John Dewey, are to be located.

Dewey's first article for the *New Republic* was printed 19th December, 1914: "A Policy of Industrial Education." He wanted, first, to "keep youth under educative influences for a longer time." Second, "The aim must be efficiency of industrial intelligence, rather than technical trade efficiency." He sees that automatic machines are on the upswing, and hence "high specialization of work will develop." *Yet:* What is needed is "to develop initiative and personal resources of intelligence."[6] "In a word," he continues, "the problem in this country is primarily an educational one and not a business and technical one as in Germany."

In order to understand the public of the *New Republic* and of Dewey, and to understand Dewey's own intellectual orientation, we have to reconstruct in broad detail certain political trends and opinions.

First of all, it is significant to these understandings that most of the movements against established power in the United States during the late nineteenth and early twentieth centuries rested socially upon agrarianism. As everyone knows, "revolts" took the form of "horizontal" sections. Jeffersonianism, and then the western movements, have been the social center of America's liberal ideology. It is in terms of this tradition and its roots that much of the thought of John Dewey is to be understood. The American tradition of opposition, of the liberal and the radical, has derived its social impetus from the agricultural population. The indigenous American road to the left, such as it has been, has led from the farm. The reasons for this situation are determinable.

After the Civil War business in the East hid behind high tariff walls and monopolized a home market. Competition was limited to the intranational, but the market was steadily growing and the businesses became entrenched in combinations. The economic situation of agriculture was quite otherwise. In St. Louis around the turn of the century Max Weber asserted that "the market is older than the producer here."[7] The farmer in America has been a small businessman. But he has been excluded from the "great chances of speculative business talent."[8] Important for our present concern is the fact that the farmer was not protected as was the manufacturer. The farmer competed on a world market. He was milked by a high price level for commodities and necessities; he paid for them with money from cereals sold on a low price market. And hence he howled, and voted. But he was not alone. Close to the termination of the nineteenth century another group was hurt economically: the petty and older bourgeoisie. The little capitalist began to suffer from the tramplings and trusts of the big capitalists. The little business men in the cities had a negative economic point in common with the farmer: anti-big business.

Out of such economic situations came the McKinley, LaFollette, Roosevelt, and the Wilson elections. That is their meaning: these parties struggled for the small capitalist, both urban and rural. These were no "class movements" in the Marxist sense. Let us not forget that "muckraking," which was the mass literary vehicle of this progressive movement, did not confine its fight against "trusts" to big business, it included labor unions as an object of its moral indignation and exposure.[9]

The charities and settlements arose in one urban portion of the movement. Populism was another, the dominant feature, of the movement. The biggest "socialist vote" (in 1912 when Debs received less than 900,000 votes) drew from populism and its agrarian backing and found a structural implementation in the smaller businesses in cities. It was into the muckraker movement[10] that large sections of the non-academic intelligentsia placed their energies, and muckraking, too, must be located in the generic struggle mentioned. They were patchers, intellectually and in politics. They were all quite wary of definite commitment to any party lines. They had no clear view of the total situation they faced or of its larger issues. The typical career line of the muckraker of "the crusading liberal" has been ably drawn by Louis Filler:[11] He was born in the 1860's somewhere in the West. He saw cities rise, felt the tide of immigration about him, saw "large rude enterprise, of industry . . . always developing." From his parents he heard about Lincoln. He went to college and he read Mark Twain. He had difficulty choosing a career. Wanting to write, he went into journalism. "Some of his ideas sounded, even to him, frightfully serious and quite unprintable."

> "Our liberal was intensely nationalistic and individualistic, yet watching the steady growth of the corporations, the octopus-spread of railroad power, he tinkered with thoughts of government ownership and regulation. He could see labor's point of view, its need for unified action; he was sympathetic with the problems facing reformers. As for religion, his work and habits allowed him little time or inclination to carry on with the church as his fathers had done, and he thought of it chiefly with disapproval of its unprogressiveness, its tendency to cling to reaction. If the world of affairs was changing, he felt that the church, too, should be modernizing its ways. With the rise of Theodore Roosevelt, the young journalist gave himself wholeheartedly to the new movement for exposure and reform. These great days kept him busy from morning to night. He bloomed; his powers were free and absolute. An eager public accorded him a hearing, praise and honor, and money.[12] He redoubled his efforts, writing the facts of contemporary life in the style that journalism had developed for him: a clear, bold, straightforward style, concerning itself with facts and figures."[13]

As a muckraker, he "dealt with facts and not with theory." He contributed to the:

> "reform literature . . . the 'people' seemed to understand;

careless of whether his work was art, or not, they read it eagerly. And the muckraker was satisfied. 'The best cure for the evils of democracy,' he used to assert, 'is more democracy.' "[14]

Parenthetically, it must be remarked that due to increased educational level and to the rising smaller middle class this individual had a public, a large one: this may be related to his faith in the "people." Lincoln Steffens got $2,000 per article, did four or so a year.

The war came and typically the muckraker supported it. "What else was there to do?" "Junkerism had to be ousted." He liked to see the Czar go down, but the Bolsheviks "conscious, intellectual, ruthless — inspired the deepest revulsion." In the twenties, a new, a Freud-discussing generation arose, a generation separating literature and sociology as he had not done; now he felt that for a "footloose intellectual . . . there was . . . no sense in trying to reform anything."

> "The ex-muckraker — for now he was truly a figure of the past — established himself comfortably with a corporation or a university. Or he remained his own master. He wrote a few books, served on a number of commissions requiring sane, informed men, thought of Woodrow Wilson with respect and some sadness. To his eyes times became stranger and stranger, a little silly, a little incomprehensible. For now, during the twenties, there was this fabulous, not entirely satisfying prosperity."[15]

Came the depression: "The old American heartiness and optimism vanished. One saw gesturing messiahs springing into prominence like dolls . . . we were still Americans. Perhaps it would all turn out well . . ."[16]

In the heyday of "progressive crusading" E. A. Ross refracted muckraking in academic terms. He stood for the farmer as an individual. He fought the big monopolies and, since he was regionally West, he especially fought the railroads. What he stood for was *Jeffersonianism.* In 1907 he translated the issues arising out of the struggles of farmers and small business vs. Big Business into the moral vocabulary of the Jeffersonian world. "Tax-dodging is larceny . . . railroad discrimination is treachery . . . Embezzlement is theft . . ."

It is this "progressive movement" that the *New Republic* inherited; it is to this movement, and the smaller business and "professional" groups which carried it, that the pragmatism of Dewey generally corresponds. In this situation earlier we find William James with his hatred of "bigness," his ambivalence toward Theodore Roosevelt, his mediation. And here we find Dewey's political anchorage. The American rural orientation of these movements and the smaller business groups in a liberal context live in his concepts and his structure of thinking. His *formality, intellectuality,* and *tentativeness* correspond precisely to the actual course and manner of the intellectuals and politicians who were active in Progressivism. Many members of the *New Republic* public had risen *because* of their education, their knowledge. It was a fight of the "best minds" against a few "undemocratic individuals" and for "the people." The liberals — Howells, Brant Whitlock, Lincoln Steffens, have, as has often been remarked, been afraid of doctrine, of commitment to party or program. The *New Republic* has never had a firm "line." Progressives have in effect, believed in the power of ideas per se. And Dewey has redefined "Ideas" so as to have their belief, and his, make sense — at least to the Progressive circle.

Everything the earlier crusading liberals, the Muckrakers, were against was *specific;* a given town's political corruption, the stock yards, a meat trust, a tobacco trust, a fake advertisement; they were against features of the big industrialization, of high capitalism. What they gave were Jeffersonian shibboleths: Was government corrupt? Civil service reform. Were there big trusts? Trust-busting. Was there an oligarchy of banks, etc.? Wilson's New Freedom — for the small capitalist, including farmers. They experimented. They were specific; they were definitely intelligent. But they were wiped out, sucked into the gyrations: the pattern of objective events, the big structural shifts to high capitalism wiped them out along with their publics and the magazines for which they wrote.

Politically, they were killed by the war, and their hopes were shattered by the peace, and their public by prosperity during the twenties. For the very "Big Business" which destroyed their little business and against which they revolted increasingly created new jobs for a newer middle class, for the sons of the older class who had gone to college and become salaried employees, or professionals Indifference to "crusading liberals" followed the new job opportunities. The magazines were killed directly by their own advertisement departments. After all *Munseys, The American, Everybodys, McClures* were business propositions for their editors and owners.[17] Individuals in the movement reacted differently to its debacle, but perhaps Steffens is not a-typical. He became so tolerant, saw various virtues in so many men that really he wasn't taking any position: Hoover, Ford, Lenin, Mussolini. Of the crusading liberal magazines only two remained after the war: *The Nation* and the *New Republic*. Financed by angels, they circulated among a very restricted audience as compared for example, to *Munseys*. In Volume 1, No. 1, page 1 of the *New Republic* we find: "Progressivism of all kinds has fared badly. The Progressive Party has been reduced to an insignificant remnant."

Like votes for the political leaders of progressivism pre-war model certain books came from the presses. They were by J. Allen Smith [*Spirit of American Government* (1907)], by Herbert Croly [*Promise of American Life* (1909)] by Walter Weyl [*The New Democracy*], Walter Lippman's early books [especially *Preface to Politics*], Charles Beard's *An Economic Interpretation of the Constitution,* Theodore Roosevelt himself [*The New Nationalism*]. Politically, the name of John Dewey falls into line with these. He was focused on a slightly different domain than were the others but he had their *hopes* and their general strategy. The *School and Society* in 1899 and then in 1916, "summarizing" his philosophy up to then, *Democracy and Education*. Put crudely, they attack, *in the sphere of education*, the enemy located by Veblen: the leisured class and the conspicuously wasteful institutions. The anti-urban orientation of Veblen is obvious. As we shall see later, Dewey's concepts definitely bear the imprint of the *rural* extraction and orientation of the earlier progressives. But let us not anticipate further. Dewey's political thought has sprung from and remains closely tied to his educational interest. Let us turn to his educational public and to certain movements within its structure setting.

In the case of education, obviously our choice of a representative display is not any of the magazines to which Dewey has contributed but the book, *Democracy and Education*. In addition to such books as *Democracy and Education,* we should indicate the following periodicals:

Journal of Education	*Elementary School Teacher*
School Review	*American Teacher*
Kindergarten Magazine	*Progressive Education*
Educational Review	*School and Society*
Proceedings of the N.E.A.	*Social Frontier*

It is clear that some of these journals are technical educational journals. Some of them were also professional organs. Dewey has, by contributions to them and to teachers' conventions, participated heavily in the building of the teaching profession in this country. It is significant that he has written scarcely anything of a quite "technical" nature: his "educational philosophy," in this context, is a *professional ideology* and a *political standpoint* predicated upon a belief in education's role in a democracy.

Perhaps the interaction of social-*political* and *educational* matters as indicated by the title, *Democracy and Education* points to an interaction of publics, viz.: the recruitment of Dewey's political audience was by way of a transfer of a public previously recruited by the educational work and prestige. A good many of the articles in the *New Republic* were on educational topics. Let us recall that, in 1931, educators constituted 34.5 per cent of the subscribers of this journal. Also the latter day "educational" journals to which Dewey had contributed, such as *Social Frontier,* have by no means been technical Dewey educational reviews. They have, as we have indicated, moved over into political opinion. Emphasis upon "education" at the social level, has fallen in neatly with one chief element of the political orientation of Dewey, indeed, it is a sociologic feature of American "liberalism": the emphasis upon a diffused reform, the reaction against big concentrations, the individuality. The positive basis of these negations is the centrality of the primary community." The concept of "culture" as used in *Freedom and Culture* performs a similar function; both "education" and "culture" are tools in the avoidance of major cleavages and correspondent problems of power.

One should mention also that *School and Society* "the most widely read and influential of Dewey's writings"[18] consists of public talks given in Chicago in order to raise money for the laboratory school described above. The parent-contributors to "progressive" schools are probably "liberal-minded," fairly well off, they have probably abandoned the faiths of their fathers, they are "open-minded" and tolerant." They are among those:

> "who favor in a mild sort of way fairly liberal programs of social reconstruction, who are full of good will and humane sentiment, who have vague aspirations for world peace and human brotherhood, who can be counted on to respond moderately to any appeal made in the name of charity, who are genuinely distressed at the sight of unwonted forms of cruelty, misery, and suffering, and who perhaps serve to soften somewhat the bitter clashes of those real forces that govern the world; but who, in spite of all their good qualities, have no deep and abiding loyalties, possess no convictions for which they would sacrifice overmuch, would find it hard to live without their customary material comforts, are rather insensitive to the accepted forms of social injustice, are content to play the role of interested spectator in the drama of human history, refuse to see reality in its harsher and more disagreeable forms, rarely move outside the pleasant circles of the class to which they belong, and in the day of severe trial will follow the lead of the most powerful and respectable forces in society and at the same time find good reasons for so doing."[19]

The publics of *Democracy and Education* must be reconstructed in greater detail. H. H. Horne, a professor of education and philosophy at New York University has written an "exposition and comment" of *Democracy and Education*, which has channelled Dewey's ideas, albeit upon a rough vehicle. Professor W. H. Kilpatrick, a disciple of Dewey's, has compiled a *Source Book*. Of these books Horne writes:

> "Dr. Dewey has exerted a great influence on education both at home and abroad. Dr. Kilpatrick's *Source Book* and Dr. Dewey's *Democracy and Education* are the texts most widely used in our country in the field of educational philosophy.[20] About one-fifth of the former book is drawn from the writings of Dr. Dewey. This situation suggests the significance of Dr. Dewey's educational views at home."[21]

Democracy and Education has been used very widely as a text then. It has been used in normal schools and in liberal art schools; it has been a handbook for the training of public school teachers. Therefore, we must examine the sociology of the profession of teaching. This will be valuable because this profession forms a public of

Dewey's and because he has followed it closely and worked active-ly for it and within it. Of all concrete groups in society, it is with this one that he has been most continuously and closely connected.

In a previous section we have set forth certain trends in U.S. educational institutions in the last half of the nineteenth century. There the emphasis was more upon colleges and universities than upon the primary and secondary grades. Now let us briefly recon-struct the situation of the educational system as a whole and, in particular, the positions of its personnel, for this was of central con-cern to Dewey. As we have said, this personnel formed a major public of Dewey and he has, both personally and intellectually, participated in its movement. Those features of the educational structure and personnel that are relevent to these participations now claim our attention.

Certain contours of Dewey's own writing set a rough limit to what we have to consider. It is the *public* schools that he has talked about and written for. The controversies over secular vs. denominational schools have not persistently claimed his attention. We have al-ready indicated the structural mechanics which led to the secular-ization of the schools; by the time Dewey came to give publication-attention to "education" they are predominantly secular, that is, public.[22]

The outstanding fact about the public schools since the last quar-ter of the nineteenth century has been their expansion. If we can grasp the *conditions* and some of the *results* of their growth, we shall have gone far in locating them structurally and grasping the posi-tions and chances of the personnel who have manned them.

Besides sheer population increase of the country at large[23] there were legal conditions for this growth, such as the legal diminish-ment of child labor.[24] The school population in secondary schools increased from 630,000 in 1900 to 4,740,580 in 1930.[25] This growth was accompanied by an occupational diversification and consequent curriculum changes. In 1890, public secondary schools offered nine subjects; in 1928, forty seven were offered.[26] This has received at-tention above; we are interested now in the teachers.

1. Compilations of Dewey's social and political essays are found in *Characters and Events*, two volumes, and *Individualism, Old and New*.

2. In the excellent obituary appendix which the NR printed on Croly, we read: "Herbert Croly . . . with the assistance of Mr. and Mrs. Willard Straight founded the *New Republic*." "Herbert Croly, 1869-1930." *New Republic* (LXIII, No. 813, Part two, July 16, 1930) pp. 243-71, contains articles revealing of the philosophy of the early NR.

3. The figures for 1928 and 1930 are from N. W. Ayer and Sons, *Directory of Newspapers and Periodicals*. The others were furnished by me by the kindness of Mr. Daniel Mebane, treasurer of the *New Republic*. The circulation of the *Saturday Evening Post* was 2,908,000 in 1930; the *Atlantic Monthly* was 133,000.

4. These data and those on income, etc., to follow were furnished by Daniel Mebane. These 828 were the only replies to a questionnaire sent to 7,000 of NR's subscribers. This is about twelve per cent. *See* next note.

5. Scientifically the figures given on the *New Republic* readership cannot be accepted as definitive.

6. *New Republic*, Vol. I, no. 1, p. 12.

7. *Congress of Arts and Science*, Vol. 7, p. 727.

8. *Ibid.*, p. 728.

9. *See* Baker's article "Labor and Capital Hunt Together," in *McClure's*, (Sept., 1903).

10. Among the top of the volumes on the muckrakers is Louis Filler's *Crusaders for American Liberalism* (1939); covering the same period and after: P. L. Haworth, *America in Ferment* (1915); John Chamberlain, *Farewell to Reform* (1932); Mark Sullivan's *Our Times (1927-35);* and of course books by Charles Beard. *See* chronology and bibliography of period in Filler.

11. *Crusaders for American Liberalism* (New York 1939), pp. 3-7.

12. "It was good to be alive and young in the years between the turn of the century and the beginning of the First World War. On the whole, the country was prosperous and gaining in prosperity. The panic of 1907 was of short duration. Unemployment was far from unknown, but it was not a chronic and devastating disease. The average young man with reasonable health, reasonable energy, and reasonable luck was at least sure of a job." — Norman Thomas, *We Have A Future* (New York 1941), p. 6.

13. Louis Filler, *op. cit.*, pp. 4-5.

14. *Ibid.*, p. 5.

15. *Ibid.*, p. 7.

16. *Ibid.*, p. 7.

17. *See* Russel, "The Magazines Soft Pedal," *Pearsons* (February, 1914).

18. Jane Dewey, *op. cit.*, p. 28.

19. George Counts, *Dare the Schools Build A New Social Order?* pp. 7-8, John Dewey pamphlet.

20. *Cf.* Henry W. Mack, "Comparative Context of Educational Philosophy Text Books," *Education*, (December, 1928).

21. H. H. Horne, *The Democratic Philosophy of Education*, (N.Y., 1963),

p. ix. Concerning Dewey's educational influence abroad: "Translations have appeared of practically all of his educational writings. One or more have been published in most of the European languages — French, German, Russian, Hungarian, Bulgarian, Greek, Italian, Spanish, and Swedish — and in Arabic, Turkish, Chinese, and Japanese, while special editions of his earlier works have been published in England. The [foreign] literature about Dewey has been slight . . . the majority . . . of recent date." Kandel, I. L., "John Dewey's Influence on Education in Foreign Lands," in *John Dewey the Man and His Philosophy* (Cambridge, 1930), p. 71, cited in Horne, *Ibid.*, p. ix.

22. Which is one of the most outstanding in the modern Western world, increasing approximately fifty-fold in about a century. From 1900 to 1930, the population increased 47,000,000. *See* Chapter I, *Recent Social Trends.*

23. See above section for articles on religion and the school, cited therein.

24. In 1870, 13.2 per cent of children between the ages of 10 to 15 were gainfully employed; in 1900, 8.5 per cent; in 1930, only 4.7 per cent were so employed.

25. Judd, *Recent Social Trends*, p. 329.

26. *Ibid.*, p. 330.

18

Professionalization of Teaching

The mark of professionalization is specialized schools, attendance in which qualifies admission into the occupational role. Between 1836 and 1860 eleven "normal schools" were created and made available to teaching personnel."[1] By 1898 there were 167 public normal schools in the United States.[2] Their existence undoubtedly was a factor increasing the prestige, social protection, and perhaps the income of the teaching population, but by no means did it boost them to the professional level and status of lawyers, doctors, or even ministers. The number of teachers grew so rapidly that normal schools could not possibly "keep up with them." In the late 'nineties there were 403,333 teachers in the United States, most of them working in the elementary schools. But during one of these years the number of teacher graduates from public and private normal schools were only 11,225; estimates of the number needed for the turnover and expansion are around 50,000.[3] More formal certification and examinations by "superintendents" grew out of the more informal qualifications of the lay committees. The functions of principals increased during the first half of the nineteenth century. At first principals were "head teachers" but later they were freed from teaching.[4] Along with the growth of the normal schools, in the middle decades of the last century, out of the conditions of the emerging profession there arose "associations" for teachers. What had been unorganized, sporadic growth, came to focus in movements and the eyes of schoolmasters and marms were upon the leaders and their minds were at the disposal of theoreticians in the normal schools. The associations and movements came into being within states, then they amalgamated to embrace sections. They agitated for normal schools and for the establishment of libraries, adult education, taxes for growing public school systems. This was perhaps their central social reason for being.[5] Some of them were supported in their aims and their pressures by organized labor, which rightly saw in the schools chances for ascent. In 1849 there was a consolidation with Horace Mann as head, while eight years later the National Teachers Association came into being at a convention in Philadelphia. This latter organization seems to have been a genuinely professional association; it constituted a medium for the dissemination of ideas. From it now could emerge parties to carry ideas into educational action and to sponsor reforms of such things as certification of teachers.

In 1870 the name was changed to National Education Association, and it absorbed other societies. Its membership fluctuated up to 1900. It had 2,729 members in 1884; 11,297 in 1895; and 4,641 in 1900.[6]

But its growth continued, and in 1919 the active membership was nearly 10,000; in 1921 the membership added 40,000; and by 1932 it totalled 220,149. In addition to the National Educational Association, there has been in existence since 1916 an American Federation of Teachers, in which year the membership was 2,800. In 1934 it comprised only 13,000 with about 125 locals. Between 1934 and 1938 it rose to 30,000 members. It has operated in the field of "public opinion" and legislation against opposition and criticism from school boards and many educators. With a slogan of "Democracy for Education, Education for Democracy" it has came out for such policies as abolition of war, recognition of the Soviet Union, abolition of child labor, attack upon bankers for their attitudes toward public education, etc.[7]

Having its roots directly in the utterances of John Dewey and Frances Parker, The Progressive Educational Association was founded in 1918-19 in Washington, D.C. Its membership has remained quite small, numbering only 10,000 in 1938. In 1929 it shifted its attention somewhat from problems of child growth to the social and economic problems of education. Its members have ranged from "mildly conservative to extremely liberal."[8] The salary increases of teachers in the last part of the nineteenth century is indicated in the following table:

TABLE 7

Weekly *Real* Salaries by Rural-Urban and Sex for 1865 and 1890°

Year	Rural		Urban	
	Men	Women	Men	Women
1865.........	$ 9.09	$ 5.99	$23.15	$ 8.57
1890.........	18.08	13.68	52.19	21.05

Adapted from a table from W. R. Burgess' "Trends of School Costs," given by Elsbree.[9]

During the same period "common labor" ranged from $8.94 to $8.82 and urban artisans increased from $14.90 to $15.64. The reason for the economic ascent of teachers displayed here is in part, merely the tremendous increase of demand, a demand augmented by the wholesale creation during this period of the high schools. In addition, the emerging profession was becoming organized and vocal and its members were, with the growth of normal schools, better (and more expensively) qualified. They were still, however, in this period, to be classed as similar to semi-skilled labor rather than professional in the occupational and class hierarchy.

Salaries have continued to increase. Judd[10] after correcting for the cost of living, gives the average of the annual salaries of public school teachers as $525 in 1914 and $851 (uncorrected: $1420) in 1930. Paul H. Douglas[11] and W. R. Burgess[12] have shown that both the earned and the real wages of teachers have rather steadily increased. Of course, they must be compared with other workers in order properly to locate them. From 1890 — 1920 teachers had a per cent increase in salary of 125 per cent, whereas *workers'* average weekly wages increased 195 per cent and *artisans'* wages showed a percentage increase of 169. It should be recalled that salaried employees such as teachers are somewhat "protected" from economic vicissitudes.

After the first World War the picture is rather different: there is a greater rise in income. Thus, from 1890 to 1937 the percentage increase in *real* wages was 277.[13] Given their initial low, it may be said that "teachers' salaries have improved more rapidly during the Twentieth Century than have the wages of most groups of workers."[14]

And the N.E.A. says: "They have suffered less decline in salary than many other groups.[15] From the World War to the depression the real income of teachers more than doubled."[16]

One of the more *specific* probable reasons for this has been indicated: the longer period of training required. The average teacher in the late thirties had twice as much professional training as in 1890.[17] Also there were more days of "school" to teach.

There is another way of locating teachers economically which Harold F. Clark has used.[18] It is possible to rank occupations in terms of their average earnings for a working lifetime, basing the expectations upon average incomes prevailing from 1920 to 1936. Placed in this way within a crudely comparative set of occupations, mainly professional, public school teaching is *eleventh* with a life expectation of $29,700; whereas medicine is first with $108,000; and college teaching is *sixth;* with $69,300. Public school teaching is next above the *skilled trades* which carry a life-expected earning of $28,600. If we place teaching upon a scale of earnings in dollars per year in terms of the average income between 1920 and 1936, we find that the skilled trades are slightly above public school teaching which stands at $1,350; whereas medicine is again number one, standing at $4,850. Medicine and law are about three-and-a-half times as economically attractive as teaching. In terms of extraction, elementary school teachers during the period of Dewey's life span have been drawn largely from the lower economic classes. The cost of college training, required for high school teachers, has tended to cause them to be drawn from slightly higher income groups. Income has probably been the deciding factor in the choice of either normal school leading to elementary teaching or college in general leading to high school. Persons training for teaching in liberal arts colleges tend to derive from "proprietary, professional, and managerial" groups.[19] Those who are aimed at teaching via training in the "teachers' colleges" predominantly derive from labor groups, about forty-five per cent of them from skilled labor.[20] They also come in large numbers from farmers and fewer from "businessmen."[21] Thus, ascent into the "profession" of teaching would seem to be rather easy, regardless of stratum of father. Certainly among professions it is the easiest to enter. Intellectually and socially the barriers are comparatively quite low. A teacher has been much more likely to be the daughter of a farmer or a tradesman than of a professional man. The studies of Hill and Moffett[22] have shown that the typical teachers' college student has derived from classes with a median parental income of $2,000 to $2,500 per year and from occupational groups such as farmers, skilled workmen, or owners of small businesses. The student has typically been reared in a rural community or a small town. The sisters of these students become stenographers, nurses, or business clerks.

To this low economic position and extraction, and as partial explanation for it, should be added the fact that steadily the proportion of men teaching has declined in favor of women. The Civil War was the first big turning point in this direction. In 1880, forty-two per cent of the 286,593 of total number of teachers were men; whereas in 1930, only 16.5 per cent of the total teaching population of 854,263 were men.[23] The occupation of high school and elementary grade school teaching has been one of the lowest paid professions. It is the profession of the lower income class. As a group it has risen some in class position; it has definitely given opportunities for ascent on the part of individuals. It has remained among the lowest paid of those occupations that are qualified by professional training and organizations.

Teachers and those concerned with them have experienced and seen the growth of "knowledge" operating as a pull toward "success," for that is one meaning of "professionalization." Not only this, but given the possibility, rather widely realized, of occupational and class ascent of people going to schools, those concerned with education, if they take the picture in a large enough stretch of time, can see class ascent operating through the vehicle of education. Not only have teachers risen, but it has been within the institutions which they run that their "clients" have risen. It has been slow perhaps, but all "progress" is slow.

Hence there is every sociological reason for the truth of the statement: "For a century the social outlook of teachers has been based upon an expanding economy."[24] It may be noted that this ascent has touched the top ranks of the teaching profession:

> ". . . a half dozen outstanding administrators in education today, drawing salaries which put them in the top 2 per cent of the distribution of national income, came from one poverty-ridden section of rural Indiana."[25]

It is clear then that "School attendance, school curricula, and school methods expressed the idea of schooling as a stepping stone to higher-economic status."[26] Nor that the mood of Dewey's style of thought has taken hold in this sphere.

The United States has, comparatively speaking, been rather unique in providing for large numbers a unilateral opportunity to go from grammar school to and through the university.[27] Dominantly it has not had a dual set of school channels resting upon differential classes. Each generation of children has tended to have increased educational opportunities. And the character of their jobs has shifted, if not in all cases, their class position. In 1890, "high schools" were viewed as the privilege of those planning to enter professions; in 1928 they were generalized to take in those preparing for manifold activities. The per cent of adolescents in secondary schools has been larger than in any other country.[28] Of great relevance to our concern is a direct result accruing from the rapid growth of education:

> "Expansions in an education system as extensive and as rapid as those [of the US] . . . inevitably give rise to problems of readjustment . . . Indeed many of these problems can be solved only through experimentation which in some cases involves the compromise or even drastic invasion of vested interests and deepseated prejudices."[29]

In a more stable educational situation, routine procedure might have been satisfactory, but a situation such as existed in the United States was tailored to an "experimental" philosophy without too much respect for "tradition," yet, given the position of teachers in communities, it could not be too "experimental." It had to be "practical" in the sense of plain political safety. But the problems simply faced could not be solved by reference to precedent or by authoritatively handed down doctrines and procedures. The members of the emergent profession who directly faced these problems of growth formed the public which gobbled up the educational philosophy of John Dewey.

That the schools are public means that the chief *source* of the income making up the situation of teachers is public taxation. This feature aids in accounting for the character of the public stands taken by teachers' organizations. It is also a reminder to anyone concerned with "education" that education is a *"public service."* When one so concerned speaks of expressions of government, of the welfare state, he includes in his statement the great bulk of teachers of the nation. From 1910 to 1930 the aggregate public service doubled its numbers; whereas the total gainfully employed expanded only thirty-four per cent.[30]

The social position and the character of the problems faced by teachers in towns of 30,000 - 100,000 are perhaps representatively indicated by examination of Muncie, Indiana.

Even the Muncie press (in 1936) reported on the difficulties of the job of teachers:

> "How are we to teach thrift to those who have lost everything? . . . teach youth to rise . . . no jobs to go to? . . . teach honesty when it has been reduced to . . . legal technicality? Today's school teacher," the editor commented, "must be wiser than Solomon."

When in doubt about "sex," "troubled parents turn for help to teachers or preachers, who are in the unhappy position when they address the children of being criticized by the parents for saying too much and of being laughed at by the children for saying too little."[31]

The type of activity and speech which can be indulged in by teachers seems to be set by the relative strength of the various interested groups of the town. The problem is to play off one against the other to satisfy as many as possible. It is a set of problems requiring "tact," mediation; only a slow "improvement" can be envisaged. Thus:

> "The D.A.R., always on a hair-trigger of watchfulness for 'disloyalty,' is reported to feel that both the high school and college have 'some pretty pink teachers'; and it is reported as characteristic of its activity that sons and daughters in the classrooms of suspected teachers have been enlisted to check upon the latter's teachings. When a social science teacher in one of the high schools spoke favorably of joining the World Court, a local editorial warned that teachers ought to remember that the schools are supported by taxes. A State law, passed by the legislature in 1935 with the backing of the D.A.R., requires a new compulsory high-school course on the Federal Constitution."[32]
>
> "The tightening of the conflict between the two philosophies of public education has resulted in a state of affairs in which mature, thoughtful, conscientious teachers not only fear what

parents or organizations may say if they follow candidly the searching questions of their students, but in which a teacher discussing these problems with a colleague may interrupt the discussion by the apprehensive remark, "But I don't know whether I should discuss these things *even with you.*"[33]

The town believes:

"That schools should teach the facts of past experience about which 'sound, intelligent people agree.' That it is dangerous to acquaint children with points of view that question 'the fundamentals.' That an education should be 'practical,' but at the same time, it is chiefly important as 'broadening' one. That too much education and contact with books and big ideas unfits a person for practical life ... That schoolteachers are usually people who couldn't make good in business."[34]

Such, very briefly, are the historical situations and the character of the problems faced by the section of the population in which Dewey has perhaps been most interested. Their situation — one of "local autonomy" open to pressuring groups, one expanding enormously — corresponds to a non-authoritarian ideology, one that is pluralistic and experimental.

1. W. S. Elsbree, *The American Teacher* (New York 1939) Chapter XII, p. 153.
2. *Ibid.*, p. 312.
3. *Ibid.*, p. 314.
4. *Ibid.*, p. 174.
5. *Ibid.*, p. 242.
6. National Education Association, Journal of Proceedings and Addresses, (Vol. XXXIX, p. 801) given in Elsbree, *op. cit.*, p. 503.
7. Elsbree, *op. cit.*, p. 577.
8. *Ibid.*, p. 514f.
9. *Ibid.*, p. 432.
10. Judd, *Recent Social Trends.*
11. *Real Wages in the United States* (Boston 1930) p. 382.
12. Trends of Social Cost, pp. 32-33.
13. Douglas, p. 382.
14. Elsbree, p. 436. *See* P. Douglas.
15. From *N.E.A. Research Bulletin,* Vol. XIII, No. 4 (1835) p. 243.
16. *Teacher and Society*, p. 144.
17. Elsbree, p. 436.

18. *Life Earnings in Selected Occupations in the United States* (New York 1937), Given by Elsbree, p. 437.

19. E. S. Evenden *et al, Teacher Personnel in the United States,* Vol. II, in National Survey of the Education of Teachers, Office of Education, No. 10, 1933, p. 20f.

20. M. Kiely, *Comparison of Students in Teachers' Colleges and Students in Liberal Arts Colleges,* Teachers' College Columbia Contribution to Education, No. 440, 1931.

21. F. L. Whitney, in *Education* XLVII. 1927. pp. 449f.

22. Elsbree, p. 549. The *following citations* from C. Hill, *A Decade of Progress in Teacher Training* (N.Y., 1927) and M. L. Moffett, *The Social Background and Activities of Teachers College Students* (N.Y., 1929), are presented in Elsbree, Chapter XXXV.

23. From a table adapted from L. M. Chamberlain and L. E. Meece, *Women and Men in the Teaching Profession* by Elsbree, p. 554.

24. *The Teacher and Society,* W. H. Kilpatrick, editor (First Yearbook of John Dewey Society 1937) p. 143.

25. *Ibid.,* p. 144.

26. *Ibid.,* p. 144.

27. *Recent Social Trends,* p. 325.

28. *Recent Social Trends,* pp. 330-31.

29. *Ibid.,* p. 346.

30. *Ibid.,* p. 292.

31. Robert S. Lind, *Middletown In Transition,* pp. 482-83, 170.

32. *Ibid.,* p. 236.

33. *Ibid.,* p. 238.

34. *Ibid.,* p. 411.

19

The Philosophic Public and Professional Ascent

In the case of technical philosophy, the journals in which Dewey published are such that only members of the academic profession of philosophy would be likely to examine. The following are representative: *The Journal of Philosophy, The Philosophical Review, International Journal of Ethics, Mind, The University of California Chronicle,* and *Journal of Speculative Philosophy.* Of these professional reviews, the *Journal of Philosophy* and the *Philosophical Review* may be taken as representative. Dewey was co-editor of the former.

The circulation of *The Philosophical Review* in 1900 was 450 copies. It remained roughly at this figure until World War I. In 1920 it circulated 525; but in 1925 it dropped to 400. In 1930 N. W. Ayers did not list it. The case of *The Journal of Philosophy* (formerly called *Journal of Philosophy, Scientific Method, and Psychology)* is similar. It was founded in 1904; in 1914 it circulated 600 copies, dropped in 1925 to 560; went up to 675 in 1930.

The subscribers to these journals are in all probability either libraries or members of the philosophical craft, *i.e.,* professional teachers of philosophy. It is not probable that one can enlarge their circulation by saying that more than one person reads library copies. I have been in a dozen libraries subscribing to *The Journal of Philosophy,* the pages of which were never cut. It is possible then to equate the public of Dewey's technical philosophy with the members of the American Philosophical Association and their advanced students, who will soon be members. This academic group has already been discussed.

In addition to these three publics, classified roughly by topic, there is another public which has continued to be in Dewey's focus throughout his career: the students he has taught or who have read his books. As far as Chicago is concerned, this matter has been discussed. There we found that twenty-four per cent of the fathers of students were professional, whereas sixty-two per cent of the students became professionals. Many of these no doubt are among the group of teachers discussed above. It is safe to suppose, in the absence of data, that the situation at Columbia University, at least up to the depression, was similar.

There are a few facts which lend probative force to generalizing the Chicago pattern. To begin with, the United States holds the record in total college and university student enrollment. It also has a higher proportion of such students to the population than has any other country. In 1932, one out of every 125 inhabitants went to college or a university.[1] That means ascent via education for large numbers of people. As far as such mobility goes, the following table adapted from Bagley is revealing:[2]

TABLE 8. COLLEGE STUDENTS BY OCCUPATION OF
THEIR FATHERS

Occupation of father	9 Mass. Normal Schools	3 La. Teachers Colleges	19 Penn. Normal Schools	4 Mich. Normal Schools	65 Liberal Arts Colleges
Business	29.7	23.4	21.3	...	44.4
Skilled Labor	39.8	10.4	33.2	...	7.2
Unkilled labor	11.4	5.0	14.0	...	.5
Farmers	7.6	34.2	18.7	33.5	24.2
Professions	5.7	6.9	9.9	6.7	18.5

In 1927-28 (prosperity) forty-nine per cent of male students were at least partially self-supporting.[3]

These facts and figures showing occupational and demographic patterns of ascent and shifting underlie the publics of John Dewey. We shall see that they lie back of his modes of thought, his values, and his apparatus of concepts. They explain how such figures are among those facts most crucial to the understanding of American cultural life.

Both within the schools and among topics of interest in the media of printed communications, philosophical topics have *declined* in the volume of attention given them.

TABLE 9. The Ratio of Articles on "Philosophical Topics" per 1,000 Articles indexed in *The Readers Guide*, 1905 - 1931.*

Item	1905-1906	1915-1918	1925-1928	1930-1931
"Philosophy"	.80	.51	.55	.87
"Logic"	.42	.21	.31	.33
"Pragmatism"	.35	.04	.05	.07
Etc.	...	...	...	...
Total	3.60	2.29	3.15	4.04

*Adapted from table by Hornell Hart in *Recent Social Trends*, p. 395.

Another study of "seven mass circulation magazines" shows a decline of interest in philosophy and logic after the war "to a level consistently lower than half the height shown in 1900."[4] Commenting in general upon these data and others, Hart writes:

> "The relative decline of attention devoted to pure science and to religion in magazine articles is allied to the partial eclipse of problems in the fields of philosophy, metaphysical psychology and psychiatry ... The philosophical topics as a whole show a fairly consistent tendency toward peaks just before the war and during the year 1930-1931. The outstanding exceptions are pragmatism and mysticism which failed to recover at the second peak... "[5]

The height for pragmatism, 1905-06, was due no doubt to William James.

> "With regard to pragmatism, it seems reasonable to suppose that it has not ceased to be discussed but rather that it has become assimilated into public thought to such an extent that special articles no longer appear on this subject. New philosophical terms, such as "instrumentalism" may have been substituted."[6]

The last sentence above makes us skeptical as to how much weight can be given these data regarding "pragmatism" in general. It should however be stressed that in the light of these data and those for university courses to be presented we can say that in the general competition of ideas the fact that John Dewey's thought and interest has not been "philosophical" in the traditional sense of the word, has implemented his diffusion. The traditionalist would call it a pyrrhic victory! These data are interesting in terms of the shift of Dewey to heavy writings on "education" and, precisely when "philosophy" goes down in volume of public focus, 1915-18, the attention given to social and political affairs.

"Education" steadily rose in volume of attention: in 1905-06 the articles per 1,000 were 29.67; in 1929-30, the ratio was 48.17. Also note that "practical science" gained over "pure science"; science gained terrifically over "religion."

Now let us take the point of intellectual competition, decline of focus on "philosophy" and Dewey's prestige, the unphilosophical character of his thought, and his focus upon other topics entirely — let us examine the point in the light of data concerning courses elected by students in schools. First, the obvious point that no "philosophy" is taught in high schools; their growth would not necessarily conduce to an increased interest in "philosophy" at the college level commensurate with the general growth. Indeed, considering the practical trends in secondary education we might expect the reverse. And we find the reverse. Fortunately, materials are available on the University of Chicago.

TABLE 10

Number of Courses in the Records of "one hundred typical members of the June graduating classes," University of Chicago, 1900 - 1930.*

Subject	1900	1910	1920	1930
Commerce and Administration	....	....	....	142
Divinity	63	88	41	86
Education	45	134	217	432
Economics	107	159	303	217
Philosophy	151	107	87	85
Sociology	98	92	121	136
Zoology	53	58	83	70

*Adapted from table by Judd, *Recent Social Trends*, p. 339.

The decline in philosophy is steady. Even Divinity rose in 1930 after a depression in 1920. To put the point crudely could it be that competition for student attention between departments had anything to do with the "non-philosophical" character of pragmatism as a blend in university philosophy given its inclusion of other domains such as education, the retention of a heavy interest in "psychology," especially a psychology drawing a great deal upon the rising social studies? Can features of pragmatism be interpreted in terms of changes in the curricula? I am *not* positive about the point but I *am* suggesting that the figures are very interesting to professional philosophers!

As intellectual differentiation has proceeded, as the volume of attention in mass communication media upon "philosophy" and "pragmatism" declines, as the number of philosophical courses chosen by university students declines, John Dewey's focus of attention, competing for public interest and for the recruitment of a public, has shifted into educational and social-political affairs. Both education and social-political affairs have risen in volume of public attention and in the number of courses chosen in the universities. And John Dewey has remained before a selected public's attention. Thus his personal foci of attention have fluctuated and shifted so as to mesh, rather to correspond with the rise in volume of those of general communications and of specific publics. Such are, in brief, the gross relations of Dewey's writings, publics and attentions — conceived formally, by topic. The content of such mechanics of intellectual life will be scrutinized.

We have now reconstructed certain *social bases for imputation* which can now rest upon four types of imputational base or upon various combinations of them:

a. *Contexts.* There are the contexts in which Dewey has moved. These include the primary extraction context, the circles and activities, the institutional, and the more voluntary ones. Here we have given, briefly, the institutional forms in their structural locations, participation in which might have conditioned the slant of his social sight and political orientation.

b. *Career.* Closely related to contexts, we have a sociological picture of his career; it is segregated here from (a) because of the *ordering* of the experiences to which it gives rise in conjunction with (a). Because of this ordering, the features of later social contexts which are responded to selectively are in part set by previous experiences in previous contexts. This must be taken into account in lining up the probative evidence for detailed imputation.

c. *Publics.* From another side, we have reconstructed some probable publics of Dewey and have indicated something of their location in the social structure and of their overlappings.

d. *Foci.* Something else has been accomplished which may serve as a guide and apparatus in the making of imputations. We have roughly set forth Dewey's foci of attention through time, and have begun the explanation of several of their obvious shifts in terms of gross career happenings.

Thus from several angles we have a sociological picture of his "positions" and foci of attention. By "position," we may refer to (a), and/or (b), and/or (c). Which of these possibilities is referred to subsequently will be made clear by the context in which the reference is made.

Lastly, the reader should recall the citations above to a theoretical discussion of the *mechanisms connective* of "positions" and doctrines. It is, in part, upon the validity of this discussion that the relevance of our work in reconstructing "publics" depends, and, in turn, it is partially upon what follows that this discussion on mechanisms is to receive a test of usefulness.

Now, after grasping these four matters and the set of connective mechanisms, we may enter into a sociological content-analysis of publications with some probability of controlling and being aware of the grounds for the imputations to be advanced.

The structural changes and the mobilities which the social world of Dewey has undergone are ascertainable. In each of the following configurations and trends (1) Dewey himself, (2) considerable portions of Dewey's publics, and (3) the groups for which he has, putatively, spoken have been well in the middle of the shifts to be indicated:

(a) In terms of *stratification,* the general picture is steady ascent on all fronts. Specifically, Dewey is born of the smaller bourgeoisie; having to borrow money for specialized training, he climbs to the upper middle class. His student publics rise from lower middle and middle to upper middle. His largest public, students who are studying to be teachers, climbs from lower classes into the lower middle. The public for his political writing is definitely upper middle class.

(b) In *occupational* terms, diversification is rapid and severe. Dewey rises in class through professionalized training, moving into a professional group from a family in small business. His students move through a similar channel: from smaller business to professions. His teacher-students move from farming and skilled workers into the least paid, most easily accessible "professional" group. His political publics are dominantly professional.

(c) *Demographically,* one general picture is from rural to urban. Dewey derives from and stays until young manhood in small towns, then moves through Baltimore to Ann Arbor, then to the pivotal years in Chicago, and later maturity in New York City. His students are precisely among those elements in the population who have gone into the growth (and occupations) of the cities; many of them have come from farms. Teachers also, of course, have followed density of population, although here, too, many are recruited from rural areas and small towns.

A second demographic fact which bears upon the conditions of intellectual work is the large increase in population. This increase, in conjunction with the diffusion of education means, in general, the possibility of a wider intellectual public. The sectors of the element of this public in which Dewey's writings found a response have already been indicated.

Third, there is the fact that society on the North American Continent during the nineteenth century continually migrated to the West. By 1890 this expansion was about closed. It would seem that, apart from an intangible mood commonly and proudly imputed to this demographic factor, its operation on intellectual life is best grasped in an indirect way. (a) For example, it would seem that its influence upon the class structure, in making chances for ascent more profuse, was the way in which it may have been connected with the expansive optimistic tenor of pragmatism. This openness of class structure was, of course, also affected in a signal way by the continual European immigration. Usually, each successive wave came in at the bottom and pushed large areas of stratification upward. (b) The frontier, demographic basis of a continually colonizing democracy also operated in the type of education pattern which, as we have seen in part and shall examine in textual detail later, has been a definite determinant in certain of Dewey's concepts. Any attempt to exploit in a *direct* way the *regional frontier* thesis in connection with the form of pragmatism will have to grapple with the fact of the strict, although, it is true, sometimes Fichtean, Hegelianism, which flourished in St. Louis and yet found itself on such a congenial basis with the New England Transcendental group. As will be clear from the reconstruction of Dewey's career-line and from what follows, it seems best to understand the factor in (a) and (b) immediately above. Both (a) and (b) can be readily seen as direct determinants of Dewey's style of thought.

Each of these structural shifts has rather specific import for the perspective of Dewey. Take the *occupational* first. Notice that the occupations (and strata ascent *through* them) undergone by Dewey and his publics *depend upon the development of knowledge ßkills.* This is one sociological clue to his heavily *intellectualist* slant. It is precisely in the professions that the dominant values of pecuniary success and social prestige are most likely to depend upon a growth of academic knowledge and symbolic skill. Notice that these persons occupy positions requiring rational decisions, and remember that Dewey is *deeply* and consistently against all corporate groups or bureaucracies, industrial or governmental, which would not distribute rationality "down the line," but rather concentrate and monopolize decision-making in certain positions. Dewey does not offer a form of thought corresponding to that type utilized and required in such corporate organizations. Although teaching staffs in America are quasi-bureaucratic, they are here of a loose-knit type; and public school teachers are, thereby, in many ways "on their own." Incidentally, the type of "problems" they face fit rather neatly with the Deweyan formulae; for problem solving and the cautiously *mediating, pluralist,* and *transitional* character of his formulae of intelligence is an indispensable feature of public school teachers. For an institutional arrangement in which much "local autonomy" remains, a teacher must compromise between many pressuring groups. Since they are without power they must rely upon persuasions. Such a situation makes quite understandable the *formalization* of the ends of education: to teach "how to think."

Take *stratification* next: the pattern all around Dewey is ascent. But the class and status ascent — with which he is most closely linked — is ascent apparently due to personal effort, it is ascent via occupations requiring personal "improvement" and "growth." But what we are concerned with in this ascent pattern is the *optimism* which prevails throughout Dewey's style. His optimism is qualified only by the possession and issue of "intelligence," which is understandable considering the specific occupational vehicles of the ascent with which he has been most involved.

The third item mentioned was *demographic,* and there we found the pattern to be "rural" and small town to "metropolitan industrial," with all that the phrases convey by way of sociological structure. This item is more complicated than the other two. And it is, perhaps, intrinsically linked to a very central and cherished value of Dewey: the "social," the "community," and it goes further in the explanation of his political viewpoint than do the other two items mentioned.

Now if we understand "optimism" in terms of the general pattern of ascent; situate "intellectuality" within the occupational compositions and professional trends mentioned; and place the category (and its broad use and implications) of the "social" within the demographic shift, we can then put the three together: this perspective is optimistic about the progress of man because it believes intelligence can win out; but it wants that intelligence to "win out" in a certain way; it wants intelligence used in the attainment of a *socially* shared democracy based on a community scale of social life. Intelligence carries too many values for Dewey for him ever to let it become a merely neutral calculation; in every statement of inquiry the community is highly favored. The statement of intelligence itself takes on a character which to be fulfilled must correspond with a homogeneous, individuated community world which is to be (re-)instituted. This recommunalization is the basic political intention of Dewey's thinking.

We have already indicated that the liberal political tradition in America, with which Dewey affiliated himself and of which he is a part, is partially to be understood in terms of the value implications of the demographic shift from rural sociality to urban corporacy.

1. Kotschnig, *Unemployment in the Learned Professions,* p. 18.

2. W. C. Bagley, "The Problem of Teacher Training in the U.S." (Education Yearbook of the International Institute of Teachers Colleges, 1927) (New York 1928), p. 584f.

3. W. J. Greenleaf, "Self-supporting College Students," *Vox Studentium,* VI, 1929, p. 175f.

4. *Ibid.,* p. 397.

5. *Ibid.,* p. 396.

6. *Ibid.,* p. 396.

20

Meanings and Moorings in Dewey

Each of the conceptions that are central to John Dewey's mind seems to be a component, in one way or another, of what he has termed *inquiry*. They have not all *arisen* within the context and needs of "logic," but it is there that they have received a statement which links them and it is there that they have developed many of their continuing characteristics. Examination of the publications of Dewey as a whole reveals the following "clusters" of concepts which as we shall proceed to demonstrate in detail, are "central" in his thought. By "cluster" we mean a set of terms which are surrogates of one another, each term being presented within a different contextual focus. If two terms are "surrogates" in the *same* contextual focus, their relation will be termed "synonymous."

> "I imagine that my development has been controlled largely by a struggle between a native inclination toward the schematic and formally logical, and those incidents of personal experience that compelled me to take account of actual material."[1]

It is the theory of logic, the general model of inquiry, which Dewey had urgently set forth since at least 1903, that we want to present first. In particular it will be necessary and expedient to tease from this model the basic categories which make it up. Choice of this feature of Dewey's thinking for presentation is, in part, based upon its chronological centrality in his focus of attentions and upon the (so far) putative reason that the statement of inquiry, and the concepts used in setting it forth, seem to pervade other areas of his thought more than do the concepts of any other context. Dewey's analysis of "thinking" constitutes the foundation of his thought.

(a) Some of the surrogates and synonyms of "inquiry," are: "thought," "reflective thought," "science," "scientific method," "reflection," "method," "the method of intelligence or of reflection," "intelligence," "reflection" or "creative," "method of democracy" or "liberalism."

(b) The chief intellectual source of Dewey's theory of logic is acknowledged to be and is plainly Hegelian. We have already detailed the circumstances of institutions, teachers, and current literature, and something of the internal affinities which were involved in his taking to Hegel. It is where he takes Hegel that now concerns us. What modifications were made by Dewey in the Hegelian statement, and why?

The answering of these questions directs us to other conceptual materials from which Dewey drew and which he set together to interact and blend in his mind with formal Hegelian categories. These materials, put in terms of concepts used, are "science," "behaviorism" (which is one important Deweyan eventuation of "Darwinism"), "everyday life" or "common sense."

(c) One outcome of our examination of these matters will consist in a cataloging and contextual examination of the components of Dewey's theory of "inquiry." To anticipate, these are: "problematic situation," "action" or "behavior," "experiment," "adaptation," "outcome of reflection."

These conceptions form the clusters to which we shall give attention. Examination of publications has indicated the central conceptions of John Dewey's thought.

Dewey's theory of "inquiry" is allegedly "empirical." What does this mean? It may mean anything from the frequent use of examples to a flat descriptive treatment of pieces of reflection. No matter what it may mean, there is little doubt but that any empirical statement is selective of which it would depict. The choice of empirical cases and the reasons for that choice are important questions. Rather slowly Dewey comes away from Hegelianism. In 1930 Dewey picked out for notice in the Preface to the *Studies in Logical Theory* as an underlying agreement of the Chicago school:

> "... that since Reality must be defined in terms of experience, judgment appears accordingly as the medium through which the consciously effected evolution of Reality goes on; that there is no reasonable standard of truth (or of success of

the knowing function) in general, except upon the postulate that Reality is thus dynamic or self-evolving, and, in particular, except through reference to the specific offices which knowing is called upon to perform in readjusting and expanding the means and ends of life. And all agree that this conception gives the only promising basis upon which the working methods of science, and the proper demands of the moral life, may co-operate."[2]

There are three features of this passage which should be noted: (1) as indicated above, it reveals the Hegelian stamp. But this immanent feature is not so important as the distinctly Deweyan features that are emerging. (2) We see here a *practicalization* of Hegelianism *via* the *specification* of the office of thought, and (3) the passage reveals a motive that is to underlie much of Dewey's thought: to get "science" and "the demands of the moral life" to "cooperate."

Coming towards his later formulations from out of Hegel's categories of the dialectic, Dewey's empiricism had two channels or two sets of categories which operated as selectives and which eventuated in the emphasis upon the "practical," upon "action" as a category.

(a) Very early the general empirical tendency was channeled by the acceptance of certain implications drawn from the biological work of "Darwin," *i.e.*, a set of biologically oriented psychological theses later to be known as Behaviorism. The result for logical theory was a location and statement of reflection in bio-functional and behavioral terms. This behavioristic psychology is one source of the category of "action" in Dewey.

(b) The other was the acceptance and nearly exclusive concern with one type of "reflection:" namely, that occurring in the "sciences." Dewey, unlike Peirce, lumped a generalized behavioral version of the procedure of laboratory science with "reflection in practical life." In his concern with the scientific mode of knowing Dewey was seizing upon a source of thought models which were accepted as dominant among many thinkers of the time.

The *empirical drive*, the *biologic emphasis*, and the *concern with the methods of physical science* are the three generic motifs in the theory of inquiry of John Dewey.

"Two motifs . . . influential in developing . . . a new type of empiricism: the practice of science . . . the radically different psychological approach that comes from looking at things objectively from the standpoint of biology rather than introspective analysis."[3]

Across a Hegelian backdrop these motifs generate the central conceptions with the aid of which Dewey has resuscitated logical theory by redefining "the problem of thought."

Against what did Dewey set forth his theory and urge the use of his conceptions? Within traditionally received epistemologies, according to Dewey and other Chicago pragmatists, "the problem of thought" has most usually been instituted *überhaupt*. On the one hand, there is Reality; and on the other, the Knower. The springs of knowing, that from which it arises, has been verbalized generically as "wonder," or, as within Cartesianism, as "general doubt." Such terms have been thought to represent a characteristic or faculty of a substance called Mind. The antecedent contexts and consequences of mind, being ignored, have made no difference to its operation and nature. And thought has made no difference in the world through which men move. Prior to Hegel, the history of thought was considered additive, *i.e.*, the advancement of ideas proceeded by the addition of new Truths to old.[4] For Truth, being absolute, is that which is not subject to correction.

The Hegelian statement of thought is of the tradition known as Absolute or Objective Idealism. From its standpoint:

> "rational thought, since it is the outcome of the processes of organic development, expresses in its own nature the essential truth of that development, comprehends . . . all . . . earlier (*aufgehoben*) stages. Hence in its unfolding it is absolutely free, self determining."[5]

To speak of its conditioning locus is to misunderstand it: "external circumstances" are unessential to its nature and movement. Man himself, as Peirce said in an Idealist vein, is the self-exemplification of a concept. "Environment" could perhaps disturb the evolution of man and things and thought. It could not condition their nature. The entire universe is to Hegel the expression of the thought of the supermind. In the philosophy of Hegel the development of mind is the same thing as the development of the world."[6]

"... all that is real ... is the manifestation ... of mind ...
metaphysics coincides with the logic which has to develop the
creative self movement of spirit as a dialectical necessity ...
the antitheses and contradictions of conceptions belong to the
nature of mind itself, and thus also to the essential nature of
reality which unfolds from it."[7]

Thus, within this Universal Mind, or Rational Process, the opposition which gives rise to thought is an opposition of two universals. The relation of things is a relation of thought; the cognitive
relation is ubiquitous, and in "Nature." Ideas come to be opposed
with each other. In the mind of a cosmic self, they come to be opposed. And the development of the universe, of an insect, of a rock,
is a process of resolving contradictions. All thinking, says Hegel,
begins "when unity has disappeared from the life of man, and
when its oppositions, having lost their vital relations and interactions assert themselves as independent."[8]

"Dewey, in his years of association with Morris in Ann Arbor,
developed the idea that there was an intermediate kind of
logic that was neither merely formal nor a logic of inherent
'truth' of the constitution of things; a logic of the processes by
which knowledge is reached. Mill's logic seemed to him an effort in this direction, but an effort that was disastrously blocked
and deflected by Mill's uncritical acceptance of a sensationalistic and particularistic psychology."[9]

The Deweyan point to be emphasized in connection with Hegel's
generic attitude toward thought is chiefly a locational one. It is
the metaphysical character of the Hegelian formulation which he
rejects: he takes "thinking activity, its empirical condition ... its
objective goal, apart from the limits of an historic or developing
situation."[10] It is a result of reading the processes of human reflection into nature. Hegel, wrote Mead later, ontologized the human reflective process. To Hegel the universe was mental through
and through, and the events exhibited therein occurred in a mental
manner. The logical categories of human speech were read into
the world, as if they were therein congealed.

Bluntly opposing such "absolutism" (which is Dewey's central
antagonism) and metaphysics, is the "naturalism" of Dewey. For
"naturalism" in philosophy consists essentially in locating empirically that to which it speaks. The naturalism of instrumental logic

displaces thought as the equipment of an absolute self, relativizing it by locating it humanistically as a specific function peculiar to
man as an animal trying to get along in an environment.

The redefinition of "the problems of logic" involved a pulveriza-
tion and location of inquiry; by it Dewey shook the detailed hold
of the "older epistemology." The instrumentalist revolt moves
against the concerns of "epistemological logic," *i.e.,* those positions
conceiving their task as dealing with an alleged wholesale relation
of "Thought" to "Reality," attempting to trace connectives of
thought at large to empirical antecedents at large. There is the
denial of a problem of Thought "in general." There is the denial
that Thought and Reality are great closed affairs complete within
themselves and absolutely finished.

What is "the logical problem" as defined by Dewey? ". . . the
very heart of the logical problem: the relation of thought to its
empirical antecedents and to its consequent, truth, and the relation of truth to reality . . ."[11] What is the perspective from which
these questions may be solved?

> "If one could get rid of his traditional logical theories and
> set to work afresh to frame a theory of knowledge on the basis
> of the procedure of the common man, the moralist and the ex-
> perimentalist . . .[12] [For] from the naive point of view no diffi-
> culty attaches to these questions. The antecedents of thought
> are our universe of life and love; of appreciation and struggle.
> We think about anything and everything . . . No one doubts
> that thought, at least reflective as distinct from what is some-
> times called constitutive, thought, is derivative and secondary.
> It comes after something and out of something, and for the
> sake of something. No one doubts that the thinking of every-
> day practical life and of science is of this reflective type."[13]

Notice that primacy, both logical and historical, is put on practice, not reflection:

> "Sticking for a moment to this naive standpoint, we recognize
> a certain rhythm of direct practice and derived theory; of pri-
> mary construction and of secondary criticism; of living appre-
> ciation and of abstract description; of active endeavor and of
> pale reflection. We find that every more direct primary attitude
> passes upon occasion into its secondary deliberative and discur-
> sive counterpart. We find that when the latter has done its

work it passes away and passes on. From the naive standpoint such rhythm is taken as a matter of course."[14]

This point of view results logically in a *specification,* in a lowering of the level of abstraction upon which the inquiry is to proceed:

> "If we were to ask the thinking of naive life to present, with a minimum of theoretical elaboration, its conception of its own practice, we should get an answer running not unlike this: thinking is a kind of activity which we perform at specific need, just as at other need we engage in other sorts of activity: as converse with friend; draw a plan for a house; take a walk . . . The measure of its success, the standard of its validity, is precisely the degree in which the thinking actually disposes of the difficulty and allows us to proceed with more direct modes of experiencing, that are forthwith possessed of more assured and deepened value."[15]

And this standpoint and institution of the problem stands polarized against another view:

> "What we have to reckon with [in "naive life"] is not the problem of, How can I think *überhaupt?* but, How shall I think right *here and now?* Not what is the test of thought at large, but what validates and confirms *this* thought?"[16]

Constructively, on the metaphysical side, Dewey utilizes the term reality in a denotative manner.[17] Logically, the orientation is within a concept of genetic logic that examines *specific acts* of thought, delineates their antecedent conditions. Inquiry, the way in which men fix beliefs, is made "the primary and ultimate source of logical subject matter."[18] The context, constitution, and behavior of "the reflective act," as well as its outcome or end become objects of empirical scrutiny. It is a logic which deals with thinking "as a specific procedure relative to specific antecedent occasions and to a subsequent specific fulfillment." Allegedly, it keeps constantly at hand the historic context of thought; attempts empirically to analyze actual pieces of thinking. On such a view, the so-called, and non-empiric, problem of the wholesale relation of thought at large to reality in general can but be considered meaningless and insoluble.[19]

On such a view, a natural-history or genetic method can be carried over from biology and utilized in the account of thinking. Since thinking is conceived as a "natural human activity," it has a natural history in the precise manner that any other object or sequential happening has. Since thinking is a response to a specific stimulus condition, it is not something in itself. It has its traits, elements, and laws only as a specific response to a specific stimulus.[20]

Thought arises from antecedent non-reflective conditions, which constitute its context. For Dewey, 1903-16, thought does not "set its own problems," nor does it arise from an implicit force or rationality designed to realize itself, nor from the Aristotelian notion that in each man there is a mind designed to know.[21] Hence, in explanation of thought, it cannot be said that it arises from "wonder" at all objects, or from universal and courageous doubt; for the antecedent, the context of thought, "has a certain structure and content of its own, setting the peculiar problem of thought, giving the cue to its specific activities and determining its object.[22]

Dewey's revolt rests upon a redefinition of the entire gamut of problems and subject matters of "logical theory." By denying the generalized problems of "epistemological logic" as genuine, and *allegedly* facing empirically actual inquiries *in situ*, new problems investigatively answerable are instituted for philosophy. His strategy is to set up different problems, entailing a denial of the legitimacy of other problems. In Dewey's own language:

> ". . . the chief divisions of modern philosophy, idealism in its different kinds, realisms of various brands, so-called common-sense dualism . . . (etc.) . . . have grown up around the epistemological problem of the general relation of subject and object . . . philosophy, consisting largely . . . of different answers to these questions. Is it not time that philosophy turn from the attempt to determine the comparative merits of various replies to the questions to a consideration of the claims of the questions?"[23]
>
> "The Essays try to show that such terms as 'thinking,' 'reflection,' 'judgment,' denote inquiries or the results of inquiry, and that inquiry occupies an intermediate and mediating place in the development of a (non-reflective) experience."[24]

It is this drive toward an empirical unit for investigation, and the emphasis upon the mundane experiential location, the empirical context, that is central in the early formulations of Dewey. It is such contentions which reset the aim, and the corpus of problems for logical theory. Its precise objective becomes the attempt to present a naturalistic characterization of actual pieces of reflection as they occur in "practical life and science."

All thought is intrinsically bound up with and conditioned by, though secondary to and derived from, the larger context of non-reflective experiences and behaviors. The stage in experience that is prior to thought is, in *The Essays*, variously designated as "social," "affectional," "technological," "esthetic," etc. This context "may most easily be described from a negative point of view: it is a type of experience which cannot be called a knowledge experience."[25] Dewey, operating on a formal level, is concerned with revolt against formalistic positions. Hence, in logical contexts, there is no focus upon, no detailed and empirical characterization of, this "non-cognitive context" of thought. Such "experience" is conceived in formal terms, left empirically residual. All revolts to a greater or lesser measure participate in, take something from, that against which they constitute a revolt. The experiential context of thought is conceived as in itself internally organized. Its organization is of a "non-logical character." It is "objectively continuous and organized," and has "infinite range of context" and specific moving "focus."[26] This situation wherein thought is located evokes thought, and "determines its object." In the passage from non-reflective to and through reflective modes of experience there is fundamental continuity.

This emphasis upon the empirical particularity and upon the context of thought is intimately related, on the one hand, to the concept of the *problematic* and, on the other, to the category of *action*. Dewey's early discussions of both these concepts lie within his attempts to determine the locus of "the act of reflection."[27] These two concepts perform the offices of conceptual levers. With their aid instrumentalism grounded "thought" by specification of it. With them Dewey outlined his constructive statement of reflection. Both are catalytic of Dewey's position precisely because both locate thought in "practice." They delimit "thought" to the domain of "man-in-nature." They are the chief components of a perspective from within which the specific conditions which call thought forth and the kind and extent of thought's observable consequences are seen.

Since the concepts of "action" and "the problematic situation" are so central in Dewey's logic, we must determine their social origins and intellectual sources, trace them through several contexts other than that of the logical theory; we must determine their uses in Dewey's perspective. Of the two concepts, "action" turns out to be much the more important.

Peirce was concerned to impute an intrinsic connection of mentation and action, but this linkage was rigorously restricted to the laboratory. We have witnessed James' generalization of the notion in a particular moral direction. In Dewey the description of the epistemological and the mental in the end finds definition in behavioral terms. This is true, in part, of the problematic context and the outcome of thought. And it holds for the general function given reflective processes. One of the basal coordinates of "pragmatism" is its "elevation" of behavior to the status of philosophic respectability. And this reaches its climax in John Dewey.

Within the *thought* of Dewey the origins of the concept "behavior" or "action" are clearly to be seen as two-fold, a certain conception of the *experimental procedures of physical science;* and a *biologically oriented* behavioristic psychology. From these "intellectual" sources has come the category of behavior, in terms of which "reflection" has found its instrumentalist formulation.

"Sources" is modified with "intellectual" because one should keep *analytically* separated pragmatism's *cultural* "sources and persuasions" from "immanent" sources. Such a segregation is, however, mainly one of convenience in presentation. For (a) the reasons for Dewey's utilizing certain "immanent" sources are not themselves explainable by immanence; nor (b) is the slant from which they are taken so explainable. Also (c) in the present instance Dewey himself is an "immanent" source of "behaviorism" as well as, to a lesser extent, of "experiment." Dewey (and Peirce and James before him) has done much to develop "behaviorism" and to isolate and accentuate the activity or "experimental" content of "science;" hence it does not explain the concept's usage by Dewey to impute it to these "intellectual trends." These "trends" themselves, and especially the "action" conceptions they make central, must be explained. "Behaviorism" and "science" should be viewed as implements which Dewey seized upon, developed and used in making "action" central to his general perspective. In the present section we want to consider a cultural source to which the concept "action" and some of its surrogates may be imputed. In this connection it is significant that the concept of action arose in Dewey's writing within an *ethical context.*

An 1891 essay on Matthew Arnold and Robert Browning deals with science, philosophy, and poetry.[28] The general problem is conceived as their respective contributions to "the supreme question concerning the right ordering of life" and more specifically:

> "Here, indeed, is just our problem. We must bridge this gap of poetry from science. We must heal this unnatural wound. We must, in the cold, reflective way of critical system, justify and organize the truth which poetry, with its quick, naive contacts, has already felt and reported. The same movement of the spirit, bringing man and man, man and nature, into wider and closer unity, which has found expression by anticipation in poetry, must find expression by retrospection in philosophy."[29]

Dewey presents a justification of science and philosophy in terms of their roles in facing this "supreme question." He does not deny a role to poetry. He states its function to be *ethical* and to lie within the limits of a "verifiable account of the universe."

> "If there is belief in the high and serious values of the universe, with what glory shall not the imagination portray and inspire life, what consolations shall not issue from it! But let intelligence lose this belief in the meaning and worthiness of experience, and poetry is but the tricking out of illusions, the devising of artifices I can well comprehend that poetry may deliver truth with a personal and a passionate force which is beyond the reach of theory painting in gray on gray. Indeed, it is the emotional kindling of reality which is the true province of poetry."[30]

Several things are important here. The *seriousness* of his attitude toward the purpose of poetry is almost Puritanical, although perhaps an attenuated strain. But notice the negations, the adjectives descriptive of what he is *against*: "trivial ... ornate ... cheap sentiment ... artificial ... evils which threaten ... from the frivolous, the sensual, the artificial . . . "[31] Over against these he places: "intelligence," "a verifiable account of the universe." Poetry:

> "can preserve its genuineness and its sustaining force . . . [by] truth, and truth alone . . . I confess I do not understand how that can be true for the imagination, for the emotions, which is not also true for intelligence."[32]

The "truth" which is to be used as a criterion of the genuineness, the purpose of poetry, is not conceived as something apart from "the supreme question," *i.e.*, questions of right "conduct." In this *ethical* context, we are given a defense of philosophy and science and in this polemic both become related to *conduct*.

> "It is easy to disparage science, it is easy to laugh at philosophy with its 'reasoning about causation and finite and infinite being.' Both are remote enough from our immediate spiritual and ethical interests. Face to face with the supreme question concerning the right ordering of life they seem ludicrously insufficient. But, after all, science means only knowledge, — philosophy, only love of wisdom, only the essay at reaching the meaning of this experience of ours. I cannot believe that the attempt to know truth, to grasp the meaning of experience, is remote from conduct, from the ideals and aspirations of life."[33]

Here "truth" and its quest by science and philosophy are seen tied to the realm of ethical action and value. And this linkage is accomplished by means of the notion of "conduct."

That the use of the category of action occurs early in Dewey's writing within such ethical contexts is also true on more technical levels of discourse. In the same year in which the above quotations were written, he wrote a "moral theory and practice" for the *International Journal of Ethics*. It is significant that one of the early contexts in which Dewey stressed the behavioral dimension of theory, of ideas and mentality, is this 1891 article concerned with "Moral Theory and Practice."[34] He remarks first that he found the subject of practice and theory "touched upon" by four writers (Sidgewick, Adler, Bosanquet, Salter) dealing with ethical questions. He objects to the "lurking idea" that "moral conduct is something other than . . . conduct itself, — understanding by conduct distinctively human action, that based upon and realizing ideas."[35] Thus he would secularize moral theory by means of intrinsically relating it to action. Here are the roots of ethics as engineering, a key metaphor in Dewey. Here we are concerned with understanding "action" as a level compelling this view. This secularization is also accomplished by stress on the everyday.

> "Moral theory . . . is all one with moral *insight*, [which] *is the* recognition of the relationships in hand . . . [This] makes moral insight, and . . . moral theory, consist simply in the everyday workings of the same ordinary intelligence that measures dry goods, drives mails, sells wheat, and invents the telephone . . . [And then, generalizing the view:] Moral theory . . . is the action *in idea* . . . [Theory as idea is] "the construction of the act in thought against its outward construction; it is, therefore, the doing . . . the act itself, in its emerging."[36]

Thus, were practice and theory linked in moral action. The hypothesis that one derivation of the concept of action is moral speculation is augmented by the fact that in this article Dewey is not sure that his remarks hold for all theory.[37] However this may be, the linkage of theory and action with moral matters is explicit, for his claim "precisely that an idea of what is to be done and moral theory are identical . . . "[38]

If we examine this article in its more technical aspects we can gain insight into the moral character of Dewey's intellectualism. As for the intellectualism, note that it, too, is intrinsically affiliated to the stress on action.

> " . . . human nature refuses to be moved except in the one truly human way, — through intelligence. Get the fresher, more open outlook, the refined and clarified intelligence, and the emotions will take care of themselves. They *are* there, and all they need is freeing. It is in power . . . the truth that makes free. Besides intelligence, I see but two means of moral emergence: that of hortatory preaching and that of some scheme of panacea."[39]

And from this standpoint of "intelligence" we encounter a most revealing sentence which is repeated in the essay: "The 'ought' is itself an 'is,' — the 'is' of action."[40] Around that sentence a great deal of the thought of John Dewey pivots. For the understanding of his total thought it is one of the most important sentences he has **ever written:**

(a) The category of the act, linked with theory, is an answer to the separation of the *is* and the *ought*. And this separation operates elsewhere as science and morals, as science and art or value, etc. It is "action" with which he gets them together.

(b) In so using the category of *action*, it becomes the repository of morals. It replaces ought.[41]

(c) And it allows an intellectualism: that is, a view that intelligence intrinsically involving *action* is all that is needed for any problem, moral, religious, or what not.

Dewey gives an example of a streetcar conductor's decision whether to join a strike or not. This anchorage of the point is very revealing:

> "The difference between saying, 'This act is the one to be done, this act will meet the situation,' and saying, 'the act *ought* to be done,' is merely verbal...[42] "Imagine [he concludes the essay] a scene of ceaseless movement; needs, relations, institutions ever moving on. In the midst of this scene appears an intelligence who identifies himself with the wonderful spectacle of action ... He puts forth his grasp, his *Begriff*, and arrests the movement ... Intelligence sees what it is like ... Then ... removes its break, its abstracting hold, and the scene moves on. That to which intelligence sees it moving is the 'ought to be' ... This, then, is the relation of moral theory and practice. Theory is the cross-section of the given state of action in order to know the conduct that should be; practice is the realization of the idea thus gained: it is theory in action."[43]

Another context of "action" is seen in its surrogate "work." The handling of this term is relevant to the moral and religious aspect of "action."

> "What is work, [Dewey asks] work not as mere external performance, but as attitude of mind? It signifies that the person is not content longer to accept and to act upon the meanings that things suggest, but demands congruity of meaning with the things themselves. In the natural course of growth, children come to find irresponsible make-believe plays inadequate ... When this point is reached, the ideas that things must be applied to the things with some regard to fitness ... For work (as a mental attitude, not as mere external performance) *means interest in the adequate embodiment of a meaning* (a suggestion, purpose, aim) *in objective form through the use of appro-*

priate materials and appliances. Such an attitude takes advantage of the meanings aroused and built up in free play, but *controls their development by seeing to it that they are applied to things in ways consistent with the observable structure of the things themselves."*[44]

And he continues:

> "In play activity, it is said, the interest is in the activity for its own sake; in work, it is in the product or result in which the activity terminates . . . Both may equally exemplify interest in an activity 'for its own sake'; but in one case the activity in which the interest resides is more or less casual, following the accident of circumstance and whim, or of dictation; in the other, the activity is enriched by the sense that it leads somewhere, that it amounts to something."[45]

And again, continuing *the ethicizing of "work" as a mode of action:*

> "The adult is acquainted with responsible labor upon which serious financial results depend. Consequently he seeks relief, relaxation, amusement. Unless children . . . have come under the blight of child labor, no such division exists for them. Whatever appeals to them at all, appeals directly on its own account. There is no contrast between doing things for utility and for fun. Their life is more united and more wholesome."[46]

In all these passages which display (a) the seriousness toward poetry and the place of "conduct" in this seriousness; (b) the ethical role of action, and, finally, (c) the "ethicizing" of work conceived as a special type of activity, we, of course, glimpse a Puritanical New England atmosphere, liberalized and sophisticated, perhaps, but nevertheless, unmistakable. It would be a mistake to forget that New England, including Vermont with its small holdings and chores, is the home of Puritanism in America.

We are, frankly, wary of placing too much emphasis upon the Yankee Puritan context of the Vermont of Dewey's first two decades. A career-line cannot be telescoped into the pre-manhood years, and the explanation of ideas and accentuated values by biographical context ought to give such functional autonomy to later periods as it can. Often such emphases upon explanation by extraction are not really grounded imputations at all. They are merely a tacit transferral of the accepted depictions of such milieux to the character of the thinker and his thought. Fortunately, in the case of Dewey, we do not have to let explanation of such Puritanism as may be seen in his intellectual production and particularly in connection with "action" rest upon vague references to the Vermont milieux. First, we have Dewey's self-reference, in a letter to James in the early nineties: "I presume to think that I am more of a Yankee and less of a philosopher than may sometimes appear." Taken in isolation, such self-references might mean only a certain regional pride. The grounds for imputations are cumulative, with each bit of evidence of probative value. Such sentiments of and value-investments in the Yankee Puritanism of New England as may have been deposited by the early milieu and sustained by regional pride were no doubt concretely implemented by happenings further along the career-line of Dewey. Their explanation rests not only upon reference to features of the cultural system of New England life up to Dewey's manhood but also upon the facilitation afforded by two experiences further along the career-line.

(a) The first factor is the association with the endeavor of Jane Addams' Hull-House. The motivation and animus underlying this venture, in which Dewey participated, has already been displayed above.

(b) The second factor is acceptance of *selected* features of the work of Thorstein Veblen's *Theory of the Leisure Class*. We cannot here enter into the detailed evidence for the Puritan texture of the standpoint of Veblen with his obvious and ironic dislike of "conspicuous consumption," "ostentatious display," "leisure class" polarized against the positively appraised "productive work" and implicitly the use of pecuniary elements for reinvestments for expansion of production. It is clear that Dewey shares this animus.

The strata orientation of John Dewey is tied to his use of the category of action, practice, use, etc., as a positive value and as a tool of analysis. Conversely, his negations of certain strata phenomena are soaked through with the negative side of the category. They are contemplation, leisure, uselessness.

(a) It is convenient to begin with a statement about contemporary society, his objections to certain selected phases of it, and the reasons back of the objection.

In one of his most striking essays, "The House Divided Against

Itself," a "review" of *Middletown*, Dewey focuses on two points which are worth noting:[47] First, he points out "the obvious contradictions between our institutions and practice on one hand, and our creeds and theories on the other, contradictions which a survey of any of our Middletowns reveals." He comes down hard and negative on the point. One almost gathers that Dewey would rather Middletowners accept and profess a rigorous selfish "Darwinism" for:

> "The philosophy appropriate to such a situation is that of struggle for existence and survival of the economically fit. One would expect the current theory of life, if it reflects the actual situation, to be the most drastic Darwinism. And, finally, one would anticipate that the personal traits most prized would be clear-sighted vision of personal advantage and resolute ambition to secure it at any cost."

Sidney Hook caught a vital strain of Dewey's pattern when he wrote that "sincerity of action is the test for sincerity of belief."[48] Thus did the pragmatic maxim of Peirce become "ethicized" as it ran over the boundaries of technical and laboratory contexts.

The point is that one of the chief objections — not the only one — to contemporary society is that it institutionalizes, as it were, the segregation of practice from creed. The fundamental and simple *honesty* of Dewey cannot bear such segregation. Action becomes routine in such a situation and hence cannot fulfill the moral science that we have seen Dewey conceives it to have. Class-isolated knowing from doing sunders theory from practice.

More to the point is the following:

> "Our materialism, our devotion to money making and to having a good time, are not things by themselves. They are the product of the fact that we live in a money culture; of the fact that our technique and technology are controlled by interest in private profit. There lies the serious and fundamental defect of our civilization, the source of the secondary and induced evils to which so much attention is given . . . old European tradition with its disregard for the body, material things, and practical concerns. The development of the American type, in the sense of the critics, is an expression of the fact that we have retained this tradition and the economic system of private gain on which it is based, while at the same time we have made an independ-

ent development of industry and technology that is nothing short of revolution."[49]

What is relevant about this passage is the tacit notion that the "private interests" are due to a philosophy of anti-practice. Also, notice that "money," a negative category, as in the rurally oriented Veblen, is linked with this private profit negation. Money is the root of evil. The implication is almost that "money" might be all right if it were used to expand production.

(b) Perhaps the majority of the negative imputations which Dewey has advanced have rested socially upon a negative concern with a leisure class, which has fostered knowing as contemplation and has divorced it from action and use.

> "The social division into a laboring class and a leisure class, between industry and esthetic contemplation, became a metaphysical division into things which are mere means and things which are ends. Means are menial, subservient, slavish; and ends liberal and final; things as means testify to inherent defect, to dependence, while ends testify to independent and intrinsically self-sufficing being."[50]

The dualistic heritage which Dewey finds central in philosophy prior to pragmatism centers for him in the dualism of thought and activity, theory and practice; he seats this dualism in the social dualism of the Greeks, and the medieval world. The leisured contemplative class is segregated by slavery from the artisan.

It is not necessary to further document the point: the objection to leisure, to a pecuniary culture, to sheer contemplation — and to the intellectual blessings which have, according to Dewey, been given them — all these negations are met positively by the category of action. This category — and its surrogates such as the ethicized notion of "work" — definitely performs a moral mission in the career of Dewey's thinking. It is not too much to hold that such an orientation is intrinsic to Puritanical New England. We are not yet through with this concept of action.

Whether or not a *sophisticated Puritanism* and its orientations and problems or the *frontier* and its social import has the greater weight in Dewey's model of action is, in a sense, a microscopic reproduction of a central problem of American history. Grossly, it is, again, the Turner thesis versus John Fiske's derivation of U.S.A. from New England. We need not decide absolutely, disjunctively. Both are operative: the frontier slant is manifest in the *biological* model of action, in the conception of "adaptation," and in the individual versus the environmental model. The Puritanical ethics, which stamps the early essays in which "practice" bridged poetry and science, was not only available during Dewey's youth but, as we have indicated, was facilitated by later persons and doctrinal contact; and this strain persists in highly technical growth down through the very last monograph on *valuation*. Let us now examine the biological model of action.

The impact of the Darwinized biological sciences upon American intellectual communities carried an iconoclastic import for traditional formulations of mind, for the character and setting of reflection. Perhaps no thinker has been more influenced by the biological intention and categories than has John Dewey. Within this biological perspective he has attempted to "naturalize" mind and to delineate thinking as a "biologic function." He has attempted to do so by viewing man as a behaving, biologic unit, and by stating the mental as an episode of such behavior.

It is in large part in biological terms that the empirical drive toward the location and specificity of "reflection" is worked out in the logical theory of Dewey. The positive features of his development are in continuity with a biologized statement of reflection. The formal restatement of focal epistemological problems proceeds in the ambit of the Darwinian paradigms. This is particularly the case in so far as the solution of these problems entails "action." Because, "from the Darwinian standpoint, the nature of thought must be explained by ascertaining the part which it plays in the life of the organism. Thought [is] a moment, or factor in [organic] development."[51]

The conception of thought as a capacity peculiar to the mind of man lifted logic from earth and from the merely animal. It was within the compass of the evolutionary hypotheses that Dewey has situated thought. Finding for it a "naturalistic" locus, he conceptualized it as a function within the adjustive behaviors of men construed as biological organisms. Against deeply set and stubborn philosophical tradition he placed thought within biologic behavior, and attempted to state the consequences of such a location for epistemology and for logical theory. Herein lies the philosophical iconoclasm of John Dewey.

It is essential to remember that "instrumentalism" is predominantly a biologistic doctrine. Applied to "logic," instrumentalism views thought as emerging, as "a mode of organic adjustment to environment," and conceives "its whole development as determined with reference to this function."[52] To every aspect of the reflective process, Dewey in the first three decades of this century applied such a method: organism-in-relation-to-environment became the keystone of his theory of knowledge, as psychology is linked with logical theory through the interpretation of the thought process as a mode of "adjustment."[53]

> ". . . the interaction of organism and environment, resulting in some adaptation which secures utilization of the latter, is the primary fact, the basic category. Knowledge is relegated to a derived position, secondary in origin (and) involved in the process by which life is sustained and evolved."[54]

Experience itself has a behavioral dimension, and everything "mental" was defined with reference to this dimension: for instance, sensations are treated as cues, "points of readjustment," involved in the on-going activity of the organism. In like manner, "reason" receives its behavioral redefinition: it is the reorganizing center from which emerge new plans of adaptive action.[55] The situation wherein thought has its origin, the problematic, is similarly construed behaviorally:

> ". . . in line with what has already been said about experience being a matter primarily of behavior, a sensory-motor matter, is the fact that thinking takes its departure from specific conflicts in experience that occasion perplexity and trouble."[56]

And again, more generally: ". . . as the philosoper has received his problem from the world of action, so he must return his account there for auditing and liquidation."[57]

".... the great exception to what was said about no fundamental vital influence issuing from books; it concerns the influence of William James. As far as I can discover, one specifiable
philosophic factor which entered into my thinking so as to give
it a new direction and quality, it is this one. To say that it proceeded from his *Psychology* rather than from the essays collected in the volume called *Will to Believe*, his *Pluralistic Universe*, or *Pragmatism*, is to say something that needs explanation."[58]

The explanation is that what was taken from James was the biologized psychology, not the pragmatism.[59]

Now we have already noted the biological emphasis of Dewey
as one of the two chief determinants for his statement of inquiry
and we mentioned briefly the centrality of the category of action
in this statement. It is the biological statement of the act which
now claims our attention. This is not the only point of view from
which the structure of the act is seen by Dewey, but it is one of
the two most important angles. It is in biological terms that the
conception of environment and its "control" through action arising
out of inquiry becomes central. It is in terms of the act biologically
conceived that the concept of "adjustment" arises. Whether or not
the origin and early function of the term "action" is for Dewey a
Puritanical reconciliation of value and science, one of the dominant forms which "action" assumes is "adjustment."

The Deweyan form given to the basic conception "behavior"
when it is used in connection with descriptions of thought in general is the form which behavior assumes in the overt manipulation
of physical objects. There is the organism. There is the environment. And behavior is the interaction set up between the two.
From impulsive beginning to consummation, the activity is kept
within the "adaptive" form and the delineation of the act proceeds
within the biological framework set by the environment and the
organism.

It is within such a framework and conception of action that "intelligence" is situated, and from its functioning within this structure, intelligence derives many of its characteristics. The manual
modes of the technician and the farmer along with the far reaches
of the mathematician's abstract reflection must somehow find their
place within and gain their cognitive character from this be-

havioral scheme of biology. We would, therefore, expect the schematum to be generalized, and so it is; but now we must examine it as a biological statement.

The leading presuppositions of the biological theory of action utilized by Dewey as basic in his account of reflection are, of course, directly derived from the general theory of organic evolution:

> "Since the human species has evolved from lower animals, all human actions, even those on the highest cultural level, have gradually developed from the original processes of biological adaptation of animal organisms to their natural environment . . . the conclusion is drawn that all human actions remain essentially similar in form and function to those organic processes in which they originated, only differing from them in such secondary, though important, characters as complexity, indirectness, range of adaptability in space and time mostly due to the development of speech."[60]

The theory of biologic origin and character of action is assumed to be basic to all theories of action. The form and generic character of what DeLaguna terms "primary behavior" are assumed to be applicable to the "secondary variations" (including "reflective activity") which have developed from it.

It is evident that the categorical principle underlying such extension is that of *continuity.* "The pattern of life-behavior," says Dewey, "definitely foreshadows the general pattern of inquiry." There is continuity of development in the "respective patterns of logical and biological forms and procedures."[61] Of such statements a certain equivocation of context and presupposition should be noted. Do such persistent statements mean: (a) that the continuity is in the life history of an individual thinker or of any given inquiry of the twentieth century so that if it were in empirical detail traced out, it would be seen to incorporate biological factors? Or does the principle as here applied mean (b) that the biological-logical continuity is to be taken historically, *i.e.,* as of a continuum in the history of culture so that among proto - and early man the form of inquiry and the items necessary to its functioning may be said to differ from those of a twentieth century urban-dominated culture in respect to extent of incorporation of consideration properly described as biological? No unambiguous stand as regards these alternatives is to be found in the extant writings of Dewey.

One reason for this ambivalence may be due to the view of society tacitly underlying the "continuity" of Dewey. Thus: mind in primitive communities is to be seen as oriented in a "biological" manner. This is seen in the "biologic" character of the statistically dominant occupations of such cultures; *e.g.*, hunting. In such an occupation "thought" is caught up in action that is directed toward the end of "hunger consummation." And it terminates in animal contact with food-objects. But even in the most primitive of such situations a biological terminology is dangerous. It is the cultural pattern that selects for perception and chases the particular objects that are food and sets the features of the hunting act.

In the more recent *Logic* it is not very clear just how much of biologism and frame of action Dewey would carry over into the sphere of inquiry and its conditions among men. But on the "b" application of continuity, the adjustment schematum remains in twentieth century cultures "the ground pattern." In his note on the Australian mind: "We have not so much destroyed or left behind the hunting structural arrangement of mind as we have set free its constitutive psycho-physical factors."[62] In like manner, but apparently within the more formal, "a", application of continuity he says that "certain general conclusions" may legitimately be drawn "as to the nature of the pattern of inquiry as a development out of certain aspects of the pattern of life-activity," particularly the "organic-environmenal integration and interaction." And there are frequent statements to the effect that inquiry can legitimately be treated "as a special mode of organic behavior."[63]

One reason underlying Dewey's incorporation of a biological view of action (and hence of inquiry) is to locate reflection naturalistically. Such a biological stress on action enables him to anchor reflection. This, however, does not take us beyond the epistemological polarization of reflection versus constitutive thought which lies upon the surface of Dewey's work, especially its earlier phases. It is the outcome of the biological statement that we must examine more carefully. Again, grossly, this outcome is the category of adjustment as adaptation. In the uses to which this concept is put, in the role which it fulfills in Dewey's perspective, in the political and ethical outcome of its use, we find the life of the term in his thought and perhaps reasons for its being there.

"Adaptation" is a focal term to the Darwinian hypothesis from which the psychology of Dewey took its rise. In Darwin, biological adaptation is simply conceived as the precondition of survival. But survival is, socially, a vague and empty concept. It means no more than continued existence, and the meaning of existence changes enormously with the subject on which it is predicated. Within the limits of biological existence and survival lies all that is diversely and extensively interhuman. To speak of survival in the biologist's sense as the end (terminal juncture) of mental life is monstrously to dwarf the realities of cultural choice. The neglect of such differentia causes a distressing if convenient ambiguity in the usage of such terms as "need" and "adjustment."

The biologic-adjustment model of action utilized by Dewey in his statement of reflection is *ambiguous* and *formal*. It is socially open and indecisive. These features fit into the larger features of Dewey's perspective in their intellectuality, but here we are not concerned with "adaptation" from this larger view.

"Adaptations" can easily be stretched to "getting along," getting what is desired. In some contexts this adaptive process has little to do with overt behavior, *e.g.*, among the natives of John Steinbeck's *Tortilla Flat* "intelligence" has norms and outcomes sharply differentiated from, *e.g.*, a segment of New England culture. I indicate this locale because in *Tortilla Flat* the cultural definition of the role of thought is extremely different from the rigorous and the action-oriented and sanctioned. Among the *paisanos* "logical activity" does not arise to implement action, but rather to prevent the necessity of it. A "problem" is a task to be performed, a duty to fulfill; a "solution" is the articulation of that *verbal* form which will permit one to avoid the task, refrain from duty's excessive demands, and yet will allow one to retain his dignity, kindliness toward all, and self-respect in the eyes of the community. If men are not clever enough to think their way out of a situation, *then* overt action is taken. By cultural definition, thought occurs in order to remove the necessity of action, and the group respects and motivates those men who with retention of honor are capable of withholding from action for the longest time. This, too, is "adjustment."

The simple fact of the matter is that the statement on every other page of Dewey to the effect that men adjust by means of reflection is never tentatively handled in a genuinely empirical manner. What empirical support is adduced is squeezed into the biological framework. The biological model of action, "adaptation," by its formality enables one to avoid value-decisions. The biological terms in which it is advanced aids the tacit assumption of cultural sanctions for activity of a certain kind.

By treating as real or at least central only that action which manipulates physical objects we are drawn to the view that the function of all action is mutual adaptation between organisms and environment. By putting the matter in biological terms, it is formalized, which is to say that the content of the end of action (and of reflection) is left open. Adaptation is the term in Dewey which stands at this level. By its usage, value-decisions as value-decisions are assimilated into the biological and hidden by formality.

> "The biological point of view commits us to the conviction that mind, whatever else it may be, is at least an organ of service for the control of environment in relation to the ends of the life process."[64]

Another intellectual usage which the biological framework of action permits and sanctions is the conceptual strain centering around "control of the environment." Behaviorism, as worked out by Dewey's pupil, John Watson (who became an advertising expert) has this theme as a central feature.

> "Behaviorism's primary contention is that . . . if organized society decreed that the individual or group should act in a definite, specific way, the behaviorist could arrange the situation or stimulus which would bring about such action (control)."[65]

In whatever respects Dewey's biological psychology differs from Watson's, there is no doubt that in this matter of "control" he agrees completely. There are many uses to which the possibilities of such a view are put by Dewey [66] but one of the sources for it might well be the fact of the waves of immigrants into the United States in the last half of the nineteenth century and early decades of the twentieth. Dewey saw this in working contact with agencies which were dominantly concerned with these immigrants as a social problem. At Hull House they were in the center of vision. Their existence, as I have indicated, was not taken as a class problem but rather they were posed by such institutions from the standpoint of a manipulative "nationalism." Within this perspective, the aim was to assimilate them to the existent society. The manner in which such a view falls in with the biological perspective and adaptation is clear. On the one hand is an individual; on the other a society. The problem is to set up a working relation between them, to adapt them to the societal environment. When we take this immigrant factor in conjunction with the educational focus of Dewey, we have a rather adequate social basis for the understanding of control-of-the-environment-through-adaptation formula of action and thought. These do not, however, exhaust the sociological possibilities.

From a larger angle the organism and environment schema may be a reflex of the general frontier situation, that is to say, of a society whose dominant occupational patterns involved men in a manipulative, controlling relation with nature. This, however, although plausible, does not seem to be as crucial as certain pragmatists would have us believe, for it is rather difficult to establish the mode of connection operation. On the other hand, the immigrant situation was participated in by Dewey at first hand. It may not be too much to suspect that the immigrants, by social selection and by experience in America in confrontation with the new experiences of the eager, rude, sudden growth of industrialized cities, might have possessed animi of a more "controlling" nature than contemplative, but this is doubtful.

Again, the occupations to which Dewey is oriented, by participation, contact, and public, tend at least slightly, to be concerned with the man-thing relations which are readily seen within an adaptation schema: farmers, skilled trades, scientists, professions — features of their experiences might be generalized into a biological model of control of the environment and of adaptation than would the life experiences of lawyers, financiers, businessmen, and typists. Certainly the primary farming community which I suspect to be the dominant social vehicle of value for Dewey would fall into such a schema more readily than would a metropolitan area.

There are several purposes which the biological model of action and the consequent statement of reflection serve. In each case this model fits into other aspects of Dewey's generic perspective; we shall, therefore, encounter these items again in other connections. They are very important.

(1) The biological model of action and reflection serves to minimize the cleavage and power divisions *within society*, or put differently, it serves as a pervasive mode of posing the problem which locates all problems between *man and nature*, instead of between *men and men*.

(2) It, therefore, aids the general attempt at intellectuality, *i.e.*, the attempt to assimilate all value, power, or human problems to a statement of the function of intelligence. The answer to all problems becomes man's use of intelligence to work "his" way out of the difficulties "he" faces. The biological, environment-organism adjustment schematum underlies the cogency of this type of "problematization" and its answer. It jibes with the drive for more education as a solution to social problems: all that is needed is the diffusion of "intelligence."

(3) Through the concept of adaptation, the biological model strengthens the drive toward specificity of problems. And this specificity implements — to put it crudely and briefly here — a *politics of reform of situation*. Adaptation is one step at a time; it faces one situation at a time.

> "Thinking is adaptation *to* an end *through* the adjustment of particular objective contents. The thinker, like the carpenter, is at once stimulated and checked in every stage of his procedure by the particular situation which confronts him."
>
> "The entire significance of the evolutionary method . . . is that every distinct organ, structure, or formation, every grouping of cells or elements, has to be treated as an instrument of adjustment or adaptation to a particular environing situation. Its meaning, its character, its value, is known when, and only when, it is considered as an arrangement for meeting the conditions involved in some specific situation."[67]

It must not, however, be thought that adjustment means "conformity." Indeed, the advantage of the concept politically considered lies precisely in its formality and non-specificity.

> "But as life requires the fitness of the environment to the organic functions, adjustment to the environment means not pas-

sive acceptance of the latter, but acting so that the environing changes take a certain turn. The 'higher' the type of life, the more adjustment takes the form of an adjustment of the factors of the environment to one another in the interest of life . . ."[68]

There are several ways in which various philosophers have approached and assimilated "science." A philosopher may allow his problems to be set by the propositional residues of certain sciences as he conceives these to contradict "common sense" or "naive realism."[69] Certain logical positivists conceive the philosopher's concern with science to be a logical analysis of the meanings carried by scientifically enunciated sentences. Similarly, but more broadly, C. W. Morris' "scientific empiricism" states the philosophic task as concerned with the semiotic process as it proceeds in the scientific continuum. Logic and epistemology become theories of signs implementing the unification of diverse sciences.[70] Philosophers have not been limited in the manner in which they take account of "science."

What approach and use of science are characteristic of pragmatists? I have suggested that Peirce took up science as *technique* and generalized it into a logical method of definition; it was also pointed out that perhaps the legal context of discussion of the Metaphysical Club might have been a feature in this slant. Now Dewey is not *too* far from Peirce in the *general* manner in which he utilizes "science."

John Dewey approaches science in its methodological dimension. He contends of this method that its *experimental* content is its basis and its signal characteristic. In contraposition to many "scientific philosophies," it is the methodological, the procedural dimension of science upon which pragmatism has seized, and it is this aspect that is treated by Dewey as the exemplary feature of the pattern of "successful" inquiry. In terms of this pattern, avowedly arrived at by, and generalized from, a behavioral analysis of *de facto* scientific procedure, the feature of reflection and inquiry are delineated. In Dewey's account a certain kind of physically controlled laboratorial action is stated as the controlling seat of all intellectual authority. The most pervasive and important conceptual outcome of the influence of science upon John Dewey's thought is the installation of experimental action at the heart of knowing. It is important not only in itself but because it offers a statement of "science"

which has high generalization potential in a specific direction. It
makes possible a use of "science" that would perhaps not otherwise be available.

> "Our main attempt will be to show how the actual proce-
> dures of knowledge, interpreted after the pattern formed by
> experimental inquiry, cancel the isolation of knowledge from
> overt action . . . knowing as judged from the actual procedures
> of scientific inquiry has completely abandoned in fact the tra-
> ditional separation of knowing and doing."[71]

One point which should be emphasized is that Dewey's statement and location of *scientific method* tends to be controlled by
biological considerations. The experimental dimension of science,
its close and intrinsic connection with theory, is there to be noted.
But in Dewey's statement the *action* content of scientific procedure is seized upon and made focal in a generalized statement
presumably covering "reflection," and the *action* and reflection are
again placed within "the adjustment of man," the control of environment.

We have seen how the concept of behavior also emerged out of
Dewey's examination of the psychological implications of Darwinian biology. In Dewey's writings the two sources, "science" and
"biology," are given about equal weight. It is a moot question as
to which of the two furnished his major channel, implemented his
wide usage of the category of behavior. It is true, however, that
his very statement of science and particularly the wide contextual
generalization that he gives "science" proceed largely in quasi-bio-
logical language. For example, and quite typically, in speaking to
the American Psychological Association in 1899 he said:

> ". . . Science, both physical and psychological makes known
> the conditions upon which certain results depend, and there-
> fore puts at the disposal of life a certain method of controlling
> them."[72]

Again, in the following quotation, may be seen the manner in which
scientific method is approached and stated in biological terms. It
is also indicative of the way in which the category of behavior
as focal to inquiry and as arising from both the analysis of scientific method and the Darwinian influence are blended, converge into the generalized category:

"Action is the means by which a problematic situation is resolved. Such is the net outcome of the method of science . . . 'Action' is the name given to one mode of interaction, namely, that named from the standpoint of an organism. When interaction has for its consequence the settling of future conditions under which a life-process goes on, it is an 'act.' If it be admitted that knowing is something which occurs within nature, then it follows as a truism that knowing is an existential overt act. Only if the one who engages in knowing be outside of nature and behold it from some external locus can it be denied that knowing is an act which modifies what previously existed, and that its worth consists in the consequences of the modification . . . now we have the model of experimental procedure before us and are aware of the role of *organic acts* in all mental processes."[73]

From the modes and forms of manual experiment in scientific procedure and of overt organic action and adaptive qualities in the biological realm of Darwin, pragmatism derives, crystallizes the generalized category of "behavior" or "action." In terms of this pervasive and key category, instrumentalism formulates all things "mental," "intellectual," the noetic.

But the discussions of Dewey proceed in two interweaving directions. There is the generalized descriptive account of "reflection," and there is the more specific account of scientific method. In the first, the concept action tends to take the form of "adjustive behavior." And in science, *experimental* action is quite usually and quite equivocally termed "practice." It is at once a "test" and an "application" of reflection.

The central feature of Dewey's descriptive account of the scientific method (or "inquiry *qua* inquiry") is the experimental activity involved therein. Since the formal paradigm of inquiry was in some sense "derived" from the description of "science," this formulation of the common pattern of valid inquiry contains at its epistemological center, "experiment." Experiment assumes the seat of intellectual authority. Let us examine this experimental action as a differential mode of behavior. It is convenient to do so in connection with the theory of meaning.

The category, experiment, as exemplified in physical science, and from the standpoint of the scientist, is basically an overt motor manipulation of physical objects. It consists in the arranging of objects so as to organize the inter-object activities and their laboratory termination as a notation on the consequences to which these inter-object activities give issue.[74] Experiment is the setting up of variant organizations of inter-thing activities so as to discover their variant consequences. The laboratory man "controls" his instrument. He does not control directly the consequences of the inter-thing activities he organizes. These are what they are; and they constitute the defining "natures" of the interacting materials.

It is these natures so arrived at which the laboratorian seeks to determine. Dewey terms them "objective meanings."[75] In an experiment, physical interaction objects are compelled to present themselves, to yield up for notation defining qualities hitherto obscured and concealed in the objects as isolated. It is these that are discovered in experimentation. And it is in terms of this type of meaning that ideas are "applied," "tested." They are "tested" as glasses are tested, *i.e.*, in the laboratory; things are looked at through the medium of specific meanings to see if hereby they assume a more orderly and cleared aspect, if they are less blurred and obscure.[76]

The distinction which Dewey draws between such "objective" or technologically determined meanings and what might be called "social meanings" is important enough to be given explicit attention. It is important because it enables us to differentiate and characterize the structure of experimental action as one among diverse forms of action.

In Dewey's theory, meaning, has its *origin* within a social-behavioral process, and meaning itself is conceived primarily as a property of human behavior. It is "a natural consequence of the peculiar form which interaction sometimes assumes in the case of human beings."[77] Such social meaning constitutes Dewey's primitive and humanistic explanatory base for all meaning. But the pattern of such meaning is "extended to all sorts of acts and things so that they become signs of other things."[78] If meaning is primarily a property of human behavior, it is "secondarily a property of objects ... The representative capacity of meanings are attributed to things in their connection with one another; not to marks (or utterances) whose meaning depends upon agreement in social use." Signs are then external to man, so to speak, and inherent in the texture of interactive continua. Signs point to the "existence" of other things;

whereas social symbols are quite often "non-existential" in reference.[79]

This account of the category of experimental action represents a hypothesis about a feature of physical science inquiry. Possibly it will be reshaped by further studies in the behavioristics of science. But as it stands, it is a *vera causa* hypothesis, *i.e.*, there is a domain of data to which it may very well be empirically applied in test. The difficulty begins when one attempts to generalize *this* category of *action*. And it begins immediately. The *generalization of experiment* is, as we have already indicated, implemented by biologistic considerations and terminology. For this formal category of experiment slips imperceptibly over into the "adjustment" and "practice" of "man" against an "environment." By stating experiment in biological terms its relevance to "life," to "practice" is brought about and "life" becomes an experiment; if it is not, knowledge is not possible.[80]

There is in Dewey the concern to understand and delineate the experimental procedures of laboratory science, the character of the category of action as exemplified in scientific inquiry. And there is the radiation of such an account into an epistemological exemplar of inquiry *qua* inquiry which is then taken out of laboratory contexts and into political uses. Even on descriptive levels in Dewey, there is ever present the drive programmatically to derive from physical science and then apply to other domains a paradigm of inquiry. Such an epistemological program carries with its fulfillment the application of the experimental mode of action to society.[81] Just as experimental action within science is seized upon descriptively as focal, so in "the common pattern of inquiry" it is given central and authoritative status.

In our discussion of "science" in Dewey we have been concerned with the way in which science was assimilated into the general pattern of "inquiry." We have seen that, like behavioristic psychology, one of its major contributions was a strengthening and shaping of the concept of action within the Deweyan model of reflection.

1. *Contemporary American Philosophy,* (New York 1930), Vol. II, p. 16.

2. Dewey, *Studies in Logical Theory* (Chicago 1903) p. x.

3. *Columbia Studies in History of Ideas,* (New York 1935) Vol. 3, p. 23. "An Empirical Survey of Empiricisms." Cf. also G. H. Mead, *Movements of Thought in the Nineteenth Century,* p. 351. ". . . the sources of the pragmatic doctrine are . . . behavioristic psychology . . . and the scientific technique."

4. Cf. G. DeLaguna, *Dogmatism and Evolution,* p. 19.

5. *Ibid.,* p. 120.

6. G. H. Mead, *op. cit.,* p. 139.

7. Windelband, *A History of Philosophy,* pp. 611, 612. In Hegel's own words, the center of the question as to the "location of thought" is clearly indicated: "Method is noways different from its object and content." *Science of Logic,* (English trans., Vol. I, p. 65). Quoted by Sidney Hook, *From Hegel to Marx.*

8. Quoted from Hegel by Hook, *op. cit.,* p. 72.

9. *The Philosophy of John Dewey,* "Biography of John Dewey" edited by Jane M. Dewey, p. 18.

10. Cf. Dewey, *Studies in Logical Theory,* p. 8, for this definition of metaphysical.

11. Dewey, *Studies in Logical Theory,* p. 1.

12. *Essays for James,* (1908) pp. 62-63.

13. *Ibid.,* p. 1

14. *Ibid.,* p. 2.

15. *Ibid.,* pp. 2-3.

16. *Ibid.,* p. 3.

17. Cf. *Creative Intelligence,* p. 55.

18. *Logic: The Theory of Inquiry,* p. 8. In 1936 Dewey "accepted" and elaborated in his own view the Peircian conception on "inquiry."

19. Cf. *Essays in Experimental Logic,* ch. 1-4.

20. *Ibid.,* p. 93.

21. *Ibid.,* p. 23.

22. *Ibid.,* p. 122.

23. *Creative Intelligence,* p. 34.

24. *The Essays in Experimental Logic,* p. 1.

25. *Ibid.,* p. 2.

26. *Ibid.,* pp. 5-7.

27. *Studies in Logical Theory,* pp. 26-27.

28. "Poetry and Philosophy," *Andover Review* (August, 1891), reprinted in *Characters and Events,* Vol. I, p. 3-17.

29. *Ibid.,* p. 17.

30. *Ibid.,* p. 5.

31. *Ibid.,* pp. 4-5.

32. *Ibid.,* p. 5.

33. *Ibid.,* p. 5

34. *International Journal of Ethics,* Vol. I, No. 2 (January, 1891), pp 186-203.

35. *Ibid.*, p. 187.

36. *Ibid.*, p. 188.

37. *Ibid.*, p. 191f. Cf. also D.T. Thomas' *John Dewey's Logical Theoory* for factual report of essay.

38. *International Journal of Ethics, op. cit.*, p. 190.

39. *Ibid.*, p. 197.

40. *Ibid.*, pp. 198 and 201.

41. *See* below.

42. *Ibid.*, p. 202.

43. *Ibid.*, p. 203. Later Dewey calls value-judgment "judgments of practice," we shall return to his ethics later.

44. *How We Think*, pp. 162-63.

45. *Ibid.*, p. 164.

46. *Ibid.*, p. 167.

47. *Individualism, Old and New*, pp. 9-18. The second point will be discussed below in dealing with "sociality." Thus, this passage is not to be taken as comprehensive of Dewey's negative orientation to phases of contemporary society.

48. *The Metaphysics of Pragmatism*, (New York 1925).

49. *Individualism, Old and New*, p. 30.

50. *Experience and Nature*, p. 124.

51. DeLaguna, *Dogmatism and Evolution*, p. 120.

52. DeLaguna, *Philosophic Review*, Vol. XVIII, No. 4 (July, 1909).

53. Cf. D. T. Thomas, *The Logical Theory of John Dewey*, p. 47.

54. John Dewey, *Reconstruction in Philosophy*, p. 87.

55. Cf. *Reconstruction in Philosophy*, Chapter IV.

56. *Ibid.*, p. 138.

57. *Influence of Darwin*, p. 274. Cf. also p. 44. It should be noted that Dewey carries the concept of act into historical reconstructions. In a pioneering essay, "The Significance of the Problem of Knowledge," he situates what is perhaps the largest dichotomy in philosophy, rationalism and empiricism, within the act: "both factors (reason and sensation) are necessary in action. One stands for stimulus, for initiative; the other for control, for direction," p. 274. Again, the mediatory function of the category of "action" is seen.

58. *From Absolutism to Experimentalism*, p. 23.

59. I have already shown that this biologized standpoint was *not* the center of James' thought, at least not of his "pragmatic" thinking.

60. Znaniecki, *Social Actions*, p. 7.

61. *Logic*, p. 34 and p. 41.

62. *Philosophy and Civilization*, p. 187. Cf. also pp. 45, 229, 87, 187.

63. *Logic*, pp. 33, 35.

64. J. Watson, *Psychology from the Standpoint of a Behaviorist*, Philadelphia and London, 1919, p. ix. [Quoting Dewey]

65. Especially in liberal social psychology. *See* Section 61.

66. "Interpretations of the Savage Mind," *Psychological Review* (May, 1902), p. 219.

67. Dewey, *Studies in Logical Theory*, pp. 81 and 65.

68. "The Need for a Recovery of Philosophy," John Dewey, *Creative Intelligence*, (N.Y. 1917), p. 10.

69. Cf. Dewey's account of Russell, *The Essays in Experimental Logic,* "The World as a Problem."

70. *See* "Foundations of the Theory of Signs," *Encyclopedia of Unified Science.* Vols. 1 and 2.

71. Dewey, *Quest For Certainty, See* pp. 36-48.

72. *Psychological Review*, Vol. VII, p. 105.

73. *The Quest for Certainty*, pp. 244-45.

74. *See* Ratner's introduction to *The Philosophy of John Dewey* (Modern Library edition, 1939) for an able secondary account of Deweyan experimentation, p. 138f.

75. *Experience and Nature,* Ch. IV. in the discussion, Peirce called them "technological."

76. *Essays in Experimental Logic,* pp. 183-216.

77. *Experience and Nature,* p. 179.

78. *Journal of Philosophy,* Vol. XXIII, p. 547.

79. *Logic,* p. 51.

80. Later we shall see the way in which an *epistemological* necessity for "action" of a certain character is transferred into the *political* sphere.

81. Dewey speaks of pragmatism in terms of the ". . . .attempt to generalize the experimental side of natural science into a logical method which is applicable to the interpretation and treatment of social phenomena." *Encyclopedia of the Social Sciences,* Vol. 9, p. 602.

21

Modulations of Action

Two related models of action may be sifted from Dewey's writings; that of *experimentation* and the *biologistic adaptive* model. These two models of action correspond to the two avowed sources of instrumentalism: natural science and behavioristic psychology. In the contexts of Dewey's thought, the two models of action are related, for the former is often stated or "interpreted" in terms of the latter, and in "the common pattern of inquiry" they are formally as one. The biological and the scientific models of action (and the statements of reflection in their terms) have in common a man-and-environment framework. This "environment" is set forth, where possible, in bio-physical terms. We may however, look at the matter of action in terms of the kinds of action socially available for use in philosophizing.

There are many types of existent action (and of thought). From them Dewey selectively focuses upon a definite few. The type of "action" his work assumes fits into a certain type of social order, and, on the other hand, does not correspond to other social sectors and types. The general type of action and thought which Dewey most pervasively utilizes and which forms his positive model in large part may be termed *technological*. This type does not:

> "have to think beyond the task immediately at hand . . . [It has] to be able to foresee the most probable consequences of an event . . . At this level man had to imagine a definite goal and then think out in advance how to distribute his activities in a given way over a certain period of time with this goal in view."[1]

Mannheim situates such modes of action and reflection in a society that is "only partially regulated." There is a socially uncontrolled selection proceeding behind the backs of individuals, and there are also administratively controlled institutions.

It may be said that liberal democracies in their organization have existed with such thought prevailing. In such a society there are bound to be unforeseen consequences involved in any reflection and action for the total organization is not under the control of enacted institutions. Yet such a mode of reflection is most likely to work out satisfactorily only in three or four kinds of situations:

(1) In man-object situations: technician-tool, scientist-laboratory, farmer-plough.

(2) In these inter-person situations one man has "authority" over other individuals due to his acknowledged technical superiority We refer particularly to a professional-client type of relation; it includes teacher-pupil; social worker-client.

(3) In "everyday situations" in which the more complex institutional arrangements are not too much in the foreground.

Now if we comb Dewey's books for the situations which (1) he adduces as examples, and (2) which are obviously implied or assumed by his references, we find a given limited number. They persist in the several contexts:

The social *action* to which Dewey overtly refers and tacitly assumes typically consists of:

(1) School teachers and administrators: school committees in Michigan, *e.g.*, or people organizing a new type of school.

(2) Scientists in laboratories and in industries.

(3) Men in occupations in which they contact "nature" and handle tools, *e.g.*, farmers or hunters.

(4) Individuals in "daily" "situations" as a man at a fork in the road, or lost in the woods.

(5) Professionals, but not so much those who handle paper, *e.g.*, lawyers, as those who handle things, perhaps technically skilled groups, *e.g.*, doctors.

Dewey's concept of "action" as "behavior" is not political action. Reality to him is seen *technologically* or *socially*, in his peculiar, complex and freighted meaning of social, which is not peculiar and complex when viewed against a small town of artisans or a farming community.

His concept of action is *of an individual*. It is not the action of a petty official nor of an administrator who is acting within "routine affairs of state."[2] It is the conduct of an individual in non-rationalized spheres or types of society. It is conduct that makes decisions about situations that have not been regulated. Perhaps the best correspondent is the action of a member of a free profession. It is conduct on the edge of social structures, such as frontier types of society that are edging out into places not hampered by social organization. It is predominantly outside the rationalized structures in which the action of individuals faces decisions, and almost by definition, decisions involving new factors that have come into the actor's horizon and path. It is here, too, that the relations of theory and practice arise as a problem, and sometimes as an issue. Perhaps the most important of such spheres of action today is political. It is most important in the sense that increasingly more and more depends upon it. Within the non-rationalized sphere, the political as here used is distinguished by its heavy concern with power and its accessibility to physical force and domination. But to these spheres, the unregulated *political* and the thoroughly *rationalized,* Dewey's concept of "action" and his model of thought do not at all correspond. Ultimately his conceptions are anchored in a social situation whose integration can occur by means of liberal individuals heavily endowed with substantive rationality.

Could the political character of Dewey's concept of action be imputed to the fact that none of the groups to which he is oriented have aspirations to rule?

Dewey's category of action is a very cautious one. To realize pragmatism's model of action, a segment of behavior has to unfold slowly, take up one thing at a time, be in continuity with the past. Adjustment is the term. It is not brute action because that would be blind, unintelligent. It is not violence, for that is "wasteful."[3] It is not repetition of "tradition," for that would be sluggish and lazy. It is not abruptly discontinuous with what has been and is, for that would be utopian, unrealistic, or, again, by divorce of ends and means, it would be "unintelligent" action. It has to go slowly in order to squeeze the meaning and values from events it encounters. It is careful. It is intelligent action.

It can be *experimental*, which in the political sphere may well mean expediency, because it trusts the grand direction of underlying patterns of change. One can trust expediency to turn out the good, when the underlying trends are moving toward the good. Thus, its optimism anchors experimentalism and also makes it possible to include values in it.

The character which Dewey gives *action* may be, in part, explained by tacit awareness, or a desire to avoid the consequences foretold in the truism that when thought gets hitched to political action, it tends strongly to become rigid, to ignore factual matters which would embarrass it by its changes. Such a situation also goes into the explanation of why Dewey has been rather liberally mugwumpish in politics, and why "action" is *not* linked with a sizable organization, a movement, a party with a chance at power. The concept of action in Dewey obviously does not cover the kinds of action occurring within and between struggling, organized political parties. Parties, as Max Weber put it, live in a house of power. They are organizations for social fighting. Their "theory," *e.g.*, platform, has to be dogmatized, not only to insure, in a time of quick mass communication, uniformity among party workers, but because they are organizations. Some party workers become functionaries, hence it is not permitted that they think through independently problems in a "free" and "intelligent" manner. In organized social action "reflection" is rather quickly frozen into "lines." It does not like political doctrines and credos, for that is "absolutism." Politically, pragmatism is less expediency than it is a kind of perennial mugwump confronted with rationalized social structures.

Dewey takes a manipulative active standpoint. In the sphere of *technology* or within a biological framework there are no difficulties for this position. When such a category is generalized, however, into the fields of political movements, it faces power problems, makes overt judgments, acts against some people, organizes itself socially and takes on a "line" — or, it ignores power issues, doesn't see them, defines issues around them, but never directly in their middle. This latter is the Deweyan slant. It is accomplished (a) by continual selection of concrete examples which are in a power context or even clearly inter-human, (b) by becoming very formal, highly abstract in its unitary model of thought, "adjustment," "control of environment," (c) by refusing to formulate concrete socio-political ends, (d) by an infinitely pluralistic view of society, (e) by methodizing *all* such problems: *i.e.*, rendering them, formally, soluble by "intelligence."

Dewey's pluralistic view of society and of "publics" goes to explain his *monistic* (hence highly abstracted) view of intelligence. The pluralism gives cogency to the view in a society with a high division of labor. The monistic paradigm of intelligence, by which all problems are to be solved, offers a "common ground," a point of mediation. The components of "intelligence" are formal and the biological standpoint aids in this formalization. Not to choose concrete sides and face the moral and power implications of such choice makes more central, and more abstract, the universal-problem-solver. It makes "method" itself the seat of value. It makes "intelligence" *the* good.

It is not only with reference to the statement of thought that formalization occurs within Dewey's liberally oriented perspective. In the field of explicit value theory also *formalization* is the key. The contents of a definite moral choice are never selected. The only criterion is the ubiquitous use of a method. It also assumes a tolerance, which is, of course, a virtue congenial to the indecisive, no matter how ironically its opposite is verbalized as a "quest for certainty."

From the strain of Puritanism in it, with its disdain of the trivial, the useless, the idle, of those "that don't earn their keep," and its value sanctioning of those who work, the men in greasy caps with alert eyes and ready hands who nurse the big machines, or the laboratorians — from this strain and with the value orientation derived from it, it leans toward "labor." But "labor" is not seen as a class, a specific group, but as an attitude, as a way of *acting*. Also since this perspective corresponds and appeals to groups that certainly do not wear overalls,[4] it does not use "labor" to designate a class and group.

All these modulations of the category of action go into the conception held by Dewey. There is one more social anchorage for the concept which must be mentioned; its link to education, through its "experimental" features.

How We Think, of 1910, is especially valuable to us, for it is a book on *logic* written expressly for *educators*. Dewey's own comments in the preface, expressive as they are of his motive for writing the book, furnish a lead into understanding the correspondence of his perspective and concepts with the educational situation. He comments on "the multiplication of studies" and the augmentation of the teachers' tasks. His book is to give some "chew of unity, some principle that makes for simplification..."[5] We have already commented upon the growth of educational institutions and the sociological reasons for their diversification of curricula. This growth meant, of course, an ever enlarging personnel facing new problems. This personnel, located above, and those who trained it, constituted one of Dewey's publics. It is not likely that those in such an enlarging situation would have been snared into acceptance of *authoritative* doctrines. No absolute, fixed end would aid them for three reasons. First, the rapidity of changes in the administrative positions they occupied; second, the diversity of these positions spread out through various regions, urban and rural. And, third, the changes and diversities in the *situations* they faced. Thus the "end," the guides given them had at once to be formal, or general, and yet possible of practice. For they were concretely involved in decision making and the outcome of their decisions were available for them and others to see.

> "This book [writes Dewey] represents the conviction that the needed steadying and centralizing factor is found in adopting as the end of endeavor that attitude of mind, that habit of thought, which we call scientific. This scientific attitude of mind might, conceivably, be quite irrelevant to teaching children and youth. But this book also represents the conviction that such is not the case; that the native and unspoiled attitude of childhood, marked by ardent curiosity, fertile imagination, and love of experimental inquiry, is near, very near, to the attitude of the scientific mind."[6]

Such a view set the seal of science, a secular seal with growing prestige, as has been explained; it meets the demands of the occupants of the new educational situation as enumerated above. It has the added advantages of avoiding too controversial social questions by tacitly rooting the attitude taken as a "growth" from what is native to the child.

Dewey is concerned with moral values; he accepts the scientific method. He has persistently endeavored to combine the two together. This intention might be affiliated with the polarization of "religion" and "science," as in James, but whatever the existent surrogate the mediation which James' pragmatism afforded him is quite different from the mediation of science and morals achieved by Dewey.

> "... as my study and thinking progressed, I became more and more troubled by the intellectual scandal that seemed to me involved in the current (and traditional) dualism in logical standpoint and method between something called "science" on the one hand and something called "morals" on the other."[7]

Dewey has overcome this "scandal," first of all, by means of a statement of what inquiry involves; he has stated inquiry or intelligence or scientific method so as to have it exhaustively assimilate moral problems. And this aim is one factor shaping his discussions of "inquiry."

> "... I have long felt that the construction of a logic, that is, a method of effective inquiry, which would apply without abrupt breach of continuity to the fields designated by both of these words, [science and morals] is at once our needed theoretical solvent and the supply of our greatest practical want. This belief has had much more to do with the development of what I termed, for lack of a better word, 'instrumentalism,' than have most of the reasons that have been assigned."[8]

In a section above we have documented the use of the category "conduct" in the mediation of art and value with science. But the category is an element in the larger logic of intelligence of scientific method itself.

We move from:

> "one of the most genuine problems of modern life . . . the reconciliation of the scientific view of the universe with the claims of the moral life . . . [to] the supreme importance of intelligence within the moral life [To achieve this Dewey has to ask] . . . how moral judgments — judgments of the ought and should — relate themselves to the world of scientific knowledge. To frame a theory of knowledge which makes it necessary to deny the validity of moral ideas, or else to refer them to some other and separate kind of universe from that of common sense and science, is both provincial and arbitrary. The pragmatist has at least tried to face, and not to dodge, the ques-

tion of how it is that moral and scientific 'knowledge' can both hold of one and the same world. [He continues:] the conception that scientific judgments are to be assimilated to morality is closer to common sense than is the theory that validity is to be denied of moral judgments because they do not square with a preconceived theory of the nature of the word to which scientific judgments must refer. And all moral judgments are about changes to be made."[9]

Thus, "scientific method" and "moral judgments" come together on the common ground of "changes to be made," in the sphere of practice, just as poetry and science come together in practice.[10]

Once Dewey:

"heard a physicist, quite innocent of the pragmatic controversy, remark that the knowledge of a mechanic or farmer was what the Yankee calls gumption — acknowledgement of things in their belongings and uses, and that to his mind natural science was only gumption on a larger scale: the convenient cataloguing and arranging of a whole lot of things with reference to their most efficacious services."

And then such a model is generalized into the "reasonable" itself: "To be reasonable is to recognize things in their offices as obstacles and as resources. Intelligence, in its ordinary use, is a practical term..."[11] These quotations are most revealing. Notice the identification of "science" and the "practical," thus making "intelligence" a "practical term." The "practical," the "ordinary use" represents here the world of value. This world is brought into the picture that science gives by a modification or particular slant toward both science and value. Both of them become matters of the practical. In this blend the way in which values are stated does not commit one to the content of any particular value, and this is so precisely because what is ordinarily termed "the value problem" is formalized by its assimilation to a kind of *biologized practice:* "obstacles and resources," "efficacious services," "belongings and uses," indeed, "gumption" itself. The reason for seeing science as practical is to allow *values* a place in the scheme of things. Dewey's empirical honesty almost gives him away in such statements as: "The perceptions of the scientist need have no such overt or 'utilitarian' uses, but surely after them *he* behaves differently, as an inquirer if in no other way..."[12]

Now this mediation of value and science not only proceeds by methodizing and "practicalizing" value problems as well as science; values also get anchored metaphysically. This metaphysics comes out best in the determination of the object of knowledge. Values are anchored metaphysically by means of a theory of knowledge.[13] Dewey's metaphysics is not at all understandable apart from his theory of knowledge[14] and from a realization of what this latter theory is designed to accomplish.

As part of the general "nominalistic program" of the "philosophers of science" the pragmatism of Dewey could seek to "reduce" abstractions to the "concrete" terms of the world of "science" or to the world of "everyday life." But Dewey's "concrete" terms go further than those of several of his fellow thinkers who belong to this general program. He does not "reduce" abstractions to what he would call the "abstractions" of "sense data" or "scientific objects." To him "immediate reality" is composed of *things*, not of abstracted *qualities*. He restores "the world of everyday life as the basis of knowledge." Now: Reichenbach makes the following penetrating assertion as to one motive for such a restoration:

". . . Dewey does not only want to establish knowledge in a better and more solid form. What he intends, and perhaps to a greater extent, is establishing the sphere of values, of human desires and aims, on the same basis and in an analogous form as the system of knowledge. If concrete things as immediately experienced are the truly 'real' world, if the scientific thing is nothing but an auxiliary logical construction for better handling of the 'real' things, then ethical and esthetical valuations are 'real' properties of things as well as are the purely cognitive properties, and it is erroneous to separate valuations as subjective from cognitive properties as objective. In persuasive language and in ever renewed form Dewey insists upon this outcome of his theory, the establishment of which seems to be the motive force in the work of this eminently practical mind, 'practical' to be taken in both its implications as 'moral' and 'directed towards action' . . . reveals the motive force of the pragmatic conception of reality. If the pragmatist considers secondary and tertiary qualities as real he does so because he wants to establish esthetics and ethics as aspects of reality comparable to physics; because he wants to show that esthetic and moral judgments are statements of facts in a sense analogous to statements of physical facts. It is the desire to establish objective esthetics and ethics, as opposed to subjective conceptions of esthetics and ethics, which stand behind the pragmatist's theory of reality."[15]

By shifting the locus of the "value problem" in a conception of "reality" and away from inter-human conflicts about action, Dewey is able to avoid the social, economic, and political trials which certainly beset the moralist, and especially a social pluralist! And it also overlooks what Reichenbach and others have correctly stated as the heart of moral questions today: the compulsory character of the judgment. But Dewey, morally, is really Socratic. He does not distinguish, make a problem of, the determination of goods and the compulsion to act in line with them. He is a neo-Socratic, with the "neo" standing for intellectuality of a kind which blurs the alleged *epistemological* requirements of knowledge and the "demands of the moral life."

The Deweyan revolt against "dualism" is a revolt proceeding in terms of a theory of knowledge which has as its objective the throwing over of Descartes' exclusion of values from the solid world. As philosophy:

> "accepts knowledge of facts and principles from those competent in inquiry and discovery, so it accepts the goods that are diffused in human experience. It has no Mosaic nor Pauline authority of revelation entrusted to it. But it has the authority of intelligence, of criticism of these common and natural goods."

But what does philosophy or intelligence do with these values?

> "It has to appraise values by taking cognizance of their causes and consequences; only by this straight and narrow path may it contribute to expansion and emancipation of values. For this reason the conclusions of science about matter-of-fact efficiencies of nature are its indispensable instruments. If its eventual concern is to render goods more coherent, more secure and more significant in appreciation, its road is the subject-matter of natural existence as science discovers and depicts it."[16]

For "it is the province of moral theory to reveal moral goods; to bring them to consciousness and to enforce their character in perception."[17] In his moral life man has only thought, but that may well be enough, for we are in nature and in nature itself there is good.

"When we have used our thought to its utmost and have
thrown into the moving unbalanced balance of things our puny
strength, we know that though the universe slay us still we may
trust, for our lot is one with whatever is good in existence. We
know that such thought and effort is one condition of the coming into existence of the better . . . in nature itself qualities and
relations, individualities and uniformities, finalities and effica-
cies, contingencies and necessities are inextricably bound together. The harsh conflicts and the happy coincidences of this
interpenetration make experience what it consciously is; their
manifest apparition creates doubt, forces inquiry, exacts choice,
and imposes liability for the choice which is made."

If men would but carry:

"into the region of values the principle now embodied in scientific practice . . . ends would be found in experienced enjoyment of the fruits of a transforming activity. In so far as the
subjectivity of modern thought represents a discovery of the
part played by personal responses, organic and acquired, in the
causal production of the qualities and values of objects, it
marks the possibility of a decisive gain."[18]

To seat value in nature, "nature" must include "humanity." This we
shall examine again in connection with the naturalistic conception
of sociality. In the meantime, note that "nature, including humanity, with all its defects and imperfections, may evoke heartfelt
piety as the source of ideals, of possibilities, of aspiration in their
behalf, and as the eventual abode of all attained goods and excel-
lencies."[19] ". . . experiences of objects had by the way of affection
and practical action," are as real as any "objects of knowledge."
The products of such experiences cannot be called "subjective and
phenomenal" for:

"all modes of experiencing are ways in which some genuine
traits of nature come to manifest realization . . . [and] the isolation of traits characteristic of objects known, and then defined
as the sole ultimate realities, accounts for the denial to nature
of the characters which make things lovable and contemptible,
beautiful, humorous, settled, disturbed, comfortable, annoying,
barren, harsh, consoling, splendid, fearful; are such immediately and in their own right and behalf . . . [They] stand in themselves on precisely the same level as colors, sounds, qualities of
contact, taste, and smell."[20]

> "In current philosophy [Dewey wrote in 1908] everything of
> a practical nature is regarded as 'merely' personal, and the
> 'merely' has the force of denying legitimate standing in the
> court of cosmic jurisdiction ... pragmatism — by which I
> mean the doctrine that reality possesses practical character and
> that this character is most efficaciously expressed in the function
> of intelligence—"[21]

Thus is revealed something about the stress on the practical in
Dewey. With it not only is his central category of intelligence or
inquiry of scientific method made to do moral service, but reality
itself is seen as practical and hence as a carrier of value.

The history of Dewey's process of getting ethical affairs within
the scope of scientific determination is interesting. It enables us to
show in this context the role of certain other notions. In 1887 Dewey denied that "physical science" is to be "the founder of the ethical system of the coming man. His reasons for this bifurcation
were threefold:

(1) "Ethics deals with an end, and there is no place for an end
in nature."

(2) "... even if there were an end in the universe, this would
not of itself constitute the ideal for human conduct ... "

(3) "Science is utterly unable to establish the essential feature
of the ethical ideal, its insistence upon the identity of humanity in
their relation to it."

The way in which this problem of morals and science operates as
a surrogate for the religion vs. science problem is amply displayed
in "the bearing" of these points, which are conceived as:

> "the profound conviction that in a world such as physical sci-
> ence takes cognizance of there is no ground for morals ...
> a spiritual interpretation of reality can alone found a truly sci-
> entific ethics and justify the living ways of man to man ...
> [And, more pointedly:] the cause of theology and morals is one,
> and ... whatever banishes God from the heart of things, with
> the same edict excludes the ideal, the ethical, from the life of
> man."[22]

The next stage in Dewey's thought may be brought out by a brief
display of an essay written eleven years after the above. In a discussion of Huxley's famous speech, Dewey "sums up" all the differences:

"between the ethical process and the cosmic process . . . [in the fact] that the process and the forces bound up with the cosmic have come to consciousness in man. That which was instinct in the animal is conscious impulse in man . . . tendency to vary in the animal is conscious foresight in man . . . unconscious adaptation and survival . . . is with man conscious deliberation and experimentation . . . [These differences mean] the whole distinction of the moral from the immoral. [In his] . . . moral struggle [man] acts not as a mere individual but as an organ in maintaining and carrying forward the universal process."[23]

The drive toward location of man in nature, the naturalism of Dewey is clearly *not* any general enthusiasm for "science" as *against* religion. Dewey's "naturalism" is a way of getting moral discussion upon an acceptable secular basis. With evolution he was able to locate the ethical within the human and to distinguish between the ethical and the cosmic as a difference between types of animals and the consequences of these differences. Moral issues could then be seen by Dewey within a biological model of human life. Some of the social results and functions of this model have been set forth above.

Now technically this same polemic and merger of the moral and the scientific arises in the question as to whether judgments of value are different from judgments of fact. "All conduct," writes Dewey in his last statement of the problem, "that is not simply blindly impulsive or mechanically routine seems to involve valuations."[24] No distinction is to be admitted by Dewey between judgments of facts and judgments of valuation. The entire question of valuations — can they be "objective propositions?" — is translated into two items: "(i) aversion to our existing situation and attraction toward a prospective situation and (ii) a specifiable and testable relation between the latter as an end and certain activities as means for accomplishing it."[25]

"Liking and disliking" are to be "considered in terms of observable . . . modes of behavior . . . " It is an "affective-motor" affair, if we do not take "affective" as "private 'feelings.' " Thus the biological. Then the technological: one way in which "ends" may be valuated is in terms of the means used to attain it. It may be "found that it will take too much time or too great an expenditure of energy to achieve it," etc.

> "There are [he says in a summary] propositions . . . which describe and define certain things as good, fit, or proper in a definite existential relation: these propositions, moreover, are generalizations, since they form rules for the proper use of materials . . . the existential relation in question is that of means-ends or means-consequences . . ."

Dewey implies that any attempt to raise a distinction between things that are good *for* something and things *intrinsically* good is not tenable because "ends framed in separation from considerations of things as means are foolish to the point of irrationality." In so far as "such" a distinction can be made, it is one between the "desired and the desirable" which means "the object of a desire as it first presents itself . . . and the object of desire which emerges as a revision of [this] impulse, after the latter is critically judged in reference to the conditions which will decide the actual result." We see the attempt to assimilate various "value-questions" to the technologized Deweyan thought model: values are properties of the objects of desires. But desires arise only when "there is something the matter." This "trouble" is conceived by Dewey as "something lacking, wanting, in the existing situation . . . an absence which produces conflict in the elements that do not exist." On the other hand "when things are going smoothly desires do not arise," and ends are not projected.

Since desires and interests must themselves be evaluated as means, they may be looked upon as *plans, i.e.,* "directive means."

> ". . . value in the sense of *good* is inherently connected with that which promotes, furthers, assists, a course of activity . . . value in the sense of *right* is inherently connected with that which is needed, required, in the maintenance of a course of activity . . . valuation-phenomena . . . have their immediate source in biological modes of behavior . . ."

In the course of Dewey's thought we began in a rather conventional manner with ethics polarized against physical science and the world which it sees. With the aid of "practicality," the theory of evolution, the biological model of action, the central emphasis upon a certain statement of scientific method Dewey is able to do two things: first, to assimilate all questions of value as "problems" thoroughly soluble by the scientific or the secular method of intelligence; second, to construct a "naturalistic metaphysic," *i.e.*, one which is compatible with science and which at the same time anchors values in the cosmic process. Underlying and sustaining the cogency of this ethical and metaphysical endeavor is the assumption of a relatively homogeneous community which does not harbor any chasms of structure and power not thoroughly ameliorative by discussion. Always there must be the assumption that no "problems" will arise that will be so deep that a third idea-plan would not unite in some way the two conflicting plans. But this model of problem posing does not concern itself with two social interests in a death-clutch. Here the biological conception does valuable service. For under this model there is the constant conception of this homogeneous "man" confronting the problems of "adapting" to nature so that supporting this assumption stands the biological model of Dewey, and the technological perspective which will be discussed below.[26]

Whenever opposing groups are confronting one another and can not be "adapted" to one another because of the structural antagonisms of society, the "answer" we get from Dewey is not a choice supporting one or the other. More than likely there is the plea that when social science develops like physical science, we can solve or obviate such problems, or define them so as to permit their solution. ". . . the ultimate fate is the fatality of ignorance, and the ultimate wickedness is lack of faith in the possibilities of intelligence applied inventively and constructively."[27]

Dewey has not taken party stands. He has stood for many "programs" and attitudes and very specific issues like the trials of Negro sharecroppers. Sidney Hook, who surely should know, has written: " . . . none of the conventional labels of left-wing politics can be affixed to him. This is what we should expect about anyone faithful to the spirit of the experimental philosophy."[28]

We can see Dewey fumbling for words that are politically neutral: "There is no word which adequately expresses what is taking place. 'Socialism' has too specific political and economic associations to be appropriate. 'Collectivism' is more neutral, but it, too, is a partyword rather than a descriptive term."[29]

Dewey in 1933 expressed the belief that the Democratic Party,

just elected, "is thoroughly incapable of doing the needed work."
He turns to Norman Thomas' socialists and, feeling that they are
not large enough to be "the efficient agent for radical political change," turns to the "League for Independent Political Action," which is "not a party and has no ambition to become a party." Speaking for the League he wrote:

> "We believe that actual social conditions and needs suffice to
> determine the direction political action should take, and we
> believe that this is the philosophy which underlies the demo-
> cratic faith of the American people . . . Our program is, in an
> ultimate sense, partial and tentative, experimental and not
> rigid . . ." The second main point of the L. I. P. A. is the belief
> "that politics is a struggle for possession and use of power to set-
> tle specific issues that grow out of the country's needs and prob-
> lems. . . .Because we desire a union of forces. . . .we are strong-
> ly opposed to all slurs and sneers at the farmers, engineers,
> teachers, social workers, small merchants, clergy, newspaper
> people, and white-collar workers who constitute the despised
> middle class."[30]

There is a "logical" parallel between Dewey's handling of *logic*
and of *morals*. In both cases he tries to derive the normative from
the existent and in both cases he ends up with a *method*. As Ralph
Barton Perry has put it, "Dewey's preoccupation with method
amounts in effect to a naturalistic panlogism, in which content *is*
method."[31] On the side of logic, Dewey of course denies any fundamental distinction between "logic" and actually operating
methodology. Inquiry itself generates normative forms for future
thought. It is very interesting to note C. S. Peirce's reaction to this
methodologizing of the normative, which is so absolutely central
in Dewey. In a review of the *Studies in Logical Theory*, printed
in *The Nation*, Peirce wrote: "Dewey . . . seems to regard what he
calls 'logic' as a natural history of thought."[32]

> "If calling the new natural history by the name of 'logic' (a
> suspicious beginning) is to be a way of pre-judging the ques-
> tion of whether or not there may be a logic which is more than
> a mere natural history, in as much as it would pronounce one
> proceeding of thought to be sound and valid and another to be
> otherwise, then we should regard this appropriation of that
> game to be itself fresh confirmation of our opinion of the urgent
> need of such a normative science at this day."

This is of course a blow at the very heart of Dewey's central thesis concerning "logic" which is that the normative is derived from operative inquiry. We may present this matter by classifying the sentences in Dewey's texts having to do with science. They may be classified in innumerable ways, for they grade from the abstract formal and the historical to the simple observational. Only two generic classes need here be indicated: (a) sentences existing on an observational, or a low level, of induction, and concerning science directly as a set of procedures, as a type of activity engaged in by a class of men; or concerning the connectives of this type activity with its larger cultural setting. Most of the sentences in this bracket are open to empirical verification. These assertions and negations as such form a contribution to the psychology and the theory, or better, a brace of hypotheses about scientific procedures. There are many other hypotheses about science and its setting which differ from those of Dewey. By no means is there clear or wide agreement as to the character, location, setting, and outcome of physical science. Nevertheless, Dewey has contributed several important and *vera causa* hypotheses about science construed as data for a sociology of science.

(b) Mingled, at times indiscriminately, with such empirical hypotheses is the ever present drive toward the articulation of a formal paradigm of "thought," a "common pattern of inquiry." For not only does Dewey present an account of scientific procedures, he generalizes it, utilizes this account as an epistemological criterion. On its basis he criticizes existent epistemologies.[33]

Often this construct is put forth in the name of "scientific method." But it is not only descriptive of *de facto* procedures in the sciences. We have indicated how this formulation of a general paradigm of inquiry is channeled by biologistic considerations. It is in terms of a biological psychology that Dewey interprets and states his model of thought as well as that from which it is avowedly "derived" — physical science.[34] This epistemological thought model is a statement of the implications of scientific procedures as viewed by the pragmatist. This "common pattern of inquiry" is a *model* of thought formulating certain conditions that must be satisfied by any inquiry if it is to yield "warranted assertions." "Logical forms," says Dewey, "are the conditions that inquiry, *qua* inquiry, has to meet." These criteria are empirical in the sense that they "have grown out of the experiences of actual (scientific) inquiry." But they possess "rational standing" and by "rational" is meant that the means are such as to have issue in warranted assertions as consequences.[35]

Thus there are really two concerns with science in Dewey's writings: (a) there is the attempt to present an empirical account of the way scientific inquiries proceed, the context from which they come, and in what their termination consists. (b) There is the set of more strictly logical, *i.e.*, normative questions, the answers to which center around a paradigm formulation incorporating the grounds for the "warranted," the valid. It is to Dewey's credit that he has opened widely and contributed substantially to the issue regarding the relation of these two concerns as we have conceptually separated them here. To Dewey, answers to the latter type problem cannot proceed without materials furnished by the former type investigations. Which is to say, briefly, that logical norms are empirically derived.

We can study inquiries as "objective data," our aim being to report "the ways in which men do think." Or we can "prescribe the ways in which men ought to think." In the history of logic such a distinction has been interpreted in terms of a difference between the "psychological and the logical, the latter consisting of 'norms' provided from some source wholly outside of and independent of 'experience.'" Dewey's "fundamental thesis" being that "logical forms accrue to subject matter when the latter is subjected to controlled inquiry, he interprets the way in which men at a given time carry on their inquiries." The difference between this and the ways in which they ought to think:

> "denotes a difference like that between good and bad farming . . . [*i.e.*] Men think in ways they should not when they follow a method of inquiry that experience of past inquiries shows are not competent to reach the intended end of the inquiries in question."

In brief, to Dewey, epistemological criteria are the abstracted structures of *successful* inquiries. The natural sciences are *assumed* to exhibit such inquiries. This notion of the rise of logical forms is contrary to the idea that they are *ad hoc*, built of "air," that they are "transcendental" or *a priori*. On the contrary: logical forms are "descriptive of something that verifiably exists." For the methods employed in natural sciences were not invented by logicians. On the contrary: science proceeds quite outside of the formulations of the logician and each step in science, as Peirce put it, has been a lesson in logic. The criteria of scientific inquiries were formulated and articulated as canons governing further scientific inquiry by scientists and the methods of science are self corrective, *i.e.*, the scientists "derive" the norms that govern their present and future work from formulations of norms abstracted from past procedures. The philosopher can but verbalize and advise these "norms" which exist as habits of the scientist.[36]

This same drive toward *methodization* (and the derivation of the *normative* from the existent) is even more apparent in the case of morals. It has been indicated above that moral questions are so stated by Dewey as to be answerable by scientific inquiry, by a technological examination of conditions and consequences. The methodization of value is another way of referring to the fact that for Dewey "inquiry," "intelligence," or "scientific method" are existent processes *and* his central *value*, his key norm, his tool for all evaluations. Always there is that happy ambivalence. That the methodization of value is another way of stating that for Dewey the notion of inquiry is central is indicated by the 1903 quotation which states a need for "a general logic of experience as a method of inquiry":

> "The value of research for social progress; the bearing of psychology upon educational procedure; the mutual relations of fine and industrial art; the question of the extent and nature of specialization in science in comparison with the claims of applied science; the adjustment of religious aspirations to scientific statements; the justification of a refined culture for a few in face of economic insufficiency for the mass — such are a few of the many social questions whose *final* answer depends upon the possession and use of a general logic of experience as a method of inquiry and interpretation."[37]

Such a quotation appears quite inauspicious, but there is a connection between the methodization of value and the suspicion confirmed in the mind of at least one pragmatist:

> "To those of us [wrote Randolph Bourne, sensitive follower

and student of Dewey until the First World War] who have taken Dewey's philosophy almost as our American religion, it never occurred that values could be subordinated to technique. We were instrumentalist, but we had our private utopias so clearly before our minds that the means fell always into place as contributory. And Dewey, of course, always meant his philosophy, when taken as a philosophy of life, to start with values. But there was always that unhappy ambiguity in his doctrine as to just how values were created, and it became easier and easier to assume that just any growth was justified and almost any activity valuable so long as it achieved its end. The American . . . content with getting somewhere without asking too closely whether it was the desirable place to get . . . You must have your vision, and you must have your technique. The practical effect of Dewey's philosophy has evidently been to develop the sense of the latter at the expense of the former."[38]

We have indicated the biological and technological turns of thought which enable Dewey to assimilate "problems of value" to the formation and use of techniques or method. All of Randolph Bourne's remarks are not wholly justified in terms of Dewey's *texts* (as over against their possible effects on various people), for "intelligence" is given by Dewey a social direction. It is a *socially loaded* method. When he speaks, *e.g.*, of "the newer morale of industry and commerce," or the "ethics of industry and of reciprocal contractual service,"[39] he assumes that this "ethics" and this "morale" are informed by "intelligence" and by "sociality," in the same way that these liberalizers of action and technique are to suffuse the school room and thus let into this social mood moral relations which will live at the center of intellectual activities.[40]

The entire issue, I believe, of Dewey's position in ethics hangs upon his following assertion: "Instruments imply . . . ends to which they are put, purposes that are not instruments which control them, values for which tools and agencies are to be used."[41] But obviously nothing of the sort is true. There is no value trademark placed upon airplanes or even upon educational procedures. By their character, physical instruments set limits to their use, but obviously the limits are very wide indeed. The professionalizing or methodizing of value and of value questions already assumes for its happy operation a kind of community that nowhere exists.

One more concept should be indicated which conspires to mask serious value conflicts and the chasms and antagonisms underlying them and at the same time leads once again to the ubiquitous "method": the concept of the "problematic situation." A quotation which displays clearly the surrogateship of "problem" for "value" is:

> "I am suspicious of all attempts to erect a hierarchy of values: their results generally prove to be inapplicable and abstract. But there is at every time a hierarchy of problems, for there are some issues which underlie and condition others."[42]

If "values" are debatable, then we can conceive of "problems" as "objective." And a problem is the "way into" Dewey's "inquiry." Let us briefly reconstruct the concept of the problematic in the course of Dewey's thought, and thus note its orientation and how it operates as a mask.

In his first statements of the problematic Dewey is quite within the routines of the post-Kantian and Hegelian tradition.[43] In 1903 he denies "constitutive" thought, for all experience is man's, but he retains a sort of leapfrogging of universals as part of the environmental structure. Such language is, of course, foreign to Dewey; he speaks of "factors," "objective elements," and "situations." But it is possible to relinquish the idealistic metaphysic, the cosmic proportions of the Hegelian statement, and still retain traces of the structure of the idealist version. That is the modification effected in 1903 at which time Dewey stated:

> "The antecedent . . . [to thought] is a situation in which the various factors are actively incompatible with each other, and yet in and through the striving tend to a reformation of the whole and a restatement of the parts. The 'situation' as such is clearly 'objective.' It is there; it is there as a whole; the various parts are there; and their active incompatibility with one another is there . . . the conflict is not only objective in a *de facto* sense (that is, really existent), but is objective in a logical sense as well; it is just this conflict which effects a transition into the thought situation — this, in turn, being only a constant movement toward a defined equilibrium. The conflict has objective logical value because it is the antecedent condition and cue of thought."[44]

The problematic, is "out there," but even in the early writings a value correlativity is sensed. For the elements in the conflicting situation may also be viewed as a "conflict in the matters of contents of an experience."[45] But it is not clear to what extent, the situation *as problematic* is *dependent* upon human factors.

That in moving from Hegel to Dewey we experience a profound metaphysical delimitation does not detract from the fact that Dewey's early restatement of the problematic retains the formalistic pattern. For objective "nature" is still the locus of "problems." Dewey states this situation as an "objectively logical one," *i.e.*, "nature" contains situations apart from the purposes of man that are in themselves problematic.

Dewey denies that the conflict initiating thought is one occurring between universals, ideas, or interests. It seems that he pictures the conflict occurring between two "objective factors," *i.e.*, elements in nature apart from man's presence.[46]

By mentioning the formalistic metaphysic of conflict we do not mean to imply that such statement of the problematic is clear-cut in Dewey; only its traces exist as half-shadowed imprints upon his pages. It is more "background" than distinctively Deweyan. For the influence of the biological conceptions is clear. In the 1916 *Essays:*

> ". . . it is the needs of a situation which are determinative. They evoke thought and the need of knowing, and it is only within the situation that the identification of the needs with a self occurs; and it is only by reflection upon the place of the agent in the encompassing situation that the nature of his needs can be determined."[47]

Both the ontological idealist and this biological statement of the problematic mask the social and value-conflicts which are, in reality, involved in "problems."[48] And he can mask from himself this fact because he has never seriously questioned a fundamental and ultimate communal homogeneity of society. What is a "problem" to one "group" is not at all problematic to another; it may well be a satisfactory "solution." "Social" conflicts and problems are "objective" only in the sense of wide-spread recognition, actual or vicarious, of certain relations and movements as "unsatisfactory." The statement of the problematic in biological categories masks this form.

Different groups of thinkers, classes, institutions have different social values and aims; they want to go different "places;" they are on the move; or they want to stand "conservatively" still; they have different work patterns and as a projection of such behavioral patterns, they encompass and pivot around different systems of objects which their activities are striving to realize and which guide their directions and hence furnish the guiding thread for the emergence of their problems. It is here that "problems" arise and obviously they often involve deep conflicts of value. Dewey's theory of value is not capable of really handling such situations. The concept of the problem aids in this process of masking.

The more explicit connection in Dewey's writing between science and a certain order of social affairs and the view that science has a social purpose arose in his early discussions of Ernest Renan. In these articles of 1892 and 1893, he sets forth such assertions as:

> ". . . the most important thing to my mind is, after all, the conception which Renan had, in 1850, of the universal — the social, the religious significance of science and his partial retraction of this faith in 1890. *The Future of Science* breathes a constant and bracing tone of optimism: *The Future of Science* is not the future of erudition nor yet of knowledge as such. It is a social future, a development of humanity, which Renan has in mind. This was the origin of the book — 'the need I felt of summing up in a volume the new (*i.e.*, social) faith which has replaced the shattered Catholicism.' "[49]

In the polarization of science with religion it is Science which is spread as to become endowed with a "social, a religious significance." Notice in the following quotations the linking of "democrat" with ". . . a believer in the universal function of science." Notice also that here might be the *intellectual* source and motive of an interest in education for all.

> "In 1871, in his *Intellectual and Moral Reform* Renan writes: 'At its outset, civilisation was an aristocratic accomplishment: it was the work of a very few — nobles and priests — who made it obtain through what the democrats call the imposition of force. The continued preservation of civilisation is also the work of the aristocratic class.' In 1848 he wrote: 'Only one course remains and that is to broaden the basis of the family and to find room for all at the banqueting table of light . . . The aristocracy constitutes an odious monopoly if it does not set before it for its aim the tutelage of the masses — their gradual

elevation.' In 1871, his tone is: 'The people properly so-called
and the peasantry, to-day the absolute masters of the house,
are in reality only intruders, wasps who have usurped possession of a hive they did not build.' "[50]

The next year Dewey, still thinking of these matters, wrote:

> "The fundamental conception of Ernest Renan's work, *The
> Future of Science*, is that science is both subjectively and ob-
> jectively social: that its material, in its most important respects,
> is to be found in the history of humanity, and that its aim is
> furthering the organisation of humanity. The relation of science
> to the welfare of man is the true text of the book; and this in
> no limited definition of welfare, but in a sense so broad as to
> include his religious attitude, as well as his intellectual and ar-
> tistic enjoyments . . . if Renan conceives the theoretical out-
> come of science to be this revelation of man to himself, his con-
> ception of its practical resultant is not less broad. The whole
> march of Europe for four centuries is summed up in this prac-
> tical conclusion: to elevate and ennoble the people, and to let
> all men have a share in the delights of intelligence.' " [And
> sums it up:] "The definition of science, then, is to know from
> the standpoint of humanity; its goal is such a sense of life as
> will enable man to direct his conduct in relation to his fellows
> by intelligence and not by chance. It is to this that I would di-
> rect special attention — Renan's faith in '48 in the social basis
> and aim of science. According to Renan the present era is
> marked by intelligence coming to consciousness of its social
> function."[51]

There is an ambivalence in this depiction of science's relation to
the social which should be noted as rather persistent in Dewey's
strategy. Science is "social" in the sense of a coordinated inquiry;
it must be "public" in the sense of scientists checking one another's observations. But also science is "social" in the welfare sense.
These two meanings of calling science "social" are, in isolated essays, made distinct, but in many other crucial contexts the distinction is blurred so that the epistemological necessities of "public"
and "social" are exploited to lend weight to the welfare or political
sense of social.[52] A quotation will illustrate the point:

> "While the humanizing of science contributes to the life of
> humanity, it is even more required in behalf of science, in or-
> der that it may be intelligible, simple and clear; in order that

it may have that correspondence with reality which true knowledge claims for itself."[53]

Thirty-five years after writing on Renan, Dewey links technology
and society in such a manner that certain traits of technology are
conceived to form the positive basis of a good society of rounded
individuals.

> "The sick cannot heal themselves by means of their disease,
> and disintegrated individuals can achieve unity only as the
> dominant energies of community life are incorporated to form
> their minds. If these energies were, in reality, mere strivings for
> *private pecuniary gain,* the case would indeed be hopeless. But
> they are constituted by a *collective art of technology,* which
> individuals merely deflect to their private ends. There are the
> beginnings of an objective order through which individuals
> may get their bearings."[54]

The features of science are a sufficient value-base; we only need
a wider diffusion of them. For example, in the following we see an
interpretation of the organization of "science" directly transferred
to a social model:

> "No scientific inquirer can keep what he finds to himself or
> turn it to merely private account without losing his scientific
> standing. Everything discovered belongs to the community of
> workers. Every new idea and theory has to be submitted to this
> community for confirmation and test. There is an expanding
> community of cooperative effort and of truth. It is true enough
> that these traits are now limited to small groups having a some-
> what technical activity. The existence of such groups reveals a
> possibility of the present . . . Suppose that what now happens in
> limited circles were extended and generalized . . . The general
> adoption of the scientific attitude in human affairs would mean
> nothing less than a revolutionary change in morals, religion, pol-
> itics, and industry. The fact that we have limited its use so
> largely to technical matters is not a reproach to science, but to
> the human beings who use it for private ends and who strive
> to defeat its social application for fear of destructive effects
> upon their power and profit."[55]
> "Take science (including its application to the machine) for
> what it is, and we shall begin to envisage it as a potential creator
> of new values and ends. We shall have an intimation, on a wide
> and generous scale, of the release, the increased initiative, in-
> dependence and inventiveness, which science now brings in its

own specialized fields to the individual scientist. It will be seen as a means of originality and individual variation . . . Because of the free working of mind is one of the greatest joys open to man, the scientific attitude, incorporated in individual mind, is something which adds enormously to one's enjoyment of existence. The delights of thinking, of inquiry, are not widely enjoyed at the present time."[56]

"Science and technology" (and not some class or party) are what is polarized against *pecuniary* individualism.

"This reference to science and technology is relevant because they are the forces of present life which are finally significant. It is through employing them with understanding of their possible import that a new individualism, consonant with the realities of the present age, may be brought into operative being. . . . The art which our times needs in order to create a new type of individuality is the art which, being sensitive to the technology and science that are the moving forces of our time, will envisage the expansive, the social culture which they may be made to serve. I am not anxious to depict the form which this emergent individualism will assume. Indeed, I do not see how it can be described until more progress has been made in its production. . . . The greatest obstacle to that vision is, I repeat, the perpetuation of the older individualism now reduced, as I have said, to the utilization of science and technology for ends of private pecuniary gain."[57]

Just how this technology is to be taken from those pecuniary individuals who now monopolize it, we are not told. The nearest approach to this question is given by stress upon "education" which "marks the most perfect and intimate union of science and art conceivable in human experience."[58]

A more general statement and understanding of this technological perspective is rendered possible by certain social historical considerations. During the nineteenth century social structures all over the world groaned with the unprecedented growth and application of science. On several levels of publics "science" attained great prestige. Let us conceive of "science" as stretching from abstract mathematics to a new type of plough. For convenience we shall call the abstracted end "science," the other end, "technology." Peirce, for reasons already set forth, assimilated science; he was a mathematical logician, and, with a vehemence not explicable in terms of purely intellectual conviction, he disclaimed the Baconian dictum. The laboratory in the name of which he set forth his views was a laboratory of "pure science" and the model of inquiry which he generalized from it turned out to be irrelevant to "practice." It is not so with John Dewey. On this matter he stands quite opposite to Charles Peirce. From Dewey's technological perspective "action" and a biological psychology mediate "science" and "technology":

> "In outward forms, experimental science is infinitely varied. In principle, it is simple. We know an object when we know how it is made, and we know how it is made in the degree in which we ourselves make it. Old tradition compels us to call thinking "mental." But "mental" thought is but partial experimentation, terminating in preliminary readjustments, confined within the organism. As long as thinking remained at this stage, it protected itself by regarding this introverted truncation as evidence of an immaterial reason superior to and independent of body. As long as thought was thus cooped up, overt action in the "outer" natural scene was inevitably shorn of its full meed of meaning; it was to that extent arbitrary and routine."[59]

For Dewey knowledge, that is, science, is power. And the strength of this statement has aided the cogency of his style and perspective. The prestige of science derives from this technology with which it has been identified. In this identification John Dewey's thought has participated.

On the surface it would seem that science and technology were morally neutral, that empirically they should be looked upon as means, which may limit the range of possible ends, but which, nevertheless, do not set them. For some time the scope of technologically possible ends has been very wide, indeed, they range from utter comfort to stark death.

Technological power is then socially neutral and those who would celebrate it must face the question: Power for what? Dewey has celebrated "man's" growth of power through science and technology; he has not clearly answered the question involved in that celebration. To do so would have committed him to face squarely the political and legal problem of the present distribution of power as it exists within this social order. And this Dewey has never done.

One sociological reason for his *not* facing up to the political problem of power in connection with science and technology, lies in the fact that up until World War I technology served an expanding economy in controlling the "forces of nature." If diverse classes got differential returns from the growth and use of science, it was no matter; practically everybody got some returns, whether they "invested" or not. The most plainly available results of science in the United States up until the First World War were precisely the shared goods which growing corporations had quickly made from the laboratories and distributed through a *growing* market.

Dewey's own social position in this growing scene was well calculated to induce a positive, and from the present standpoint, inadequate incorporation of science into an intellectual orientation. For the groups with which Dewey had most frequent contact and to whom he addressed himself were rising into professional and skilled positions. It was precisely these groups who were closely involved in scientific practices and technological skills and who by their practices raised themselves in the class and status structure of the industrializing society.

The biological conception of the human individual must be mentioned as fitting into the positive appraisal of technology *per se* which Dewey manifests. For this model of action placed the individual against "nature" (the "environment") and within it the action that is implemented by science is more readily conceived as "adaptive to nature" than the conflict of the organization and movement of individuals for conquest of nature. The "existential transformation" that is the outcome of thought is a transformation of "nature," a field ploughed more quickly, a husked grain of a cereal plant, a strong steel road bridging a river, or one of concrete plunged through a mountain.

In short, the assimilation of problems of political power and of moral goods to a statement of thinking, of method, to a model of action and thought imputed to "science," occurred within the social context of a growing industrialization that was spreading across a physical continent and from the position of one in close, daily contact with the rising professional and skilled groups who were central in the implementation of this conquest of nature by machine.

This model was highlighted by the many fingers pointing at the technological results of science and from the success of the professions implemented by them. But the model is generalized by Dewey into education and into the discussions of politics. In these contexts and particularly in the latter, "scientific method" becomes "the *method* of intelligence" and this method is equated with "liberal democracy."

The World War of the second decade made publicly available the facts of the neutrality of technology. Prior to this time its products were not so easily questioned. It was after and during the war that Dewey began to write for political journals. It was clear that technology could be used against nations. Could its differential distribution among classes make for other "unsocial, unhumanitarian" use? One of the questions was: has "the method of intelligence" failed?

If one continues to focus upon technology as a *means* and yet as *the key good*, assimilating questions of ends to questions of means, then politically one should expect an implemented aimlessness. We are reminded of Mead's "We don't know where we're going but we're on our way," a statement which there is no reason to believe Dewey would not accept.

Now a crucial question to a liberal who is trying to view things from a technological perspective is the place of violence in the scheme of things. Dewey strives to state and to solve problems of power and of the legitimation of violence from within his *technological* perspective. He wants to accomplish a statement wholly from within this perspective, without any "moral" residue. The essay that is central here was printed on the eve of America's entrance into World War I, about a year after the sinking of the Lusitania, and the stand taken in it goes far to explain Dewey's support of the war effort.[60]

First, Dewey asks the standard questions, such as: Are the Tolstoyans right? Is all law really coercion? Is it a curtain for violence? Are the direct-actionists in industry correct? And so on. Such empirical cases as are given are largely drawn from penal practices, industrial disputes and war.

Second, he differentiates the "three conceptions of power or energy, coercive force, and violence." Now:

> "Any political or legal theory which will have nothing to do with power on the ground that all power is force and all force brutal and non-moral is obviously condemned to a purely sen-

timental, dreamy morals. It is force by which we excavate sub-
ways and build bridges and travel and manufacture; it is force
which is utilized in spoken argument or published book. Not to
depend upon and utilize force is simply to be without a foothold
in the real world."

And then, within this technological standpoint, he defines "violence" so as to rule it out: "violence" is "waste." "Energy becomes
violence when it defeats or frustrates purpose instead of executing
or realizing it." Whereas:

> "coercive force [occupies] we may fairly say, a middle place
> between power as energy and power as violence. To turn to the
> right as an incident of locomotion is a case of power: of means
> deployed in behalf of an end. To run amuck in the street is a
> case of violence. To use energy to make a man observe the rule
> of the road is a case of coercive force."

Then "law" is defined within this framework. Again "violence" becomes "waste," and "organized force" becomes "efficiency."

> "Law is a statement of the conditions of the organization of
> energies which, when unorganized, conflict and result in vio-
> lence — that is, destruction or waste. We cannot substitute rea-
> son for force, but force becomes rational when it is an organized
> factor in an activity instead of operating in an isolated way or
> on its own hook. For the sake of brevity, I shall refer to the or-
> ganization of force hereafter as efficiency, but I beg to remind
> you that the use of the term always implies an actual or poten-
> tial conflict and resulting waste in the absence of some scheme
> for distributing the energies involved."

The whole set of questions then becomes capable of being judged
by the canon of "efficiency." "Ends" become assumptions necessary to the formulations of "means," and therefore the canon of
efficiency can hold sway. Thus: " ... the only question which can
be raised about the justification of force is that of comparative efficiency and economy in its use."

> "It is, in substance, a question of efficiency (including econ-
> omy) of means in the accomplishing of ends. If the social ends
> at stake can be more effectively subserved by the existing legal
> and economic machinery, resort to physical action of a more di-
> rect kind has no standing. If, however, they represent an inef-

> fective organization of means for the ends in question, then re-
> course to extra-legal means may be indicated; provided it real-
> ly serves the ends in question — a very large qualification be
> it noted."

The principle of *legalized* force (juridical) is, at least tacitly, defended by naming it "impersonal," and "efficient in use of means,"
by polarizing it against "personal," which is read back in time as of
the "primitive methods," and, which is by implication, inefficient:

> "Thus the bias against any doctrine which seems under any
> circumstances to sanction resort to personal and primitive meth-
> ods of using force against the more impersonal juridical contri-
> vances of society turns out to be *prima facie* justified on the
> principle of efficiency in use of means . . . This conclusion that
> violence means recourse to means which are relatively waste-
> ful may be strengthened by considering penal measures."

But law itself, of course, is to be judged by the canon of "efficiency," of means and ends. Dewey thus comes upon his "main point":

> "No ends are accomplished without the use of force. It is
> consequently no presumption against a measure, political, in-
> ternational, juridical, economic, that it involves a use of force.
> Squeamishness about force is the mark not of idealistic but of
> moonstruck morals. But antecedent and abstract principles can
> not be assigned to justify the use of force. The criterion of value
> lies in the relative efficiency and economy of the expenditure of
> force as a means to an end."

And then, with the enlightenment shining through (and striking us
today as a little suspicious) he continues:
"With advance of knowledge, refined, subtle and indirect use of
force is always displacing coarse, obvious and direct methods of applying it. This is the explanation to the ordinary feeling against the
use of force."
This feature, which we have seen to be central to Dewey, is most
interestingly displayed in the context of this problem: in so far as
"moral" considerations enter (compare the above use of "end") they
are assimilated to the "intellectual":

> ". . . the so-called problem of "moralizing" force is in reality
> a problem of *intellectualizing* its use: a problem of employing

so to say neutral instead of gross muscular force as a means to accomplish ends . . . An immoral use of force is a stupid use."

Here "efficiency" intersects with "intelligence" (non-"stupid") and "the decisive question is the level of efficiency and economy upon which the deploying of forces goes on."

Yet we must consider the other side of the question, the other contention and see the non-resistance argument within the same Deweyan canons, for:

> "Only upon such a principle of expediency can the doctrine of non-resistance be urged, without committing ourselves to the notion that all exercise of energy is inherently wrong — a sort of oriental absolutism which makes the world intrinsically evil. I can but think that if pacifists in war and in penal matters would change their tune from the intrinsic immorality of the use of coercive force to the comparative inefficiency and stupidity of existing methods of using force, their good intentions would be more fruitful."

More positively, *upon this ground* of "efficiency," such organizations as the closed shop would be justified: "It may turn out in the future that the movement for the closed shop is an incident of an organization of labor which is itself in turn an incident in accomplishing a more efficient organization of human forces." Even such ideals as "liberty" would be positively viewed within technological canons:

> ". . . it is as an efficiency factor that its value [liberty] must intimately be assessed. Experience justifies the contention that liberty forms such a central element in efficiency that, for example, our present methods of capitalistic production are highly inefficient because, as respects the great body of laborers, they are so coercive."

We shall call this standpoint technologism. First, it shall be remarked that it would be difficult to find a better standpoint for a liberal in war time. Randolph Bourne understood this. At any rate, the consequence of this view for Dewey's later action was support of the war.[61]

Second, it is only from a technological perspective, such as we have traced in several other contexts above, that these quoted passages can be grasped.

Third, it is with this standpoint, along with such terms as "education" and the anthropologist's "culture" and by varying the level of abstraction, that Dewey avoids a really definite recognition and statement of the problem of political power.

Technologism is itself caught up in a larger intellectualism and forms a major point of support and ingredient of his methodological rationalization of value.

1. In a discussion of "planning" Mannheim has indicated some features of such thought, which he calls the "inventive." *Man and Society in an Age of Reconstruction*, p. 151.

2. For an adaptation of this phrase of Shäffle and a distinction between conduct and "reproductive" behavior, *See* K. Mannheim, *Ideology and Utopia*, p. 101f.

3. *See* below.

4. Cf. *The Encyclopedia of the Social Sciences*, "Business Schools," *i.e.*, to the extent they are "democratically professionalized."

5. *How We Think*, p. iii.

6. *Ibid.*, p. iii.

7. "From Absolutism to Experimentalism," p. 22.

8. *Ibid.*, p. 22.

9. *Essays for William James*, pp. 63, 64.

10. *See* below.

11. *Essays for William James*, p. 60.

12. *Ibid.*, p. 61.

13. The most penetrating resume of this matter has been given by Hans Reichenbach, *Philosophy of John Dewey*, p. 159f.

14. *See* H. E. Murphy's essay, *Philosophy of John Dewey*, p. 197.

15. Hans Reichenbach in, *Philosophy of John Dewey*, pp. 162-63, 178.

16. *Experience and Nature*, p. 408.

17. *Ibid*, p. 432.

18. *Ibid.*, pp. 420, 421.

19. *The Quest for Certainty*, pp. 276, 306.

20. *Quest for Certainty*, pp. 24, 79; *Experience and Nature*, pp. 24, 21, 96.

21. John Dewey, "Does Reality Possess Practical Character?", *Essays Philosophical and Psychological in Honor of William James* (N.Y. 1908), pp. 54, 58.

22. Ethics and Physical Science," *Andover Review*, Vol. VII, (June, 1887) pp. 591, 577.

23. *The Monist* Vol. 8, pp. 340, 341. (April, 1898).

24. "Theory of Valuation," *International Encyclopedia of Unified Science*, Vol. II, No. 4. The following quotations are from this source with specific pages corresponding to the following order: 13 and 14, 24, 25, 26, 32, 33, 53, 57, 64.

25. Italics are in the original; they portend the emphasis upon such technological propositions which blend with the biological framework.

26. *See* below.

27. *Characters and Events*, Vol. II, p. 719.

28. Sidney Hook, *John Dewey: An Intellectual Portrait*, (N.Y., 1939), p. 162.

29. *Individualism — Old and New*, p. 36.

30. *Nation*, "The Future of Radical Political Action" (January 4, 1933) pp. 8-9.

31. Perry, *op. cit.*, Vol. II, p. 515.

32. Vol. 79 (Sept. 15, 1904), p. 220f.

33. One example from among many: in criticizing a statement of the antecedent conditions of thought... "Such statements cannot be verified by reference to a single instance of thought in connection with actual practice or actual scientific research." *Logic*, p. 124.

34. Peirce's work on "science" differs from Dewey's in that not only is there more description of the laboratorian's behavior (as data) but inferences about what occurs in the laboratorian's mind (including functioning of certain canons) is not guided as directly by any particular psychology or theory of mind as are Dewey's. This is not to deny that Peirce's work in the psychology and sociology of science does not imply and/or presuppose a "behavioral" psychology.

35. *Logic*, pp. 14, 15, 9, 10; the following quotations are from this source and correspond to its pagination in the following order: 103, 101, 103 and 104, 102 and 5.

36. I have stated the implications of such a view of logical norms for the sociology of knowledge in the *Am. J. of Sociology*, (November, 1940).

37. *Studies in Logical Theory*, pp. 19, 20.

38. Randolph Bourne, *Untimely Papers*, reprinted from essays in the *Dial*.

39. *See Characters and Events*, Vol. II, p. 607.

40. "Ethical Principles Underlying Education," *Third Yearbook of the National Herbart Society* (1897), pp. 7-33. "The School as Social Center," *NEA, Proceedings*, (1902), pp. 373-83.

41. *Essays in Experimental Logic*, pp. 1-2.

42. *Individualism — Old and New*, p. 141.

43. *See* especially the *Psychology* (1887), pp. 233, 204.

44. *Studies in Logical Theory*, pp. 38-39. Cf. also *The Essays*, p. 121f.

45. *Studies in Logical Theory*, p. 49 also p. 40.

46. Cf. *Quest for Certainty*, pp. 234-36. See also *The Essays*, pp. 108-22.

47. *Essays*, p. 70.

48. In the *Psychology* (1887), an adumbration of something similar to the "biologic" formulation is present, *not* in the discussion of knowledge and thinking, but in the chapter on "Volition." Here there is talk of an internal conflict of desires, a "conflict of himself with himself" where in a man "is the opposing contestants as well as on the battlefield." pp. 364-65. Only later does this notion get carried into the realm of cognition, with the difference that it is correlated with the situation. This correlativity is stressed

throughout Dewey's works in all discussions of the biologic. But cf. the 1938 *Logic*, pp. 105-06. "We are doubtful because the situation is inherently doubtful."

49. In the *Open Court* in 1892, reprinted in *Characters and Events*, Vol. I, p. 21. The following quotations are from this source, in the following order: 21, 22-23, 23 and 24.

50. *Ibid.*, pp. 22-23.

51. *Ibid.*, pp. 23-24.

52. In Mead this matter perhaps amounts to more definite blurring. *See* "The Individual Thinker and Scientific Method" in *Creative Intelligence*, Ed. by J. Dewey.

53. *Experience and Nature*, p. 164.

54. *Individualism — Old and New*, p. 65 [My italics].

55. *Ibid.*, pp. 154-55.

56. *Ibid.*, pp. 160-61.

57. *Ibid.*, pp. 98-100.

58. *My Pedagogic Creed*, p. 16.

59. *Experience and Nature*, p. 428.

60. "Force and Coercion," *International Journal of Ethics* (April, 1916) reprinted in *Characters and Events*, pp. 782-90. The quotations which follow are from this source. They correspond to its pagination in the following order: 784, 789, 784 and 785, 789, 785 and 786, 787, 788, 789.

61. "I have been a thorough and complete sympathizer with the part played by this country in this war, and I have wished to see the resources of this country used for its successful prosecution." Dewey, *The American Teacher*, (January, 1918), Vol. VII, p. 8.

22

In 1939 Dewey wrote *Freedom and Culture*. The conception of "culture" is utilized widely in this work. Its use shifts attention from the "political and legal" which are "effects, not causes" to a wider "complex of conditions . . . summed up in the term, culture."[1] This shift sets the "theme" of the analysis. The term, culture, thus used, makes for, fits into, or implements (1) a *pluralistic* conception of political problems; thus "culture" is an element of a generic perspective which would proceed (2) *specifically, step-by-step* and (3) which does *not see chasms, irreconcilable antagonisms, between a limited number of empowered structures.* Sociologically, it doubtless has general roots in the essential regionalism of a continental nation, in the diverse structures of various governmental units, and in the extreme heterogeneity of the population of the United States.

Monism, or the view that "one factor. . . is so predominant that it is *the* causal force," stands negated in this perspective. Monism is conceived as "wholesale reasons" from which we must escape for they are "as totalitarian as are the states ruled by dictators."[2]

(a) The polemic against Marxism arises in a context in which Marxism is taken as "typical . . . of the absolutism which results when the one factor in the interaction is isolated and made supreme." This "absolutism" is positively replaced by Dewey by a view of society which sees "social events . . . as *interactions* of components of human nature on one side with cultural conditions on the other."[3] Marxism is conceived as absolutism, as a "monistic block-universe theory of social causation," and as reducing "the human factor as nearly as possible to zero."

426

(b) Dewey does not oppose "the historian's" economic theory of history but against his statement of Marxism he puts the acceptable formulation as follows:

> ". . . historians have been content to point to our specific economic conditions operating in specific emergencies . . . The generalization to which historians have pointed is rather a practical maxim: If you wish to secure a certain political result, you must see to it that economic conditions are such as to tend to produce that result. If you wish to establish and maintain political self-government, you must see to it that conditions in industry and finance are not such as to militate automatically against your political aim."[4]

He does not "aim" to deny:

> "the role of economic factors in society nor at denying the tendency of the present economic regime to produce consequences adverse to democratic freedom. These things are rather taken for granted. Criticism aims to show what happens when this undeniable factor is isolated and treated as *the* cause of *all* social change."

(c) Another point made against Marxism is that it tends to block "investigation." Against this a cultural interactionist procedure is set forth:

> "To adopt and pursue this method would be in effect to abandon the all-comprehensive character of economic determination. It would put us in the relativistic and pluralistic position of considering a number of interacting factors — of which a very important one is undoubtedly the economic."

Apparently overlooking the ideological necessities of mass movements, Dewey sees Marxism as "unscientific" for:

> "it supposed a generalization that was made at a particular date and place (and made even then only by bringing observed facts under a premise drawn from a metaphysical source) can obviate the need for continued resort to observation, and to continual revision of generalizations in their office of working hypotheses. In the name of science, a thoroughly anti-scientific procedure was formulated, in accord with which a generalization is made having the nature of ultimate 'truth,' and hence holding good at all times and places."

(d) In connection with this and the point anent "absolutism," Dewey sees Marxism as similar to "theological systems of the past" for:

> "all absolutisms tend to assume a theological form and to arouse the kind of emotional ardor that has accompanied crusading religions in the past . . . the monolithic and in itself speculative Marxist doctrine took on immediate practical coloring in connection with existing economic conditions and new forms of oppressions they have produced."

(e) Dewey objects to calling Marxism "scientific," but the "probability and pluralism" of his own "cultural" view are conceived as "scientific."

> "For just as *necessity* and search for a *single* all-comprehensive law was typical of the intellectual atmosphere of the forties of the last century, so *probability* and *pluralism* are the characteristics of the present state of science."
>
> "Henceforth it is . . . pure willfulness if anyone pretending to a scientific treatment starts from any other than a pluralistic basis . . ."[5]

It is obvious that Marxism as a doctrine and movement has linked practice and theory; Dewey believes that intelligence or science combines these two. He wants to deny science and intelligence to Marxism and yet he has to admit that it, too, blends action and and thought. He does so by dating Marxism as "scientific practice" and by denouncing the character of its thought. Thus:

> "The inventor who translates an idea into a working technological device starts from examination of special materials and tries special methods for combining them. The practical techniques derived from the Marxist single all-embracing law of a single causative force follow the pattern discarded in scientific inquiry and in scientific engineering."

(f) Linked to several of the above enunciated objections (especially Dewey's restatement of "economic determinism") is the crushing blow:

"Marxism . . . in the name of science, denied moving power to human valuations."[6] [It] "throws out psychological as well as moral considerations. Whether the theory is in fact able to live up to this claim — without which its 'materialism' is meaningless — is another matter. For it would seem as if certain organic needs and appetites at least were required to set the 'forces of production' moving. But if this bio-psychological factor is admitted, then it must *interact* with 'external' factors, and there is no particular point at which its operation can be said to cease."[7]

The absence of this pluralist interactionist viewpoint in Marxism-as-seen-by-Dewey operates polemically; positively the view is identified with "democracy," which is possible for those "trained to take for granted the operation of an indefinite plurality of social tendencies, many of which are neither political nor economic..." And then the pluralistic view of causation is mated with equilibrium:

"If the result with us is often looseness of cohesion and indefiniteness in direction of action, there is generated a certain balance of judgment and some sort of equilibrium in social affairs. We take for granted the action of a number of diverse factors in producing any social result. There are temporary waves of insistence upon this and that particular measure and aim. But there is at least enough democracy so that in time any one tendency gets averaged up in interplay with other tendencies. An average present qualities that are open to easy criticism. But as compared with the fanaticism generated by monistic ideas when they are put into operation, the averaging of tendencies, a movement toward a mean, is an achievement of splendor."

And against this stands "monism," which "is accompanied in its practical execution by one-party control of press, schools, radio, the theater and every means of communication, even to effective restrictions imposed on private gatherings and private conversations."

In order fully to display Dewey's reasons for rejecting "Marxism," as well as "communism," the following points may be presented. Using "communist" to mean the "pattern set in the U.S.S.R." Dewey advances five reasons for the title, "Why I Am Not a Communist":[8]

(1) Such communism neglects the "specific historical backgrounds and traditions" of America.

(2) It is a "monistic and one-way philosophy of history" and neglects the "deeply rooted belief in the importance of individuality."

(3) Dewey is "profoundly skeptical of class war as *'the* means" of settling "class conflicts."

(4) The "emotional tone and methods of dispute" accompanying communism is repugnant.

(5) "A revolution effected solely or chiefly by violence can in a modernized society like our own result only in chaos."

The next major conception which is aided by the term "culture" is the reduction of the level of abstraction or narrowing of the sphere to be observed so that specific attacks on specific problems are indicated as the "correct" and "scientific" procedure for the handling of all political questions. The explicit linkage of pluralism and specificity of attack is displayed when Dewey tells us that:

> "We should forget 'society' and think of law, industry, religion, medicine, politics, art, education, philosophy — and think of them in the plural. For points of contact are not the same for any two persons and hence the questions which the interests and occupations pose are never twice the same . . . There is no society at large, nor business in general. Harmony with conditions is not a single and monotonous uniformity, but a diversified affair requiring individual attack."[9]

A monistic theory of causation is typically calculated for the arousal of mass action; a pluralistic view approaches political affairs in another manner. The necessities of exhortation in the case of mass action makes for monism but such action as a pluralist view may sustain is composed of many smaller acts. To be sure, even in pluralism the need or the wish for action might foster a Deweyan definition of "the cause" as that factor which is manipulated will bring about a proposed change. This conception is not quite politically consistent with a pluralism of Dewey's type and intention for it might lead to a conspiratorial theory in which a small compact force could make societal shifts possible by action against key positions in a social structure.

"Adequate experience" does not set up "wholesale theories." It fosters "intelligence" for the "first necessity is study of the scientifically cooperative type." Then perhaps we can gain:

"clearer recognition of the different interests . . . that have to be harmonized in any enduring solution."[10] "Any monolithic theory of social action and social causation tends to have a ready-made answer for problems that present themselves. The wholesale character of this answer prevents critical examination and discrimination of the particular facts involved in the actual problem. In consequence, it dictates a kind of all-or-none practical activity, which in the end introduces new difficulties."

Again this specificity, blended with a "democratic method," is manifest in the finale of this particular book:

"We must know that the dependence of ends upon means is such that the only *ultimate* result is the result that is attained today, tomorrow, the next day, and day after day, in the succession of years and generations. Only thus can we be sure that we face our problems in detail one by one as they arise, with all the resources provided by collective intelligence operating in co-operative action. At the end as at the beginning the democratic method is as fundamentally simple and as immensely difficult as is the energetic, unflagging, unceasing creation of an ever-present new road upon which we can walk together."

This drive for specification is central to Dewey's social philosophy and directly carried over from his logic. This matter has opposite sides. Negatively, and this is:

"the heart of the matter, [it opposes] various theories [which] suffer from a common defect. [Namely] they are all committed to the logic of general notions under which specific situations are to be brought. [Social philosophies have been] general answers supposed to have universal meaning . . . Hence they do not assist inquiry. They close it. [Furthermore] In transferring the issue from concrete situations to definitions and conceptual deductions, the effect, especially of the organic theory, is to supply the apparatus for intellectual justification of the established order."[11]

Apparently Dewey overlooks many abstract statements including Dewey's own quite general theory which proceeds in general definitions and concepts.[12]

Positively, the stress on specification in social philosophy means that social philosophers should be:

"helping men solve problems in the concrete by supplying them hypotheses to be used and tested in projects of reform. [He should address himself to] the concrete troubles and evils. The region of concrete difficulties, where the assistance of intelligent method for tentative plans for experimentation is urgently needed, is precisely where intelligence fails to operate. In this region of the specific and concrete, men are thrown back upon the crudest empiricism, upon short-sighted opportunism and the matching of brute forces. In theory, the particulars are all neatly disposed of . . . But in empirical fact they remain as perplexing, confused and unorganized as they were before. So they are dealt with not by even an endeavor at scientific method but by blind rule of thumb, citation of precedents, considerations of immediate advantage, smoothing things over, use of coercive force and the clash of personal ambitions."[13]

"Social theory" must be not "an idle luxury," but a "guiding method of inquiry and planning." "In the question of methods concerned with reconstruction of special situations rather than in any refinements in the general concepts of institution, individuality, state, freedom, law, order, progress, etc., lies the true impact of philosophical reconstruction." Which is to say, that positively, not a "logic of general notions" but inquiry, "intelligence," "scientific method" are to be used. In these contexts we grasp the heart of Dewey's social position, and we see again the political meaning of "inquiry." The kind of theory and inquiry that is urged is one that can catch the *kind* and the *scope* of the "action" that is contemplated.

"What is needed is specific inquiries into a multitude of specific structures and interactions."[14] Now it is fairly obvious that such inquiry and theories, if the word may be used here, would not be very well suited for action, *e.g.*, of revolutionary scale, nor indeed for the large scale planning of a society. It fits into a conception of many reform movements. For, "the object of knowledge" is "to gain the kind of understanding which is necessary to deal with problems as they arise."[15] It covers Hull House, for instance, or a Seabury investigation.[16] It is also rooted in a liberal desire to save or to reconstruct individuality.

"Individuality is inexpungable because it is a manner of distinctive sensitivity, selection, choice, response and utilization of conditions. For this reason, if for no other, it is impossible to develop integrated individuality by any all-embracing system or program."[17]

Dewey's own rationale, however, is not dominantly stated in political terms. *What he tries to do here as elsewhere is to state this political matter as an epistemological necessity of following the scientific method.* In the 1903 *Studies in Logical Theory* he wrote that if we follow:

> "practical deliberation and scientific research [we must adhere to the fundamental principle . . . that every reflective problem and operation arises with reference to some *specific* situation, and has to subserve a *specific* purpose dependent upon its own occasion."[18]

And in *Creative Intelligence* he links "science" and specificity of approach and of action:

> "For the growth of science has consisted precisely in the invention of an equipment, a technique of appliances and procedures, which, accepting all occurrences as homogeneously real, proceeds to distinguish the authenticated from the spurious, the true from the false, by specific modes of treatment in specific situations."[19]

Besides the general model of "science" which requires such specificity, there is also *the* element of this model, action, which points toward the "doing of something in particular."

> "Scientific method would teach us to break up, to inquire definitely and with particularity, to seek solutions in the terms of concrete problems as they arise. It is not easy to imagine the difference which would follow from the shift of thought to discrimination and analysis. Wholesale creeds and all-inclusive ideals are impotent in the face of actual situations; for doing always means the doing of something in particular."[20]

The conception of the problematic has already been noted as a mask for certain value-conflicts and the kind of structural antagonisms in society which generate them. The conception also operates in the tendency to specification. In the 1903 *Studies* we read:

> ". . . idea that this antecedent [which is not reflectional in character] has a certain structure and content of its own setting

the peculiar problem which evokes thought and gives the cue
to its specific activities . . . it is this latter point upon which we
would insist . . . "21

The wavering political force (and its polarization) of "scientific
method," and more specifically of "experiment," is finally set forth
in *Freedom and Culture:*

> "What purports to be experiment in the social field is very
> different from experiment in natural science; it is rather a proc-
> ess of trial and error accompanied with some degree of hope
> and a great deal of talk. Legislation is a matter of more or less
> intelligent improvisation aiming at palliating conditions by
> means of patchwork policies. The apparent alternative seems to
> be a concentration of power that points toward ultimate dicta-
> torship . . . the real problem is that of building up an intelligent
> and capable civil-service under conditions that will operate
> against formation of rigid bureaucracies."22

It should be clear that a drive toward specification, a pluralist
interactionist standpoint and a denial of "absolutist," "wholesale"
theories — that the angle of sight of these conceptions are not conducive, indeed prohibit, the discernment or the reconstruction of
power-issues and structural antagonisms. The role of "culture,"
e.g., in the mode of problem solving is sharply visible:

> ". . . the issue will define itself as utilization of the realities
> of a corporate civilization to validate and embody the distinc-
> tive moral element in the American version of individualism:
> Equality and freedom expressed not merely externally and
> politically but through personal participation in the develop-
> ment of a shared culture. 'Culture' here stands as 'community'
> within which 'the distinctive moral element' can live."23

Blending well with these conceptions is the idea of "experiment"
as it is manifested in social-political contexts. "It is not irrelevant,"
writes Dewey, ". . . that . . . Jefferson refers to the American Government as an *experiment*." It is not irrelevant to our purpose that
Dewey should recall this. For not only does the term culture serve
to guide attention and analysis into the three channels men-
tioned24 but it — and the slant which it implements — fits into
an orientation which sees the good society organized *communally,*
moreover, in a way that is unmistakably rural. Realizing that this

type of community is gone, this orientation is apt to become sad. Dewey often writes of how individuals:

> "find themselves in the grip of immense forces whose work-ings and consequences they have no power of affecting. The situation calls emphatic attention to the need for face-to-face associations, whose interactions with one another may offset if not control the dread impersonality of the sweep of present forces. There is a difference between a society, in the sense of an association, and a community. . . .Economic forces have im-mensely widened the scope of associational activities. But it has done so largely at the expense of the intimacy and directness of communal group interests and activities."[25]

He quotes from a previous book of his own, thus indicating the centrality of the point in his own mind.

> "Evils which are uncritically and indiscriminately laid at the door of industrialism and democracy might, with greater intel-ligence, be referred to the dislocation and unsettlement of lo-cal communities. Vital and thorough attachments are bred only in the intimacy of an intercourse which is of necessity restricted in range . . . It is possible to restore the reality of the less com-munal organizations and to penetrate and saturate their mem-bers with a sense of local community life . . ."[26]

The passage continues in *The Public and Its Problems:*

> "Democracy must begin at home, and its home is the neigh-borly community. It is outside the scope of our discussion to look into the prospects of the reconstruction of face-to-face com-munities. But there is something deep within human nature it-self which pulls toward settled relationships."[27]

So strong is this strain in Dewey that "community" is not only ideal-ized but it is almost identified with sociality itself:

> "anything that can be called a community in its pregnant sense there must be values prized in common. Without them, any so-called social group, class, people, nation, tends to fall apart into molecules having but mechanically enforced connec-tions with one another."[28]

And in this passage he does so identify communally oriented ac-tions with "society":

"Society is of course but the relations of individuals to one another in this form and that. And all relations are *interactions,* not fixed molds. The particular interactions that compose a human society include the *give and take of participation,* of a *sharing* that increases, that expands and deepens, the capacity and significance of the interacting factors . . . I often wonder what meaning is given to the term "society" by those who oppose it to the *intimacies of personal intercourse,* such as those of friendship. Presumably they have in their minds a picture of rigid institutions or some set and external organization."[29]

This communal orientation is not difficult to understand sociologically, given the shift in social conditions of character formation during the nineteenth century: a movement from a rural and small village economy to an industrial world dominated by metropolitan aggregations. It should be recalled that in general Dewey's career, as well as many of the careers of those making his publics, follow this structural transformation. No doubt this view on this point interacts with educational experience:

"We trust, and shall continue to trust, to the social spirit as the ultimate and controlling motive in discipline. We believe, and our past experience warrants us in the belief, that a higher, more effective, more truly severe type of personal discipline and government may be secured through appeal to the social motives and interests of children and youth than to their anti-social ones . . ."[30]

In the late thirties, invited to write a brief account of the meaning of democracy, it is understandable that Dewey should select the following point:

"When I think of the conditions under which men. . . .are living in many foreign countries . . . I am inclined to believe that the heart and final guarantee of democracy is in free gatherings of neighbors . . . For everything which bars freedom and fullness of communication sets up barriers . . . democratic way of life is undermined."[31]

In a chapter in *The Public and Its Problems* entitled "The Eclipse of the Public," he states the social composition originally underlying democracy of the conception he entertains:

> "American democratic polity was developed out of genuine community life, that is, association in local and small centers where industry was mainly agricultural and where production was carried on mainly with hand tools . . . Pioneer conditions put a high premium upon . . . neighborly sociability. The township . . . was the political unit . . . The state was a sum of such units. . . . "

Now with industrialization, things are bigger and more impersonal and "the Public seems to be lost; it is certainly bewildered."[32]

> ". . . The local face-to-face community has been invaded by forces so vast, so remote in initiation, so far-reaching in scope and so complexly indirect in operation, that they are, from the standpoint of the members of local social units, unknown."[33]

In the *Public and Its Problems*, Dewey sets out to grasp the conditions necessary for a reinstatement of a communal orientation of the democratic society. This is one of the central aims of the book. The other is the effort to save the individual and yet to advocate "social control."

The argument combines the demographic orientation to community with certain rationalist characteristics of the conception of "action." Rooted in a democracy which has lived in small homogeneous face-to-face and self-controlled communities, Dewey faces the impersonal industrial world. He begins characteristically with a consideration of human action. Human actions have consequences of two kinds: those which affect persons directly engaged in trans-actions and others which have effects beyond those so directly engaged in trans-actions and others which have effects beyond those so directly engaged. Action of the first type is private; the latter, public. The distinction is in terms of the extent and scope of the consequences of actions. When the latter type, that with indirect consequences, is recognized and regulated, we have the germ of a state.[34]

> ". . . the state is the organization of the public effected through officials for the protection of the interests shared by its members."

One thing Dewey is doing here is magnifying the conception of "an intelligent act." He is conceiving of society and of its elements as articulated elements serving a function within an intelligent action.

> "The public consists of all those who are affected by the indirect consequences of transactions to such an extent that it is deemed necessary to have those consequences systematically cared for. Officials are those who look out for and take care of the interests thus affected. Since those who are indirectly affected are not direct participants in the transactions in question, it is necessary that certain persons be set apart to represent them, and see to it that their interests are conserved and protected."

And, apparently assuming a homogeneous "monistic" view of society (or environment), he writes that "every serious political dispute turns upon the question whether a given political act is socially beneficial or harmful." In line with these conceptions, he conceives of the basis *of authority* not to reside in the "official" or in a "collective will" but in "consequences" which "private" persons can't control. The private and public is:

> ". . . not a difference between single human beings and a collective impersonal will. It is between persons in their private and in their official or representative character. The quality presented is not authorship but authority, the authority of recognized consequences to control the behavior which generates and averts extensive and enduring results of weal and woe. Officials are indeed public agents, but agents in the sense of factors doing the business of others in securing and obviating consequences that concern them."

The "state" is "the organization of the public"; the legitimation for this and its cause is as follows:

> "The characteristic of the public as a state springs from the fact that all modes of associated behavior may have extensive and enduring consequences which involve others beyond those directly engaged in them . . . Consequences have to be taken care of, looked out for. This supervision and regulation cannot be effected by the primary groupings themselves. For the essence of the consequences which call a public into being is the fact that they expand beyond those directly engaged in producing them. Consequently special agencies and measures must be formed if they are to be attended to; or else some existing group must take on new functions."

The very "formation of the states must be an experimental process," and:

> ". . . since conditions of action and of inquiry and knowledge are always changing, the experiment must always be retried; the State must be rediscovered."

This "alteration of political forms" can only be "directed" by "the use of intelligence to judge consequences" and therefore:

> "There is no antecedent universal proposition which can be laid down because of which the functions of a state should be limited or should be expanded. Their scope is something to be critically and experimentally determined."

In this "experimental" process and in the instrumentalizing of all forms of official action or of authority to "the public" even laws are not to be "viewed as commands." For:

> "Rules of law are in fact the institution of conditions under which persons make their arrangements with one another. . . . 'The law' formulates remote and long-run consequences. It then operates as a condensed available check on the naturally overweening influence of immediate desire and interest over decision. It is a means of doing for a person what otherwise only his own foresight, if thoroughly reasonable, could do."

The rationality implicit in this conception of authority as necessary to realize a Big Intelligent Act is not the only feature of this standpoint which deserves attention. For just as we began with the breakup of "communities" the analysis — and specifically the conditions for rationally based authority — is a re-institution of the *community* under the title of "public," which is identified with democracy:

> "What are the conditions [Dewey asks] under which it is possible for the Great Society to approach more closely and vitally the status of a Great Community, and thus take form in genuinely democratic societies and state? What are the conditions under which we may reasonably picture the Public emerging from its eclipse?"

Here we also discern the blending and the *mutual necessity for one another* of "intelligence" and "communal life" and their identification with "democracy":

"... one thing is certain. Unless local communal life can be restored, the public cannot adequately resolve its most urgent problem: to find and identify itself. But if it be reestablished, it will manifest a fullness, variety and freedom of possession and enjoyment of meanings and goods unknown in the contiguous associations of the past."

"The problem of securing diffused and seminal intelligence can be solved only in the degree in which local communal life becomes a reality. [For] Ideas which are not communicated, shared, and reborn in expression are but soliloquy, and soliloquy is but broken and imperfect thought."

"There is no limit to the liberal expansion and confirmation of limited personal intelligence endowment which may proceed from the flow of social intelligence when that circulates by word of mouth from one to another in the communications of the local community. That and that only gives reality to public opinion. We lie, as Emerson said, in the lap of an immense intelligence. But that intelligence is dormant and its communications are broken, inarticulate and faint until it possesses the local community as its medium."

This emphasis (in analysis and evaluation) upon the face-to-face village form of communal life is so strong in Dewey that he can write: "The invasion of the community by the new and relatively impersonal and mechanical modes of combined human behavior is the outstanding fact of modern life." That this term "community" is not merely a descriptive one is obvious enough; that community *is* democracy is equally obvious:

"... democracy is not an alternative to other principles of associated life. It is the idea of community life itself ... Wherever there is conjoint activity whose consequences are appreciated as good by all singular persons who take part in it, and where the realization of the good is such as to effect an energetic desire and effort to sustain it in being just because it is a good shared by all, there is in so far a community. The clear consciousness of a communal life, in all its implications, constitutes the idea of democracy."

Dewey's relativistic pluralism (as against absolutistic monism) is predicated on the fear of the impotence of individuals under a strong and controlling "state." Yet Dewey recognizes that "pecuniary" individualism is simply rule by corporations. By an *instrumental* view of the state, typical of most liberalisms, *and* a pluralist view of society, Dewey can allow "state" control and yet retain a sphere of freedom for the individual. This is further implemented by a definition of the state not only as instrumental, but as an organization of the *public*, which is to say, of the *community*. It is only in the community that individuality of the Deweyan type can live free of "external" and "mechanical" controls.

What are the means *by which* we get from the "impersonal" and "unintelligent" industrial society with its subordination of the individual to the "intelligent," "scientific," "democratic" *community* in which individuals can "share" and hence be coordinated? Dewey's answer is that social scientists must research on the current scene and that this research should be presented to the "masses" by "artists." For in order to "organize," the "public" must first "discover" itself. Since the social picture is now "impersonal" and not "community based," since "there are too many publics," this discovery is difficult. Therefore "the problem of a democratically organized public is primarily and essentially an intellectual problem, in a degree to which the political affairs of prior ages offer no parallel."

This "intellectual problem" cannot be "solved" even conceptually unless social scientists share their findings, for:

> ". . . a thing is fully known only when it is published, shared, socially accessible. Record and communication are indispensble to knowledge. Knowledge cooped up in a private consciousness is a myth, and knowledge of social phenomena is peculiarly dependent upon dissemination, for only by distribution can such knowledge be either obtained or tested. A fact of community life which is not spread abroad so as to be a common possession in a contradiction in terms . . .[sic!] Communication of the results of social inquiry is the same thing as the formation of public opinion."

It need not be elaborated here that the argument that "knowledge" requires communication and "sharing" by those that are to know, and therefore only if the findings of social scientists are *widely* diffused is "knowledge" possible, is thoroughly specious. Its motive is to make the end of gaining knowledge one with the creation of a "community;" it thus reinforces the tie-up of "democracy" and rational thinking.

It should be noted that "communication" (like community and "communion") is a word of great value for Dewey, for it is involved in the process of knowledge and in the sharing of the community.

> "... the Great Society is to become a Great Community; a society in which the ever-expanding and intricately ramifying consequences of associated activities shall be known in the full sense of that word, so that an organized, articulate Public comes into being. The highest and most difficult kind of inquiry and a subtle, delicate, vivid and responsive art of communication must take possession of the physical machinery of transmission and circulation and breathe life into it ... Democracy will come into its own, for democracy is a name for a free and enriching communion ... It will have its consummation when free social inquiry is indissolubly wedded to the art of full and moving communication."

Thus does "intelligence" involve "community" and with them both "democracy" is a reality.

Those occupations which would allow for Dewey's rationally thinking individual have declined since 1900. The social structure which they formed has undergone serious changes in the direction of bureaucratization. To the extent that his type of thought and action, and his call for its universal advocacy, correspond only to "liberal and free," knowledged occupations, he is "calling for" a reinstatement. He is fighting the drift into corporate forms of organization, fighting what formal rationality does to his liberal, individual thinking man. For in a deep sociological sense, in terms of occupational structure, John Dewey's perspective corresponds to a Jeffersonian social composition.

Two passages may briefly be examined in this connection: one, the comments and high praise of Jefferson himself, in *Freedom and Culture*:

> "I make no apology for linking what is said in this chapter with the name of Thomas Jefferson. For he was the first modern to state in human terms the principles of democracy. . . .The chief reason is that Jefferson's formulation is moral through and through . . ."[35]

And the following is very interesting. It is from "The Interpretation of Savage Mind."

"In conclusion, let me point out that the adjustment of habits to ends, through the medium of a problematic, doubtful, precarious situation, is the structural form upon which present intelligence and emotion are built. It remains the ground-pattern . . . we have not so much destroyed or left behind the hunting structural arrangement of mind, as we have set free its constitutive psycho-physic factors so as to make them available and interesting in all kinds of objective and idealized pursuits — the hunt for truth, beauty, virtue, wealth, social well-being, and even of heaven and of God."[36]

In the social-political sphere, Dewey's general slant is linked through the demographic shift to the concept "social." The "social" as a key and pervasive value in Dewey finds its correspondence in a rural past. He has talked much about the future, but his historical time-sense is such that he has tried to adapt ideals of a community long past to a present condition, although he has not considered the matter in just this form.

Dewey's use of the *social* cannot be *merely* welcomed as a contribution to "a sociological viewpoint." To take it merely as such would be to give up an important analytic lever which may yield added insight into his perspective. The term "social" in the thought of John Dewey has many shades of meaning. It is polarized against several other terms. It is not accidental that his stress upon it occurs in a cultural context which is beginning to deny in fact an individualistically organized society, yet a society in which individualism and independence are a dominant ideology. Psychologically, John Dewey's stress on the social, and the peculiar surrogates and synonyms he assigns to it, is rooted in a reaction against a growing *alienation* of which he is acutely aware.

We have seen the psychological reception given by Dewey to the thought of Hegel. It unified him and gave him a blend of "emotion and intellect" which he had not attained in any adolescent religion. It is directly from Hegel that he derived his concept of sociality. It is in American village life that it reposes. "In social feeling," Dewey wrote in 1887, "we merge our private life in the wider life of the community, and in doing so, immensely transcend self and realize our being in its widest way."[37] Sociologically, the concept for Dewey is anchored in a reaction against the isolation and the growing cleavages in a social framework that is entering high and corporate capitalism.[38] The orientation of Dewey strives to recognize and to make a value out of *interdependence*. He would have the character of this interdependence of a *Gemeinschaft* order. The social is the "shared," that which is of "common interests." "Communication" is the social and we share it, we "participate" in it.[39] Dewey's emphasis upon the social represents a cry to reinstitute (Dewey would never put it this way) that type of sociality that is Jeffersonian, that is rural.[40]

The clearest statement of the social in Dewey's writing occurs in *Democracy and Education*. It occurs, be it noted, under the title, "Criteria for a Good Society." Those who constantly write that Dewey has never set forth criteria may be referred to the following:

> ". . . the need of a measure for the worth of any given mode of social life . . . the problem is to extract the desirable traits of forms of community life which actually exist, and employ them to criticize undesirable features and suggest improvement. Now in any social group whatever, even in a gang of thieves, we find some interest held in common, and we find a certain amount of interaction and cooperative intercourse with other groups. From these two traits we derive our standard. How numerous and varied are the interests which are consciously shared? How full and free is the interplay with other forms of association?"[41]
>
> "The two points selected by which to measure the worth of a form of social life are the extent in which the interest of a group are shared by all its members, and the fullness and freedom with which it interacts with other groups. An undesirable society, in other words, is one which internally and externally sets up barriers to free intercourse and communication of experience. A society which makes provision for participation in its good of all its members on equal terms and which secures flexible readjustment of its institutions through interaction of the different forms of associated life is in so far democratic. Such a society must have a type of education which gives individuals a personal interest in social relationships and control, and the habits of mind which secure social changes without introducing disorder."
>
> "The isolation and exclusiveness of a gang or clique brings its anti-social spirit into relief. But this same spirit is found wherever one group has interests 'of its own' which shut it out from full interaction with other groups, so that its prevailing purpose is the protection of what it has got, instead of reorganization and progress through wider relationships. It marks na-

tions in their isolation from one another; families which seclude their domestic concerns as if they had no connection with a larger life; schools when separated from the interest of home and community; the divisions of rich and poor; learned and unlearned. The essential point is that isolation makes for rigidity and formal institutionalizing of life, for static and selfish ideals within the group."[42]

Such passages clearly indicate the "communal" orientation of John Dewey's perspective and the role of sociality in securing it.

1. *Freedom and Culture*, p. 6.

2. *Ibid.*, p. 39.

3. *Ibid.*, pp. 75-76 and 75.

4. *Ibid.*, p. 53; for following quotations *see* this source; pp. 76, 77, 87; 83 and 84.

5. *Psychological Review*, Vol. 24, p. 269.

6. *Freedom and Culture*, pp. 86 and 80.

7. *Freedom and Culture*, pp. 98-99; *see* this source for next three quota- pp. 94, 94-95, 89-90.

8. *The Meaning of Marx*, edited by Sidney Hook, (New York, 1934), pp. 88-90.

9. *Individualism —Old and New*, pp. 166-67.

10. *Freedom and Culture*, pp. 72-73. See this source for next 2 footnotes, pp. 100, 176.

11. *Reconstruction in Philosophy*, p. 188 and pp. 188-89.

12. However, in so far as Dewey has influenced "political science," as an academic discipline, he has been an influence making for specific studies. *See* Geo. H. Sabine, "The Pragmatic Approach to Political Science," *American Political Science Review*, (24, Feb.-Nov., 1930), pp. 865-86 for an account of the influence of Dewey's general position upon Veblen and W. C. Mitchell, and, in law, upon W. W. Cook and H. Oliplant. The net impact is seen in detailed empirical studies viewed as instrumental to reshaping institutions in terms of given "purposes."

13. *Reconstruction i nPhilosophy*, p. 192.

14. *Ibid.*, pp. 193, 198.

15 John Dewey, editor, *New York and the Seabury Invesgigation: A Digest and Interpretation.* Published and copywritten by "The City Affairs Committee of New York," 1933. The mixture of civil service and "politics" — results in "inefficient and incompetent" officials, "waste of taxpayer's money;" in addition the "power of the dominant political machines ... has developed in many people a feeling of indifference and cynicism." — These are "the Significance of the Seabury Disclosures." pp. 38-39.

16. *Individualism — Old and New*, p. 168. A more precise linking of

pluralism (polarized against monism) with the attempt to preserve individuality will be set forth later.

17. *The Quest For Certainty*, p. 17; *see* also pp. 42-43 and 48.

18. *Ibid.*, p. 50.

19. *Studies*, p. 37.

20. *Studies*, p. 4.

21. Dewey, "The Need for a Recovery of Philosophy," p. 58.

22. *Freedom and Culture*, p. 65.

23. Dewey, *Individualism Old and New*, pp. 33-34.

24. That is, a pluralist-interactionist view of society, and hence, specific action on specific "factors" and avoidance of confrontation with political issues in larger structural and power terms.

25. *Freedom and Culture*, pp. 159-60.

26. *Ibid.*, p. 160. Quoted from *The Public and Its Problems*, pp. 212-13.

27. *The Public and Its Problems*, p. 213.

28. *Freedom and Culture*, p. 12.

29. *Individualism Old and New*, pp. 85-86. My italics.

30. *A Treasury of Democracy*, Norman Cousins, Ed. (N.Y., 1942), p. 194.

31. *The Public and Its Problems*, pp. 111, 116.

32. Dewey, in 1904, quoted by Mayhew and Edwards, *The Dewey School; The Laboratory School of the University of Chicago 1896-1903*, p. 16.

33. *The Public and Its Problems*, p. 131.

34. *The Public and Its Problems*, (N.Y., 1927), p. 12. This is the source of the following quotations. The following pages correspond to them in the order given: 33, 15 and 16, 15, 18 and 19, 27, 33-34, 45, 74, 53 and 56, 157 (*see* also 142), 216, 217-18, 219, 98, 148-49, 126, 176-77, 184.

35. *Freedom and Culture*, p. 55.

36. *Philosophy and Civilization* (N.Y., 1931), p. 187.

37. The "pecuniary" is much disliked by Dewey precisely because of its *impersonality*.

38. Note that increased *participation* tends to be a solutional model for the existence of immigrants; this "problem" was in Dewey's Hull-House focus.

39. The other major orientation and meaning of the social is in a psychological context. This will be documented below. Here only the demographic orientation of the concept is to be indicated.

40. *Democracy and Education*, p. 96.

41. *Psychology*, 515f.

42. *Ibid.*, pp. 115 and 99.

23

Social Psychology: Model for Liberals

"Social Darwinism" and instinctivist psychology were a thorn in the political flesh of liberalism. Both these inferences from evolution fitted a laissez-faire faith and a traditional policy of individualism. The neo-Comteanism of Ward — its utilitarian view of science, its social meliorism and telesis of progress, its foresight formulation, and its faith in education — all these were anti-Spencerian, anti-laissez-faire.[1]

Now there were two features of the general instinctivist view which liberals wished to overcome or to replace: they wanted to give mind, rationality, a place in nature and in the psychology of human affairs; and they wanted to see human nature as modifiable through the reconstruction of the social "environment." They wanted substantive rationality to prevail and to be diffused by mass education, but they wanted to deny the political implications of historical individualism.[2] It is between these two poles that the social psychological tradition of pragmatism is worked out.[3] In William James the substantive rationality is so played up and so wedded to individualism that the "social" in the psychology suffers badly, and his political views are not as "social" as are Dewey's.

Dewey is entirely too "generous" when he writes:

"The objective biological approach to the Jamesian psychology led straight to the perception of the importance of distinctive social categories, especially communication and participation. It is my conviction that a great deal of our philosophizing needs to be done over again from this point of view, and that there will ultimately result an integrated synthesis in a philosophy congruous with modern science and related to actual needs in education, morals, and religion."[4]

Dewey could see this "led straight" only because his social slant and motives refracted his understanding of James so as to stress the plasticity in the view and lead to recognition of the social to an extent which James would never have accepted.

Now it is precisely the importance of the accomplishment of Dewey, and in this connection even more so of G. H. Mead, that the *social* angle is intrinsically knit to the *rational*: the answer to the tension is a *social* theory of *mind*. And this is the mudsill of the liberal psychology of Dewey. With this recognition of *social* influences as molding the person, the fate of the individual who must carry the *rationality* is jeopardized. That is why this tradition from Ward, through Dewey, to W. I. Thomas and Mead has gone in for education. For this tension between the substantive rationality of an individual and the "anti-individualist" orientation and implication of social influences makes a social education of the individual come squarely to the front. *Biological individualism*, classically put in modern times by instinctivism, is replaced by *sociological* rationality: by a perspective which makes rational mind, individuality itself strongly dependent upon social "education."[5]

> "If mind [Dewey writes] in any definitely concrete sense of that word, is an offspring of the life of association, intercourse, transmission, and accumulation rather than a ready-made antecedent cause of these things, then the attitude of polite aloofness of condescending justification as to social institutions has its nerve cut, and with this the intellectual resources of sanctified conservatism disappear." [Mind is a product of the] shared life of the place and time, [and the kind of mind that develops] depends upon the kind of objects of attention and affection which the specific social conditions supply."[6]

That answered both a biological determinism and a laissez-faire type of calculating individualism. No wonder that Dewey has said that his philosophy was best expressed for a long time by his educational writings, which are, of course, strongly imprinted by social psychological views.

In England, Graham Wallas[7] retreated from an earlier instinctivism in the name of its anti-intellectuality; he wanted a view of "thinking" that is no "mere servant of the lower passions." He refused to polarize and separate "instinct" and "intelligence," preferring a hyphenated form, "instinct-intelligence." Thus intelligence itself becomes "elemental," biologized as it were, and thought is reinstated in the range of man's actions. Hobhouse also wishes to "effect a complete revolution in the position" assigned to "mind."[8] Both of these English liberals made an effective challenge to Spencer, and they did so in terms of the Darwinian model. But Dewey and the other pragmatists exceeded them.

That Dewey's social psychology is conceived as a contribution to morals in the eighteenth century sense is an important fact in grasping this social psychology and, indeed, of Dewey's larger style of reasoning.[9] The stated point of view is the Humean one:

> "that a knowledge of human nature provides a map or chart of all humane and social subjects, and that with this chart in our possession we can find our way intelligently about through all the complexities of the phenomena of economics, politics, religious beliefs, etc."

To Hume's angle is added the recognition of "the pervasive and powerful influence of what anthropologists call culture in shaping the concrete manifestations of every human nature subject to its influence."

In a 1929 preface Dewey brings to the fore the nature-nurture controversy: he states that he wants "to keep the two forces in balance." And then, very significantly:

> "There is, I hope, due emphasis upon the power of cultural habitude and trend in diversifying the forms assumed by human nature. But there is also an attempt to make clear that there are always intrinsic forces of a common human nature at work; forces which are sometimes stifled by the encompassing social medium but which also in the long course of history are always striving to liberate themselves and to make over social institutions so that the latter may form a freer, more transparent and more congenial medium for their operation. 'Morals' in its broad sense is a function of the interaction of these two forces."

We can formulate a socially oriented principle which underlies all that Dewey says on this issue. With it we can explain and predict what he will say on given issues. It is this: *he will always take a view that leaves man's biologized nature plastic enough to make social reforms possible, but he will try to keep it unitary enough*

to be the seat and anchor and implicit standard of certain values.
He will deny fixed "instincts," but keep modifiable "impulses," and
thus steer clear of determinism on either side and allow for freedom. In the last analysis, human nature will be good if it is left
alone, but to be good it must have a good society. A good society
is one "congenial" to the "potentiality," "growth," the workings of
human nature. Again, he will not lose the individual, the center of
"intelligence" and the agent of social change, but the individual
will not become a passionate, instinctive animal. He will be a "social" creature, and in this sociality will reside some of his goodness
and his rationality. He will avoid social determinism of man and of
morals, because this would mean "the level of colorless conformity;"
it would mean loss of individuality and loss of a "standard" rooted
at least loosely in man. Yet, on the other hand, he does not "roman-
tically glorify" individuality: for, "subjection to passion" is not "a
manifestation of freedom."

Each of the key concepts of the statement serves a definite function in presenting and sustaining the orientation of these underlying propositions.

The political slant of liberalism overtly crosses the psychological
when "two schools of social reform" are set forth and a third, a mediatory conception, is advanced by Dewey: on the one hand we
have a:

> "notion of a morality which springs from an inner freedom,
> something mysteriously cooped up within personality. It asserts
> that the only way to change institutions is for men to purify
> their own hearts, and that when this has been accomplished,
> change of institutions will follow of itself. The other school de-
> nies the existence of any such inner power, and in so doing
> conceives that it has denied all moral freedom. It says that men
> are made what they are by the forces of the environment, that
> human nature is purely malleable, and that till institutions are
> changed, nothing can be done."

But Dewey finds the way out by the concept "interaction":

> ". . . all conduct is *interaction* between elements of human
> nature and the environment, natural and social. Then we shall
> see that progress proceeds in two ways, and that freedom is
> found in that kind of interaction which maintains an environ-

ment in which human desire and choice count for something.
There are in truth forces in man as well as without him. While
they are infinitely frail in comparison with exterior forces, yet
they may have the support of a foreseeing and contriving intelligence. When we look at the problem as one of an adjustment to be intelligently attained, the issue shifts from within
personality to an engineering issue, the establishment of arts of
education and social guidance."

This passage seems quite significant, for:

(i) it permits "intelligence" to save the individual, while at the
same time it recognizes "environmental" forces.

(ii) Because of the latter recognition, it shifts the issue to a technological level. It is an "engineering issue." This, of course, opens
a space for the appeal to science. Notice in the following the biological conception of this science in a moral posture:

> "Each sign of disregard for the moral potentialities of physi-
> cal science drafts the conscience of mankind away from con-
> cern with the interactions of man and nature which must be
> mastered if freedom is to be a reality."

The same strategy, moving from the nature-nurture issue to the
liberal and engineering standpoint is evidenced in later chapters
of *Human Nature and Conduct*. In his more extended treatment
of the plasticity of "human nature," we recognize the basic dialectic
of Dewey's style of reasoning, culminating in a liberal mediation
of "extremes." On the one hand, John Locke and other "early re-
formers" were:

> "inclined to minimize the significance of native activities, and
> to emphasize the possibilities inherent in practice and habit-ac-
> quisition. There was a political slant to this denial of the native
> and a priori, this magnifying of the accomplishments of
> acquired experience. It held out a prospect of continuous de-
> velopment, of improvement without end."

On the other hand, the conservative:

> "has thought to find in the doctrine of native instincts a sci-
> entific support for asserting the practical unalterability of hu-
> man nature. Circumstances may change, but human nature re-

> mains from age to age the same. Heredity is more potent than environment, and human heredity is untouched by human intent. Effort for a serious alteration of human institutions is utopian."

Dewey accepts neither. For:

> "the radical reformer rests his contention in behalf of easy and rapid change upon the psychology of habits, of institutions in shaping raw nature, and the conservative grounds his counter-assertion upon the psychology of instincts. As a matter of fact, it is precisely custom which has greatest inertia, which is least susceptible of alteration; while instincts are most readily modifiable through use, most subject to educative direction."

Both the shortcut revolutionist and the die-hard conservative are mistaken in their views of human nature and *therefore* in the tempo and possibilities of human change which they respectively envision. For "actual social change is never so great as is apparent change." Then Dewey proceeds to take the question of historical change out of the context of psychology *per se:* to locate it in "customs."

> "Those who argue that social and moral reform is impossible on the ground that the Old Adam of human nature remains forever the same, attribute however to native activities the permanence and inertia that in truth belong only to acquired customs."

He then goes into a social and pluralist view of history and institutions. And the problem is again seated within "interactions."

> "Pugnacity and fear are no more native than are pity and sympathy. The important thing morally is the way these native tendencies interact, for their interaction may give a chemical transformation not a mechanical combination."

After indicating that war is not rooted in any one or even two "instincts," but is "a function of social institutions" he cites James' essay on war approvingly and states: "A general social re-organization is needed which will redistribute forces, immunize, divert and nullify." It should be noticed here that his own analysis leads him away from a specification of the locus of war-making forces. He is pushed upon a high and general level of abstraction, a level incommensurate with his epistemological exhortations.

> "History does not prove the inevitability of war, but it does prove that customs and institutions which organize native powers into certain patterns in politics and economics will also generate the war-pattern. The problem of war is difficult because it is serious. It is none other than the wider problem of the effective moralizing or humanizing of native impulses in times of peace."

Dewey's larger model in terms of which "social problems" are conceived is (a) on the *social* plane, that is, he rejects a psychological definition via instincts, *e.g.*, and more precisely, on this social plane difficulties are defined in terms of:

(b) the "lag" of habits in the face of change, more especially, technological change. This leads to a "truer psychology" for "the trouble lies in the inertness of established habit."

In putting the problem on a social plane he gets away from the conservative who would seal the status quo in the nature of man. In recognizing the force of habit and custom he avoids the "short cut revolutionary" who would urge a change of conditions very quickly. For, writes Dewey, "Man is a creature of habit, not of reason nor yet of instinct."

The conception of habit, which is one of the three key terms of Dewey's psychology, is ideally calculated to mediate the instinctivist with a conservative political implication, and extreme environmentalism with its revolutionary import, "Habit" could almost have been deduced by Dewey to fulfill this mediation.

Habit is *acquired* and it is *not* merely "repetition." Dewey wants to keep man modifiable; even from the "acquired" side he wants no ball-and-chain conceptions.[10] He wants to make habit a lag which sets problems (and hence constitutes a limen for intelligence), and, at the same time, he wants adaptability to be a feature of human nature. The meaning of habit is shaped by these two motives.

In order to avoid the "repetition" meaning of habit Dewey bends over backwards to make it dynamic: "habit means will."[11] It is a motivational affair as well as a stabilizer, for, taken consecutively, one's habits form one's character. There are several meanings given to habit, as G. W. Allport has noted, there are no criteria advanced by Dewey for distinguishing between habit as motivational and dynamic, and habit as a lagging repetition.[12] We are, however, not surprised to realize that Dewey's concepts can deal better with adaptive shifts and changes in personality than with its more stable aspects.

This seating of motivation within the ambivalence of the conception of habit gets Dewey away from the wild animal man of James, with his uncontrollable passions. It makes easier, as we shall see, a view of man's rationality and, more importantly, it definitely implements a Socratic ethic. For if Dewey's account of habit is accepted, it becomes more difficult to raise the question of motivation for acting upon the good after it is discerned. Indeed, we are further along than that. It tends to seat the good in the easy workings of released impulses controlled by intelligently composed habits.

> "The word habit may seem twisted somewhat from its customary use when employed as we have been using it. But we need a word to express that kind of human activity which is influenced by prior activity and in that sense acquired; which contains within itself a certain ordering or systematization of minor elements of action; which is projective, dynamic in quality, ready for overt manifestation; and which is operative in some subdued subordinate form even when not obviously dominating activity. Habit even in its ordinary usage comes nearer to denoting these facts than any other word."[13]

Given this action of habit (which is identified with "attitude" and "predisposition") what is then needed is only a release of "positive forms of action" (*i.e.*, good ones).

> "If we perceive that they [attitude and disposition] denote positive forms of action which are released merely through removal of some counteracting 'inhibitory' tendency, and then become overt, we may employ them instead of the word habit to denote subdued, non-patent forms of the latter."[14]

The tacit assumption underlying these passages and forming the perspective in which they are to be understood is that "human nature" is good. It is a literal faith in man's goodness if "he" is let alone to grow under proper community conditions. This assumption is again evident in the conception of "growth" which is used as a norm within educational theory.

All orientations and tensions in the social psychology have their reflexes, at least, in the educational context.

First, of course, is the fact that this psychology's stress on the modifiability of human nature opens wide the possibility of improvement by means of the educational enterprise. The classification of "psychology" into *physiological* or *social* obviously suits the stress on modifiability, indeed, it opens the way for a *social* theory of mind, which is at once the chief outcome of Dewey's social psychology and which is slanted specifically to *educational* endeavors. It is significant that Dewey credits Mrs. Young, with whom he was associated primarily in an educational context, with inspiring this view: "I owe chiefly to association with Mrs. Young the depth of my conviction that all psychology that isn't physiological is social."[15]

This educational wish to see man as modifiable has its implication for the focus of Dewey, his selective omission of certain topics. Despite the fact that educators have been absorbed in capacity testing, Dewey has never been interested in I.Q. tests. *Anyone* is capable of thinking, of securing his adaptation. "Barring physical defect or disease, slowness and dullness in all directions are comparatively rare."[16]

In more technical debates concerning choice of curricula, it should be recalled that "faculty psychology" buttressed the discipline idea of certain formal subjects. The shift in occupational structure within which educational institutions are anchored was antagonistic to these subjects, clamored for a different set. In going against faculty types of psychology and the theories of mind underpinning them, Dewey was, therefore, aiding the newer occupational imperatives for education.

The modifiability of man is a leverage precisely for reform and "universal education" becomes thereby a psychologically possible and portentious ideal. The psychology of habits thus connects with an education interest.

> "... the cold fact of the situation is that the chief means of continuous, graded, economical improvement and social rectification lies in utilizing the opportunities of educating the young to modify prevailing types of thought and desire. The young

are not as yet as subject to the full impact of established customs."[17]

But the matter does not end here, for this focus upon the young makes possible the tacit anchorage of *values* in the child. The fact of the modifiability of the young is construed as a source of potential social value.

> "The combined effect of love of power, timidity in the face of the novel and a self-admiring complacency has been too strong to permit immature impulse to exercise its reorganizing potentialities. The younger generation has hardly even knocked frankly at the door of adult customs, much less been invited in to rectify through better education the brutalities and inequities established in adult habits."

Thus:

> "Original modifiability has not been given a fair chance to act as a trustee for a better human life. It has been loaded with convention, biased by adult convenience. It has been practically rendered into an equivalent of non-assertion of originality, a pliant accommodation to the embodied opinions of others."

And the character of this value inherent in modifiability is independent individuality: "That the most precious part of plasticity consists in ability to form habits of independent judgment and of inventive initiation has been ignored." In the following, read the plus-adjectives of Dewey's vocabulary as used in his "description" of a child's life.

> "Yet [even adults] wish a different life for the generation to come. In order to realize that wish they may create a special environment whose main function is education. In order that education of the young be efficacious in inducing an improved society, it is not necessary for adults to have a formulated definite ideal of some better state. An educational enterprise conducted in this spirit would probably end merely in substituting one rigidity for another. What is necessary is that habits be formed which are more intelligent, more sensitively percipient, more informed with foresight, more aware of what they are about, more direct and sincere, more flexibly responsive than those now current. Then they will meet their own problems and propose their own improvements."

Here the notion of habit as dynamic, plus the values implicitly seated in the nature of the child, again makes less possible the raising of the moral question as to what values we are to "teach" in educational enterprises. This item comes out more explicitly in the concept of "growth," which operates as a norm under the guise of a description. For the:

> "aim of education is to enable individuals to continue their education [or] . . . the object and reward of learning is continued capacity for growth. Now this idea cannot be applied to *all* the members of a society except where intercourse of man with man is mutual, and except where there is adequate provision for the reconstruction of social habits and institutions by means of wide stimulation arising from equitably distributed interests. And this means a democratic society. In our search for aims in education, we are not concerned, therefore, with finding an end outside of the educative process to which education is subordinate. Our whole conception forbids."[18]
> "Education is thus a fostering, a nurturing, a cultivating, process. All of these words mean that it implies attention to the *conditions of growth* . . . the ideal of growth results in the conception that education is a constant reorganizing or reconstructing of experience. It has all the time an immediate end, and so far as activity is educative, it reaches that end — the direct transformation of the quality of experience."[19]

When "growth" is defined, Dewey gets very formal. The possibility of "good growth" and "bad growth" is not entertained, nor does "educational growth" tell us how to decide between them.

> "Our net conclusion is that life is development, and that developing, growing, is life. Translated into its educational equivalents, this means (i) that the educational process has no end beyond itself; it is its own end; and that (ii) the educational process is one of continual reorganizing, reconstructing, transforming . . . Growth is regarded as *having* an end, instead of *being* an end . . . Since in reality there is nothing to which growth is relative save more growth, there is nothing to which education is subordinate save more education.[20]

Dewey repudiates the notion of education as "unfolding," or as "preparation." Either view would lead to questions of goal setting. But education as growth is calculated to avoid just such questions. The same strain has Rousseauian political eventuations. What he stands for, liberalism, here consists in "the development of the inherent capacities of individuals . . ."[21] He cites Emerson approvingly:

> "Respect the child. But not too much his parents . . . Also respect yourself . . . The two points in a boy's training are, to keep his *nature* and train off all but that; to keep his *nature*, but stop off his uproar, fooling, and horseplay; keep his nature and *arm it with knowledge in the very direction* it points.[22]

Throughout Chapter IV of *Democracy and Education* he underplays the degree to which the adult sets the child's learning. For this purpose, the concept of "growth" is useful. All of his concepts in this chapter are positive: "immaturity," is the "ability" or "power" to "develop" or to "grow." "Dependence" means "interdependence;" it also means "plasticity" which does not signify "putty," but "power to develop dispositions." Again, "habits" are not mechanical but, in this context, become "expressions of growth." A habit is "a form of executive skill, of efficiency in doing . . . and ability to use natural conditions as means to ends."[23] This conception aids in keeping the child as a center of Deweyan social change. He wants *not* to throw educational issues upon the moral, political plane where decisions between adults must be made. He wants to root change as well as its directions in the child. Seeing the child as "social" implements this motive, as does Dewey's seating of "social control" in "the situation." Indeed, Dewey thinks it might be well if adults would or could get back to the child's world in certain moral and intellectual matters: they "must become as little children."[24]

Lastly, it should be noted that the educational and psychological concepts of Dewey mutually buttress one another in the conception of the place of intelligence. For since intelligence plays a dynamic, yet mediatory, role in the changing social situations, there is a still firmer basis for a faith in education which will foster the growth of intelligence. Morally and politically, intelligence is enough, and education builds it.

The three central categories of Dewey's psychology are habit, impulse, and intellect. Each of these categories stands in a definite relation with each of the others. In the most general way, the schema runs like this: action runs along on habit, some obstacle blocks the action, impulse arises and tries to make its way to action. Prior habit and now impulse are in conflict. A problem then exists. Enter intelligence, which mediates between impulse and habit, thus facilitating the release of action, which will be a projection of existent habits newly combined so as to satisfy the stymied impulse. Several other relations between habit, impulse, and intelligence are possible, but they are to be scorned. Impulse may not get to "useful production" and this, in the Puritanical conception of the place of such things, is not so good: "Castles in the air like art have their source in a turning of impulse away from useful production . . . fancy remains an end in itself."[25]

Habits are necessary for thought; they restrict its reach, "fix its boundaries" but they are also "positive agencies"; "formed in . . . exercising biological aptitudes" they are agents of "observation, collection, foresight and judgment . . ." Although they do not "know" the obstacles they override, "we may . . . be said to *know how* by means of our habits."[26]

What is Dewey doing here? He is seating rational processes in biology. On the one hand, we have the eighteenth century "man is a rational creature;" on the other, we have the nineteenth century, "man is animal." But Dewey would have man rational, or at the very least would make for the possibility of man as rational *because* he is an animal. Conscious rationality is not operative in habitual behavior no matter how "rational" habits grounded in biological aptitudes may be. A "disturbed adjustment of organism and environment" must come about before an "old habit and the new impulse" can come to terms.[27]

Impulse is seated in an individual. It is this impulse which "determines the direction of movement;" it "defines the peering, the search, the inquiry" which will release it by that reconstructing of habit and impulse known as intelligence. In this deliberation we dramatically rehearse (in imagination) "various competing possible lines of action." "Choice" consists in "hitting in imagination upon the object which furnishes an adequate stimulus to the recovery of overt action." Mind is then "unified." Again the side workings of the scheme which have been pointed out are avoided:

"We may not look far enough ahead because we are hurried into action by stress of impulse; but we may also become overinterested in the delights of reflection; we become afraid of assuming the responsibilities of decisive choice and action, and in general be sicklied over by a pale cast of thought. We may become so curious about remote and abstract matters that we give only a begrudged, impatient attention to the things right about us. We may fancy we are glorifying the love of truth for its own sake when we are only indulging a pet occupation and slighting demands of the immediate situation."[28]

We are "irrational" if either habit or impulse wins out. And "end" should not be "so fixed, a passion . . . so absorbing, that the foresight of consequences is warped to include only what furthers execution of its predetermined bias." We are "rational" if by deliberation "old aims and habits" are remade, and thus a "love of new ends and acts" is instituted.

In this biologized and Puritanic schema of the place and meaning of rational thought the adjustment of man to nature is reproduced in microcosm of the rational individual. The political controls which operate on this statement are constant:

"The oscillation between impulse arrested and frozen in rigid custom and impulse isolated and undirected is seen most conspicuously when epochs of conservatism and revolutionary ardor alternate. But the same phenomenon is repeated on a smaller scale in individuals."

It is also true that this statement is so made as to give foundation for a moral theory which will break down the distinction between the expedient and the moral.[29] "Morality," writes Dewey, "is an endeavor to find for the manifestation of impulse in special situations an office of refreshment and renewal. The endeavor is not easy of accomplishment."[30]

However, intelligence, and intelligence alone, can accomplish it:

"There is but one issue involved in all reflection upon conduct: The rectifying of present troubles, the harmonizing of present incompatibilities by projecting a course of action which gathers into itself the meaning of them all. The recognition of the psychology also reveals to us the nature of good or satisfaction. Good consists in the meaning that is experienced to belong to an activity when conflict and entanglement of various incompatible impulses and habits terminate in a unified orderly release in action. This human good, . . . [is] a fulfilment, conditioned upon thought . . ."

With "rigid habits" and traditions there is no meaning at all. And since the world changes, they will plunge us in "disaster." Again, when the ends of impulse are "frozen and isolated" they cannot operate in the quest for good. That the moral issue is loaded with assumptions is clear by the very definition of intelligence. For instance it is interesting to see "business calculation" ruled out[31] because it is:

"obviously of the kind where the end is taken for granted and does not enter into deliberation. It resembles the case in which a man has already made his final decision . . . His end-in-view already exists; it is not questioned . . . Deliberation *is* not free but occurs within the limits of a decision reached by some prior deliberation or else fixed by unthinking routine."[32]

And hence:

"A radical distinction thus exists between deliberation where the only question is whether to invest money in this bond or that stock, and deliberation where the primary decision is as to the *kind* of activity which is to be engaged in."

Morally, this is:

"the substantial fact: Ends are foreseen consequences which arise in the course of activity and which are employed to give activity added meaning and to direct its further course. They are in no sense ends *of* action. In being ends of *deliberation* they are redirecting pivots *in* action."[33]

And thus, the "categorical imperative" does "so act as to increase the meaning of present experience."[34] The moral ideal is, therefore, the thoughtful life in Dewey's special meaning of thoughtful as the intelligent. We thus end, as we began, with a view of intelligence as central precisely because its statement is shaped to fit the moral, educational, and political values of Dewey's style of liberalism.

1. *Dynamic Sociology.* Many passages of this book could almost have been written by John Dewey.

2. In this connection, *see* Baldwin's blast, *Social and Ethical Interpretations in Mental Development*, p. 96f.

3. The structure of Mead's conceptual apparatus is clearly a bridge of this tension: Specifically, the "I" of a liberal individual and the "me" of a sociologized conscience. In terms of this tension between rationality and individuality Mead would stand opposite James, for Mead would seat rationality itself in the social process; for him mind became a little parliament, or an "inner forum." Both celebrate the self. But Mead's celebration of the self is a social fiesta, James' is the celebration of a man alone. Mead's "me" is closest approximated in James by "habit" which although socially acquired is a very definite possession of the individual. For James, society is held together by habituated individuals; for Mead, individuals are held together by the social process. "Habit," wrote James, "is thus the enormous fly wheel of society." *Principles of Psychology*, Vol. I, 21. However, *see* James' discussion of the "social self" which is tied *organically* at all points. It should also be kept in mind that for James the self is "the sum total of all that he [the individual] can call his." *Ibid.*, Vol. I, p. 291.

4. "From Absolutism to Experimentalism," pp. 25-26.

5. "... 'mind' ... represents something acquired ... It is a formation, not a datum; a product, and a cause only after it has been produced." *Psychology Rev.*, Vol. 24, p. 271.

6. *Ibid.*, p. 274.

7. *The Great Society*, pp. 39, 42-43, 53.

8. *Development and Purpose*, pp. 10-12.

9. *Human Nature and Conduct*, (Mod. Lib. ed.), Preface. This is the source for the following quotations. These pages correspond to the paginations in the order given: vi, vii, viii, viii-ix, 5-6, 7, 9, 10, 11, 106, 106-7, 107, 108, 109, 111, 115, 115, 115, 125, 125, 41.

10. See G. W. Allport in *Philosophy of John Dewey*, p. 270.

11. Human Nature and Conduct, p. 41.

12. *Philosophy of John Dewey*, p. 275.

13. Human Nature and Conduct, pp. 40-41.

14. *Ibid.*, p. 41.

15. McManis, *E. F. Young*, p. 121.

16. *How We Think*, p. 35. G. W. Allport has noted Dewey's lack of interest in any "capacity psychology." "Dewey's Individual and Social Psychology," *The Philosophy of John Dewey*, P. A. Schilpp. Ed., p. 277.

17. *Human Nature and Conduct*, p. 127. The quotations which follow are from this source and correspond to its pagination in the following order: 96, 97, 97, 127, 128.

18. *Democracy and Education*, p. 117.

19. *Ibid.*, p. 12, 89.

20. *Ibid.*, pp. 59-60.

21. *Liberalism and Social Action*, p. 32.

22. *Democracy and Education*, p. 62.

23. *Ibid.*, p. 55.

24. *Ibid.*, p. 50; *see* also p. 58.

25. *Human Nature and Conduct*, pp. 163-64.

26. *Ibid.*, pp. 172, 175, 176, 177.

27. *Ibid.*, p. 179.

28. *Ibid.*, pp. 190, 192 and 197-98.

29. *Ibid.*, pp. 98, 169-70, *See* page 210.

30. *Ibid.*, p. 169. The quotations which follow are from this source, in the following order: 210, 211, 227.

31. Yet note the ambivalence: "A business man proceeds by comparing today's liabilities and assets with yesterday's, and projects plans for tomorrow by a study of the movement thus indicated in conjunction with study of the conditions of the environment now existing. It is not otherwise with the business of living.

32. *Ibid.*, p. 215.

33. *Ibid.*, pp. 217 and 225.

34. *Ibid.*, p. 283.

POSTSCRIPT

Some Last Reflections on Pragmatism

It would surely signify either ignorance or hypocrisy to consider this endeavor to be a complete sociological account of pragmatism. It is perhaps the major fragment of such a task. I do not wish to apologize for this acknowledged incompleteness, but for future reference what is lacking must be recorded. To supply these deficiencies is, I have felt in the process of the work, beyond the confines of the usual expectations of a single book. The sociological account of American pragmatism is most likely a good two-volume opportunity. What must be made is a brief anticipatory statement of the outlines of this task and of what it will require. If it should be somewhat personal in nature, that is due to my desire for self-clarification concerning future work.

1. An account of George H. Mead must be included. It is true that many features of Mead's thought are treated by the consideration given to the work of John Dewey. However, in view of the course of the pragmatic movement and of Dewey's differential evaluation of Mead and James, the inclusion of James and the omission of Mead is an unrepresentative act that is intellectually unwarranted.

2. This specific omission is linked with an equally important, though more diffuse, inadequacy: the architecture of the entire presentation as it now stands. There is needed a more concise *phraseology and development statement* of the course of the movement as a whole as it lies within a changing social structure. This omission involves three considerations: (a) it must, of course, wait

upon the account of Mead. (b) It will require a *larger* conception of the course of the entire movement of pragmatism from Peirce to Mead than I have here permitted myself. (c) This entire matter must wait upon an increase of the writer's knowledge of the political, economic, and social history of the United States since the Civil War as it may bear upon the conditions of the total intellectual life. The sort of knowledge really required can only come with a constant working of the facts over a considerable period and from many detailed studies. The lack of this sort of knowledge is a major reason for such deficiencies as these materials may have. It is because of this personal deficiency, which can only be remedied by work in time, and because of the omission of Mead, that I have refrained from an attempted over-all reconstruction of "pragmatism" in a concise field at this time. Within the limits of such scholarly conscience as I possess, I cannot now undertake such an attempt. I thought it wiser, first, to focus upon detailed statements of each major pragmatist tied down as closely as possible to their actual texts. Only after this should one attempt to formulate the developmental phases of the movement as a whole and to state the commonalities and variations in foci, style, and result of respective pragmatists.

3. Such an overview and total grasp of the movement also waits upon at least three specialized inquiries, aspects of which have certainly been touched upon in the above, but which require systematic and more thorough consideration. (a) One is what might be called the regional or "the frontier hypothesis of pragmatism." The reader will realize from what has already been written that I am not prepared lightly to accept this so far unverified theory. It is, however, believed that the matter is capable of a refined statement, one that will permit detailed and empirical, rather than rhetorical and romantic, testing. Indeed, such a statement and test is required. This task involves a sociological portrayal of the St. Louis school. (b) Another over-all hypothesis, suggested by Mannheim and others, although not established by anyone as yet, conceives "pragmatism" as representing a "democratization" of criteria. (c) There is the often carelessly made imputation of pragmatism as a rationale of a crude commercialization of American cultural life. As is the case with (a) and (b) this matter is believed capable of yielding its full fruit only after it has been restated in terms

of concrete data and connective mechanisms. These matters may be conceived as portions of the job of systematizing and stating the "friendly" explanations of pragmatism given by such men as Sidney Hook, Horace Kallen, and, above all, G. H. Mead.

4. There is also required more definitive data upon the extraction and general social composition of the academic personnel of philosophy (and of certain non-academic intellectuals) since the Civil War. This lack, as well as the omission of an account of Mead, is primarily due to the fact that research funds are needed to obtain required data.

5. A broader matter of at present unknown importance must be examined: the relations, if any, and their character, between pragmatic elements of thought and the New Deal government, especially its earlier phases. Certain important actors in the New Deal, such as Henry A. Wallace and Rexford Tugwell, have been influenced by Dewey's writings. At the same time it would seem that those so placed have also been close readers of Thorstein Veblen and that this has influenced their understanding of Dewey. To get at the bottom of this problem, one must ascertain more precisely the influence of Charles Peirce on the young Veblen and the influence of Veblen upon Dewey. Veblen heard Peirce lecture at Johns Hopkins, and Dewey was in at least reading contact with Veblen at Chicago. An important clue to the matter resides in what I have termed technologic meanings in Peirce, which became one facet of Dewey's theory of meaning. Sociologically, the problem can most easily be approached by direct interviews with the relevant men of the early New Deal government.

6. The major critics at various stages in the development of pragmatism should be considered in a systematic and sociological way. The correct performance of this task, which at a minimum should include Bertrand Russell, Carl Schurz, A. E. Murphy, Lewis Mumford, Waldo Frank, as well as those who so valiantly fought by Dewey's students and colleagues, waits upon a more detailed understanding such as is indicated. It would culminate in a more explicit and close account on the competition of ideas throughout the period.

7. It is also the opinion of the writer that such an endeavor as the present one should by all means be accompanied, when completed, with detailed methodological self-reflections. In the present

stage of research in sociology of knowledge there is a need for every substantive attempt to be accompanied by *explicit* self-awareness both of detailed procedure and of larger epistemological concerns. Advance in sociology of knowledge will not follow from substantive work alone, for every such piece of work involves methodological issues, whether we endeavor to hide them or whether we take the risk of crossing intellectually outmoded academic fences. I am by no means satisfied with the methodological basis and rationale of such concrete work in sociology of knowledge as lies within my awareness. The writer has not been unaware of these problems and has, indeed, filled many margins of pages with such reflections. Their omission in the present work is in large part due to irrelevant considerations for this statement.

8. It is perhaps not indispensable, but it would certainly be interesting and in all probability revealing, to examine the non-American refractions and criticisms of pragmatism. In Italy, especially, as well as in England, France, and Germany, there has developed, since the time of William James, a literature on this topic. In this connection it would be significant to trace the receptions of Dewey's work in the hands of Orientals and scholars of non- or only semi-industrialized countries, especially those of China and India, as well as of Mexico and Turkey.

9. There remains the present situation of pragmatism in America. Perhaps never before in its eighty years' existence has this style of thinking been so under attack as it has since the world crises which came to fruition in the late thirties. The attack has been in "spiritual" or "religious" terms and also on "political" grounds. No volume that in any sense could be called major has as yet resulted from these reactions. The personal and political reasons for such a course of events must be examined from a standpoint as removed from these reasons as is possible. To so examine it would offer the possibility of a fundamental understanding of the conditions for the future development of philosophy in the United States.

C. WRIGHT MILLS
1943

Abbott, Francis E., 84, 86-92, 97, 103, 105, 114-15, 201, 242, 271
Abelard, 129, 200
academicians; social ascent of, 354-55; social origins of, 76-80
Adams, Herbert, 286
adaptation, biologistic, 379, 382, 391
Addams, Jane, 307-12, 371
Adler, Mortimer J., 367
Adorno, Theodore, 13, 23
Affiliated clubs of graduate students, 71
"agapism" (evolutionary love), 189, 196-99
Agassiz, Louis, 45, 216, 219
agnosticism, 84
agrarianism, 328, 329
Allport, Gordon W., 454
ambiguity, 146
(The) American, 332
American Association for the Advancement of Science, 45, 71
American Economic Association, 71
American Federation of Teachers, 339
American Historical Association, 71
American Journal of Mathematics, 123
American Mathematical Society, 71
American Philological Association, 70
American Philosophical Association, 71, 81-82, 313, 347

American Political Science Association, 71
American Psychological Association, 71, 313, 384
American Sociological Society, 71
American Teacher, 333
American universities, 175-76; decline of philosophy in, 348-50; enrollment in, 348; social origins of students in, 348
Amherst College, 79
(The) Andover Review, 325
Angell, J. B., 57, 58, 62, 292, 312
anomie, 21
Anti-Imperialist League, 11, 26, 267
Appleton, William, 86
Aristotle, 129, 132
Arnold, Matthew, 318, 366
Asia, 325
(The) Atlantic Monthly, 64, 325
Ayers, N. W., 347
Ayres, Clarence E., 29, 319-21, 324f.

Bacon, Francis, 417
Bain, Alexander, 84, 106, 283
Baldwin, James Mark, 136
Bancroft, George, 72
Barnard, Henry, 67
Barnes, Albert C., 313, 318
"Barnes Foundation", 318
Baum, Maurice, 224, 225

Beard, Charles, 21, 44, 332
Becker, Howard, 30
behaviorism, 357, 358, 365-67, 391
Bentham, Jeremy, 84
Berkeley, George, 129, 177, 237
Big Business (in U.S.) 327-31
biological theory of action, 375-78, 391
Blaine, J. G., 261-62
Boehm, Jacob, 133
Boole, George, 132
Bosanquet, Bernard, 312, 367
Bourne, Randolph, 222, 409-10
Bowditch, Henry P., 134
Bradley, F. H., 234, 312
Brattle, William, 38
Bromberg, F. G., 261
Brooks, Van Wyck, 21
Brown University, 43, 79
Browning, Robert, 318, 366
Buckham, 283
Burgess, W. R., 340
Bureau of Applied Research, 29
Butts, R. Freeman, 40, 46

Cabot, J. E., 133
Calvinism, 98, 242, 253
Cartesian conception of doubt, 150-55, 161, 163, 194
Carnegie Andrew, 58
Castro, Fidel, 26
categorical imperative, 461
Cattell, J. McKeen, 78, 313
Catholicism, 413
Causes of World War Three, 23
Chicago; social condition in, 308, 310; University of, 43, 50-51, 53f., 59-60, 62, 68, 77, 297-98, 306f., 311-12, 316, 348, 350, 466
China, 317
Chipman, Alice, 293-94
(The) Christian Century, 325
Clark, Harold F., 341
Clark University, 68
Clarke, James F., 123
Clay, Henry, 92
Clifford, William K., 93

Cogswell, J. G., 72
Cohen, Morris, 109
Columbia University, 43, 45-46, 48, 68, 77, 79-80, 313, 316, 348
Commager, Henry S., 31
(The) Common Law, 109
Common Sense, 325
communism, 429-30
Comte, Auguste, 282, 291
Cooper, James F., 39
Cornell University, 79
correspondence schools, 651
criteria for a good society, 444-45
Critique of Pure Reason, 129, 130
Croly, Herbert, 326, 332
Cronze, Edward, 200
culture, 426, 430, 434
(The) Current History Magazine, 325
Curtis, Benjamin R., 123

Dartmouth College, 46, 48
"Dartmouth College Case", 44
Darwin, Charles, 84, 93, 94, 198-99, 237, 263, 357-58, 372, 374, 379, 384, 385
Daughters of the American Revolution, 344
Davidson, Thomas, 312
Debs, Eugene V., 329
Dedekind, Richard, 139
DeLaguna, Grace, 377
De L'Utilité du Pragmatisme, 30
Democracy and Education, 332-34, 444, 458
Democratic Party, 405-06
Democritus, 237
Descartes, Rene, 38, 150-55, 359, 400
Dewey, Jane, 307, 308
Dewey, John, 11, 13, 15-21, 23-25, 27, 30, 36, 43, 46, 58, 60, 63, 75, 76, 80-81, 101, 109, 113, 145-46, 184, 186, 189, 206, 207, 210, 223, 232, 243, 272, 277-463
(The) Dial, 325

Dictionary of American Biography, 75-76

Dictionary of Philosophy and Psychology, 136

doubt, as origin of inquiry, 150-65

Douglas, Paul H., 340

Durkheim, Emile, 12, 24

(An) Economic Interpretation of the Constitution, 332

Education (in America); adult, 49; and business schools, 48-49; and growth of universities, 34-53, 335; household arts in, 49; and state universities, 44, 50

Educational Review, 333

elective system, 40, 50, 72

Elementary School Teacher, 332

Elements of Logic, 128

Eliot, Charles W., 40, 57, 62, 80, 93, 134, 219, 264

Emerson, Ralph W., 88, 133, 216, 271, 440

(The) Emotions and the Will, 106

empiricism, 362-64

Essays and Notes, 105

ethics, 184-85, 402

evangelism, and the development of colleges, 43

Everett, Edward, 72

Everybody's, 332

evolution, 93-95, 97, 244-45, 282; and individualism, 104

Experience and Nature, 113

experimental process, in politics, 439

experiential school, 299-302

experiment in science, 385-87, 391

Fay, Harriet M., 135

Filler, Louis, 329

Fisch, H. M., 106-08

Fisher, G. P., 133

Fiske, John, 22, 84, 89, 92-95, 97, 101, 114-16, 133, 199, 242-43, 373

Follen, Charles, 73

Ford, Henry, 332

Foreign Affairs, 325

Forum, 325

Foundations of the Theory of Signs, 15

Frank, Waldo, 466

Frankel, Charles, 23

Franklin, Benjamin, 71

Free-floating intelligentsia, 85

"free religious association," 87, 89

Freedom and Culture, 11, 14, 27, 426, 434, 442

French, J. F., 78

Freud, Sigmund, 21, 29

(The) Future of Science, 413, 414

gemeinschaft, 444

Georgia, University of, 42

(The) German Ideology, 16

German universities, 176, 243

Gerth, Hans, 13, 23, 29

Gilman, Daniel C., 50, 57-58, 60-62, 133

Godkin, E. L., 217, 260-61, 268

Göttingen, 71-72

graduate schools, 67-73; and professionalization, 71-73; Germans and Americans in, 72-73

Granet, Marcel, 14

Grant, Ulysses S., 52

Gray, Asa, 45, 218

Gray, John C., 107, 114

Green, E. B., 92

Hackett, Francis, 326

Hall, G. Stanley, 286

Hamiltonianism, 84, 95-96

Harper, William R., 57-59, 302

Harris, W. T., 89, 284

Harrison, Frederick, 282

Hart, Hornell, 349

Hartshorne, Charles, 144

Harvard University, 37-38, 43, 45, 46, 48, 58, 62-65, 67, 72, 80, 88, 93, 96, 114, 123-24, 175, 238, 313, 314

Hegel, Georg W. F., 130, 202, 281-

82, 284, 286, 288, 289-92, 315, 357-60, 411-12, 443

Hemingway, Ernest, 12

Herschel, John Frederick, 101

(The) Hibbert Journal, 325

historical criticism, 243

Hill, Thomas, 63, 341

Hobbes, Thomas, 129

Hobhouse, L. T., 449

Hofstadter, Richard, 31

Holmes, Oliver W., 21, 36, 47, 84 85, 106, 107-15, 123, 193-94, 268

Hook, Sidney, 317, 373, 405, 466

Hoover, Herbert, 332

Hopkins, Johns, 61

Horkheimer, Max, 13, 23

Horne, H. H., 334

How We Think, 395

Howells, William D., 331

Hull House, 307-12, 371, 381, 432

Hume, David, 271, 449

Hunt, W. M., 218

Huxley, Thomas H., 62, 93-94, 195, 243, 282, 402

"immigrant problem", 323f.

immigrants, second generation estrangement of, 310

imperialism, 264-65

(The) Independent, 325

Ingersoll, Ralph, 243

Institute of Social Research, 13

intellectuals, and World War II, 20-21

International Journal of Ethics, 88, 347, 367

instinctivist psychology, 447

intuition, 151-52; and religion, 205f.

I. Q. tests, 455

James, Henry, Sr., 215-17

James, Henry, 96, 134-35

James, William, 12, 13, 19, 23, 26, 36, 58, 75-76, 80, 84-86, 88, 94, 96-97, 107-09, 112-15, 134-37, 141, 145-46, 187-88, 210, 211, 213-76, 289, 296, 297, 312, 314, 331, 349, 365, 376, 396, 447, 454, 467

Japan, 317

Jefferson, Thomas, 434

Jeffersonianism, 328, 330-31, 442, 444

Jevons, Stanley, 312

John of Duns (Duns Scotus), 105, 129, 130

John of Salisbury, 129

Johns Hopkins University, 39, 45, 58, 62-63, 65, 123, 144, 285-86, 313, 466

Journal of Education, 332

(The) Journal of Philosophy, 347

Journal of Speculative Philosophy, 40, 284, 347

Judd, 340

Jung, Carl G., 200

Junkerism, 330

Kallen, Horace, 466

Kant, Immanuel, 85, 89-90, 106, 129-31, 190, 210, 289, 411-12

Kerouac, Jack, 12

Kilpatrick, W. H., 334

Kindergarten Magazine, 333

Kunkel, B. W., 76

labor intellectuals, 19-20

laboratorian, 424f.

LaFollette, Robert M., 328

Laski, Harold J., 111

League for Independent Political Action, 406

Leisure class, 373

Lenin, Vladimir, 332

Lewes, George Henry, 93

liberalism in America, 327-28

Lieber, Francis, 73

Lippmann, Walter, 326, 332

Listen Yankee, 26

Lloyd, A. H., 75, 296

Locke, John, 101, 129, 225

Logic: The Theory of Inquiry, 14, 16, 378

Lotze, Rudolph H., 312

MacLeish, Archibald, 21
Malraux, Andre, 12
Malthus, Thomas Robert, 111
Mann, Horace, 42, 339
Mannheim, Karl, 15-17, 21, 24, 26, 465
Marshall, Chief Justice, 44
Martineau, Harriet, 282
Marx, Karl, 13-17, 21, 24, 26, 28-29
Marxism, 23-24, 426-29
Massachusetts Institute of Technology, 46
Mather, Cotton, 37
Maury, Matthew F., 45
Mead, George H., 15, 17, 21, 24-25, 36, 43, 46, 58, 60, 75-76, 167f, 184, 252, 275f, 296-97, 312, 360, 419, 448, 464-66
mediationalism, 257f.
Metaphysical Club, 13, 47, 142, 178, 225, 280, 383; biographical composition of, 84-116; lawyers in, 106-08; and science, 142-43
Mexico, 317, 318; establishment of University in, 37
Michels, Robert, 12, 20, 28
Michelson, Albert, 73
Michigan, University of, 67, 292-93
Middletown, 372
Mill, John S., 84, 95-96, 101, 103-04, 130, 312, 360
Miller, A. C., 48
Mind, 347
Moffett, 341
monism, 426, 429-30
Moore, A. W., 76, 312
moral theory, 368-70
Morison, S. E., 38
Morrill Act (1862), 47, 49
Morris, Charles W., 15, 18, 383
Morris, George S., 286-89, 291-93
muck-rakers, 28, 328-31
"mugwump", 261
Mumford, Louis, 21, 466

Munseys, 332
Murphey, A. E., 466
McClures, 332
McCosh, 103, 271
McKinley, William, 328

National Academy of Science, 123-24
National Education Association (formerly N.T.A.), 339; *Addresses and Proceedings of,* 333
National Liberal League, 87
(The) Nation, 88, 97, 136, 217, 260-61, 269, 325-26, 332
nature-nurture, 449-52
(The) Nautical Almanac, 95, 123, 125
Nebraska, University of, 68
Needham, Joseph, 14
neo-Comteanism, 447
neo-Machiavellian school of Franco-Italian sociology, 25
Neumann, Franz, 13, 23
New Deal, 466
(The) New Democracy, 332
(The) New Men of Power, 18
(The) New Nationalism, 332
(The) New Republic, 317, 322, 325-27; reading public of, 326-27, 330-33
New York Evening Post, 196, 261
Newcomb, Simon, 197
Newton, Isaac, 101, 102
nominalism, 90-91, 199-204, 207, 272
Norton, Charles Eliot, 98

Pareto, Vilfredo, 12
Parker, Francis, 339
Parrington, Vernon L., 93
Peirce, Benjamin, 123-24, 129,131, 142
Peirce, Charles S., 13, 15, 16, 23-24, 29-30, 36, 38, 45-47, 58, 63, 75-76, 80, 84-86, 88-89, 94-99, 103, 105-06, 109, 114-15, 121-212, 216, 219-20, 223-25, 242-43, 248-

49, 256, 268-69, 271, 286, 312, 326, 365, 373, 383, 406, 409, 465-66
Peirce, James M., 124, 129
Perkins, G. H., 281
Perry, Ralph B., 31, 80, 108, 222, 224, 255, 272, 406
Perry, T. S., 94
Peru, establishment of University in, 37
(The) Philosophical Review, 40, 81, 347
"planning", 423f.
Plotinus, 133
pluralism, 430
political parties, 394
political science, Dewey's influence on, 445f.
Popular Science Monthly, 85
populism, 328-29
Porter, Noah, 283
power elite, 21
(The) Power Elite, 22-23
Power, Politics, and People, 14
practical philosophy, 169-71
pragmatic maxim, 13, 100, 177-81, 183-86, 189
pragmatism, *passim;* and American impact, 28; and European Fascism, 24; history of, 35-37; on language, 15; and lawyers, 106-07, 115; and personal involvement, 26; and relation to universities, 36-37
Pragmatism, 112, 222, 224-25, 249, 251, 296
Preface to Politics, 332
Prescott, William H., 39
Princeton University, 43, 48, 67
Principles of Psychology, 297
professionalization; of philosophy, 29, 33, 79; of science, 62; of teaching, 338-345, 351
Progressive Education, 333
(The) Progressive Educational Association, 339
Progressive Party, 332

progressivism, 328-32
Promise of American Life, 332
Protestant Ethic, 175-77
publications in early America, 39-40
(The) Public and its Problems, 435-37
public schools (in America), 41, 335; and Catholics; development of, 338; growth of, 338; local autonomy over, 345; as means for mobility, 342-43; opportunities for attendance, 343; and religion, 42; teachers' salaries, 340
Puritans, 37-38, 242, 271, 315, 370-71, 373-74, 376, 395, 459, 460

Ratner, Joseph, 319-21, 323f.
realism, 199-203
Reichenbach, Hans, 399-400
Reid, Thomas, 271
Religion, Dewey on, 317-18
Renan, Ernest, 413-15
van Rensselaer, Stephen, 45
Rensselaer Polytechnic Institute, 45-46
Richardson, 110
Rockefeller, John D., 58-59
Roosevelt, Theodore, 26, 108, 264, 328-29, 331-32
Ross, E. A., 330
Rousseau, Jean Jacques, 458
Rowland, Henry A., 62
Royce, Josiah, 80, 88, 234, 260
Russell, Bertrand, 466
Russia, 317, 330

Saint Augustine, 129
St. John Green, Nicholas, 84, 94, 105-06, 114
Saint Louis movement, 33, 465
Salter, 367
Santayana, George, 72, 40, 257
Schelling, Friedrich W., 133
Schiff, Philip, 73
Schiller, F. C. S., 135
Schlötel, 139, 148f.

School and Society, 332-33

(The) Schoolmasters Club of Michigan, 294

School Review, 333

Schurz, Carl, 466

Science; and belief, 169; and morality, 396-98, 403; and philosophy, 169-73, 366; and relation to the social, 414; and religion, 226, 416

Scientific Theism, 89

Scottish Common Sensism, 203, 207

Seabury, 432

Selkirk, Alexander, 138

(The) Seven Arts Magazine, 325

Shröder, 193

Sidgewick, Henry, 367

Silliman, Benjamin, 45, 61

Simmel, Georg, 24

Sinclair, Upton, 28

Smith, J. Allen, 332

Smith, Mary, 307

Smithson, James, 45

Smithsonian Institute, 45, 123

Social Darwinism, 447

Social Frontier, 333

social psychology, 447 328

(The) Sociological Imagination, 11, 17, 24-25

sociology of knowledge, 15-16, 19, 142, 159

sociotics, 15

solipsism, 90

Sorel, Georges, 30

Spanish American War, 264-66

specialization, and professionalization of higher learning, 40-41, 47

Spencer, Herbert, 93-94, 101-103, 130, 233, 235, 240, 288, 297

Spirit of American Government, 332

Steffens, Lincoln, 28, 330-32

Steinbeck, John, 379

Straight, Willard, 326

Studies in Logical Theory, 312, 357, 433

Sumner, William, 44

(The) Survey, 325

Tappen, H. P., 51

Tarbell, Ida, 28

teachers (in American public schools); problems of, 344; salaries of, 340; social origins of, 341-42; in Vermont, 303f.

technologism, 422-23

Theory of the Leisure Class, 371

Thomas, Norman, 406

Thomas, W. I.,448

Thoreau, Henry D., 217

Tichnor, George, 72

Titchener, 312

Torrey, H. A. P., 283-84

Tortilla Flat, 379

Transcendentalism, 33, 133, 271, 353

Tufts, James, 60, 75, 295-96, 297, 312

Tugwell, Rexford, 466

Tyndall, John, 93

Turkey, 317, 318

Turner, 373

types of university "developers"; educator, 57; philanthropist, 58

Twain, Mark, 329

unemployment, 336f.

United States Supreme Court, 47

(The) University of California Chronicle, 347

values, in science, 11, 399-401

(The) Varieties of Religious Experience, 251

Veblen, Thorstein, 12, 17, 29, 63, 184, 311-12, 332, 371, 373, 466

Venn, 312

Vermont, 280, 283-84; University of, 281

Virginia, University of, 43

Vivas, Eliseo, 18

Von Holst, H. 73

Wallace, Henry A., 466
Wallas, Graham, 448
war, 266-67, 331
Ward, Lester, 447-48
Warner, Joseph, 84, 88, 106-07, 114
Watson, John, 380
(The) Way Out of Agnosticism, 88
Weber, Max, 12, 20-21, 24, 28, 41,
 244, 328, 394
Weiner, Philip P., 31
Weiss, Paul, 144
Wells, H. G., 318
Wenley, R. M., 287
Weyl, Walter E., 326, 332
Wharton School of Finance and
 Economy, 48
Whately, Richard, 128
Whewell, 126
White, A. D., 61
White, Morton, 31
White Collar, 20-21
Whitlock, Brant, 331
Who's Who in Philosophy, 75

William and Mary (College), 43
William of Ockham, 129
Wills, E. V., 46
Wilson, Woodrow, 328, 331
Wisconsin, University of, 13, 23,
 79, 313
Wissenssoziologie, 17
Witherspoon, 271
woman's suffrage, 105
Worcester Polytechnic, 46
(The) World Tomorrow, 325
World War I, 317, 419
Wright, Chauncey, 36, 84-85, 95-
 105, 109, 114-15, 125, 130, 142
 179, 200, 219-20, 243, 248, 268-
 69
Wyman, Jeffries, 218-19

Yale University, 43-46, 48, 59, 67,
 313
"Yankee" tradition, 285, 370-71
Youmans, E. L., 94
Young, Ella F., 302, 455